FAT-PROOF YOUR CHILD

OTHER BOOKS BY JOSEPH C. PISCATELLA

FAT-PROOF YOUR CHILD

BY JOSEPH C. PISCATELLA
RECIPES BY BERNIE PISCATELLA

WORKMAN PUBLISHING • NEW YORK

Library of Congress Cataloging-in-Publication Data

Piscatella, Joseph C.
    Fat-proof your child / by Joseph C. Piscatella.
        p. cm.
    Includes index
    ISBN 1-56305-150-8
    1. Children—Nutrition. 2. Obesity in children—Prevention.
3. Cookery. I. Title.
RJ206.P57   1997
613.2'083—dc21   97-9065
                                                 CIP

Workman books are available at special discounts when purchased in bulk for premiums and sales promotions as well as for fund-raising or educational use. Special editions or book excerpts can also be created to specification. For details, please contact the Special Sales Director at the address below.

Workman Publishing
708 Broadway
New York, NY 10003-9555

Manufactured in the United States of America

10 9 8 7 6 5 4 3 2 1

The material in this book is provided for information only and should not be construed as medical advice or instruction. Always consult with your physician or other appropriate health professionals before making any changes in diet and/or physical activity.

FOREWORD

J oe Piscatella knows how to write a book. His four previous books have been pleasures to read, and I— and my patients—have learned much from them. In my opinion, no one has done a better job of educating the public with "how-to" information on lifestyle and health. It is no wonder that thousands of hospitals use his books to help people lose weight, lower cholesterol and get into better shape.

Fat-Proof Your Child is no exception. It focuses on one of the most critical public health issues facing this nation: the overweight and out-of-shape condition of American children and teens. *It is the first book to focus on this major health problem.*

Overweight is one of the greatest health problems for American adults; indeed, one-third of the adult U.S. population is considered obese. But being overweight can no longer be considered exclusively a problem for adults. As this book illustrates, it is a significant problem today for children and adolescents as well. Since the 1960s, the number of seriously overweight children and teens has more than doubled. This is a disturbing trend. There are now more than 20 million overweight children in the United States, and some 5 million of these children are severely overweight. In fact, 80% of 10-year-old girls have a "fear of fatness," and 40% of them are already trying to lose weight. As for teens, some 40% are over their ideal body weight, and about 20% are approaching obesity.

This situation is serious because studies show that overweight children "track" into overweight adults. And overweight adults are more prone to heart disease, certain cancers, high blood pressure, diabetes and obesity. So, as

Joe Piscatella counsels parents, weight loss is not the goal. Fitness and health is the main objective.

Fat-Proof Your Child is a tremendous resource for parents. It focuses on the overweight child and teen, the reasons behind the problem and the role of parents. The book emphasizes that parents are the single most influential factor regarding how active and healthy their children will be. This is because children emulate their parents as role models. Advice on healthy living from parents with poor lifestyle habits is simply meaningless. Children do what parents do, not what parents say. This book examines what parents can and should do as personal examples of a healthy, active lifestyle.

Joe Piscatella offers splendid advice about two key areas: physical activity and healthy eating. Lack of physical activity is a prime reason for the decline of fitness in American children and adolescents. Today the average teenager exercises no more than 15 minutes a day; moreover, physical fitness peaks in teenagers at the age of 14 and goes downhill from then on. The book examines many of the reasons for this circumstance, among them increased television viewing, increased computer use, lack of physical education programs in schools and societal changes that have restricted the unchaperoned use of parks and playgrounds by children. But more important, it provides specific, realistic things that parents can do to help their children (and themselves) to become more physically active.

Eating habits are given the same thorough treatment. American children consume too much fat (about 38% of calories eaten come from fat). In examining what children are fed, from fast food and school lunches to frozen dinners, Joe educates parents to the sources of that fat. But rather than recommending a restrictive diet, he provides seven simple steps that parents can take to moderate fat and to change their children's eating habits. And he makes great sense. Instead of recommending that parents introduce unfamiliar low-fat foods to their children,

Joe shows how familiar meals can be made lower in fat. And he backs it all up with "kid-friendly" recipes developed by his wife, Bernie.

All in all, *Fat-Proof Your Child* is one of Joe Piscatella's best efforts—easy to read, based on accepted medical science and full of practical advice. I highly recommend this book to all parents, to all teenagers and to all members of the medical profession.

William C. Roberts, M.D.
Executive Director,
Baylor University Cardiovascular Institute
Editor in Chief, *The American Journal of Cardiology*

CONTENTS

PART IV
DIET: THE SEVEN-STEP SOLUTION   175

INTRODUCTION

We all have a nagging suspicion that kids today, raised among the temptations of sedentary computer games and fast food, are more overweight and out of shape than kids were just a generation ago.

It's not our imagination. Recent reports from the experts confirm that the number of seriously overweight children and adolescents in the United States has more than doubled over the past three decades, with most of the increase occurring since 1980. This means that today's adults—with their considerable and well-documented health problems, including heart disease, obesity and high blood pressure—actually were more fit and had healthier headstarts than our children!

The reality is that in the age group 6 to 18, there is an epidemic of overweight and out-of-shape kids. And if current habits and lifestyles do not change, these children and teenagers may be doomed to a lifetime of chronic health problems.

This is of such concern that the recent Surgeon General's Report on Physical Activity cites it as one of the most challenging public health issues of the next century. In other words, the health and fitness of our children today is of the utmost importance to our society tomorrow. The economically fragile medical system in the United States is currently strained by serving a population that was more fit and less overweight in youth. How will it handle a generation raised to be overweight and out of shape at an earlier age?

Of course, we don't have to wait for the future to see how this situation penalizes many children and teenagers now, especially those who are overweight. Often, over-weight kids have problems with sports, self-esteem and socializing. And if they remain overweight and out of shape as adults, they can find themselves well along the road to heart disease, diabetes and other obesity-related health problems.

But it doesn't have to be that way. These problems are largely avoidable. And the earlier your child develops healthy lifestyle habits, the more these choices become just that—habits—and the greater the short- and long-term benefits. That's what this book is about. Its purpose is to give parents and others who care for kids a simple plan for getting children and teens to understand, enjoy and even make their own healthy lifestyle choices.

For me, this issue is not simply an academic one. I know what it's like to make the wrong decisions about diet early in life and then pay the price later. Like most children growing up in the post-World War II era, I ate the typical American diet—one recommended for "strong bones and healthy teeth." This diet was touted for being rich in protein and calcium, but no one ever pointed out that its dominating feature was fat—a feature that contin-ues to prevail in what our children eat today.

I ate that diet into adulthood, and as a result my weight and cholesterol steadily increased over the years. Then, in 1977, dietary excesses caught up with me and I underwent coronary bypass surgery. I was 32 years old. My children were young. My daughter, Anne, was six; my son, Joe, was just four.

In retrospect, my surgery may have been the best thing that happened to them because it led me to a better understanding of the link between lifestyle habits and health. I no longer had a choice. I had to change the way I was living to lose weight, lower cholesterol and increase physical fitness. So I moved from a high-fat diet and sedentary habits to a lifestyle of healthy eating and regu-lar physical activity.

And so did they.

Physical activity as a family affair became the standard, not the exception. I had to walk and jog for my heart, and I loved it when they would come with me. Healthful meals, eaten together, were a family habit. Sure, there was time for a pizza after a ballgame, but as a rule our meals were healthy and delicious. By supporting my health habits, our kids produced for themselves a lifestyle designed for fitness. Today in their mid-20s and out of college, they have maintained healthy eating and exercise habits.

My experience with healthy eating and exercising in the real world is shared in the four books I've written over the last decade. These books were directed to adults— heart patients, people who wanted to lose weight and reduce cholesterol, and those who just wanted to get fit and improve health.

This book is also for adults. But it's about children. It helps parents and caregivers to identify the problems of overweight and lack of fitness as well as the reasons for those problems. More important, it provides specific things that parents can do to help their children and themselves.

- It's simple because it doesn't involve any drastic changes in the lives of family members. Instead, it provides parents who are already out of time and feeling guilty with realistic ways to help their children. For example, it doesn't make much sense to advise parents never to take their children to a fast-food restaurant. It must be recognized that in this society fast food is a fact of life. Thus the suggestions include a section on how to help your child make the best fast-food choices.

- It's effective because it relies on proven dietary and exercise guidelines, based on current science and heavily laced with practical experience.

- It's easy because it contains family-tested recipes, and meal plans that feature foods kids like to eat. Research shows that it's easier to modify kids' favorite foods than to introduce unfamiliar foods. Adults may experiment with new foods in an attempt to eat meals very low in fat, but kids generally won't eat strange stuff. So, the book includes over 100 recipes developed by my wife, Bernie, which show parents how to lighten up favorite meals— Spaghetti with Meatballs, Southern Fried Chicken, Noodle Casserole with Tuna, Combination Pizza and many more. In addition, Bernie has provided entire menus (many of which can be made in under 30 minutes) as an aid to creating nutritionally balanced meals.

Parents are in the best position to influence the dietary and exercise habits of their children. But they need to do it in a "real world" way. This book is a blueprint for action. It will make it easier to raise low-fat kids in a high-fat world.

Joseph C. Piscatella

PART I

OUR OVERWEIGHT KIDS

CHAPTER 1

A POPULATION OUT OF CONTROL

Americans have never been as health-conscious as we are now. Fitness is not just healthy— it's also fashionable. Joggers, walkers and bi-cyclists clog streets and pathways. People are huffing and puffing on exercise machines, stepping and sweating in aerobics classes.

And everyone, from Oprah to the man on the street, is concerned about fat. Supermarket shoppers recite their mantra— "lite, low-fat, no fat"—before reading labels and selecting foods. We eagerly buy the latest diet books (over 400 in print at last count). We spend billions of dollars annually on weight-control devices—pills, liquid meals, special foods and powders. And there's a booming busi-ness in diet movements, 12-step diet programs, and diet franchises complete with celebrity TV endorsements and calorically correct prepackaged meals, snacks and desserts.

But somewhere between Dad's jog and Mom's fat-free cookies, a strange thing happened to our children.

They got fat!

Research conducted by the American Health Founda-tion shows that no less than a quarter of America's youth can be classified as overweight. And this alarming fraction is increasing each year at an inordinate rate.

Significantly, as overweight has increased in kids, fitness has decreased. The result is that children and teens today are more sedentary, weigh more, have more body fat and are less fit than children 20 years ago. This does not bode well for their future health given the fact that overweight children are prone to heart disease, high blood pressure and diabetes as adults. And, for a nation battling health care costs, it is an economic time bomb.

A MODERN PHENOMENON

The picture of families exercising and eating better is an illusion. Americans may be more aware of the need to exercise and eat less fat, but that knowledge has not been put into practice. "We want to lose weight, and be fit and healthy," says Thomas Dybahl of *Prevention* magazine, "but we see the steps to weight loss and fitness as painful and unpleasant, and consequently we don't do a lot of them." Indeed, an ongoing federal survey recently confirmed that we're getting fatter faster. From 1960 to 1980, one in four American adults was obese. Since 1980, that number has ballooned to one in three adults, or almost 60 million people. Says Dr. F. Xavier Pi-Sunyer of Columbia University Medical School, "The proportion of the population that is obese is incredible. If this were about tuberculosis, it would be called an epidemic."

An overabundance of food, combined with sedentary lifestyles, has created an overweight, unfit population in the United States. The actuality is that this is a nation in which most people discuss the latest diet book over Danish pastry and lace up their running shoes only to trot to the refrigerator. And our children are following suit. In too many families, kids are likely to be found munching on potato chips in front of the TV set rather than snacking on an apple between outdoor physical activities.

The products of this high-fat, sedentary lifestyle—overweight, obesity and lack of fitness—have never been as evident in kids as they are today.

WHAT'S WRONG WITH THIS PICTURE?

The fattening of American children did not take place overnight. If you looked at a class picture of high school freshmen in the 1960s and then looked at one from today, you'd find a lot of differences. Ignore the surface stuff like hairstyles and clothing. These things come and go. The most obvious difference is that many more kids in today's photo will be pudgy. And others will be downright fat.

Undeniably, time has produced a rampant overweight problem in our children. Says Dr. Suzanne Oparil, former president of the American Heart Association, "We estimate that there are a minimum of 20 million overweight young children in the United States—more than ever before. And those numbers are rapidly rising."

Children's Weight Ranges (Ages 6–12) 1984–1991

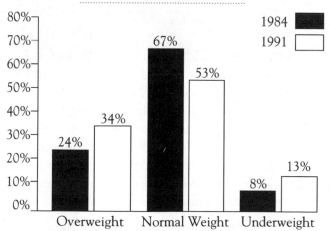

Source: Harris survey for *Prevention* magazine.

And it's no better for teenagers. The percentage of overweight teens held steady at about 15% through the 1970s. By 1991, however, the percentage had climbed to 21%, and that figure is rising today at a faster rate than the increase for adults.

Weights at Which Teenagers Are Considered Overweight

Height (in inches)	Cutoff Point (in pounds)		
	Ages 12–14	Ages 15–17	Ages 18–19
Females			
54	97	103	107
56	104	111	115
60	120	127	132
64	136	144	150
68	154	163	170
72	173	183	190
Males			
54	95	101	107
56	103	108	115
60	118	124	132
64	134	142	150
68	151	160	169
72	170	179	189

Source: American Medical Association.

This disturbing trend holds true for the fattest kids as well. The National Center for Health Statistics reports that almost five million American youths aged 6 to 17 are "severely overweight." That is about 11% of that age group, more than double the percentage of "severely overweight" kids in the 1960s. States Dr. William Klish of the American Academy of Pediatrics Committee on Nutrition, "I'm not surprised by the increase, but I'm surprised by the *degree* of the increase. It's a very significant jump."

But it doesn't take sophisticated studies alone to show

that a weight problem exists. The evidence is observational as well. Consider the following:

- Many grade schools, particularly those in rural areas, have been using classroom desks made in the 1940s. They can no longer do so. It seems that the increasing size of the young American posterior prevents many of today's grade-school students from fitting the school desks of 50 years ago.
- Jeans, the uniform of American youth, have grown larger. A major manufacturer has again recut dies to accommodate the increasingly larger sizes of American children and adolescents.

Many parents complain that not only are kids today more overweight, but they're also less fit than ever. At a youth baseball game where both teams sported more "extra-large" than "small" uniforms, I overheard one dad complain, "These kids can't run from first to third without being winded. We're raising a generation of out-of-shape butterballs." That observation is validated in numerous studies. Says Dan Haydon, former executive director of the Governor's Commission on Physical Fitness in Texas, "Kids are less fit now than at any other time data has been taken."

FROM "BABY FAT" TO OBESITY

The problem is not a few extra pounds of "baby fat." The image of a smiling baby with pudgy cheeks, chubby thighs, and rolls of flesh around wrists and ankles is taken as a picture of good health. Perhaps this is related to the extra fat that helped babies survive lean times. And the problem is not necessarily the "chunky" child or teen. Many kids grow out of temporary weight gain. And some, despite the extra weight, may actually be more fit than their leaner counterparts.

But today it is recognized that the chubby baby frequently becomes the overweight child, who in turn becomes the obese adult. The fact is that many children and adolescents have already moved well beyond the chubbiness stage to the more serious conditions of obesity and extreme obesity.

These harsh terms—obesity and extreme obesity—often bring knee-jerk negative reactions, particularly when used to describe our children. However, they are not arbitrary labels but conditions that carry medical definitions. Generally, health professionals categorize people as "obese" if they are more than 20% above the ideal weight for their age, height and gender. So, if Johnny should weigh about 100 pounds but tips the scales at 122 pounds, he is considered obese. People more than 40% over their ideal weight are categorized as "extremely obese." If Mary should weigh about 100 pounds, but her weight is 145 pounds, she is considered extremely obese.

Unfortunately, these terms apply to too many of our children and teens. According to Dr. William Dietz, a pediatrician at Tufts University School of Medicine who specializes in childhood nutrition, *one in five American children is obese*. He found that compared with the 1960s, obesity among today's children and adolescents has skyrocketed.

Increase in Numbers of Obese and Extremely Obese Children and Adolescents

	Ages	
	6–11	12–17
Obese	+54%	+39%
Extremely obese	+98%	+64%

Can these figures be correct? Are there almost twice as many "extremely obese" kids aged 6 to 11 than there were in the 1960s?

Unfortunately, the answer is yes. Indeed, the ongoing, 22-year Bogalusa Heart Study of 14,000 children and young adults has produced similar data showing that the number of overweight kids has more than doubled in the last two decades.

Certain segments of young American society also seem to be at greater risk for obesity. African-American girls and Mexican-American boys, for example, have been found to be more prone to obesity or extreme obesity at a young age, as have the children of poorer families. Even location may make a difference. One study of children aged 6 to 11 found that a 9-state northeastern area had almost twice the percentage of overweight children as a 17-state westward stretch starting at Kansas.

Where Children Are Overweight

Region of the U.S.	% of Children Who Are Overweight
Northeast (Pennsylvania, New York, New Jersey, New England)	22.8%
Midwest (Illinois, Indiana, Iowa, Michigan, Minnesota, Missouri, Ohio, Wisconsin)	18.6
South (ending at the borders of Texas and Oklahoma)	15.3
West	13.9

The message is clear. The average child of the 1990s weighs more, has more body fat and is less fit than the average child of the 1960s. A dangerously high percentage of American kids today are overweight at an early age, and the trend is that these kids become obese and extremely obese adults.

Baby fat, it seems, is now old enough to drive.

OUTLOOK FOR
THE FUTURE

One of the tragedies of this situation is that many
overweight children are condemned at an early age
to a life of obesity. Says Dr. Leonard Epstein, a specialist
in childhood obesity at the State University of New York
at Buffalo, "We should be concerned about childhood and
adolescent weight because it predicts adult weight. Obese
children go on to become obese adults."

The evidence for this is overwhelming. The predictability of excessive weight extends all the way back to
early infancy. A 1976 report in the *New England Journal of
Medicine* offered proof that chubby infants were more
likely to become obese adults. And more recently the
Bogalusa Heart Study found a strong "tracking" tendency
in lean, obese and extremely obese children. That is to
say, lean children tend to stay lean, and chubby children
tend to remain heavy—all the way to adulthood.

A critical factor seems to be the age at which obesity
begins. The older the child, the greater the risk that obesity will continue into adulthood. Overweight in girls during early adolescence (after puberty) is closely related to
overweight at age 50. According to pediatrician Dr. Laura
Nathanson, an obese infant has a 1-in-10 chance of
becoming an obese adult, while an obese preschooler has
a 1-in-4 chance. Says Dr. Leonard Epstein, "About 40%
of obese seven-year-olds become obese adults."

This trend is echoed by Dr. Robert Suskind, a pediatrician at Louisiana State University, who found that 70%
of children considered obese at ages 10 to 13 will go on to
become obese adults. And the pattern continues through
adolescence. The National Research Council reports that
more than 80% of obese adolescents remain obese in
adulthood.

A second important factor is the degree of obesity

involved. Research on seven-year-olds illustrates the predictability of adult obesity:

- Of those who are 30% to 45% over their ideal weight, almost half will be obese in adulthood;
- Of those who are 46% to 65% over their ideal weight, about four in five will be obese in adulthood;
- Of those who are 65% or more over their ideal weight, virtually all will be obese adults.

Because overweight kids are likely to become overweight adults, early intervention is imperative to help children control weight, increase fitness and reduce the risk of future health problems. As emphasized by Laurel Mellin, director of the Center for Child and Adolescent Obesity at the University of California at San Francisco, "Problems related to obesity are very treatable in childhood, less treatable in adolescence and almost untreatable in adulthood."

CHAPTER 2

ESCALATING HEALTH RISKS

One of the principal reasons for concern about overweight kids is the impact of excess weight on their future health. Too often, appearance has been the chief focus of overweight. This is, after all, a nation where you cannot be "too rich or too thin." But health professionals are now calling for a fundamental change in public thinking. Former Surgeon General C. Everett Koop says, "Excess weight should be regarded not as a cosmetic problem but as an important, chronic, degenerative disease that debilitates individuals. It is responsible for 300,000 premature deaths in the U.S. each year. In children, it is the earliest sign of poor health."

Childhood and adolescent overweight can lead to a variety of adult diseases: coronary heart disease, stroke, hypertension, diabetes, certain cancers, gallbladder disease, arthritis, gout and restricted mobility. In addition:

- When suffering with the same illness, overweight children are sicker longer than their normal-weight counterparts.
- Both overweight children and adults are more susceptible to complications from surgery, infections and delayed healing of wounds.
- Overweight girls are more prone to menstrual problems.
- Overweight adults die from all causes at an earlier age than adults of normal weight.

Says Dr. Gilman Grave at the National Institute of Child Health and Human Development, "Overweight children and adolescents, particularly those who are obese or seriously obese, are clearly facing a doubling of the risk for adult diseases later in life."

Overweight is connected to three significant health concerns: heart disease, cancer and poor self-image/self-esteem. Because their symptoms are not usually evident in childhood, heart disease and cancer (discussed later in this chapter) are not generally identified with children. But today we know that childhood habits can impact adult outcomes. It just takes a wait of 20 to 40 years before these diseases manifest themselves.

This is not the case with emotional health issues impacted by obesity, such as poor self-image/self-esteem, which can penalize the overweight child as well as the obese adult.

SELF-IMAGE/SELF-ESTEEM

High self-image/self-esteem is critical to positive human development. Research shows that people who think well of themselves have greater confidence, achieve more satisfying results and are happier in life. Unfortunately, this is a society that tends to equate physical characteristics with character, intelligence and self-worth, and overweight people often suffer the consequences. To paraphrase Will Rogers, "It's no sin to be fat, but it might as well be." Writes Lisa Grunwald of *Life* magazine, "In our closets, hanging like old calendars, are the dresses and suits we wore a few winters ago, when we were 10 pounds thinner, but still not thin enough. Thin enough for what? The answer is stupid and simple: thin enough to be loved."

Children receive this message early in life. Overweight children frequently stand out among their peers and are made to feel different and inferior. They are easy targets for gibes, jokes and ugly names. Children of "normal" weight often have a low opinion of overweight children. One study showed that even preschoolers were already determining the worth of their classmates based on weight. Amazingly, these young children characterized their fatter peers as "ugly, stupid, mean, sloppy and lazy, prone to lying and not to be trusted."

Many adults have similar views. Rude strangers feel free to make comments about "chubby" children, and teachers sometimes reject and ridicule the overweight children they are supposed to be helping. In a landmark study published in *Parents Magazine*, both children and adults were asked to rank "different" children. An overweight child was included in the list. The overweight child received a lower ranking than a child in a wheelchair, a child with a disfigured face and a child with one hand missing. Indeed, some parents of overweight kids report that they feel ashamed of their children—even parents who are overweight themselves!

No wonder overweight children, sensing others' low opinion of them, tend to become social outcasts—self-conscious, passive and withdrawn. Rarely do these children get to star in school plays or become class presidents or team captains. Many choose to underachieve. Researchers find, for example, that overweight kids don't do as well on reading and math tests as their thinner counterparts. Even when they make an effort to do better, their efforts are often met with further rejection. Author Vicki Lansky described the experience of one overweight youngster:

> When I was in seventh grade, I finally worked up the courage to try out for the class musical. Even though I was fat, I could sing! I made the chorus and couldn't wait to start reheasals. I thought looks wouldn't matter. I was wrong. On the first day the director divided us up into two groups. In the first group were all the pretty,

popular, thin girls and good-looking boys; they got to stand in front. The rest of us stood in the back, where the audience wouldn't see anything but our heads.

Overweight children learn to make themselves the butt of jokes as part of an elaborate defense system. This results in poor self-image/self-esteem, which carries into teen and adult years. Many will face outright discrimination later on at school, at work and in society. Being overweight at an early age takes both a social and emotional toll in childhood and usually in adulthood as well, setting the stage for long-term health problems.

CORONARY HEART DISEASE

Coronary heart disease is the major cause of death in the United States today. Every year there are 1.5 million heart attacks, yielding more than 500,000 deaths. One American suffers a heart attack every minute. Unhealthy lifestyles such as poor diet, lack of exercise, and cigarette smoking are the major environmental problems that contribute to the disease.

The mechanics of coronary heart disease are quite simple. The heart needs blood to function (after all, it beats more than 100,000 times a day). It receives this blood through a surrounding lacework of tiny coronary arteries. At birth these arteries are like thin-walled rubber tubes that expand and contract as the heart pumps, but over time layers of cholesterol and fat can form "fatty streaks" on the inner walls, much as rust accumulates in an old water pipe. The walls thicken and harden, causing the arteries to lose their ability to expand and narrowing the channel through which blood flows to the heart. Should the blood supply be so restricted that the heart no longer functions normally, a heart attack can result.

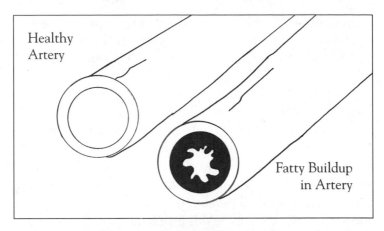

Healthy Artery

Fatty Buildup in Artery

A prime characteristic of coronary heart disease is its slow and silent progression over many years, usually with no outward signs or symptoms. This is why so many people are surprised by the "sudden" heart attack. In reality, the disease is not sudden at all. According to experts at the National Cholesterol Education Program, compelling evidence exists that "cholesterol buildup begins in childhood and progresses slowly into adulthood, at which time it frequently leads to coronary heart disease." Dr. Guy Reiff at the University of Michigan puts it in plainer terms: "Heart disease starts in the first grade."

The first changes of coronary heart disease, fatty deposits in the coronary arteries, begin appearing by age three in children eating a typical American diet. By age 12, nearly 70% of children are affected—and more advanced deposits rapidly appear throughout the teens. By age 20, deposits are nearly always present.

The link between diet and heart disease in young peo-. ple surfaced in studies based on autopsies of American soldiers killed during the Korean and Vietnam wars. Despite an average age of 22, many of the soldiers suffered from coronary heart disease. It was estimated that some 45% of these young men were well on their way to a heart attack because of their diet. More recently, autopsies of children and teens who died accidentally confirm that coronary artery blockages exist even in youth. Considered a rare finding in the past, fatty deposits are being found today in the arteries of children and teens with increasing frequency.

A 1997 study shows why this is happening. Autopsies of male and female teenagers found dramatic differences in the severity of fatty deposits on arteries, depending on whether or not they ate a fatty diet. Fatty streaks were found in the coronary arteries of young people with high levels of cholesterol in their bood. The amount of fatty deposits increased with age, and the difference between subjects with high and low cholesterol showed up as early as age 15.

"What this illustrates," says Dr. Basil Rifkind of the National Heart, Lung and Blood Institute, "is that the problems of diet and heart disease start early in life. A childhood diet rich in fatty foods can begin the progression toward heart disease later in life. Children who eat a lot of cheeseburgers and milk shakes increase their risk of heart attacks if they do not change their dietary habits by young adulthood." Dr. Gerald Berenson, director of the Bogalusa Heart Study, concurs: "The disease that produces a full-blown attack in adulthood often starts during childhood and the teen years. We believe that half or more of today's kids are at cardiac risk, and unless we do something about their diet and exercise habits, our children will become the next generation of heart attack victims. By the year 2020, heart disease will claim 1.5 million lives each year of today's 60 million children."

KIDS AND CHOLESTEROL

It is well known that the higher the level of blood cholesterol, the greater the risk for heart disease. An individual with a cholesterol level of 260 mg/dl has four times the risk of a heart attack as an individual with a level of 200 mg/dl. Unfortunately, more and more American kids are demonstrating elevated cholesterol. The American Heart

Association estimates that 36% of children and teens, aged 2 to 19, have high cholesterol. Says Dr. Susan Oparil, "We've found elevated cholesterol levels in children as young as eight years old. One study of 5,000 Iowa schoolchildren showed half to have cholesterol levels that can be considered a risk for future heart disease."

Children with elevated cholesterol tend to "track" in later life to adults with high cholesterol. And, of course, adults with high cholesterol tend to develop coronary heart disease. So, blood cholesterol levels in childhood play a major role in the development of heart disease and stroke later in life. In fact, trials show that in every nation of the world where children have elevated cholesterol levels—especially Finland, Northern Ireland, Scotland, England and the United States—there is also a high death rate from coronary heart disease among adults. Conversely, wherever children's cholesterol levels are low, there is very little risk of coronary heart disease later in life. It appears that children's cholesterol levels predict heart disease several decades before the first symptoms are likely to show.

What should your child's cholesterol level be? The following tables show risk levels for children and teens according to the American Heart Association. (Adult levels are included for the purpose of comparison.)

Total Cholesterol Risk Levels

Adults	Classification	Children/Adolescents (Ages 2–19)
Below 200*	Desirable	Below 170*
200–239	Borderline risk	170–199
240 and over	High risk	200 and over

*It should be noted that many health professionals believe optimal cholesterol is under 150 mg/dl.

The age at which children should be screened is still a matter of controversy. The American Heart Association advocates cholesterol screening for children who have at least one parent with high risk, or whose parents or grandparents are known to have had heart disease before the age of 55. Other groups, such as the Bogalusa Heart Study, strongly recommend screening for all children older than age two.

Parents should consult with their child's doctor before making a decision.

LDL Cholesterol

Children who have a high total cholesterol level should also have their LDL cholesterol evaluated. LDL cholesterol, or low-density lipoprotein, is known as "bad" cholesterol because "fatty streaks" tend to build up in the arteries when it reaches a high level.

The table below expresses the link between LDL cholesterol levels and cardiac risk for children and adolescents.

LDL Cholesterol Risk Levels

Adults	Classification	Children/Adolescents (Ages 2–19)
Below 130	Desirable	Below 110
130–159	Borderline risk	110–129
160 and over	High risk	130 and over

Because LDL cholesterol is very sensitive to dietary fat, particularly saturated fat, an expert panel of 42 major U.S. health and professional organizations—including the American Academy of Pediatrics and the American Heart Association—recently issued recommendations that all healthy children above the age of two eat a low-fat diet to stave off heart disease later in life. A heart-healthy eating plan specifies a diet with no more than 30% of total calories from fat and less than 10% of total calories from saturated fat. The recipes and menu plans in this book will help parents to accomplish this goal for their families.

HDL Cholesterol

HDL cholesterol, or high-density lipoprotein, is known as "good" cholesterol because it acts as arterial Drano, removing harmful LDL cholesterol from the bloodstream and helping the body to excrete it. Removal helps to prevent "fatty streaks" from building up in the arteries. The more HDL a person has, the lower the cardiac risk.

The table below expresses the link between HDL levels and cardiac risk for children and teens.

HDL Cholesterol Risk Levels

Adults	Classification	Children/Adolescents (Ages 2–19)
Over 45*	Desirable	Over 45*
35–45	Borderline risk	35–45
Below 35	High risk	Below 35

*According to the National Cholesterol Education Program, the "most desirable" HDL level is over 60 mg/dl.

HDL is sensitive to physical activity. People who exercise regularly and are fit generally have higher levels of HDL. Conversely, sedentary people tend to have lower levels. This is one reason for establishing physical activity goals for children and adolescents.

KIDS AND OVERWEIGHT

While cholesterol receives most of the press, extra weight also increases the risk for heart disease. According to recent estimates from the National Institutes of Health, one-quarter of cardiovascular disease can be linked to overweight. New research shows that even modest weight gains in adulthood raise heart attack risk. An eight-year study of more than 115,000 American women aged 30 to 55 revealed that those as little as 5% overweight were 30% more likely than their lean counterparts to develop heart disease. That risk increased to 80% in those who were moderately overweight, while obese subjects were over 300% more likely to develop coronary heart disease.

As illustrated in Chapter 1, today's overweight kids tend to become tomorrow's overweight adults. And overweight adults are disposed to have a greater risk for heart disease. Says Dr. Alvin M. Mauer of the American Academy of Pediatrics, "Childhood obesity may be a greater risk than elevated cholesterol. During childhood and adolescence, obesity is a critical determinant of future cardiovascular risk." In a nation that experiences more deaths each year from coronary disease than from AIDS, cancer and auto accidents combined, this is not a small consideration.

It is not presently clear whether childhood overweight by itself is a risk factor for adult heart disease or whether the lifestyle habits that contribute to overweight are the real culprits. It may be a combination effect. In addition, genetics can be a factor. But for most people there is little doubt that high-fat dietary habits learned early in life, coupled with a national propensity for inactivity, bear much of the responsibility for the American epidemic of heart disease.

CANCER

Overweight is also a significant risk factor for certain types of cancer found in adults. In a long-term study of 750,000 men and women conducted by the American Cancer Society, the rate of cancer was significantly higher among people 40% or more overweight. For men, this mainly involves cancer of the colon and rectum. For women, there are higher death rates from breast and endometrial cancer, as well as cancer of the gallbladder and cervix. Researchers think the reason for the strong tie between overweight and breast and endometrial cancers

is that obesity tends to increase the production of estro-
gen, the female hormone that can enhance tumor growth
at these sites.

Perhaps a more important link is shown in evidence
suggesting that the high-fat American diet, which contributes so greatly to childhood and adolescent overweight, also contributes to long-term cancer production.

According to the National Cancer Institute, fat is the
dietary substance most strongly linked to cancer. About
one-third of all cancer deaths in the United States are
related to diet, or about the same percentage caused by
smoking. Says Dr. Bruce Ames of the University of
California at Berkeley, "Toxic waste and alar may grab the
headlines, but lowering dietary fat will do more to reduce
cancer than eliminating pollutants." So, what our children eat not only can make them fat today, but can also
set them up for cancer in adulthood.

Numerous population studies and trials strongly suggest that a high-fat, low-fiber diet directly increases the
risk specifically for colon, breast and prostate cancers—
after lung cancer, the second, third and fourth causes of
cancer deaths in the United States. These three types of
cancer account for almost 40% of all new cancer cases.

Dietary fat contributes to cancer risk in three ways:

- It acts as a cancer promoter in cells. Fat is not a car-
cinogen itself, but in many people it stimulates tumor
growth.
- It contributes to overweight and obesity, an independent risk factor for certain cancers.
- Foods rich in dietary fat often displace healthier
foods in the diet pattern, such as fresh fruits, vegetables
and whole grains, i.e., foods rich in protective fiber and
antioxidant vitamins.

According to Dr. Oliver Alabaster, director of cancer
research at George Washington University, there is evidence that 60% of cancer in women and 40% of cancer in

men is caused by diet. But will the fat your child eats today trigger cancer later in life? No one knows for sure, although some studies indicate that childhood diet pattern is immensely important. The National Research Council's Committee on Diet and Health, for example, states that "fat intake early in life may have a greater influence on breast cancer risk than later in life." And the National Research Council's 1989 Diet and Health Report concluded: "The weight of evidence suggests that what we eat during our lifetime strongly influences the probability of developing certain cancers."

Few studies, however, have looked at the impact of dietary patterns in children and the impact of these patterns on cancer risk later in life. Part of the problem is cancer's typically long latency period and the inability of researchers to follow thousands of children over their entire lifetime. Should parents, then, disregard diet until all the evidence is in? "No," says Dr. Myron Winick of Columbia University. "If we extrapolate from the studies that have already been done, then add a dose of common sense, I think you can make a strong case that long-term eating habits will affect cancer risk."

BAD NEWS / GOOD NEWS

Dr. Lloyd Kolbe of the Centers for Disease Control and Prevention states that "The major health problems facing our nation today are caused, in large part, by behaviors established during youth. The greatest health risks for today's children are those of heart disease and cancer as adults. Such diseases, responsible for more than half of all adult deaths, are not an inevitable part of growing older. Both are related to a child's dietary and physical activity habits."

In summary, the news is both bad and good. The bad news is that overweight children tend to become obese adults with a higher risk of coronary heart disease, cancer and self-image/self-esteem problems.

The good news is that much of the obesity in youngsters can be traced to lifestyle, particularly physical activity and dietary habits. And lifestyle habits can change. By helping your child now to improve diet and exercise habits, you can prevent or correct a weight problem. More important, you'll be helping your child to develop a lifestyle that will reduce the risk for future disease.

Dr. John Knowles of the Rockefeller Foundation aptly sums it up: "Ninety-nine percent of us are born healthy and are made sick as a result of personal misbehavior or environmental conditions. The ability to lengthen one's life depends first on the capacity not to shorten it."

CHAPTER 3

WHAT PARENTS CAN DO

The first step in dealing with any health condition (and childhood and adolescent overweight and obesity *are* health conditions) is to make a distinction between noncontrollable risk factors and controllable risk factors.

Noncontrollable risk factors are those that are out of our hands—beyond our ability to make a difference. A family history of heart disease, for instance, is a noncontrollable risk factor for heart attack. We can't change our parents, even though we might not like their legacy. People with a genetic history of heart disease are simply more prone to developing it than are those with a family history free of the disease.

Controllable risk factors, on the other hand, are just that—controllable. For example, anywhere from 20% to 40% of all cardiac deaths are attributed directly to smoking. But smoking is a choice. The individual is in control, which makes smoking a controllable risk factor.

With respect to overweight and obesity, both noncontrollable and controllable factors come into play. The most important noncontrollable factor in this regard is, of course, heredity.

THE ROLE OF GENETICS

Does the shape of your genes dictate the shape of your jeans? The truth is, some families have a genetic predisposition to excess weight. Such a hereditary burden can have a significant influence on the weight of children and teens and can, in some individuals, predispose obesity. A certain percentage of children will end up stockier, or heavier, than others even if they eat relatively small amounts of food and engage in a fair amount of vigorous physical activity.

The role of genetics in overweight is complex and not fully understood. However, many population studies show a strong inheritance factor. The common thread appears to be that overweight parents tend to produce overweight children.

Chances of a Child Being Overweight

- If both parents are of average weight   15%
- If one parent is overweight   50%
- If both parents are overweight   80%

Says one pediatrician, "If an overweight child has lean parents and two slim siblings, there is a good chance that he will grow into his weight. But if both parents and other siblings are overweight or obese, the chances for that child to slim down are few."

Genetic predisposition to obesity has been illustrated in a number of studies. One such study involved pairs of identical twins. In some pairs, the twins had been raised together; in others, the twins had been separated early in life and raised apart from each other. The findings of the study included data showing that the twins who had been raised apart were just as similar in weight as those who had been raised together.

GENETICS AND OVERWEIGHT

As researchers try to figure out why some people gain weight and others do not, it is becoming increasingly apparent that heredity may be an influence in a number of ways.

Genetics can decrease metabolic rate.

Genetics can influence metabolism, the rate at which a person burns calories. Calories from food are a source of energy for the body. They are burned to fuel exercise, physical activity and basic bodily functions. Calories that are not burned are stored as body fat. In effect, stored fat becomes a fuel tank for the body. When 3,500 extra calories have been accumulated, one pound of body fat has been stored.

As long as the amount of calories consumed is in balance with the amount of calories burned, excess body fat will not accumulate. So, on the surface, it seems as if losing weight should involve nothing more than balancing that equation in our favor by consuming fewer calories. This would be true if we all burned calories at exactly the same rate. But we do not.

Maintaining a proper balance has a lot to do with our personal metabolism, or what some term the body's "idling speed." Some people simply burn more calories than others when they're doing the same things, or doing nothing at all. If you could look inside two kids who are lying down resting, you might find that their bodies are using calories in completely different ways. One child might be burning up calories to produce body heat, while the other might be storing calories as fat.

The fact is that certain people naturally have a high metabolism and, like luxury cars with big engines, burn fuel at a rapid rate. These people tend to be lean. Others have a sluggish metabolism that processes calories like a small, fuel-efficient car. Their problem, of course, is that it's easy to store body fat. People with low calorie-burning capacities tend toward overweight and obesity.

Some research suggests that, to a certain extent, metabolism is influenced by heredity. So, for some people, a predisposition to be overweight could be the result of genetically influenced slow metabolism.

Genetics can influence setpoint weight.

Genetics may play a role in creating a "setpoint" weight, which is a predetermined weight that the body works to keep. Proponents theorize that the brain contains a weight-regulating mechanism that chooses the amount of body fat it considers ideal for a person's needs. It then works tirelessly to defend that weight by controlling how much the person eats and how much body fat will be carried.

Even if one is successful in losing weight on a diet, the body will strive to get back to its setpoint weight. According to Dr. Theodore Van Italie of the Obesity Research Center at St. Luke's Hospital in New York, "It's clear that if you lose weight, adaptations come into play that make it possible to regain that weight more efficiently."

In other words, a person may be programmed to have his or her weight stay at a certain level. When setpoint weight is threatened by a cut in calories, the mechanism increases appetite and lowers metabolic rate by 15% to 25%. By reducing the rate at which calories are burned, the body becomes more energy-efficient and weight loss is harder to achieve. This may be the reason that many people reach a "plateau" in their weight-loss results.

Genetics can influence fat cells.

Studies find that genetics may have an impact on fat cells, the body's storage containers for fat. It is now known that an average healthy baby is born with 5 to 6 billion fat cells. An adult of normal weight has 30 to 40 billion fat cells. And an obese adult carries some 80 to 120 billion fat cells. The more fat cells there are, the "heavier" the body wants to be and the harder it becomes to keep weight down.

The number of fat cells a person has is, in part, genetically determined, but experts are not certain about the impact of heredity. What is clearly understood is that the development of too many fat cells during childhood may signal the beginning of a lifelong weight problem. According to Dr. Charles Attwood, "The increased number of permanent fat cells created during infancy and again during adolescence is probably the chief reason for the gradual weight gain in adults as they age."

In addition, once a fat cell is created, it's forever. Fat cells shrink and swell like sponges with the amount of fat inside them. You can reduce the *size* of fat cells by restricting caloric intake, thus forcing the body to use up the fat stored in cells. But you can never reduce the *number* of fat cells. They merely shrink, not disappear, and lie in wait for the chance to swell up again.

Contrary to popular thought, crash diets do not melt fat cells. In fact, when the body is starved, says Dr. Irving Faust of Rockefeller University, "fat cells appear to be as fully protected as brain cells. They can become smaller but never totally vanish."

HEREDITY IS NOT DESTINY

To answer the question why so many kids are overweight and out of shape, we should focus on the controllable factors of lifestyle that have a direct impact on the problem. The great importance of such controllable factors is recognized in light of the fact that

- Obesity and poor fitness in American youngsters is a modern phenomenon, and
- Kids in many other parts of the world are not as overweight as American children and teens.

Have our genes changed dramatically from the 1960s to produce this modern epidemic? I don't think so. Are our children biologically different from other kids in the world? The answer is no. For most overweight children, the problem is lifestyle, not genes.

There is no doubt that genetic factors may predispose a child to be overweight. However, most health professionals agree that genetics does not cause most kids to be overweight. A study at the Medical College of Wisconsin in Milwaukee found that genetics accounted for only 12% of overweight people, while cultural and environmental influences were more important influences by far.

Lifestyle changes can, in almost all cases, alter the effects of a person's genetic blueprint. Metabolic rate, for instance, may be depressed because of heredity, so it's easy to blame obesity on inherited low metabolism. But nearly all research indicates that for most people low metabolism is the *result* of obesity rather than the *cause*. Most overweight people started out life with perfectly "normal" metabolisms. As they gained weight, they developed a lower metabolic rate, making it easier to gain pounds and harder to take them off.

Is it possible to return metabolic rate to "normal"? Experts advise that regular exercise is the best way to speed up a sluggish metabolism. Performed on a routine (rather than occasional) basis, exercise can boost metabolism by 20% to 30%. A University of Southern California study, for example, showed that people who exercised had a metabolic rate up to 28% higher than if they did not exercise.

The setpoint theory is discouraging because it implies that we don't have much control over our weight. While setpoint may be a valid genetic factor, studies show that when a prudent diet is combined with physical activity, the setpoint can be favorably changed. "The body seems to sense that an active person needs to be thin," says Dr. Dennis Remington of Brigham Young University, "and it reacts by adjusting its concept of what constitutes the proper amount of body fat. Lowering the setpoint allows the body to process calories more efficiently."

And while the base number of fat cells may be genetically determined, that number is less important to weight control than their size and content, both of which are influenced by diet and exercise. Does an overabundance of fat cells doom us to obesity? Not necessarily. An individual with a high number of fat cells can be of average weight—if those fat cells are very small. Does a scarcity of cells guarantee slimness? Not at all. Someone with minimal fat cells can be overweight—if those fat cells are very large. In the final analysis, the amount of fat contained in the cells dictates body weight, and cell content is a product of lifestyle choices.

According to Dr. Thomas Wadden of the University of Pennsylvania School of Medicine, the steady increase in percentage of overweight and obese Americans during the 20th century shows that environment exerts the major influence. "Our gene pool isn't changing," he states. "Rather, it's that our environment now supports fatness. Because our society encourages people to eat more and more and to exercise less and less, those people who are genetically predisposed to become fat will do so. For every dollar spent by the Surgeon General and researchers to prevent and treat obesity, a hundred dollars is spent by the food industry to lull people into eating more fattening foods. We're being fattened up by the food industry and slimmed down by the billion-dollar-diet-and-exercise industry. That's great for the capitalistic system, but it's not so great for the consumer."

Genetic "baggage" does not guarantee overweight. However, when pro-fat heredity combines with a high-fat diet and sedentary lifestyle, overweight is invariably the result. "Remember," says Dr. Charles Attwood, "lifestyle changes can alter a child's genetic blueprint manyfold. A family history of adult onset diabetes, for instance, may double a child's risk for eventually developing the disease. However, when the same child has poor lifestyle habits resulting in obesity, the chances of becoming a diabetic increase by 50 times."

Genetic history is important to a child's weight. But it is not as significant as the child's lifestyle. Dr. Louis Aroni of Columbia University says, "It's usually not a too-slow metabolism that makes us fat, but a too-fast fork. Studies clearly link childhood obesity to many of the same factors that cause adult obesity, including poor diet and inadequate exercise. Look at the Pima Indians. Those in the U.S. are obese; those in Mexico are thin. Their genetics are the same. It's their lifestyle that differs."

Dr. William Connor of the Oregon Health Sciences University sums it up: "Too often, when children are overweight, genetics is blamed. My experience is that children usually are overweight as the result of eating patterns and sedentary habits learned from their parents. If parents won't change, the child won't change."

A CHALLENGE TO PARENTS: LOOK IN THE MIRROR

The ancient Greek scholar Demosthenes never struck his students when they made a mistake; instead, he smacked their parents. His theory was that children learn by example and are therefore blameless if they do wrong. Never has this been more applicable than in the lifestyles and health of children and teens today.

Actually, children start out with healthy lifestyle habits—good inclinations to eat right and be active. Infants are born with the ability to regulate their caloric intake; babies fed a high-calorie formula will drink less than those given a diluted liquid. Toddlers and preschoolers rarely overeat; they too can regulate how much food and drink they need, often enjoying a variety of fruits and vegetables. Left to their own devices, children are naturally active. Running and jumping are a way of life.

So where do they pick up all those bad habits? Parents should take a look in the mirror. As caregivers and role models, many parents have set their kids on the path to overweight and poor fitness. Susan Kalish, author of *Your Child's Fitness*, writes:

If we complain about our children's terrible eating hab-its, remember that they didn't crawl into a fast-food restaurant for their first visit—someone took them. If we lament that our children watch too much televi-sion, who first turned the set on and sat them in front of it? The fact is, it's easier to watch over children who are watching TV rather than playing outdoors. It's eas-ier to keep children at home than to take them to a recreation center to play ball. It's easier to hand chil-dren a bag of chips than to make a sandwich. And so we take the easy way out—at our children's expense.

Columnist Susan Estrich echoes this perspective: "The ability to regulate food intake found so naturally in babies and toddlers can be destroyed by well-meaning parents who use food as a bribe or a reward, treat certain foods as forbidden or insist on clean plates regardless of hunger." We must recognize that many of our caregiving decisions have moved our children away from healthy foods and an active lifestyle to a high-fat, sedentary way of life.

In addition, today's children are bombarded with un-healthy messages, attitudes and behaviors in the media. The advertising budget for M&M's, for example, is twice that for the National Cancer Institute's entire "Five-A-Day" program, which promotes the consumption of fruits and vegetables. Is it any wonder, then, that young children ask for candy instead of fruits and vegetables? Parents must combat these messages and attitudes to posi-tively influence their children's fitness.

And finally, parents have a responsibility as role mod-els. This means that your attitude and actions about food and fitness have an enormous impact on your child.

PARENTS LEAD . . .

It's nice to believe that children do what parents say. They do not. They do what parents do. For many kids, this means picking up unhealthy lifestyle habits at an early age. What messages are you giving your kids? If you smoke, you can preach all you want to about not smoking, but it will fall on deaf ears. If your only exercise is to jog from the TV to the refrigerator during commercials, your child may not much care about exercise, either. If you live on fast food and eat a high-fat diet . . . chances are, so will your child. *Parents are the single most influential factor regarding how active and healthy a child will be.*

This is a nation where slimness is seen as a virtue and overweight as a character flaw. Wake up a pound thinner and you feel better—not just physically but morally and perhaps spiritually. Wake up a pound heavier and you confirm your worst fears—you're turning into the person you secretly knew you were going to be all along. Worth and weight seem to have an inverse relationship. We feel bigger when we're smaller, smaller when we're bigger.

Says author Kim Chernan, "In this era, when inflation has assumed alarming proportions and the threat of nuclear war has become a serious danger, when violent crime is on the increase and unemployment a persistent social fate, 500 people are asked by pollsters what they fear most in the world and 190 answer that their greatest fear is 'getting fat.' "

An unhealthy obsession with weight already exists, particularly among females. Consider this:

- In 1972, 23% of women in the United States said they were dissatisfied with their overall appearance; today that figure has more than doubled to 48%.
- Surveys show that 9 out of 10 people think they weigh too much.
- Gallup reports that one-half of American women are on a diet at any given time.

. . . AND CHILDREN FOLLOW

Children are not immune from this culture. A shocking 80% of 10-year-old girls suffer from fear of fatness. According to a recent survey, 40% of 9- and 10-year-old girls—many of whom are of normal weight or even under-weight—are trying to lose weight. In extreme cases, some even diet, binge and show signs of anorexia. Reports one teenage baby-sitter, "I was baby-sitting for this little girl—she couldn't have been more than eight—and she asked me how many calories a bottle of Clearly Canadian had. She's eight years old! What does she need to be thinking about that for?"

Dr. Ronald Kleinman, a pediatric nutrition expert at Massachusetts General Hospital, suggests that these children are just mirroring adult attitudes. "They see thin women everybody considers gorgeous, and they make tons of money, and girls want to be like that."

By the fifth grade, American children have received the message, directly and indirectly, that any accumulation of fat—regardless of the reason—is undesirable. And the problem is even greater with teens. One of the hall-marks of adolescence is a preoccupation with appearance and body image. As children reach the teen years, their increased awareness of society's emphasis on having the "perfect" body, coupled with what is often an acute or exaggerated sense of how their bodies differ from the ideal, makes many of them feel worthless and depressed.

Much of this perception is fueled by television and the print media (where you could bounce a quarter off the well-toned abs of cast members on any number of "twenty-something" programs, and fashion magazines are filled with airbrushed photos of emaciated models), which are defining what constitutes beauty or even an acceptable body as virtually inaccessible. The result? Many Americans are feeling worse and worse about the workaday bodies they actually inhabit. And the people be-ing hurt most are the ones who are the most vulnerable:

adolescents. "If teens compare themselves with these unrealistic standards," says Dr. Cash, "they can only conclude they are born losers."

Girls are particularly prone to obsessing about the shape of their bodies, but boys are not exempt. Consider that over 40% of the more than 900 12- to 22-year-old males questioned at a clinic in Tacoma, Washington, said they were dissatisfied with their weight; one out of three was not happy with his body shape. Indeed, studies show that the increased use of anabolic steroids by high school boys is based on a desire for a better "body image."

It is within this atmosphere that parents must work to help their children, but to do so without causing alarm or stress, or sending the wrong message. Berating children and teens about their weight or body shape can destroy self-esteem and be counterproductive. "It's not effective or appropriate to tell your child she should be unhappy with her body," says Dr. Ronna Kabatznick. "If you comment on the child's appearance or give her looks in a sorrowful or reproachful way, this will make her feel worse and she may eat more. The goal of thinness needs to be replaced by the goal of fitness. If you really want to influence your child, set a good example."

KEEP A HEALTHY PERSPECTIVE

Many of us feel guilty for not doing more about the way kids live today. We see that America's young people are becoming overweight and out-of-shape adults before they know it. We understand that television and video games, which for some children consume over 50 hours a week, keep them from being physically active. We realize that kids have easy access to high-calorie fast foods and junk foods, rich in harmful fat and cholesterol. And we know that teenagers, especially girls driven by a desire to be thin, are smoking in record numbers. "The underlying cause of these activities," says Dr. Donald Benson, "is that children adopt lifestyles that are parallel to those of their parents."

"Do what I say" just doesn't go as far with kids as "Do what I do." Dr. Richard Keelor sums it up best: "The only person's fitness and health you can change is your own. If you want to be an influence on the health and fitness of those you love, take care of yourself. There is a compelling influence in the power of personal example that will ripple outward to your family. Health is more infectious than disease."

Are you to blame if your child is overweight and out of shape? Of course not. Parents are already stretched too thin with a myriad of activities and responsibilities. The last thing we need is another guilt trip. Instead, parents need to think of themselves as part of the solution, not the problem. For most children, overweight is a product of lifestyle habits, particularly eating and physical activity. Emphasis, then, should not be on weight or appearance, but rather on changing the lifestyle habits that impact on weight and appearance. The proper perspective is not to produce a slim child, but to foster healthy lifestyle habits that produce fitness and health for a lifetime.

Problems of overweight need to be examined rationally and unemotionally. Parents should not criticize their children for being overweight. They should not panic and put their children on restrictive diets or force them to run 10 miles to "shape up." No matter how correct a parent's motivation, such diets are *not recommended* by health professionals. Indeed, many now say that subjecting children to weight-loss regimens does more harm than good. "Putting a child on a diet is the worst thing a parent can do," says dietitian and family therapist Ellyn Satter. "Actions to control weight should be taken only for the right reasons: to produce better health and fitness in your child. Losing weight is a by-product of that effort."

The chapters that follow will set out ways to make physical activity and healthier eating a natural part of your child's (and your family's) life. But these steps must be taken within a framework that focuses on effective lifestyle changes. Remember, *fitness and health, not weight loss, is the goal.*

The purpose of this book is to help you meet that goal. That's why it's not just about what children and teens can and should do to develop healthy lifestyle habits. It's also about what parents can and should do. It's for your kids. And it's for you.

PART II

PHYSICAL ACTIVITY: A FAMILY AFFAIR

CHAPTER 4

KIDS NEED EXERCISE

Regular physical activity is well recognized as a necessary component of a healthy, fit lifestyle. Unfortunately, this recognition has not been translated into action for American kids. Studies show, for instance, that the percentage of teenagers who exercise regularly has continued to drop—from 24% in 1987 to 21% in 1994. Such a decline in physical activity, a trend found in all age groups, caused the American Health Foundation to lower the health "grade" of the nation's youth from a C– in 1994 to a D in 1995. "This downward trend is significant," says Dr. James Rippe of Tufts University School of Medicine. "Many health problems and chronic diseases have their roots in childhood inactivity. With three out of four children living a sedentary lifestyle, they may be sacrificing a healthy future."

Ironically, an overwhelming majority of parents today believe their children are in good physical shape. According to a 1992 survey in *Prevention* magazine, 85% of parents polled said their child was "physically fit." Only 14% admitted their child was "out of shape." This may be the most troubling finding to come out of the current body of public opinion research. Unless parents recognize the problem, the current patterns of inactivity among children is likely to continue.

Why are children and especially teens less active today? They certainly have the same energy as youth in the past. But society has changed, and it's harder for

41

young people today to use that energy and become fit than it was for their counterparts in the 1960s. Television marketers have targeted young audiences, and kids have responded by watching 25 to 30 hours of TV a week. Computer games gobble up enormous amounts of time that used to be spent outdoors. In this age of single parenthood and two working parents, there is less free time available for parents to be active with their children. And, because of societal changes, parents don't feel safe letting kids go to the park or play on their own.

Often it's an organized activity . . . or nothing. Even when children engage in organized sports such as youth soccer, Little League or gymnastics, they seldom get enough exercise, frequently waiting for a turn at bat or watching other teammates take their turn. The result is that most children are not exercising at even the lowest acceptable levels for health, and inactivity becomes more habitual as they age. And as a consequence, many of today's kids are more sedentary, overweight and out of shape.

A CRITICAL SITUATION

It is estimated that, on average, *youngsters now get less than 15 minutes of activity a day.* Studies involving millions of kids aged 5 to 17 show that two-thirds fail to meet minimum fitness criteria. In fact, according to experts, most reach their fitness peak, such as it is, at age 14—and it's all downhill after that.

Kids, it seems, believe that the message to get fit doesn't apply to them. "While we're watching our weight," says parenting expert Vicki Lansky, "they're watching TV. While we're running around the block, they're walking to the refrigerator. While we're bending and stretching, they're sitting or sleeping."

As a result, more kids are starting off on a sedentary lifestyle earlier than ever before. "The concern is that the pattern of inactivity of adults is already well established by adolescence," says Dr. Gregory Heath of the Centers for Disease Control and Prevention. "The trend is that the proportion of young people who are inactive continues to increase." We're going to reap what we sow. And we appear to be sowing an inactive lifestyle that will reap untoward health consequences."

In the opinion of many experts, American kids are in worse shape than ever before in our history. Not only do the boys and girls of today weigh more than their same-age counterparts in the past (on average, a 12-year-old today weighs 11.4 pounds more than a 12-year-old in 1973), but they also don't measure up on tests of endurance and strength. In California, more than one-third of kids participating in a pilot aerobics program couldn't do 10 minutes of aerobic exercise. In Florida, kids scored lower on fitness tests than their counterparts did a decade earlier. In Texas, half the children scored "poor to weak" in the 600-yard run.

The findings of a study directed by the University of Michigan's Dr. Charles Kuntzleman, an authority on children and physical activity, are astounding. Some 19,000 boys and girls aged 6 to 17 were involved. Nine standard tests were used in the study, including sit-ups, pull-ups, a 50-yard dash, and walking/running. Dr. Kuntzleman found that one-third of the boys and one-half of the girls couldn't run a mile in 10 minutes or less, and that one-quarter of the boys and three-quarters of the girls were unable to do one pull-up. According to this study, American children would rank about 20th among nations worldwide. As the President's Council on Physical Fitness and Health cryptically reports, "The fitness boom never reached our children."

This situation is critical for four specific reasons:

- It is well known that physical inactivity is a significant predictor and cause of obesity in children and teens, independent of nutritional habits.

- Physical inactivity in children and teens is a significant predictor of coronary heart disease, cancer and other adult diseases.
- Poor fitness produces low self-esteem, poor body image, and not enough energy to be their best.
- Physical inactivity in childhood tends to "track" into adulthood. The sedentary child tends to become the sedentary adult.

But the reverse is also true. *The physically active child tends to become an active adult.* The challenge, then, is for parents to identify and remove the barriers that stand in the way of their kids' being more active.

THE BENEFITS OF EXERCISE

Experts tell us that kids do not exercise for the health benefits derived from physical activity. They run, jump and play organized sports to have fun, improve their skills, compete and be with their friends. But parents should understand the benefits of exercise in order to be able to combat unhealthy societal messages. They need to let their kids know that fitness is an important family priority and that physical activity, like brushing teeth, is a lifetime activity.

Being physically active is a crucial lifestyle factor in losing weight, controlling weight and increasing cardiovascular health. The 1996 Surgeon General's Report on Physical Activity and Health states that "the importance of promoting physical activity among youth is based on growing evidence that physical activity is associated with enhanced physical and psychosocial health." The report cites physical inactivity as a "major cause of overweight and obesity," a concern echoed by the U.S. Public Health

Service, the American College of Sports Medicine, the American Academy of Pediatrics, the American Heart Association and the American Medical Association.

Says Dr. Richard Troiana of the Health Statistics Center, "Certainly high-fat food plays a part in the increasing trend to more and more overweight children and teens, but the main cause for the increase can be attributed to children and teens not being very active." Dr. Kuntzleman puts it in simpler terms: "Active children rarely become overweight."

Health care professionals have long understood the importance of physical activity to promote good health. Active people enjoy a number of health benefits such as increased cardiovascular stamina, lower heart rate, lower blood pressure, increased bone density, enhanced glucose tolerance, reduced body fat, greater muscle strength, increased metabolism, better ability to cope with stress, better self-image/self-esteem and greater longevity. Indeed, exercise has traditionally been prescribed as a treatment for children suffering from chronic diseases like asthma, cystic fibrosis and insulin-dependent diabetes.

Until recently, most studies on physical activity were conducted on adults. But new research shows that the level of childhood physical activity may affect both the current and future health of a child. Dr. James Sallis of San Diego State University comments that "Diseases such as obesity and coronary heart disease for which sedentary behavior is a likely risk factor are lifelong processes with origins during childhood. So, physical activity habits established early in life may persist into adult years."

In other words, the inactive child tends to become the inactive adult, thus raising the risk for obesity and heart disease. Conversely, the active child tends to become the active adult, thus reducing health risks.

Exercise reduces body fat.

Although much concern is focused on "overweight" kids, the real problem is kids who are "overfat"—those who carry an excess of body fat. Because physical activity is what burns calories, it's the single best way to reduce body fat. More important, it can prevent an "overfat" condition. Says Stanford University's Dr. William Haskell, "There has been an overemphasis on calories consumed, and too little emphasis on calories being burned. The major culprit in weight gain for people of all ages is lack of physical activity."

How do kids become "overfat"? Here's how it works. Essentially, body fat is simply the storage of an excess of calories consumed. The food your child eats contains calories that his or her body uses as fuel. But when your child takes in more calories than are used, those excess calories are stored as body fat. Body fat accumulates primarily under the skin and around internal organs, where the body can readily draw on it as needed. When your child takes in and stores 3,500 extra calories, a pound of body fat has been created. And an energy expenditure of 3,500 calories will be needed to use up this pound of fat.

Despite the dieting propensity of Americans, the fact is that *body fat cannot be dieted away*. As millions of people have learned, crash diets—particularly low-carbohydrate, high-protein diets—produce fluid loss but not fat loss. Merely reducing caloric intake by dieting alone doesn't cause lasting results. "The best reason not to diet is simple: diets don't work. Experience and statistics show that the majority of people who lose weight by dieting alone will gain it back almost as quickly," says Dr. Evette Hackman, a registered dietitian. "About 9 out of 10 adults who go on a weight-loss diet gain back the lost weight (and usually put on more) within two years. And for children specifically, stringent diets are not recommended. To be sure, low-fat eating habits are necessary, but they work best in concert with physical activity. It takes exercise to squeeze the fat out of fat cells and burn it as fuel."

So, for kids who are "overfat," the message is to become physically active. Mild-to-moderate physical activity burns calories and uses fat as a source of energy.

Only when a child or teen is physically active will his or her body utilize its stored fat as fuel. Over time, this can result in a substantial amount of calories burned and body fat reduced.

An even more important message for kids, however, is to be physically active on a regular basis early in life to prevent a buildup of body fat. This advice will serve them well throughout their youth and into adulthood.

The following chart estimates the number of calories a 100-pound individual would burn in different activities.

Activity	Calories Burned per Hour
Aerobic dance	300
Baseball and softball	185
Basketball	375
Bicycling	
6 mph	160
12 mph	275
Cross-country skiing	465
Dancing	
Moderate	160
Vigorous	280
Downhill skiing	235
Football	360
Gymnastics	180
Hiking and backpacking	265
Ice and field hockey	360
Jogging	
5.5 mph	495
7 mph	615
Jumping rope	500
Racquetball, handball, squash	500
Rowing	
Leisurely	195
Vigorous	520
Running (10 mph)	855
Running in place	435
Skating (ice, in-line, roller)	200
Soccer	360

Activity	Calories Burned per Hour
Swimming	
25 yards per minute	185
50 yards per minute	335
Tennis (singles)	265
Walking	
2 mph	160
3 mph	215
4.5 mph	295

Source: American College of Sports Medicine.

To estimate the number of calories your child would expend in any of the activities listed above, do the following calculations:

			Example
1. Write down your child's weight. Since the chart is based on a weight of 100 pounds, divide your child's weight by 100.	Your child's weight ÷ 100 = calorie factor		125 lbs. ÷ 100 = 1.25
2. Multiply this number by the number of calories burned per hour in a specific activity.	calorie factor × _____		1.25 × 360 calories (soccer) _____
3. This is the estimated number of calories your child will burn when engaged in the activity.	=		= 450 calories burned

(Use this same calculation to figure out the calories you burn in your favorite physical activity.)

Exercise raises metabolism.

If burning calories directly were the only benefit, exercise would not be a very efficient way to reduce body fat. Because it's such a highly concentrated form of energy, it takes a long time to burn a pound of body fat. A 150-pound person, for example, would have to walk for more

than 9 hours at an aerobic pace (4 mph) in order to burn
3,500 calories.

But regular physical activity does more than just burn
calories. It also raises metabolism, the rate at which the
body processes calories. In effect, exercise revs up the
body's engine and keeps it running (burning calories) for
hours at a higher level. This means that even after exercise stops, even during rest, the body needs more calories
to function. Physically active kids can burn excess calories literally while they sleep.

How and why exercise increases metabolism is not
clear, in part because metabolism is hard to measure and
can vary greatly among persons of the same weight, age
and sex. What is clear, however, is the positive effect of
physical activity. One study showed that people who
exercised had a metabolic rate up to 28% higher than if
they had not exercised and that the higher rate continued
for four hours after they stopped.

Exercise causes the metabolic furnace to burn at a
higher level and, in doing so, makes it harder for the body
to conserve calories and easier for it to lose weight. This
process may also cause any setpoint barrier to be adjusted
downward, making it easier to lose weight and keep it off.
Says Dr. Jack Wilmore, an exercise expert at the University of Texas, "If exercising regularly changes your metabolism even slightly, so that you burn an extra 100 calories
a day, that small change can add up to 10 pounds of
weight loss a year."

Crash dieting can produce the opposite effect: reduced
metabolism. That's because diet alone can deplete the
lean muscle that is so effective in burning fat. "When
caloric intake is drastically slashed, as with a crash diet,
the body reacts defensively by slowing down metabolism,
burning calories at a lower rate and making weight loss
more difficult," says nutritionist Dr. Audrey Cross. "Your
body has a sense of survival. Restricting calories makes
your body's metabolism more thrifty. It adjusts to the calories you take in."

Exercise creates fat-burning muscle.

Exercise creates and maintains muscle tissue. Not only is this important in terms of strength and tone, particularly for growing kids, but it is also a critical factor because muscle burns fat. Building up lean muscle tissue through regular exercise dramatically increases the body's ability to burn calories and to utilize body fat as energy.

In addition, body fat needs fewer calories to maintain itself than does lean muscle tissue. Studies show that overweight people need one-third to one-half fewer calories to maintain their weight than do people of normal weight. This is why, of two people who eat the same amount of food, the fat person gets fatter and the lean person stays thin.

"Diet can't build muscle tissue," counsels Georgia Kostas, R.D., of the Cooper Clinic. "But exercise will. We're not talking about weight lifting, which is inappropriate for kids. We're talking about building and toning muscles through normal childhood and adolescent games and physical activities like walking or swimming. Such activities produce muscle, and the more muscle you have, the easier it is to burn fat—even while sitting down."

Exercise increases cardiac health.

Physical inactivity is linked directly to coronary heart disease. "Since couch potatoes run nearly twice the risk of heart disease as people who are physically active," states Dr. William Haskell, "a sedentary lifestyle just doesn't pay. Sedentary people are at the same risk for heart attacks as the obese and heavy smokers." While physical inactivity by itself may not trigger a heart attack, studies show that a fundamental connection exists. Conversely, these same studies suggest a strong correlation between physical activity—even if moderate—and protection from coronary disease.

A landmark study of the lifestyles of Harvard University alumni, conducted by Dr. Ralph Paffenbarger, Jr., revealed that active men reduced their risk of heart attack by 35% and lived longer than their sedentary classmates. Benefits began to appear as soon as the men expended 500 calories a week in exercise, with peak benefits at 2,000 to 3,500 calories a week. The study also showed that benefits dwindled after 3,500 calories, thereby making regular, moderate exercise the best prescription.

A study by Steven Blair of the Aerobics Institute in Dallas yielded the same results. Dr. Blair followed over 10,000 men and 3,000 women for eight years and found that even a minimal amount of exercise, such as a brisk half-hour walk daily, provided significant cardiovascular protection.

One of the important cardiac benefits of regular exercise is that it produces increased cardiovascular stamina and fitness and improves the strength of the heart. People who exercise have more energy and more endurance, and can do more physically with less strain on the heart. Exercise also increases the all-important HDL cholesterol. This type of cholesterol is protective, and high levels are very desirable. Conversely, low levels of HDL are a cardiac risk. Regular exercise is the most effective action a person can take to raise HDL.

Exercise enhances emotional health.

There is strong evidence that physical activity enhances emotional health, particularly in adolescents. Exercise can help to throw off stress, produce less anxiety and depression, and create greater self-image/self-esteem. Described as nature's own tranquilizer, exercise may be the most effective method of dissipating pressure, reducing tension and increasing endorphins (natural painkillers produced by the brain). Psychologist Dr. Thomas Steven comments, "Anxiety, depression, anger and other stressful emotions are banished through physical activity."

Exercise also helps to change stress-related eating habits, a source of much psychological self-flagellation. Food often becomes a consolation to adults who feel their lives are out of control, that life is happening to them. It is well known that overeating is often dictated by stress and anxiety. There is an axiom that "when under stress, all roads lead to the refrigerator." Most of us know from our own experience that this is true. When we're hurried and harried, anxious about what is to come and depressed over what is already here, we often make poor lifestyle decisions. It is at such times that we overeat, binge, or live for days on a fast-food diet. The same is often true for children and teens, who have less control over their lives and thus have fewer options in responding to emotional peaks and valleys. They too may be prone to changing the way they eat as their moods and behavior change.

One of the results of exercise is better control over eating habits. A calm, relaxed, de-stressed person is less likely to "pig out" on brownies or ice cream. Studies show that physically active people choose to eat more healthful foods and fewer high-fat foods than do sedentary people. In addition, exercise creates an environment for success that bolsters self-confidence and self-esteem. With the focus on what we can do rather than on what we can't eat, exercise serves as a positive distraction, giving us something to concentrate on besides food.

THE BEST MEDICINE

Says Dr. Robert Butler, former director of the National Institutes on Aging, "If exercise could be packaged into a pill, it would be the single most widely pre-scribed—and beneficial—medicine in the nation."

The benefits of physical activity are numerous:

- More energy and capacity for work and leisure ac-tivities
- Greater resistance to stress, anxiety and fatigue, and improved self-image/self-esteem and outlook on life

- Increased stamina, strength and flexibility
- Loss of extra pounds of body fat
- Increase in metabolic rate

Although kids may not be interested in such outcomes as a rationale for physical activity, parents should communicate these benefits in an ongoing and appropriate way. (That means no nagging.) Kids will pick up the message over time that physical activity is important, especially if their parents set an example by being physically active themselves.

Do these benefits come only from formal exercise workouts? No. Children, teens and young adults do not have to set up regular exercise routines or attend aerobics classes to receive these benefits. They can just have fun riding bikes, in-line skating, roller skating, dancing or running around with pets in the backyard (more about this later). The important thing is for parents to get their children active now and set them on the road to staying active throughout their lifetime.

CHAPTER 5

HOW MUCH IS ENOUGH?

The many benefits of exercise provide the foundation for a call by health professionals for *all* Americans to be more physically active. The Surgeon General, the American College of Sports Medicine and the Centers for Disease Control and Prevention have acknowledged the importance of lifestyle physical activity as a means of reducing disease risk. But what does this mean in practical terms? In other words, how much exercise is good for your child?

Guidelines have been established for children and adolescents. It is important for parents to know these guidelines. By avoiding the "one size fits all" exercise prescription, parents can better help their kids into physical activities that match their interests and capabilities. What a teen is interested in and capable of doing may be a far cry from what a young child enjoys and can do.

EXERCISE GUIDELINES FOR CHILDREN

The guidelines for children are just that—guidelines. They are not based on hard-and-fast numbers. One reason for this broad approach is that most children, particularly younger ones, are physically active by nature and do not need the more formal guidelines suggested for adolescents and adults.

THE BASIC GOAL

The 1996 Surgeon General's Report on Physical Activity and Health suggests that the minimum standard, or basic goal, is for daily "mild-to-moderate" activity. Parents should not assume that school recess will meet the minimum standard. It may take an additional commitment to childhood games and activities like walking, riding a bicycle or performing physical tasks around the house such as raking leaves or helping to wash the car.

Minimum Activity Standard for Children

Frequency: Daily. Frequent activity sessions (3 or more) each day.

Intensity: Moderate. Alternating bouts of activity with rest periods as needed or moderate activity such as walking or riding a bike to school.

Time: A total of about 30 minutes or more of active play or moderate sustained activity that may be distributed over 3 or more sessions.

This standard is easily attainable for most children. You can help your child to meet it by becoming acquainted with some of the basic concepts outlined below.

Being outdoors is basic to increasing childhood physical activity.
Maximize the time your child spends outside. This is clearly the most important thing the parent of a young child can do. Children are inherently active, and the more time they spend outdoors, the more active they are. This may be a better way of dealing with young children than a formal exercise prescription. So, if you do nothing

else, make an effort to get your child outside. Take a walk, build a snowman, ice-skate, swim, fly a kite, go bike riding—there are hundreds of activities to share. And be sure to offer encouragement to your child as well as opportunity.

Childhood activity is often intermittent and sporadic in nature.

Children act in bursts of energy. Be aware that your child will not likely do prolonged exercise without rest periods, and select your activities accordingly. In addition, children are concrete rather than abstract thinkers. A child may be unwilling to persist in a physical activity if he or she sees no concrete reason to do so. The message to parents is to be flexible.

Intermittent bursts of activity add up.

Total volume is a good indicator of childhood activity. A single activity is not what's important—it's the sum of all the activities. This is why the standard calls for three or more sessions. Consider all of them when judging whether or not your child is physically active.

Physical activity patterns vary with children of different developmental and ability levels.

Your young child, for instance, may not be attracted to high-intensity exercise. On the other hand, your more highly skilled older child may see its value for enhancing performance in sports. Match the activity to the ability and interest of the child.

THE OPTIMAL GOAL

Experts say that it is not unreasonable for parents to establish an optimal goal of more "moderate-to-vigorous" activity for their children, such as jumping rope, swimming or playing soccer. This optimal goal gives parents additional flexibility in helping their children to achieve physical fitness.

Optimal Activity Goal for Children

Frequency: Daily. Frequent activity sessions (3 or more) each day.

Intensity: Moderate to vigorous. Alternating bouts of activity with rest periods as needed or moderate activity such as walking or riding a bike to school.

Time: A total of about 60 minutes or more of active play or moderate sustained activity that may be distributed over 3 or more activity sessions.

"This more intense goal is appropriate," says Dr. Chuck Corbin of Arizona State University, "because it is during childhood that children learn basic motor skills that provide the basis for lifetime activity. Proper skill development requires substantial practice time and energy expenditure. If motor skills are not learned early in life, such skills may never be developed and the opportunities for lifetime activity will be limited."

SENSIBLE PARAMETERS

There are some sensible parameters when it comes to children and physical activity that parents should know. Dr. Ken Cooper, the father of aerobic fitness, counsels parents to link the child's activity level with his or her developmental age. "Remember," he states, "developmental age and chronological age may not match. Each child is an individual. Some kids do things early; some later. Know what activities are appropriate for each stage of your child's development."

The First 2 Years

Praise and encourage everything your child does in order to build self-confidence and curiosity. Try to create an environment where the child can play and interact without danger. This minimizes activities that force you to say "no."

Ages 2 to 5

Teach your child the basic skills of throwing, kicking, catching and jumping. These important skills provide the basis for the child's physical activity later in life. At ages two to five, children will enthusiastically repeat these skills again and again to please you and themselves. Don't worry about proficiency—yours or your child's. Your goal is to help your child understand the basic skills and to find fun and confidence in their execution.

Ages 5 to 8

Children in this age group run, jump and play sports as a natural part of life. They don't keep track of the score or play only to win. They want to improve their skills, have fun, be with friends and burn off energy. Parents should support fitness by making sure there is adequate time and space for their children to be as active as possible.

Ages 8 to 10

These are the ages when children discover team sports—soccer, basketball, swimming and the like. They have mastered basic physical skills, and they are quick to learn the application of those skills to team sports. Parents' chief concern should be to make sure their children enjoy a variety of activities with friends. Because physical development varies greatly in the 8-to-10 age group, parents should be sure their children play in environments where they are physically, mentally and socially ready for the activities. Be sure to stress activity over competition. This helps to avoid burnout at an early age. Kids who drop out of sports now may never come back.

Ages 10 to 14

These are the ages of puberty for most children. However, puberty does not follow a set course. For some children it starts at age 10, for others at age 14; for some it ends at age 14, for others at age 18. Parents' first concern, therefore, should be to make sure their child has access to playing sports with others who are at his or her stage in the development of motor skills, endurance and social abilities. "Look for programs that match development, not age," says Dr. Cooper. "Sometimes sports that focus on individual development, such as bicycling or hiking, are better. The point is that we want to help the child have a positive experience. A foul taste of fitness at this age can last a lifetime."

Puberty can be an emotional roller coaster. Girls in particular should understand that an increase in body fat during puberty is natural, a preparation for childbearing later in life. Parents should remember that an active lifestyle is associated with a positive self-image, confidence, a feeling of control and a reduced risk of depression—all helpful for the child and the parent in surviving the puberty stage.

EXERCISE GUIDELINES FOR ADOLESCENTS

While children are physically active by nature, their inclination for physical activity declines with age. The average drop in physical activity for males is 2% to 3% per year from age six on. This means that during the school ages of 6 to 18 boys decrease their activity by at least 24%. In other words, grade school boys are 24% more active than high school boys.

The picture is even worse for girls. A 1993 Harvard University School of Public Health study of girls in grades

5 through 12 suggests that as girls get older, the less likely they are to be active. The average drop in physical activity for females is 3% to 7% per year over age six. This means that during the school ages of 6 to 18 girls decrease their activity by at least 36%. The other side, however, is that girls who keep active past age 14 are much more likely to be active adults.

It has become clear that interventions are necessary to halt the age-related decline in physical activity, and in 1993 the International Consensus Conference on Physical Activity and Adolescents responded by recommending the following two guidelines for adolescent physical activity.

GUIDELINE 1: "MILD-TO-MODERATE" ACTIVITY

All adolescents should be physically active every day, or nearly every day, in the context of family, school and community activities—including play, games, sports, work, transportation, recreation, physical education or planned exercise.

Teens should engage in a variety of physical activities as part of their daily lifestyles—such as walking up stairs, riding a bicycle for errands or doing them on foot, having conversations with friends while walking along with them, parking at the far end of the lot, and performing household chores. Such activities should be enjoyable, involve a variety of muscle groups and include some weight-bearing activities. The intensity or duration of an activity is probably less important than the requirement that energy be expended and a habit of daily activity be established. "There is not a specific recommendation about the amount of time for daily activity for adolescents," says Dr. James Sallis, "but the recommendation for adults of a minimum of 30 minutes a day is reasonable for adolescents as well."

GUIDELINE 2: "MODERATE-TO-VIGOROUS" ACTIVITY

In addition to daily lifestyle activities, the recommendations call for three or more sessions per week of activity requiring "moderate-to-vigorous" levels of exertion and lasting at least 20 minutes at a time.

"Moderate-to-vigorous" activities are those that require at least as much effort as brisk or fast walking. Diversity in activities that use large muscle groups is recommended as part of sports, recreation, chores, transportation, work, school physical education or planned exercise. Examples of appropriate activities include brisk walking, jogging, stair climbing, basketball, racket sports, soccer, dance, swimming laps, skating, strength training, jumping rope, lawn mowing, strenuous housework, rowing, cycling and cross-country skiing.

Dr. Cooper suggests that parents of adolescent children should help them to identify and focus on lifetime fitness goals. "For ages 14 to 17," he writes, "help your child see where exercise and sports play a role. Set a fitness goal and map out a plan for the child to work out regularly. The American College of Sports Medicine counsels that:

- Fitness is *improved* if a person exercises more than three days a week.
- Fitness is *maintained* with a routine of exercise three days a week.
- Fitness is *lost* when a person gets exercise less than three days a week.

"Know what your child's school does—and does not do—for physical education. Be certain that your child is taking advantage of community recreational opportunities. Make certain he or she understands that fitness is a family priority."

THE ACTIVITY PYRAMID

Being active yourself, and teaching your child to be physically active, is among the most important of parental responsibilities. Don't restrict your thinking to formal workouts. Look for ways that you and your child can be more physically active on a daily basis.

A good way to picture such activities is the following "activity pyramid" developed by Park Nicollet Medical Foundation in Minneapolis:

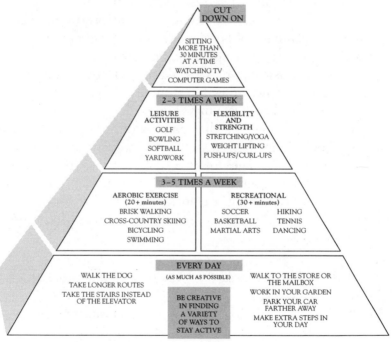

© 1995 Park Nicollet Medical Foundation.

If your child is inactive, you can help increase activities from the *base* of the pyramid by:

- Taking the stairs together instead of the elevator;
- Working together in your yard or garden;
- Parking your car farther away and walking to your destination together.

If your child is somewhat active, use the *middle* of the pyramid to:

- Find activities she likes;
- Schedule activities into her day;
- Set realistic goals she can stick with.

If your child is active at least four days a week, use the *whole* pyramid to:

- Help him change his routine to keep from getting bored;
- Explore new activities.

The importance of physical activity in the lifestyle of your child cannot be overemphasized. But it won't come about unless you plan for it. Below is a blank activity pyramid. Fill it in with an activity plan for you and your child.

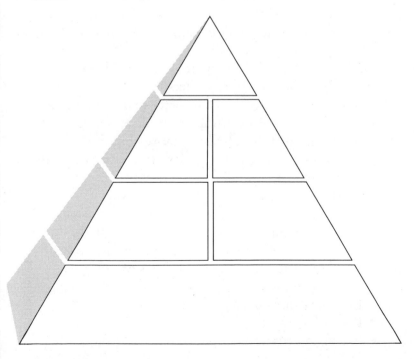

CHAPTER 6

INFLUENCES ON PHYSICAL ACTIVITY

B y this point in the book, you should need little persuasion that a sedentary lifestyle can penalize the health of your child. Conversely, you should understand that increasing your child's physical activity can aid fitness, health and weight control. But it's one thing to know that exercise is important; it's quite another to incorporate it into everyday life. The question for many parents, then, still remains: How can I motivate my child to be more physically active?

Before starting to work with your child on fitness activities, it makes sense to understand what influences children and teenagers. In identifying increased physical activity as a national health goal for all Americans, the Surgeon General has called for more research on the determinants of physical activity in youth. In other words, what motivates children and teens to be physically active? And conversely, what gets in their way?

Physical activity is affected by multiple internal and external factors. Parents need to understand these influences to better help their children be more physically active. Experts cite three important areas of influence:

- Biological and developmental factors
- Psychological factors
- Social and environmental factors

BIOLOGICAL AND DEVELOPMENTAL FACTORS

It appears that *gender* is an important determinant of physical activity in youth, although male-female differences may reflect cultural forces more than biological ones. The fact is that from preschool through adolescence, boys are usually more physically active than girls.

Part of the explanation for gender differences is rooted in culture. "Our culture rewards boys for strenuous activity and athleticism," says clinical psychologist Kate Hays at the University of New Hampshire. "But when it comes to girls, only the most successful or spectacular athletes are encouraged."

As they reach puberty, young girls often find that athleticism doesn't fit the traditional feminism image. "Many say they don't participate in gym because they're afraid of not seeming cool," states Harvard dietitian Anne Wolf. "Others say they don't want to ruin their makeup." In addition, different cultural views of femininity or an emphasis on academics over sports may account for Hispanic and Asian girls' relative inactivity.

This gender difference persists throughout the adult years. In a *Prevention* magazine survey, 45% of men said they exercise vigorously three days a week, but only 30% of women reported doing so. When girls stay active past age 14, however, there is a greater chance that they'll exercise regularly as adults.

Given the data, the parents of boys need to take advantage of a natural inclination to be physically active by affording opportunity and encouragement. The parents of girls may need to do more. In addition to encouraging physical activity, they must work for more opportunities for women in sports and ensure that school physical education activities are appropriate and acceptable for both girls and boys. Being a positive role model for fitness (working out yourself, supporting your child's sports activities) also sends the right message to girls that physical activity and fitness are important and appropriate. Parents of females need to make sure that the message is not "Get thin," but "Get fit."

Age also has an impact on physical activity. Young children appear to be the most active segment of society. They love to play. They seem to have boundless energy. They race each other, throw and kick balls, and jump rope. Simply put, a child's natural inclination is to be active. However, physical activity declines with age. Whether this is grounded in biology or in culture (one thought is that sedentary kids may be inactive because they've picked up clues from the world around them) has not yet been determined.

It is important, then, for parents to understand that a highly active child will not naturally maintain a high level of physical activity into adolescence. The most effective way for parents to promote lifelong physical activity in their children is to start early, working together to develop such activity as a habit. It's far easier to prevent a decline to low levels than to reinstate physical activity in kids who have become sedentary.

And finally, being overweight has an impact. Parents need to be aware that overweight children may not always like the same physical activities as those of normal weight. Overweight kids rate endurance activities more negatively than do their lean peers, so they're less likely to choose (or enjoy) jogging, for instance, as an activity.

On the other hand, overweight kids will exercise, although they're much more apt to maintain low-intensity rather than high-intensity activities. Indeed, these children lose more weight when they're assigned low-intensity activities, such as walking, than when they're asked to do regular aerobic exercise.

Parents of overweight children should factor such preferences into their efforts to promote physical activity. Overweight kids should never be forced into activities they don't like or feel they cannot perform. The point is to help your children move from doing nothing to doing something, to find a physical activity that is fun and effective.

PSYCHOLOGICAL FACTORS

A variety of psychological factors have been studied as influences on physical activity in children and adolescents. The research on children is incomplete, but the findings so far clearly indicate that young kids are turned on to sports and physical activities by having fun, playing with their peers, feeling successful, sharing the experience with family, experiencing a variety of activities, and being physically active with their siblings and parents.

In a recent survey, elementary school boys and girls ranked the top reasons they play school sports. And guess what, they do it to have fun!

Top 5 Reasons to Play School Sports

Boys	Girls
1. To have fun	1. To have fun
2. To improve skills	2. To stay in shape
3. Excitement of competition	3. To get exercise
	4. To improve skills
4. To do something I'm good at	5. To do something I'm good at
5. To say in shape	

Parents should note that winning, the most publicized goal of sports, is a poor motivator. It ranked 8th among boys and 10th for the girls. Having coached boys' and girls' youth soccer for 10 years (and having dealt with "soccer parents"), I feel strongly that parents need to keep sports positive and fun, never ridicule or put pressure on children to win or perform, and be good coaches and cheerleaders. What do kids want to play? According to a *Sports Illustrated for Kids* survey of 8-to-12-year-olds, the top-scoring sports include:

Boys: Basketball, baseball, football, soccer, karate, in-line skating, swimming/diving, ice skating, biking, fishing

Girls: Swimming/diving, basketball, gymnastics, roller skating, ice skating, softball, biking, baseball, soccer, volleyball

Research on adolescents reveals that personality characteristics such as achievement motivation, social adequacy and self-confidence are not associated with physical activity or sports participation. Therefore, enduring personality traits are probably not strong influences on teens' physical activity. And neither is knowledge about the health effects of physical activity. Parents should understand that, unlike adults, teens do not exercise because it's "good for them." They simply do not view disease and risk factors as adults do. How many 15-year-olds fear serious illness or death? Most think they are immune.

So, what psychological factors *do* motivate teens to exercise? Experts have identified a number of such factors that parents should take into consideration:

- *A desire to have fun.* As with their younger counterparts, fun ranks high with teens as a physical motivator.
- *A desire to be in shape, look good and feel better about themselves.* Females, in particular, fear obesity. Teens see physical activity as a way to tone muscles and control weight.
- *The impact of peers.* Teens like to be with friends who share similar interests and activities. If their friends exercise regularly, so will they.
- *Confidence in their ability to perform the exercise.* Teens like to do things they're good at.

What gets in the way of physical activity? Adolescents identify the following factors:

- Not enough time.
- A conflict between sports and academic demands and/or jobs.
- Missing out on social occasions because of sports.
- Not enough fun.
- Not getting to play or be active enough.
- A feeling that practice is too much like work.
- Not enough help with improving skills.
- Too much emphasis on winning.

SOCIAL AND ENVIRONMENTAL FACTORS

While biological and psychological factors are important, experts believe that social and environmental factors provide most of the barriers to physical activity in youth. This area offers the most potential for parents.

Today's parents need to realize that kids have not always been sedentary. In the 1940s and '50s, children had greater opportunities for outdoor play. Children in the 1960s had television but still were involved in a great deal of outdoor activity. Starting in the 1970s, however, kids became captivated by television and video games, and had less opportunity for outdoor activities due to societal changes. Each succeeding decade has produced fatter and less physically fit youth.

This is often a surprise to parents. For most of us, physical activity was a natural part of growing up. Running and playing were intrinsic to our childhood. We played all kinds of games and participated in organized sports throughout our early lives. Walking and bicycling were our primary modes of transportation. And as we've aged and focused on our own physical well-being, many of us have assumed that our children are also running and playing.

They are not. And a variety of lifestyle factors have made this so.

Modern lifestyle promotes inactivity.

Before World War II, much of America was a blue-collar society, working with its hands and burning up substantial calories naturally. This lifestyle affected children as well, in the performance of their chores and the way they got from one place to another. After the war, automation eased the physical workload in fields and factories, as did labor-saving devices in the home. The country progressively became more of a white-collar society. And as the age of industrialization gave way to the age of information, work—and workers—became more sedentary.

"What has occurred," says Dr. Michael Jensen, an obesity expert at the Mayo Clinic, "is the culmination of a century of invention and industrial development. Technology has taken the majority of people out of fields and factories and plopped them behind desks—and in front of computers. With more and more conveniences, we're doing less and less manual work."

The labor-saving features of modern life—automobiles, elevators, escalators, electric garage-door openers, food processors, computers instead of manual typewriters, lawn mowers to ride instead of push, car windows with electric buttons, push-button telephones, drive-in windows—have contributed to our physical decline. Coupled with an increase in television viewing and the building of the information highway, modern life encourages us to be still.

"We've become a push-button society—pressing, clicking, tapping away, erasing the need for any body movement," says Dr. Charles Kuntzleman. "Everywhere you look, buttons do it all: from the PC to the elevator, from the microwave to remote control. Modern technology has robbed us of what little effort we once expended to crank up the car window. With each flick of a switch, our

American lifestyle becomes more sedentary." The TV remote control is a perfect example of technology gone amok. According to the Consumer Electronics Manufacturers Association, there are about 400 million remotes in use today—or 4 for every household in America! "No single labor-saving action saves a lot of calories," says Dr. Kelly Brownell, an obesity expert at Yale University. "But add them all up and the number is significant. The amount of energy people used to expend even a decade ago is enormous compared to what they expend today."

Four facets of contemporary life have particularly contributed to the decline in physical activity of American children and adolescents:

- Television
- Automobiles
- Societal violence
- Less free time for parents

On balance, most people would consider television and automobiles to be beneficial. At its best, television can educate, communicate and entertain. And while cars can pollute, who would want to give up the freedom of motorized transportation? The problem, for our children and ourselves, is too much of a good thing. It is estimated that the average American child watches between three and seven hours of television a day. (TV is such an important drain on time for physical activity that it is covered in detail on pages 74–77.) Add to this the fact that the average child rides about 22 miles a day in a car, bus or other form of motorized transportation.

As a result, kids are sitting down for a minimum of 3.5 hours a day, every day. That's not bad by itself, but combine it with school (sitting for 6.5 hours) and sleep (9 to 10 hours), and most of the day is spent sitting or lying down.

Another facet of modern life that works against physical activity is the increase in acts of violence against children. This has caused parents to keep their children close to home. While for youngsters of past decades "after school" meant playing unsupervised in a park, not many parents today would feel easy with such an arrangement. In addition, kids in the past rode their bikes to the park. What parent feels comfortable with that? Today if kids get to the park, they do so in a car or bus. Children cause their parents less worry when they're playing video games at home than when they're playing basketball somewhere in the neighborhood. This is tragic because time spent outdoors is one of the most important determinants of physical activity.

And finally, many parents are simply out of time and families are feeling the stress of overcommitted and over-scheduled lives. Not too many years ago, in the typical American family, only the father worked outside the home. Usually the mother was the homemaker and was there to greet the children when they came home from school. But there have been dramatic changes in that picture. Today, the mothers of nearly 70% of children over age five are in the workforce. Two wage earners and working single parents are no longer the exception.

This is not a negative. Indeed, it is an economic necessity for many families and a financial boon for others (extra money for vacations and school tuition). In addition, studies find that women who work outside the home describe themselves as having higher self-esteem and a greater sense of authority. But there is also a downside. Family lifestyles today are often shaped by a drastically increased pace of life—extended work hours, rotating shifts, longer commuting times, household chores done at night. People are living on the run with less time for their children, each other and themselves than people had in the past. In the 1960s and '70s, for example, families typically had dinner together, then went to the park or into the backyard to have a catch, kick a soccer ball or shoot a few hoops. This is no longer the pattern. Parents have to shop after work, family dinners have fallen by the wayside, kids need to be picked up from day care or school and transported to piano lessons . . . who has time for playing catch?

The diminishing of parents' free time has translated into fewer opportunities to be physically active with their children. It is a prime reason why three-quarters of parents today are involved in physical activity with their children less than once a week.

As a consequence of modern lifestyle, children's normal activity patterns are greatly restrained. TV programs and video games today baby-sit many "latchkey" children until parents come home from work. (As an aside, a study by the University of Southern California School of Medicine of 5,000 students show that latchkey children who spend time alone at home are far more likely to engage in unhealthy, risky behaviors—such as alcohol, smoking or marijuana—than are kids who have adult supervision.) While children of the 1960s walked or rode their bikes to the ball field for an informal pickup game, children today need uniforms, referees and a parent to drive them to the field or they won't come out of their room—especially if it has a TV or a computer.

Moreover, there has been a change in what is seen as important. A great emphasis on being computer-literate in the information age, it seems, has taken precedence over physical performance. Kids used to go to summer camp to learn to swim, hike or ride horses. Now they go to learn how to run the latest computer programs. More kids know about bytes than batting averages. Instead of spending endless hours outside catching a baseball, many kids today would rather "play" baseball on a video game. Says one mother, "Both my children have gained 10 pounds since I bought a laptop. They're glued to the computer." Again, there is nothing wrong with mastering a computer or playing video games. But while they may enhance fine motor skills, they are absolutely incompatible with physical activities that are required for health-related fitness.

TVs, computers and autos, crime in the streets, high-density living with little open spaces, working parents with little time for outdoor supervision—none by itself is the cause of our children's sedentariness. But taken together, as they are in our modern lifestyle, they conspire to keep children indoors after school playing video games instead of outdoors playing tag or soccer.

Television means sitting, not doing.
Increased television viewing is one of the facets of modern life that has significantly diminished physical activity in children. Experts agree that spending too many hours in front of the "tube" contributes to the obesity that now afflicts more American children than ever. Dr. William Dietz states that "Excessive television viewing is responsible for about one-quarter of the recent increase in child and adolescent obesity."

Studies at the University of Michigan found that children spend more time watching television than doing anything else except sleeping. In a survey conducted by YOUTH Research on six-to nine-year-olds, almost 25% of the children said they seldom play outside, even when the weather is nice. More than 80% reported that they watch TV every day after school and on Saturdays.

According to Nielsen Media Research, the average weekly viewing of television by age group is appalling:

Television Viewing by Children and Adolescents

Age	Hours of TV per Week
2–5	28
6–11	24
12–19	22

And remember, these figures do not include the additional time spent watching movies on the VCR or playing video games. Thus the average child likely spends 25 to 30 hours plunked in front of the TV set each week, and millions of children spend many more. Says Dr. Steven Gortmaker of Harvard University, "For many kids it adds up to 40 hours a week. That's equivalent to a full-time job in front of the TV screen."

Using data from the Health and Nutrition Examination Survey (HANES), Dr. Dietz discovered a direct relationship between a child's weight and the number of hours spent watching television. He concludes that *the prevalence of obesity increases by 2% for each additional hour of television watched.*

How does TV encourage obesity? Time spent in front of the screen is time taken away from calorie-burning physical activities. Instead of running and jumping themselves, they're watching TV characters run and jump. Instead of taking a swim at the YMCA, they're tuned in to *Baywatch.* Children who spend a lot of time watching television tend to exercise less after school than their peers who spend little time with TV. They're also more likely to shun team sports. Teenagers in particular are far more likely to devote time to television than to exercise.

Another reason, according to pediatric specialist Kurt Gold at the University of California at Irvine, is that watching television is stressful. "Children are sitting, but often they're not really relaxing," says Dr. Gold. "They may be expending tremendous mental energy processing the audiovisual messages TV is throwing at them. Prolonged TV watching can be very exhausting and make people less likely to engage in physical activity later on."

Television can also reduce the ability to burn calories. Research shows that when children watch TV, their metaolic rates decline to rates even below those found in youngsters who are simply resting. In a study from Memphis State University and the University of Tennessee, published in the medical journal *Pediatrics,* 32 girls aged 7 to 11 watched a 30-minute episode of *The Wonder Years.* Half the girls were of average weight and half were obese, but all of them experienced a drop in metabolic rate—from 12% to 16%—after watching the show. Researchers concluded that "Television viewing has a fairly profound effect on metabolic rate and may be a primary mechanism for the relationship between obesity and amount of television viewing."

Of critical importance is the fact that kids usually snack while watching television, but not on fruits and vegetables. Potato chips, cookies and candy are the more likely snacks. Youngsters who watch TV for long stretches of time see one commercial after another for high-calorie, high-fat foods that can contribute to obesity—and then act on the impulses the commercials create. "The American food industry generates 3,700 calories a day for every man, woman and child and spends $36 billion a year to advertise its products," says Dr. Brownell. "A typical child is blasted with up to 10,000 food commercials a year. Most are for sugary, fatty or salty food. Think how parents would feel if on Saturday morning television, children were seeing 10,000 commercials for alcohol."

Marketers of children's products love television because commercials bypass parents and directly grab the target audience: kids. Kids ask their parents to buy whatever they see advertised, such as sugared cereals, soft drinks, candy bars, fast-food hamburgers and pizza, and other foods high in fat, sugar and salt. "Television advertising is influencing the buying and eating habits of both children and their parents," says Dr. Lisa C. Cohn, nutrition director of the Children's Cardiovascular Health Center at Columbia University. Dr. Cohn found that a youngster who watches five hours of TV during the peak Saturday morning children's viewing time sees a food commercial about every five minutes. As an example, a recent Nielsen report showed that for a one-week period, 4 of the top 10 advertisers in prime-time TV were McDonalds (#1), Burger King (#2), Wendy's (#4) and Kentucky Fried Chicken (#10). "Overall, about 38% of all food ads are for fast food, and 41% of all food ads are for high-fat foods," Dr. Cohn adds. "Parents should be aware that their children are being exposed to a lot of advertising for high-fat foods."

In additon, television shows themselves promote some of the worst aspects of the American diet. Says Dr. Mary Story of the University of Minnesota, "Our research on top-ranked comedies and dramas concluded that the prime-time diet of fast food, junk food and eating on the run is inconsistent with dietary guidelines for healthy Americans."

The American Heart Association has also reported a link between television viewing and high cholesterol in children, based on findings that the more TV watched, the greater the chance for a high cholesterol level. Many pediatricians are now asking about a child's TV viewing habits as a regular part of a physical exam to assess risk of premature heart disease.

So, just to set the record straight, excessive television viewing increases the risk of childhood obesity, keeps kids from exercising, increases their stress, decreases their metabolism, causes them to crave junk food, contributes to high cholesterol, and bears much responsibility for the lost art of family communication. Would you hire a baby-sitter with such a resumé?

School P.E. programs have declined.

Physical education (P.E.) programs historically have been an integral part of the American educational system. Because almost all youngsters aged 6 to 16 attend school, it is an ideal setting to learn the value of being active, the rewards of teamwork and the rules of fair play.

Less formal in elementary school recess, more formal in junior high and high school P.E. classes (my printed instructions as an incoming high school freshman told me to show up with "a white T-shirt, blue athletic shorts and white athletic socks"), physical activity was offered to vir-tually all children and teens in the past at least once during the school day. Teachers and parents generally

subscribed to the "mind-body" connection, and consequently P.E. programs were numerous and well supported.

But times have changed, and the number and quality
of P.E. programs have diminished. The number of P.E.
programs in schools has been drastically reduced in the
last two decades. Faced with budget cuts and the movement back to "the three R's," some schools have found
physical education an unaffordable luxury. In many districts, P.E. is often the first subject cut when budgets need
to be trimmed. In California, for example, three-quarters
of all schools surveyed have terminated or reassigned
physical education teachers. A growing number of U.S.
high schools have made P.E. optional, but less than half
the kids participate in optional physical education classes.
Today Illinois is the only state that requires daily P.E. programs for kindergarten through 12th grade.

This situation has produced devastating results. In
1964, 90% of elementary school children had daily physical education classes. Today, according to the National
Children and Youth Fitness Study, the figure is less than
30%. In addition, many elementary schools do not organize recess activities, so large numbers of kids just sit
around and talk or eat a snack. Some schools place 60 to
80 children in a gymnasium, creating an impossible
teaching situation. The downward trend continues as
children get older. Almost half of all students in grades 9
through 12 reported that they were not enrolled in physical education classes. Only one-fifth of all high school
students attend P.E. classes on a daily basis, and most of
them are ninth graders.

Researchers describe what they call "disturbing declines" in participation in school physical education
programs. On the average, children in fifth grade and
above in the United States spend only 3% of their school
day in physical education or physical activity. The comparable percentage in Japan is 18%.

Where P.E. does exist, the quality of instruction is
often called into question. Says Susan Kalish, Executive

Director of the American Running and Fitness Association, "It is important that P.E. be taught by certified physical education instructors, trained professionals. In many schools P.E. is just added on to a teacher's activities. It's seen simply as a way for kids to blow off steam. If the instructor is untrained, P.E. can become nothing more than organized recess."

"These are missed opportunities," says Dr. Gregory Heath. "And what's really amazing is that even when P.E. is offered, one-quarter of the students enrolled don't even do any real physical activity." It is estimated that between roll call, changing clothes, getting instructions and setting up lessons, on the average less than 9% of physical education class time is being spent in vigorous activity. For example, in a typical 30-minute kickball game, the average child will catch, kick and throw a ball one to two times each. For a child who takes 30 minutes of P.E. three times a week, that comes to about 8 minutes of exercise.

"In addition," says Dr. Heath, "the kind of exercise being offered doesn't promote physical fitness. Many physical education programs do not emphasize the most basic motor skills of running, jumping, throwing, catching, skipping, hopping and swimming. They center on competitive sports rather than lifetime fitness activities." This often means that only some of the kids fully participate, and none of the kids may develop the perspective of physical activity as a lifetime skill. Well-run programs focus on the process, not the product.

Even playing on a varsity team does not necessarily mean that a student is getting regular, vigorous exercise. Sports such as football, basketball, baseball, softball and volleyball are not considered aerobic because they don't require sustained hard exercise. Running, swimming, walking, jogging, aerobics and bicycling are what count; these are the exercises that burn fat, enhance cardiopulmonary health and start kids on a lifelong fitness program. Says one health expert, "The fallacy of promoting team sports is that they are not all vigorous activity."

According to a report from the American Physical Therapy Association, "More than half the children participating in organized athletics today cannot pass basic physical fitness tests."

A great part of the increasing problem of childhood and adolescent obesity can be traced to the decline of physical education programs in schools. Several recent studies, such as the SPARK study, the Project Heart Study, the CATCH Study, and the Class of 89 Study, show that increased efforts on the part of schools can increase the activity levels of children.

Parents need to question school administrators on their priorities. Does the school district offer P.E. on a regular basis? Is it being taught by a professional? Does the program stress lifestyle skills over competitive athletics? School officials should know that you expect the education of your child to be based on the mind-body model—academics *and* physical activity. After all, the school is probably funded by local tax dollars. You and other parents are in a great position to be a strong advocate for quality physical education as part of the basic curriculum.

Community programs have declined.

In an era of declining school P.E., community programs have become more important. For many kids, these are the only programs that teach and encourage physical activity. Over 20 million children and teens play sports in organized programs sponsored by the YMCA, YWCA, scouts, Little League, police athletic leagues, parks and recreation teams. Most of these programs are very good, but some problems do exist.

Fewer community programs are available today. Like the schools, state and local recreation programs have less and less money allocated to them. The result is that the availability of organized teams or programs and the access to facilities such as parks, gyms and swimming pools have declined. One major city in California, for example, had after-school recreation leaders at 97 elementary schools in

1978. Today that city has none. So, for many kids, the opportunity for extracurricular physical activity is just not there.

This is particularly evident in poor urban areas where programs have been cut. Many kids in these areas lack the fundamentals: bats, balls, a safe field. Where programs do exist, low-income families and children with working parents may not have the time or money to participate.

Another problem is that many programs emphasize competitive sports, which usually means that only elite athletes benefit from the resources of the organization. Winning becomes the all-important focal point. Such programs should instead enhance the goal of regular physical activity for all children and adolescents. Says Dr. Russell Pate of the University of South Carolina, "We should judge the YMCA, YWCA, Little League and other community organizations by the number of children involved in sports and exercise, not on their won-lost record."

Dr. Charles Kuntzleman agrees: "We often have our priorities backward with community sports teams. It's not who played that day and did we have fun; it's about who won. That needs to change. Community programs should be about participation and fun. And look at the message we give with respect to physical activity and food. If a team wins a game, we take them out to eat. We celebrate the home run with food. But if they lose a game, drop a ball or miss a tackle, we tell them to take laps and do push-ups. Children learn very quickly. They view food as a reward, physical activity as punishment."

Inactive parents are poor role models.

Parents' exercise habits are crucial because no other factor so strongly motivates kids to exercise. Research shows, for example, that children of active moms are two times as likely to be active as children of inactive mothers. Fathers seem to have an even greater influence. Active fathers are three and a half times more likely to have active kids than sedentary dads. And if both parents exercise, children are almost six times as likely to exercise themselves.

Unfortunately, many parents could do a better job of being a role model. An estimated 45% of American adults are sedentary. Inactivity is especially marked among blacks, Hispanics, low-income people and the unemployed. Of adults that claim to exercise, fewer than one in three are doing it on a regular basis. Says one exercise expert, "Americans do not exercise. We just buy exercise stuff!" The reality is that more than 70% of parents with children in grades one through four exercise moderately less than three times a week. More than 42% never exercise. And children mirror their parents.

The truth is, many parents are negative role models because of their own lack of exercise, and this needs to change. It will not be easy. In this fast-paced, modern way of life, the last thing many parents want to do is exercise. In a society where most jobs do not require many calories to be expended, you have to be willing to burn off extra calories the hard way: by playing organized sports, going to aerobics classes and climbing onto the StairMaster, and by including your children in your physical activity. Not only is this beneficial for you, but it also sets an example for your child that physical activity is important.

CHAPTER 7

WHAT PARENTS CAN DO

P roblems are always easier to identify than to solve. It is quite evident from scientific studies and simple observation that many American kids are out of shape and carrying unwanted, unneeded pounds. That's surely a problem—for the kids themselves, for their parents, and for all of us as a society.

But it doesn't have to be that way. If your child falls within this group (or, perhaps more important, if you want to *prevent* your child from an overweight and unfit life), you don't have to shake your head sadly. There are many ways for parents to set a good example, be a role model and do the right things so your kids will, too.

Children can be taught physical activity as a lifetime skill. The younger they start, the easier it is for them to maintain an active lifestyle as adults. Parents are the key to success. You are in the best position to teach your child to understand that physical fitness is a family priority. By practicing and supporting a physically active lifestyle, you help your child to ward off couch-potato societal messages and espouse physical fitness.

Remember, your role is to encourage exercise—not to force it. But simply telling a child to "go exercise" won't help at all. The best approach for getting youngsters to exercise is for parents to exercise. You can't tell kids that being active is fun. You have to show them. And that means getting off the couch to take your kids hiking, biking, dancing, sledding, swimming and skating.

SIX STEPS TO SUCCESS

A study published in the *American Journal of Diseases of Children* found that parents can promote fitness in children by encouraging them to play, by playing with them and by serving as good role models. Some of the specific things parents can do to develop healthy lifestyle habits in their kids are outlined below.

Be physically active yourself.

Moms and dads are the best motivators for kids to be active. As a parent, it's up to you to play the biggest part—bigger than the part played by a teacher, more important than the part of a coach. Your child looks to you for examples in how to talk, dress, act and lead a physically active—or inactive—life.

Being active is perhaps the most important step that parents can take because it demonstrates a clear message to children: fitness and health are part of the family culture. When I began jogging after heart surgery, my young children would come along for part of the run. Although my basic reason for jogging was to strengthen my heart, to do something for myself, I also knew that making time for regular physical activity was a way of saying that our family values health and is willing to do things to preserve it. My kids got that message. "Teaching kids personal responsibility," says one educator, "is probably the most important thing that parents can do."

Parents need to take care of themselves for their own health as well. For me, the underlying motivation was "Who will take care of my family if I'm not around?" Look for areas where you can be more physically active in the natural course of a day. Not only will an increase in physical activity help you to look better, feel more relaxed and have more energy, but it will also give your children a positive role model.

A minimum goal for adults is at least 30 minutes of physical activity a day. Schedule a regular time throughout the week for physical activity. Bear in mind that little things add up:

- Take a walk after dinner.
- Use stairs instead of an elevator.
- Park at the far end of the lot.
- Walk to the store.
- Play catch or kick a ball with your child.
- Carry your own groceries.
- Dig and plant in the garden.
- Chop and stack wood.
- Get off the bus a few stops early and walk.

It is also important for adults to be involved in vigorous, aerobic exercise at least three times a week, for a minimum of 20 minutes each time. This is the form of exercise that burns fat and provides cardiovascular conditioning, so it benefits people of all ages. Set a good example for your children by finding an aerobic activity you like and sticking with it. There are many to choose from, such as walking, bicycling, aerobics classes, swimming, jogging, exercise machines and rowing.

Involve your child.

Including your children in your own physical activities— exercising as a family—is a great way to influence them. Indeed, when parents actually participate with their children in physical activities, rather than just "commanding" them to be more active, the children's activity levels go up. "The family is a powerful influence on several health-promoting behaviors, including exercise," says Paul F. Rosengard, director of the SPARK Physical Education

Program. "Family involvement appears to be a key to children's physical activity patterns."

Younger children in particular acquire cognitive skills and new patterns of behavior by observing the performance of others. When parents are active, young children learn that physical activity is part of their family's routine and begin to emulate it. Unfortunately, most mothers and fathers never exercise with their children.

While it's true that competing demands from work, school and other involvements make it difficult to schedule family exercise, there are two easy ways to involve your children in your physical activity. The first is simply to look for daily activities that you can do together. In our house, depending on the season, after-dinner activity was usually catching a baseball or kicking a soccer ball. (Our grass never looked too great, but it was well worth the sacrifice.) There are many things to do with your kids. Take a bike ride together. Go to the park on a Saturday. Play wiffle ball in the backyard. Shoot baskets in the schoolyard. If feasible, walk with your child to school. Throw a Frisbee. Help your teenager to wash the car. Work in the yard or garden as a family. Go skating. Rake the leaves and then jump into the pile. Shovel snow and build a snowman. Play hopscotch, jump rope and tag with your children. Take a family pet for a walk or jog.

"We need exercise in order to die young as old as possible," says health expert Heinz Lenz. "One way that everyone can do this is by continuing to do what he or she has done since about age one—walk!" Some families like to use a walking log so that children can measure their progress. You can also use weekend outings to try different activities, such as hiking or bike riding. Keep exercise interesting by varying the location, even if it's just a different neighborhood or park. You can even take a walk through the mall. The list is endless.

As a bonus, shared activities give parents an opportunity to communicate. As Bernie, my wife, often said to me, "I enjoy snow-skiing with our kids. But the best part is that I have an opportunity to talk to them on the chair-lift with no TV, telephone or other interruptions. As a parent, it's a great chance to listen and to teach."

The second way is for parents to involve their kids in their own workouts. Take your son or daughter along on your bike ride. Go to the YMCA together (many Y's have excellent adult and youth programs conveniently conducted at the same time). Swimming, bicycling and other traditional exercises are great, but so are hiking, backpacking, skating and skiing.

Be sure to keep a sense of perspective when you exercise with your child. On my jogging program, I made sure there were days when I exercised alone or with an adult friend in order to get the cardiovascular conditioning I needed. But on the days when I jogged with my children, my main concern was to provide a positive physical opportunity for them and to send a message that exercise is fun. Primarily, it was a chance for us to be together and to share a good time.

Parents should try to avoid competition, discipline and embarrassment—things that can turn good times into moments of dread. Don't "take over" a shared activity or make it too regimented. "It worries me," says family therapist Ellyn Satter, "the way some parents are imposing exercise on their children. Instead of being too regimented, parents should 'play it by ear' in finding ways for kids to be more active. In some cases, that means forcing them to go outdoors and figure out something to do. It may be just the boost they need. In other cases, you may have to use a gentler approach—help a shy child learn to ride a bike or a scooter." Either way, she advises, parents should phase themselves out: "Get the child started gently, if need be, but then let the activity become his or her affair."

Remember, exercising with your child is different from exercising with other adults. Don't expect the child to be able to keep up with you or to have excellent form. Be sure to keep the activity at a pace that's comfortable for children. And be lavish with praise. It's important for children to feel successful. Praise your kids for trying. Praise them for doing. Someday, when they're grown and you exercise together, they'll make allowances for you!

Only 6% of mothers and fathers exercise with their children regularly. With the increasing demands of modern life, finding time to work out with your children is not easy. Perhaps that's why so few parents do it. But those who find the time exert a great influence on the long-term attitudes and actions of their kids.

Limit television and video viewing.

Too much TV is not only detrimental to intellectual development but also fosters overweight. Parents whose youngsters spend hour after hour in front of the set would do well to curb the habit. The American Academy of Pediatrics suggests limiting television time to no more than two hours daily as well as encouraging children to participate in after-school activities that require physical exertion.

Consider the following suggestions for reducing television viewing for young children:

- Move the television set from the main family gathering place. Out of sight, out of mind.
- Offer positive reinforcement for non-TV activities. For example, have your children track the number of books they read and reward them with a movie when they meet the standard you've agreed upon.
- Buy toys that promote physical activity.
- Invest in art materials for home use. Try taking them out and getting a project started before the TV set gets turned on.
- Look into community organizations that offer afternoon activities for children, such as arts and crafts classes, Girl Scouts and Boy Scouts.
- Have a family fun night once a week when members of the family turn off the TV and play games together or go visit the local library.

- Make a "deal" with your kids that for every hour of TV they watch, they'll spend an hour doing something active.
- Designate indoor and outdoor play areas where rolling, climbing, jumping and tumbling are allowed.

One of the best things you can do is set a good example for your kids. Instead of spending the evening in front of the TV set, find some activity that will keep you moving. Says the American Council on Exercise, "In warm weather, bike outdoors; if it's too cold, get a stationary bike, a treadmill or a trampoline." According to Kathryn Armstrong, Coordinator of the Children in the Schools program in the Office of Disease Prevention and Health Promotion, "The kids who are the leanest and most physically fit have parents who are very active physically and watch less TV."

In our house, the amount of television viewing was naturally governed by our commitment to physical activities and school/community sports. Much of our free time was spent throwing a football or baseball, playing "keep away" with a soccer ball, or playing an entire nine-inning baseball game in the front yard with a plastic ball and bat. While walking out the back door to play works well in suburbia, however, parents in urban settings may turn to nearby activity areas such as a park, bike path, tennis court, swimming pool or basketball court.

Some parents combine TV time with exercise time. One mother told me, "My children know that 30 minutes spent playing in the backyard or taking a walk with me is worth one hour of television."

Not all experts believe that parents must supply activities to counter television. "We're creating a generation of children who don't know how to entertain themselves," cautions Dr. Dietz. "Parents should just turn off the TV set and tell children that it's up to them to figure out something to do. What did children do before there was television? They are just as capable today as they were back then. Boredom from a turned-off television set generates self-reliance and creativity."

Dr. C. Everett Koop, former U.S. Surgeon General, points out another problem. "I think with television, we've lost a great hunk of family life. There's absolutely no one-on-one family enjoyment with looking at TV. You may be edified if you are watching a particularly artistic or educational film, but for people to say, 'I'm going to have a wonderful evening at home with the children and then TV, that's a fraud. With television there's no fellowship, no conviviality, and no back-and-forth exchange of information between parent and child."

Support your child's fitness activities.

Be sure your child has at least one favorite activity that provides regular exercise, and schedule for it. For many kids, it's an organized sport such as swimming, soccer or gymnastics. But it doesn't have to be. Some children prefer biking or in-line skating. Other kids may prefer working in the yard or walking the dog. Keep at it with your child until you find the right fit.

Parental involvement is critical, but so is parental perspective. "The key to helping your kids be fit is to help them find sports or activities they really like," says Judith Young, president of the National Association for Sports and Physical Education. "Offer continuous encouragement. Help children to develop confidence in their skills and a desire to improve to the next level. Help them find time for physical activities. Family support for exercise does make a difference in kids' exercise habits. The simplest form of support is verbal, and the best time to give it is just after a workout. Heartfelt praise after exercise is more effective than a reminder before exercise. Active support is even more effective."

Supporting your child's fitness activities sends the message that his or her well-being is important to you. Be sure to meet all deadlines for league sign-ups. (Many leagues are booked as early as Broadway shows.) Spending

time outdoors with younger children, providing member-
ship fees and transportation, volunteering as a coach,
scrubbing wheels at the team car wash, stressing participation rather than competition . . . these are things that
parents can do to demonstrate the importance of physical
activity. "Parents can convey explicit or subtle expecta-
tions to their children regarding participation in physical
activities," says Dr. Pate. "Active children report that parents expect them to be active."

This is not always easy, and it's particularly hard for
single parents or in families where both parents work.
"Balance is the key," says Susan Kalish. "Just let children
know you think it's important, help them when you can
and find a significant other who can help them when
you're not around. That's what you've got to do."

One of the most significant factors in developing fitness in kids is parents' willingness to provide transportation to and from activities. Says Dr. James Sallis:

> Many kids live in urban apartments or in suburban
> communities with microscopic yards. If kids are going
> to be active, they've got to go somewhere else. And in
> most cases, their parents are going to have to take
> them. Kids today are really quite constrained in what
> they're able to do. We tell them, "Don't play in the
> street, don't go to the park by yourself, don't go outside
> when you're home alone." And these restraints, moti-
> vated by our desire to protect children, have the effect
> of limiting their opportunities to be active. In modern
> society, there are many barriers to kids' physical fitness.
> Parents need to take specific steps to overcome those
> obstacles—like driving the soccer car pool.

Parents should help children to learn basic skills so
they can participate in a variety of activities. "Don't overlook the simple act of teaching about a physical activity,"
advises Dr. Kuntzleman. "Knowledge of the health effects
of exercise is not important to kids, but knowledge of how

to be physically active is of great importance. Kids want to know how to do the activity well. They don't want to embarrass themselves. So, even if you're not a great athlete or a physically active person, you can still work with your child to build skills and confidence, and help that child choose physical activity for a lifetime."

One thing not to do is to make competitive sports too important, particularly with young children. This can send the wrong message to the child. If the most excited and most positive behaviors exhibited by parents come when their children hit a home run or score a goal, then the children can get the wrong idea about what sports are about. They think, "Man, this stuff is really important. I'd better do this right, or I'm going to be the biggest loser ever." Parents need to keep a big-picture perspective.

Sports psychologist Rick Wolff suggests that parents use a sliding scale when it comes to competition with youth sports. "The younger the child, the less emphasis upon competition," he says. "In fact, with children ages 5 or 6, you shouldn't even bother keeping score. These kids are more concerned about simply getting into the game than they are about its outcome. By the time they're 9 or 10, however, they should be learning about both the winning and losing experiences. And by the time they're in junior high, they should come to understand that competing is not the end-all of sports, but just part of the game."

Work for quality P.E. programs in schools.

"Parents are the key ingredient in making sure that schools provide appropriate experiences for children to develop physical fitness and physical competence," says Dr. Judith Young. "As a result, parents need to take as much interest in a child's physical education activities as in his or her academic coursework."

One of the first things parents can do is to evaluate the quality of their children's P.E. program. Dr. Kuntzleman suggests the following grading system based on specific criteria.

How Does Your Child's School Measure Up?

Points

Low   High

1   2   3   1. Does the school provide at least one period per day of vigorous exercise that lasts at least 20 minutes?

1   2   3   2. Does the school offer at least 75% of physical education instruction in lifetime activities such as walking, running, swimming, bicycling, aerobics, tennis, badminton, skiing, weight training, stretching and the how and why of fitness?

1   2   3   3. Does the school provide tests to determine which children might lack flexibility, strength and cardiovascular endurance?

1   2   3   4. Does the school provide physical activity opportunities for the obese, unfit and unskilled?

1   2   3   5. Does the school provide physical education programs for the mentally and physically handicapped?

1   2   3   6. Does the school have a prescribed source of study for physical education that the teachers are required to follow? Is P.E. teaching monitored?

1   2   3   7. Does the school's physical education program emphasize fun, participation and relevance (fitness and motor skills) rather than sports skill development and competition?

1   2   3   8. Does the school put physical education first and athletics second?

1   2   3   9. Do the physical education teachers look fit and participate in personal fitness programs?

1   2   3   10. Do your children enjoy, speak highly of and look forward to physical education classes?

1   2   3   11. Does the school not threaten to cut physical education when budget cuts are considered?

1   2   3   12. Does the school integrate physical education concepts with classroom concepts?

After you've given a rating for each standard in the list, add up the points you've assigned. If the total score is below 30 points, the school needs to reevaluate its direction in physical education.

Next, once the quality of the P.E. program has been determined, you can take the following steps:

- Meet with your child's P.E. teacher. Learn about your child's P.E. activities and find out how to become more involved.
- Write and speak with school administrators to express your support for quality P.E.
- Encourage school officials to provide opportunities for students to be physically active before school, during lunch hour and after school.
- Volunteer to help with P.E. events at school.
- Make it clear to the local school board that physical education should be made a priority at every grade level.
- Encourage the school P.E. department to coordinate family evening and weekend activities.
- Prompt school officials to offer assembles, field trips and special events to promote physical activities.
- Get the local parent-teacher association to sponsor P.E. events.

In the final analysis, quality physical education is no longer a "given" in most American school districts. Parents must be willing to invest time and talent with other parents and educators to ensure that quality physical education is part of their children's curriculum. But help is available. Many organizations now offer curricula and programs that can be used by schools to help provide quality physical education. Some of these organizations include the CATCH (Child and Adolescent Trial for Cardiovascular Health) Physical Education Program, the Project SPARK Physical Education Program and the Bogalusa Heart Health Program.

Support your community athletic programs.
Community programs can be an integral part of developing fitness habits in children and teens. Not only do such programs encourage kids to play and have fun, but they also teach the rules of the game and how to play together. Millions of kids play sports in community programs such as Little League, YMCA, YWCA, police athletic leagues and park departments.

As a parent, you can support community athletic programs in a variety of ways. First, work for facilities and programs. Make sure your community has fields, leagues and coaches available for your children. Don't think just in terms of organized sports. Promote the development of neighborhood parks, bike paths and walking trails in your community. Second, don't obsess about winning/losing or performance. One expert suggests critiquing your child's sports performance for no more than one minute per event. Instead, focus on what your child is getting out of the process, whether it's learning athletic or social skills, or just being outdoors. Strive for a goal of wide participation instead of won-lost records. Make sure it's fun. Teaching kids to relish the mere act of playing is more likely to foster a long-lasting interest in being active. Third, support your child by attending games and practices whenever you can. Be your child's own cheerleader. Volunteer to help the coach as a team mother or dad. By being part of the experience, the child learns that this activity (not the score, but the activity) is important.

SUMMING UP

Times have changed, but the need for physical activity has not. In fact, it has never been more important. "Parents need to understand that physical activity is the key," says Dr. Gortmaker. "We can help to keep children from becoming overweight and out of shape. We can help to keep 'chubby' kids from becoming obese and can actually help them to slim down. Both diet and physical activity are important. But of the two, physical activity is paramount. For many youths, the solution is to let them grow into their overweight. Cut down on dietary fat, but not on calories. Children and teens need a good supply of calories during crucial growth spurts. But increase activity levels. Children see physical activity all the time—but mostly on TV. Parents need to make it a part of a child's, indeed a family's, lifestyle. Increased physical activity is the solution to our epidemic of obesity."

Give your children the right start. It will be easier for them to maintain an active lifestyle as an adult if they start young. There is plenty that parents can do. Simply providing opportunities for your children to play outside (rather than encourage them to stay inside) goes a long way. It's not always easy to find activities they can enjoy, but it's well worth your effort. Says Dr. James Sallis, "Parents should ask their children each year what they like to do, then help them do it. By helping your kids get involved, you send the message that physical activity is a high priority for you."

Help your kids get involved in organized activities and take them there. It doesn't matter so much whether it's a team sport, dance class or martial arts lessons. What matters is that you take the time to make physical activity possible for your children. And remember, *if you can't do it all, do something!*

PART III

DIET:
THE PROBLEM

CHAPTER 8

WHAT KIDS EAT IS HAZARDOUS TO THEIR HEALTH

I t is well recognized by scientists and health professionals that dietary habits are a significant factor in weight loss, weight control and fitness. However, what our kids are eating today parallels (and sometimes exceeds) the worst aspects of the U.S. adult diet: too many foods rich in fat, calories, sugar and sodium, and not enough fruits, vegetables, grains and legumes rich in complex carbohydrates and fiber.

The long-term relationship between diet and health is also clearly recognized. This, of course, is of no interest to kids. Children and especially teens do not choose foods based on nutritional value. Instead, they make dietary choices based on impulse, advertising, convenience, economics, status, taste and cravings. (And frankly, so do most adults.) Health risks do not motivate children or teens to become more physically active or to eat better. The result is an eating style that sets up many kids at an early age for weight problems and health risks.

How important is diet? Parents should know that the way we eat is linked to 5 of the 10 leading causes of death in the United States. A recent Report on Nutrition and Health paints a picture of Americans gobbling their way to the grave.

Says Dr. C. Everett Koop, "As the diseases of nutritional deficiency have diminished, they have been replaced by diseases of dietary excess and imbalance. After smoking, the choice of diet can influence long-term health prospects more than any other factor."

In 1996, because of these significant factors, the U.S. Department of Agriculture and the Department of Health and Human Services published Dietary Guidelines for Americans two years of age or older. The recommendations include:

- Eat a variety of foods.
- Balance the food you eat with physical activity—maintain or improve your weight.
- Choose a diet with plenty of grain products, vegetables and fruits.
- Choose a diet low in fat and saturated fat and low in cholesterol.
- Choose a diet moderate in sugars.
- Choose a diet moderate in salt and sodium.
- If you consume alcoholic beverages, do so in moderation.

These recommendations are reflected in the USDA's Food Guide Pyramid, which outlines what types of foods to eat each day. The wide base of the pyramid contains the foods we should eat in greater quantity, and the narrow peak contains the foods we should restrict. Picturing food selections in pyramid form helps to proportion choices among the different food groups. For example, by emphasizing fruits, vegetables, grains, pasta and breads in its broad base, the pyramid promotes foods with vitamins, minerals, complex carbohydrates and fiber.

Food Guide Pyramid

A GUIDE TO FOOD CHOICES

> **KEY** • Fat (naturally occurring and added)
> ▾ Sugars (added)

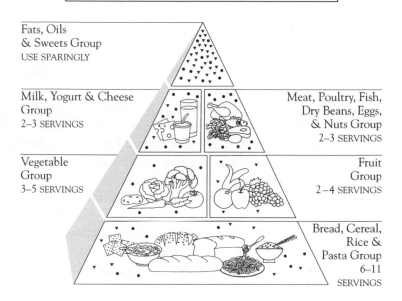

Fats, Oils
& Sweets Group
USE SPARINGLY

Milk, Yogurt & Cheese
Group
2–3 SERVINGS

Meat, Poultry, Fish,
Dry Beans, Eggs,
& Nuts Group
2–3 SERVINGS

Vegetable
Group
3–5 SERVINGS

Fruit
Group
2–4 SERVINGS

Bread, Cereal,
Rice &
Pasta Group
6–11
SERVINGS

The Dietary Guidelines tell us what we *should* eat for better health. However, when contrasted with what kids (and most adults) *do* eat, a wide gap exists. And that gap has much to do with the overweight and out-of-shape condition of American youth.

The Bogalusa Heart Study, which has been monitoring kids' eating habits for over 20 years, provides a good picture of the changes in their diet—and the contrasts are staggering. Twenty years ago, most kids had a home-cooked breakfast and dinner. Fast food and frozen meals were only occasional. Sugar cereals and pastry were popular breakfast choices, but so were nutritious dry and hot cereals, toast, milk, fruit and juice. Dinner was a family affair and usually included milk, salad and vegetables. And although everyone complained about school lunches, brown-bag or cafeteria, most offered some nutritional balance by including milk, fruit and vegetables.

Compare that scenario with kids' eating patterns today. Dr. Theresa Kicklas, director of dietary studies for the Bogalusa Study, notes what one 17-year-old boy ate in a 24-hour period:

> For breakfast, he had a fast-food egg and bacon sandwich and orange juice on the bus to school. Many of his friends left the school campus for lunch at a fast-food place. But he ate lunch at school—chicken nuggets, baked potato with butter and cheese, two rolls, a canned pear and whole milk. His other choices were pepperoni pizza and a cheeseburger with fries. His afternoon snack took place at a deli—a chicken sandwich globbed with mayonnaise and a bag of potato chips. Dinner at home was two fried pork chops, another baked potato and two slices of bread. The fact that he didn't eat a single green vegetable in a 24-hour period, and only a little fruit, doesn't surprise us. Unfortunately, this today is more the rule than the exception. This is how teenagers eat.

Survey results for elementary school children do not differ substantially. Children reported typical food selections that included six pieces of pizza for dinner; biscuits, sausage and tater tots for breakfast; and fast food and snacks throughout the day.

The Bogalusa Study results should give parents much cause for alarm because it shows our kids being placed at risk for future heart disease, cancer and obesity. Health professionals cite four areas of concern with the way American children and teens eat.

- Too much fat
- Too much sodium
- Too much sugar
- Not enough complex carbohydrates and fiber

TOO MUCH FAT

While many aspects of food and health continue to be debated, there is a consensus among medical experts when it comes to the greatest hazard of the American diet—*too much fat*. Reducing total fat (and with it cholesterol-raising saturated fat) has become the nation's highest dietary priority.

What's wrong with fat? If the truth be known, nothing. In itself, fat is not harmful and actually plays an important role in good health. Along with protein and carbohydrate, fat is one of the main classes of foods necessary to the body. Polyunsaturated fat (primarily from vegetable oils) supplies the body with linoleic acid, an essential fatty acid.

Dietary fat is also used in the transportation of important fat-soluble vitamins into the body. Without fat in the diet, we would not be able to absorb vitamins A, D, E and K. And at 9 calories per gram, fat supplies more than twice the energy as the same amount of protein or carbohydrate. This is especially important for children, particularly those under two years of age, who can use the higher energy from fat to meet increased growth needs.

In addition, fat makes food taste better. It helps to distribute flavors throughout the mouth, keeps them there longer and provides texture. It also makes food moister, causing it literally to "melt in your mouth." And because fat is digested slowly, it provides an enjoyable feeling of satisfaction after a meal.

There is nothing wrong with dietary fat *when consumed in the proper amount*. And that is precisely the root of the issue. Despite their awareness of its harmful effects, Americans eat too much fat. The problem, then, is dose-related. From a nutritional standpoint, the daily requirement for fat can be fully satisfied by consuming the equivalent of one tablespoon of vegetable oil. The average American, however, eats eight times that amount—between 800 and 1,000 calories, or about the equivalent of one stick of butter a day. It is estimated that the average family of four consumes 400 pounds of fat in a year!

SOURCES OF DIETARY FAT

The top three sources of dietary fat for Americans are 1) meat, poultry and fish; 2) visible fats such as cooking and salad oils; and 3) whole-milk dairy products such as cheese and butter. Other significant sources include baked goods such as cookies and doughnuts, fast food such as hamburgers and pizza, snack foods such as chocolate candy and potato chips, and convenience foods such as luncheon meats and frozen meals. In addition, frying and deep-fat frying are favorite methods of cooking that add fat, while fatty sauces and gravies are routinely used as flavor enhancers.

American kids are not immune to this diet pattern. Indeed, their yearnings for favorite foods are acquired from parents and society. It should be no surprise then that children get most of their fat from:

- Hamburgers, cheeseburgers and meat loaf
- Hot dogs, ham and processed luncheon meats
- Whole milk, ice cream, cheese and other whole-milk dairy products
- Commercial baked goods
- Fried foods such as fried chicken and French fries

Health experts—including the American Heart Association, the National Cancer Institute and the American Academy of Pediatrics—recommend that everyone over the age of two eat a diet that receives no more than 30% of its calories from fat. For people who wish to lose weight and/or reduce blood cholesterol, a diet with no more than 25% of calories from fat would be even better.

But what most Americans eat is a long way from those recommendations. According to the USDA, dietary fat made up just 27% of calories consumed at the turn of the century. Today, fat accounts for 34% of calories for adults. And it's worse for kids. "About 4 out of 5 children eat a diet well over 30% fat," says Dr. Gerald Berenson. "It is estimated that the average American child aged 1 to 19 gets 38% of calories from fat."

Some would say that even though we eat a lot of fat, it's less than in the late 1970s, when fat constituted over 40% of calories. "Not so," says Bonnie Liebman, a registered dietitian at the Center for Science in the Public Interest. "Fat reduction is a myth. What we're eating today is not a lower-fat diet. It's a higher-calorie diet. We are actually eating slightly more fat today than in 1991, but we're eating a lot more calories. So, the percentage looks better, but the actual amount of fat has not fallen. The recommendation to cut back on fat means just that: eat less fat. If these numbers reflect what people are eating, we're in trouble."

DIETARY FAT AND OVERWEIGHT

Along with physical activity, dietary habits have long been seen as a lifestyle factor with a critical impact on weight. The link between excessive dietary fat and obesity is particularly strong. Too much dietary fat contributes to overweight in a variety of ways.

Fat is rich in calories.

Food is consumed for many reasons, but essentially it is necessary to supply the body with energy in the form of calories. If calories consumed (what you eat) is in balance with calories expended (what you burn in exercise, physical activity and basic metabolism), all is well. But when caloric input is greater than the output, the extra calories are stored as body fat. (Think of all those fat cells soaking up the extra body fat like sponges.) It takes 3,500 extra calories to create one pound of body fat.

For most of us, gaining weight takes place over a period of time. A few more calories going in, a few less going out, is what causes body fat to accumulate. As few as 50 extra calories a day, a single chocolate-chip cookie, can add 350 calories a week. That doesn't sound like much, but it equates to a gain of 5 pounds in a year, or 52 pounds in a decade.

A diet that is rich in fat helps this to happen because of the caloric concentration, or density, of fatty foods. A high-fat diet by nature produces a lot of calories because fat contains twice as many calories as the same amount of protein or carbohydrate.

- 1 gram of fat contains 9 calories.
- 1 gram of protein or carbohydrate contains 4 calories.

Compare 3 ounces of high-fat rib roast with the same amount of low-fat, light-meat chicken cooked without the skin. The rib roast has 375 calories; the chicken, about 100. *Ounce for ounce, fat really is fatter.*

Fat packs a lot of calories into a modest amount of food. In fact, people who eat high-fat diets actually take in less food but a lot more calories, and therefore gain weight. Consider this: you could consume 250 calories by a) eating a small package of M&M peanut candies, or b) eating an entire pound of apples. So, while it's possible to gain weight by overeating any type of food, high-fat foods contribute the most simply because they contain more calories. (The one exception is "fat-free" baked goods, which are discussed later in this chapter.)

Dietary fat turns easily into body fat.

For many years, scientists believed that "a calorie is a calorie is a calorie." A growing body of research now suggests that this simple rule of dieting dogma doesn't always hold true. As Dr. Eric Jequier of the University of Lausanne in Switzerland has observed, "The body doesn't treat dietary fat the way it treats carbohydrates or protein."

Some of the calories we consume are utilized immediately as fuel. Those not used right away are converted to body fat and stored for future use. The process of converting calories into body fat takes energy, and some of the calories being converted are burned to produce that energy. Think of it as a "handling cost" to turn calories into stored fuel.

Not all foods call for the same amount of energy in the conversion process, so not all have the same "handling costs." Studies at the University of Massachusetts Medical School found that almost one-fourth (23%) of the calories found in carbohydrates are burned off when converted to fat. So, if you eat 100 calories of baked potato, just 77 calories are available to be converted into body fat.

It is not the same for dietary fat, which burns just 3% of calories in the conversion process. Eat 100 calories of butter and 97 of them are available to become body fat. "What it boils down to," says obesity expert Dr. Elliott Danforth, Jr., "is that calorie for calorie, fat is more fattening. A high-fat diet simply makes it easier to store body fat."

THE WRONG TYPE OF FAT

In addition to the amount of fat we consume, a second concern is that we eat too much of the wrong type of fat—saturated fat, the type of fat that can raise cholesterol and increase the risk of heart disease. This is particularly important in light of the estimate that 36% of American children aged 2 to 19 have high cholesterol.

All fats and oils can be described as saturated, polyunsaturated and monounsaturated. These distinctions are important because, from a cardiac standpoint, not all fats are equal.

Saturated Fat

Because it elevates "bad" LDL cholesterol, saturated fat is the most harmful to cardiac health. It is found in animal foods such as the visible fat on steak, bacon drippings, cheese, lard and butter. A rule of thumb is that saturated fat stays hard at room temperature. This type of fat is also found in three vegetable oils: palm oil, palm kernel oil and coconut oil.

According to the National Health and Nutrition Examination Survey, saturated fat makes up about 13% to 14% of calories of the diet of American children. Adults consume slightly more, about 16% to 18% of calories. However, data show that for many Americans, saturated fat makes up as much as one-third of total calories.

Since it is a major influence on the production of harmful LDL cholesterol, experts now recommend that saturated fat constitute no more than 10% of calories. "Please remember," says Dr. Virgil Brown, a past president of the American Heart Association, "that 10% is an upper limit. A better goal is in the 7% to 10% range—and below that if you have heart disease or a parent or grandparent with heart disease."

Unsaturated Fat

The unsaturated fats—both polyunsaturated and mono-unsaturated—tend to remain liquid at room temperature. These fats are better for cardiac health because they do not raise cholesterol and indeed may reduce it.

Polyunsaturated fats, found chiefly in vegetable oils such as safflower, soybean, corn, cotton and sesame oils, can help to lower LDL cholesterol. One caution regarding these oils is to avoid those that have been hardened or stiffened into solid form through a process called *hydrogenation.* This process produces trans fatty acids, which, like saturated fats, can elevate LDL cholesterol. So, while soft, tub-type corn oil margarine doesn't harm cardiac health, stick or cube margarine can. Hydrogenated or partially hydrogenated vegetable oils are also used to make solid shortening, cookies, crackers, potato chips and other processed foods.

One source of polyunsaturated fat that does not carry this drawback is seafood, including shellfish. Omega-3, a fatty acid found in fish oil, has been shown to protect against heart disease by reducing the risk of clot formation within coronary arteries. In addition, fish oil markedly lowers high triglycerides. According to the *New England Journal of Medicine*, eating "as little as two fish dinners a week (about 7.5 ounces of fish) may cut the risk of dying from heart attack in half."

Monounsaturated fats are found in olive, canola, peanut, avocado and nut oils. Studies show that these fats keep the blood from clotting, reduce LDL cholesterol and preserve HDL cholesterol when substituted for saturated fats. Olive oil and canola oil in particular are associated with a reduced risk of heart disease. This may explain the low incidence of heart problems among Mediterranean populations who use olive oil and Asian populations who use canola oil.

The Right Perspective

There is no doubt that polyunsaturated and monounsaturated fats are "more healthful" from a cardiac standpoint than is saturated fat. However, there is no need to overconsume any fat, whether it comes from a steer or an ear of corn. Indeed, there is evidence that too much fat of any kind can contribute to the development of artery blockages.

And remember, too much of any kind of fat, even the so-called "healthy oils," can increase the risk for obesity and breast, colon and prostate cancers. People who load up on margarine instead of butter, or who fry food in an inch of olive oil, miss the point. The proper perspective is this: when you eat fat, substitute unsaturated fats for saturated fats. But the bottom line is to eat less fat. Period.

WATCH OUT FOR "FAT-FREE" FOODS

The quest to cut fat has spawned a multitude of "fat-free" foods, including cookies, candy and even ice cream. And with the introduction of the fat substitute olestra, more "fat-free" snack foods—including potato chips—will be available. It is estimated that each year more than 5,900 new food items that claim to be "fat-free" or "low-fat" are introduced. To offset the loss of flavor and texture that accompanies fat reduction, manufacturers often increase the amount of sugar in their products. This automatically increases calories, and as a result these foods may have comparable—and sometimes higher—calorie counts than ordinary snacks. This is why a small "fat-free" chocolate cookie can contain 50 or 60 calories. *"Fat-free" does not mean "calorie-free."*

Health experts see a troublesome and perhaps inevitable trend. A growing number of people are overdosing on fat-free foods. Unfortunately, those who have incorporated an abundance of "fat-free" snacks into their food plan are finding it difficult to lose weight. "People perceive fat-free food as good and think they can eat as much as they want and then feel better because they avoided fat," observes Cathy Nonas, R.D. "But adding extra, empty calories to non-meal times spells danger. Snacking all day long can rack up as many calories as eating a meal, but without providing any of a meal's nutritional benefits. In the fight against fat, many people have conveniently forgotten that to lose weight you've got to keep the number of calories lower than the number you burn."

When the government called for a reduction of fat in the diet to reduce the risk of heart disease, cancer and obesity, no one anticipated an aggressive food industry going gangbusters on marketing the concept. Nor did anyone consider human nature and its tremendous ability to make irrational justifications. "We kept the fat message simple, and the food industry did what was asked," says Nancy Ernst, nutrition coordinator of the National Cholesterol Education Program. "But we said nothing about calories. So what we have is high-sugar, no-fat products that don't help weight maintenance, and in some cases may translate into weight gain. People have taken once-a-week high-fat favorites and substituted the no-fat version every day." The big problem is that low-fat and no-fat still mean calories—especially if you eat half a fat-free cherry pie (2.5 slices, 675 calories).

Products made with olestra, which appear under the brand name Olean, are of particular concern to many health professionals. Because olestra is not digestible, a large intake can cause diarrhea and prevent the body from absorbing certain fat-soluble vitamins such as A, D and E. But the real issue, says Dr. Fredric Pashkow, a cardiologist at the Cleveland Clinic, is whether or not a fat substitute will help people to better manage their weight.

Will people take this opportunity to cut back on fatty foods and lower their daily calories to lose weight or maintain a healthy body weight? Or, will people use the advent of olestra to indulge in eating even more foods, or larger portions, and rationalize their indulgence because the food doesn't contain any fat. If our experience with artificial sweeteners is duplicated with fake-fats, we could be in trouble. During the decades since the release of sugar substitutes such as saccharin, Americans have gotten fatter and fatter. The much-touted non-nutritive sweeteners have had no impact whatsoever on the problem of excessive calorie intake.

In fact, research shows that people tend to eat larger quantities of no-fat foods because they offer far less satiety than their high-fat counterparts. Chris Rosenbloom, professor of nutrition at Georgia State University, states:

"Research shows that if people are told the food is fat-free or lower in fat, they tend to eat more of it. The bottom line is that if you're looking to lose weight, loading up on fat-free foods may not be beneficial." So, you might be better off figuring out what you really want and eating less of it. Says registered dietitian Ann Litt, "I'd rather have people satisfy themselves with a couple of Oreos than go on a binge with a box of SnackWell's."

A WORD OF CAUTION: LITTLE JACK SPRAT SHOULD EAT *SOME* FAT

While the reduction of fat must be a priority, we should not make the mistake of taking the low-fat message to mean no fat or very little fat. "We're a society of extremists. We tend to take things a little too far sometimes," says dietitian Faye Berger Mitchell. "People are told by their doctors to 'eat less fat,' so therefore they think 'if I eat *no* fat,' it'll be even better for me." Health experts are alarmed about this distortion of the low-fat message by a subset of fat-conscious Americans who are forgoing fat altogether.

The fact is that we do need some fat in our diet. Health professionals say they are seeing patients today who have cut dietary fat so dramatically that dry skin, brittle hair, gastric problems and menstrual irregularities have resulted. "People have to know that the radically low-fat diets *may* be fine for patients with heart disease," says obesity expert Dr. C. Wayne Callaway of George Washington University. "But these diets are not for mainstream use."

With children in particular, it is important not to penalize those who need fat. Infants and children under age two, for example, need high levels of fat for growth and development. If parents reduce fat too early, there is a possibility that there will be problems in terms of maturation of body organs like the liver, spleen, kidneys and brain. In a few extreme occurrences, parents have cut their infants' fat consumption to the point where growth was stunted.

"Parents need to be careful even with children over two years of age," cautions Dr. Nicklas. "We do need to get kids to eat less fat than they are now consuming. In order to do that, parents need to identify the sources of fat in the diets of their children, and how often these foods are eaten. Usually it's fatty meats, high-fat cheese, whole milk products, baked goods, fast foods, convenience foods and snacks. But don't restrict your child's diet to less than about 25% of calories from fat because of ongoing growth needs. In addition, focusing on low-fat is not enough. Equal attention needs to be given to the importance of a well-balanced diet. The problem is not just what kids are eating—high-fat fast food, snacks and such. It's also what they are not eating—fruits, vegetables and grains."

TOO MUCH SODIUM

The American diet supplies far more sodium than anyone needs. As with dietary fat, there is nothing inherently harmful about sodium. In fact, a certain amount is needed in the diet for good health. Sodium is the chief regulator of the body's fluid balance, a factor in proper metabolic functioning. But health professionals counsel that consuming too much sodium can put children on the road to health problems later in life. Two of the most significant are high blood pressure and osteoporosis.

Over 63 million Americans are afflicted with high blood pressure, or hypertension, which causes over 100,000 deaths annually. High blood pressure is a major threat for heart attack and stroke. Like heart disease, it progresses silently. Blood pressure can increase slightly year after year until quite suddenly, usually in middle age, the condition appears. By this time it is often too late to repair the damage done to the heart, kidneys and blood vessels. Chronic illness and death often occur. It is estimated that 45% of Americans with high blood pressure are unaware that they have the condition.

The causes of high blood pressure are not fully understood. Some factors include age, weight, stress, genetics and diet. However, perhaps nothing is more important to the promotion or avoidance of high blood pressure than sodium intake. Studies show that in low-sodium societies hypertension is virtually nonexistent. But in sodium-rich societies, such as Japan and the United States, hypertension is rampant. In Japan, where sodium consumption is 20 times that of the West, high blood pressure is the leading cause of death.

Osteoporosis is a second significant condition that can arise from excessive sodium. Researchers have confirmed that the more sodium (or salt) you eat, the more calcium you lose from your body and the more prone you become to debilitating fractures as you age. In a two-year study of postmenopausal women, the group most prone to osteoporosis, those who took in the most sodium lost the most bone in hips and ankles.

Not all of us are sodium-sensitive. Indeed, an estimated two-thirds of the population could eat at a salt lick without any harmful effects. But there is no procedure for identifying those who do have a genetic weak-link, so eating a sodium-rich diet means rolling the dice with your health.

Much of our sodium comes from salt. Salt and sodium are not the same. Sodium is a mineral that occurs naturally in almost all foods. Salt is sodium chloride, a compound that is about 40% sodium. Thus a diet that is high in salt is also rich in sodium.

The Bogalusa Heart Study, already mentioned in connection with its work on children and heart disease, has produced much of the evidence linking excessive salt to high blood pressure in children. States study director Dr. Gerald Berenson, "About 25% of 12-year-olds have high blood pressure. The condition begins in childhood, and diet is a major factor. As with cholesterol, children who have elevated blood pressure 'track' into adults with high blood pressure." According to Dr. Alan Sinaiko at the University of Minnesota Medical School, who has studied the impact of sodium on the blood pressure of children in fifth to eighth grade, high-salt food is a significant factor.

The message to parents is this: children who eat a high-sodium diet develop a taste for salt that will stay with them as they grow into adulthood. And this puts them at increased risk for high blood pressure and osteoporosis later in life.

HOW MUCH ARE KIDS EATING?

Like many aspects of the American diet, the problem with sodium is dose-related. The National Research Council recommends that everyone over age two consume no more than 2,400 milligrams of sodium daily. (Roughly 2,300 milligrams is the equivalent of one teaspoon of salt.)

American kids typically eat about 5 to 10 times the amount of sodium they actually require. A one-year-old child, for example, needs only 225 milligrams of sodium daily, and an 18-year-old needs about 500 milligrams. However, the average child of two eats almost 2,700 milligrams of sodium daily, while the average teen eats almost 3,700 milligrams.

Why do kids eat so much salt? Parents should understand that a taste for salt is acquired. The more salt children eat, the more they crave. "Salt appetite is determined by early dietary habits and has no relationship to salt need," says Dr. Lot Page, a Harvard hypertension specialist. "Many babies and young children learn to like the taste of salt when their mothers feed them commercial baby food with added salt, or salt their food. But learning to like salty food is an affinity that can be prevented in babies and reversed in children and teens."

The key for parents is early action. As Dr. Jeffrey Cutler at the National Heart, Lung and Blood Institute points out, "Tastes are acquired early. Once acquired, they can be changed, but changing them is harder than not acquiring them in the first place. If you're used to eating food relatively low in salt, it won't take much added salt to make certain foods taste better. But the more you're used to, the more it takes to get that pleasurable taste. To me, that all points in the direction of an early approach."

SOURCES OF SODIUM

Where does all this salt and sodium come from? About 15% derives from natural sources such as meat, fish, dairy products, vegetables and drinking water. Another 35% comes from the salt shaker for use as a condiment or cooking spice. But fully 50% is from processed foods and fast foods.

Salt and other sodium products are used as a curative for fish and meats, as a brine for pickles, olives and sauerkraut, as a leavening agent in bread and crackers, and as a fermentation agent in cheese. Essentially, however, salt is a "flavor enhancer." Americans like the taste of salt, a fact not lost on the food industry. That's why you'll find it in a range of foods, from potato chips to canned soups to fast-food hamburgers. Says Vice President Albert Gore, "There is a tremendous competitive advantage to loading food with salt and not telling people about it."

Using 2,400 milligrams of sodium a day as a guideline, it's easy to see in the following table how processed and fast foods can cumulatively produce an overabundance of sodium.

Food	Milligrams of Sodium
½ cup frozen peas	70
1 oz. Lay's potato chips	95
1 oz. Planters salted cashews	110
1 cup milk	120
15 potato chips	135
1 tbsp. ketchup	155
1 order McDonald's large French fries (4.3 oz.)	200
1 hamburger bun	230
2 slices white Wonder Bread	240
2 tbsp. peanut butter	260
1 slice Oscar Mayer Ham and Cheese Loaf	290
1 oz. American cheese	335
1 oz. corn flakes	350
4-oz. serving of Healthy Choice spaghetti sauce	380
½ cup cottage cheese	445
1 hot dog	450
½ serving of chicken-flavor Stove Top stuffing	580
2 oz. bologna	655
2 oz. salami	655
1 cup Kraft Macaroni and Cheese	710
1 McDonald's Egg McMuffin	710
1 oz. Snyder's Very Thin pretzels	730
4-oz. serving of Ragú Old World Style spaghetti sauce	740
3-oz. serving of Hardee's Crispy Curl French fries	840
1 cup Campbell's Chunky chicken noodle soup	870
1 McDonald's Big Mac	890
1 Subway 6" Tuna Sandwich	905
1 Taco Bell Taco Salad	910
4-oz. serving of Prince spaghetti sauce	1,030
1 Jack in the Box Fish Supreme	1,040
2 slices of Domino's Cheese/Pepperoni Pizza (16")	1,042
1 cup Campbell's Chunky Manhattan Clam Chowder	1,055
2-oz. serving of salted popcorn	1,100
3-oz. serving of ham	1,115
Chef Boyardee Spaghetti 'n Meatballs in Tomato Sauce	1,140
2 slices Domino's Pepperoni Pizza	1,150

Food	Milligrams of Sodium
1 Burger King Double Whopper with Cheese	1,245
8 oz. Betty Crocker Bisquick	1,475
1 Jack in the Box Ultimate Cheeseburger	1,476
7.5 oz. Hormel Corned Beef Hash	1,480
1 Arby's Bac 'N Cheddar Deluxe Roast Beef Sandwich	1,672
1 cup sauerkraut	1,755
1 Carl's Jr. Double Western Bacon Cheeseburger	1,810
1 large dill pickle	1,940
1 oz. soy sauce	2,075
2 slices Pizza Hut Super Supreme Pizza (large)	2,197
French's Au Jus Gravy Mix (¾ oz.)	2,400
Shake 'n Bake Chicken Coating (2⅜ oz.)	2,557

It's no surprise that many of these foods contain sodium. After all, they *taste* salty. What is a surprise is the number of foods naturally low in sodium that are turned into high-sodium products. A medium potato, for example, has just 5 milligrams of sodium; processed into potato chips, it contains 1,560 milligrams. One-half chicken breast has 70 milligrams of sodium; a fast-food chicken dinner can have 2,250 milligrams. According to figures published in *Consumer Reports,*

- One ounce of corn flakes has nearly twice the sodium found in an ounce of salted peanuts.
- Two slices of white bread contain more sodium than 14 potato chips.
- One-half cup of prepared chocolate pudding has more sodium than 3 slices of bacon.

And it isn't just "salt" that supplies sodium. An examination of ingredient lists on food labels shows sodium in its many guises: baking soda, baking powder, celery salt, garlic salt, monosodium glutamate (MSG), onion salt, seasoned salt, sea salt, sodium ascorbate, sodium benzoate, sodium caseinate, sodium citrate, sodium erythorbate, sodium nitrate, sodium phosphate, sodium proportionate, sodium saccharin and sodium tripolyphosphate.

EASY CHANGES

A later chapter will deal in detail with what parents can do to change family eating habits. But for now, here are some of the most practical ways to reduce sodium:

Cut down on table salt.

The salt shaker is the most obvious source of salt, so it's logical to start there. A simple solution would be to just put the salt shaker away. For many families, however, this is easier said than done. Your family may find saltless food to be bland by comparison. Try spicing up foods with herbs and seasonings like black pepper, garlic, tarragon and lemon juice. Many commercial sodium-free seasonings, such as Spike and Mrs. Dash, are also available. Children's taste buds can adjust with time. If you must use salt at the table, consider using a one-hole shaker.

Cut down on salt in cooking.

As a general rule, you can reduce salt in recipes by one-half with no change in taste. (If a recipe calls for ½ teaspoon, use ¼ teaspoon.) Replace sodium-rich seasoned salts and garlic salt with fresh/dried herbs and spices, flavored vinegars and lemon juice. If you use soy sauce (in a marinade, for instance), use a low-sodium variety.

Eat more fresh foods/fewer processed foods.

Processed foods contribute half the sodium we consume, so it's important to use fresh foods whenever possible. Fresh peas, for instance, have less than one milligram of sodium per one-fourth cup. The same amount of canned peas has 230 milligrams. Watch out for high-salt foods like pickles, olives, potato chips and salted nuts.

Read food labels for sodium content.

Remember, it's best to stay under 2,400 milligrams of sodium for an entire day. One glance at the label will tell you if the food will help you do that. In addition, advertising descriptions on food labels now have more meaningful definitions:

- *Low sodium* means 140 milligrams or less per serving.
- *Very low sodium* means 35 milligrams or less per serving.
- *Sodium-free* means less than 5 milligrams per serving.
- *Reduced sodium* means at least a 25% reduction from the regular food.
- *Unsalted* means no salt added (but not necessarily no sodium added).

Watch out for fast food.

Fast food is a way of life for many children and teens. While it's usually condemned because of fat content, parents should be aware that sodium is an issue as well. Most fast-food hamburgers and cheeseburgers, for instance, run between 800 and 1,800 milligrams of sodium—and that's without French fries and a shake! Parents can help their children make smarter choices. A hamburger with small fries (or better yet, a baked potato) and juice is better than a double cheeseburger with large fries and a shake. Also, on fast-food days, the sodium load can be lightened up at home to provide better balance.

TOO MUCH SUGAR

Americans—especially kids—love sugar. Unfortunately, we consume it in excessive amounts, and this is a significant dietary problem. "America's sweet tooth is out of control," says dietitian Bonnie Liebman. This is recognized in the 1996 Dietary Guidelines, which counsel to "watch the intake of sugar."

It seems to be hard for many of us to do because almost everyone craves sugar, and it is a particular problem for children. Research shows that at least in early childhood, there seems to be a biological basis for this preference. Young children simply like sugar more than adults do. Even infants show a strong desire for sugary foods. "Virtually all humans are born with an innate liking for sweets," says Dr. Leanne Birch of the University of Illinois. "And it stays with us as a strong preference during our early years." Indeed, no other animal (with the possible exception of cats) demonstrates such a powerful inclination for sweet taste.

For most of history, this craving for sweetness was met by eating fruits, berries and other foods with natural sugar. Since they also contain important vitamins, minerals and fiber, these foods provided the best of both worlds—sweet taste plus nutrition. But in the last century or so we have progressively moved from foods containing natural sugar to those rich in refined sugar, including pastry, candy and soft drinks. And we can't seem to get enough of it. As we've eaten more, we've craved more, so increased sugar is needed to satisfy. In 1875, the average American consumed 40 pounds of refined sugar per year. By 1910, the annual figure had risen to 70 pounds. Modern Americans have taken the fondness for sweetness to an extreme. The average adult now consumes about 148 pounds of refined sugar and sugar concentrates per year. That's more than one-third of a pound, 600 calories, each day! What's troubling is that this is about 20 pounds more than we ate in 1985, and almost 30 pounds more than in 1975. Even in this age of artificial sweeteners, which are supposed to substitute for sugar, our intake of sugar continues to rise.

And it's worse for children. According to studies conducted at Washington State University, the average child consumes more than 12 ounces of sugar a day—*or about 275 pounds a year!* It should be no surprise that our children get almost 25% of their daily calories from sugar.

SOURCES OF SUGAR

We seem to be undergoing an unrestrained escalation in consumption of sugar-rich foods, from gloppy grape candy to oversize syrupy restaurant desserts. Even SnackWell's, America's most popular fat-free cookies, are almost 72% sugar.

Researchers estimate that Americans get an average of 20% to 22% of calories from sugar. Where does all this sugar come from? Contrary to popular belief, the sugar bowl is not the chief culprit. Table sugar is responsible for just one-third of sugar intake. It is used mostly in drinks such as coffee or lemonade, in cooking and baking, and as a condiment on fruit or cereal.

About two-thirds of the sugar we eat comes in processed foods, now a staple of the U.S. diet. Sugar, particularly in the form of high fructose corn syrup, has become the nation's most popular food additive and is readily found in many of our kids' favorite foods, including soft drinks, pies, pastry, ice cream, cookies, candy and chocolate.

Here are a few examples:

Food	Teaspoons of Sugar
Coca-Cola (12 oz.)	9
Jelly beans (14)	9
Commercial fruit pie (1)	6
Kellogg's Frosted Flakes (¾ cup)	3

"It isn't hard to see where some of it comes from," says Jane Putman of the Department of Agriculture. "Look at these 64-ounce soft drinks, especially in the fast-food places. You can't find a 12-ounce Coke. You have to buy a 20-ounce size."

Of course, you'd expect to find sugar in jelly beans or a Coke. But most people are shocked to find it as an ingredient in cured meats, salad dressings, peanut butter, ketchup, flavored yogurt, baked beans, tomato and spaghetti sauces, soups and bread.

Consider the following:

Food	Teaspoons of Sugar
Spaghetti sauce (½ cup)	3.5
Baked beans (½ cup)	3
"Fat-free" fig bar (2)	2.5
French dressing (2 tbsp.)	2
Polish sausage (3.5 oz.)	1

"Sugar is everywhere," says one dietitian. "It's where you expect it and it's also in foods you would never associate with sugar. If you eat a lot of processed foods, chances are you're eating a lot of sugar."

The five principal sources of sugar for Americans include:

- *Soft drinks*, which contribute 21% of total sugar calories. For those aged 15 to 34, it's even higher: 32% to 40%. Americans drank an average of 43 gallons of non-diet carbonated soda in 1994, compared with 29 gallons in 1984. (And that's not counting fruit drinks and sweetened ice teas.) Most regular 12-ounce soft drinks contain 9 to 12 teaspoons of sugar.

- *Sweets* such as syrups, jellies, jams, ices and gelatin desserts. One-quarter cup of maple syrup, for example, has about 7 teaspoons of sugar. Sweets contribute almost 19% of total sugar calories.

- *Bakery goods* such as cakes, cookies, pies, pastries and crackers. A package of Hostess Twinkies, for instance, has about 6 teaspoons of sugar. Baked goods contribute about 13% of total sugar calories.

- *Milk products* such as ice cream, chocolate milk, milk shakes and flavored yogurt. A 10-ounce McDonald's chocolate shake has about 9½ teaspoons of sugar, while

one cup of Dannon's Lowfat Raspberry Yogurt has about
10.5 teaspoons. Milk products contribute about 10% of
total sugar calories.

▪ *Bread and grain foods* such as pasta, rice, cereals and
crackers make up about 6% of total sugar calories.

Cold cereal alone contributes 5% of total calories from
sugar on the American diet. For children aged one to 10,
however, cold cereal supplies double that amount. The
sugar content of many favorite cereals tells you why. A
number of them contain 3 or more teaspoons of sugar in a
one-cup serving. By way of comparison, a child would
consume about 5 teaspoons of sugar by drinking one-half
can of a soft drink.

Sugar Content of Common Cereals

Cereal (1 cup)	Teaspoons of Sugar
General Mills	
Apple Cinnamon Cheerios	3.5
Booberry	3.5
Cocoa Puffs	3.5
Count Chocula	3.5
Golden Grahams	3.0
Honey Nut Cheerios	3.5
Lucky Charms	3.0
Nature Valley 100% Natural Cereal	
(all flavors)	4.5
Super Golden Crisp	4.0
Trix	3.0
Kellogg's	
Apple Jacks	3.5
Cinnamon Mini Buns	3.5
Cocoa Krispies	3.5
Corn Pops	3.0
Double Dip Crunch	3.0
Froot Loops	3.5
Frosted Flakes	3.5

Cereal (1 cup)	Teaspoons of Sugar
Fruity Marshmallow Krispies	3.5
Honey Smacks	5.0
Nut & Honey Crunch O's	4.5
Raisin Bran	4.5
Post	
Alpha-Bits	3.0
Cocoa Pebbles	3.5
Frankenberry	3.5
Fruity Pebbles	3.5
Grape Nuts	3.0
Super Golden Crisp	4.0
Ralston Purina	
Bill & Ted's Excellent Cereal	3.5
Cookie-Crisp Chocolate Crisp	3.5
The Jetsons	3.5
Slimer! and the Real Ghostbusters	4.0
Teenage Mutant Ninja Turtles	3.0
Quaker Oats	
Cap'n Crunch	4.0
King Vitaman	3.0
Quisp	3.0
100% Natural Oats & Honey	7.0

SUGAR BLUES

A number of health problems are linked to eating too much sugar. First, *sugar helps to promote childhood obesity* by adding calories to food. Actually, a teaspoon of sugar has just 16 calories, which makes it no more fattening than protein or carbohydrates and less than half as fattening as fats or oils. But if enough teaspoons are consumed, calories pile up. Processed foods, for instance, allow for tremendous amounts of sugar to be packed into small quantities of food, making the product high in calories.

That's why a small milk-chocolate bar (1.5 oz.) has about 230 calories and a 12-ounce cola has about 150 calories—or about the same as a bottle of beer.

Non-diet beverages in particular can be a great source of sugar calories:

Beverage	Calories
Clearly Canadian, Mountain Blackberry (11 oz.)	130
Crystal Geyser Mountain Spring Sparkler, Peach (10 oz.)	111
Fruitopia (Fruit Integration) (16 oz.)	240
Minute Maid Orange Juice (16 oz.)	230
Ocean Spray Cranapple (10 oz.)	200
Snapple Ice Tea, Lemon Flavored (16 oz.)	220

In addition, sugar is rarely consumed by itself. Instead, it comes wrapped with fat (and thus calories) in favorite foods like candy bars. The fat content of these "sugary" foods produces a double whammy on kids' weight. Another problem is that most foods rich in sugar also provide very little mass, which means kids receive no signal that they've had enough. A diet rich in sugary foods often results in the simultaneous extremes of being overfed yet still feeling hungry.

A second problem is that *sugary foods often displace more nutritious foods.* Almost anything contains more nutrition than refined sugar, because this kind of sugar has "empty calories," which means it contains no vitamins, minerals, protein or fiber. So, if the average child or teen is consuming one-quarter of his or her calories from sugar, the other three-quarters must provide 100% of nutrition.

This is difficult to achieve. For example, it's well established that children need a good supply of calcium for "strong bones and healthy teeth" and that milk is one of the best sources of calcium. But many children and teens consume soft drinks instead of milk at mealtimes, and this dietary habit can play havoc with an adequate supply of calcium. Indeed, the USDA reports that children who consume one or more soft drinks a day tend to consume about 20% less calcium than children who do not drink soft drinks.

Furthermore, many overweight kids do not *replace* nutritious foods with sugary foods. Instead, they *add* sugary foods to their diet, thus producing an abundance of calories. As Dr. Madeleine Sigman-Grant, professor of food science at Pennsylvania State University, warns: "The real danger lies in the substitution of high-sugar foods with low nutrient values for foods high in complex carbohydrates."

Third, *excessive sugar can elevate triglycerides*, a blood fat that can work like cholesterol to clog coronary arteries. About 20 million Americans have a genetic predisposition to high triglycerides, which can be triggered by excessive sugar in the diet. "Studies show that when sugars rise to about 20% of calories," says Judith Hallfrisch of the USDA, "there are elevations in blood pressure, triglycerides, total and LDL cholesterol, uric acid, glucose and insulin responses. We think that at present levels of sugar consumption, the risk for heart disease and diabetes is higher than it would be if people replaced those sugars with complex carbohydrates."

And finally, *sugar has a profound effect on our taste*. Says chef Alice Waters of Chez Panisse restaurant in Berkeley, California, "Instead of finding fruits that have flavor, for instance, people will add sugar to compensate. So it allows you to eat inferior ingredients and not have the pleasure of food flavors. It's very discouraging the way things are doctored up with sugar, even savory dishes."

If our children grow up knowing only the flavor of sugar, how will they ever develop a taste for simple, natural foods?

EASY CHANGES

A later chapter will deal in detail with steps that parents can take to change family eating habits. But for now, here are some of the most practical ways for parents to reduce sugar:

Put the sugar bowl away.

Removing the sugar bowl from the table is important because many kids are moved to routinely use table sugar simply because the bowl is in sight.

Eat more fresh fruit.

Satisfy your child's "sweet tooth" with fresh fruit rather than sugary snacks. Frozen grapes, a ripe peach, a crispy apple, ice-cold watermelon wedges—these are better choices than cookies, candy and ice cream. Watch out for "fat-free" baked goods.

Cut down on soft drinks.

Many soft drinks are extremely rich in sugar. Try keeping a pitcher of ice water with sliced lemons and limes in the refrigerator. Also, dilute fruit juice with carbonated mineral water or club soda for a refreshing drink.

Read food labels for sugar.

Remember, 4 grams of "sucrose and other sugars" equals one teaspoon of sugar. If the label tells you a breakfast cereal has 12 grams of sugar per serving, you know it contains 3 teaspoons of sugar. This is a more graphic and practical way to view sugar content.

Like sodium, sugar has many names. You have to look for it on ingredient lists as corn solids, corn sweetener, corn syrup, date sugar, dextrose, fructose. glucose, high-fructose corn syrup, honey, invert sugar, lactose, malt, malted barley, maltose, maple syrup, molasses, raw sugar, sucrose and turbinado.

NOT ENOUGH COMPLEX CARBOHYDRATES AND FIBER

Foods rich in complex carbohydrates and fiber—such as fruits, vegetables, legumes and whole grains—should be the primary source of calories in the diet. Indeed, the advice of the Surgeon General, the American Heart Association and other experts to cut down on fat, salt and sugar is also a call to eat more foods rich in complex carbohydrates. Specifically, it is recommended that the intake of complex carbohydrates make up at least 55% of total calories.

The National Research Council's Committee on Diet and Health advises all Americans to "Every day eat five or more servings of vegetables and fruits, especially green and yellow vegetables and citrus fruits, and eat six or more servings of a combination of breads, cereals, pasta, rice and legumes." Younger children should eat smaller servings but still try for five a day. Additionally, everyone over age two should eat an adequate amount of fiber— 20 to 30 grams a day for adults and adolescents.

WHY THESE FOODS ARE IMPORTANT

Worldwide studies show that people who habitually consume a diet rich in plant foods have lower risks for cardiovascular diseases and certain cancers. This is probably because this kind of diet is usually low in cholesterol-raising animal fat and higher in protective antioxidants— vitamin C, vitamin A and beta-carotene. Moreover, there is evidence that a high-fiber diet, particularly one rich in green and yellow vegetables and citrus fruits, produces a decreased susceptibility to colon cancer. And finally, there is a wide body of evidence showing that replacement of high-fat foods with complex-carbohydrate foods is linked to weight loss and control.

Weight Control

Experts advise that foods rich in complex carbohydrates aid in weight control. In general they are not calorically dense (think of the previous example of calories in a pound of apples vs. a pound of M&M's), so your child can eat more food without taking in a lot of calories. This is an important consideration for growing teenagers. Like protein, complex carbohydrates contain 4 calories per gram, while the same amount of fat has 9 calories. So, while high-fat spareribs contain about 112 calories per ounce, cooked rice has only 30 calories per ounce. Fruits, grains and vegetables by their nature contain fewer calories.

In addition, complex carbohydrates contain mass, which means that kids can be filled up before they eat too much. Foods that need a lot of chewing, like apples and carrots, allow sufficient time (about 20 minutes) for satiety to be attained. These foods also absorb water in the digestive system, thereby helping to create a feeling of fullness and satisfaction that forestalls overeating. The fact is that most overweight people cannot eat enough complex carbohydrates to maintain their weight. They lose weight automatically when they replace fatty foods with fruits, grains and vegetables.

One of the dietary myths adopted in particular by younger females is that starchy complex carbohydrates can make them fat, so they avoid bread, potatoes, rice and pasta. Nothing could be farther from the truth. Indeed, nutritionists counsel just the opposite: to lose and control weight, eat more starchy foods and fewer fatty ones. What can turn starchy foods from low-calorie to high-calorie is added fat. A medium-size baked potato, for instance, contains just 110 calories. But add fatty toppings like butter, margarine, sour cream, bacon bits, or cheese and the calories jump to 400! It isn't the potato that adds pounds—

it's the added fat. It isn't the rice that causes weight gain—it's the butter sauce. And it isn't the pasta—it's the sausage, cheese and cream sauce.

Look at the effect of added fat on a potato:

Food (8 oz.)	Calories	Calories per Ounce
Baked potato	170	21
French fries	620	78
Potato chips	1,200	150

Says Dr. Jean-Pierre Flatt of the University of Massachusetts Medical School, "In reality, you get fat not from overeating carbohydrates but from overconsumption of fat."

Good Health

A diet rich in complex carbohydrates and fiber is also instrumental in promoting good health. Consider the following facts:

- *Fruits and vegetables* (particularly citrus fruits and green and yellow vegetables) provide important antioxidants—especially vitamins C and E and beta-carotene—that may substantially reduce the risk of heart disease, stroke and cancer. The Harvard Nurses Study, for example, found that those subjects who ate at least five servings a day of fruits and vegetables lowered their risk of heart attack by 33% and of stroke by 71%. Among the best choices are sweet potatoes, carrots, carrot juice, pumpkin, cantaloupe, mangos, oranges, spinach and other greens, squash, broccoli, apricots and red peppers.

- *Fiber,* often called roughage, bulk or bran, is the nondigestible part of plant food. It aids weight control because it passes through the digestive system intact, which means that not all calories consumed stay in the body, and promotes satiety. In addition, high-fiber foods reduce the risk of colon and rectal cancers by pushing food through the digestive system faster, thereby reducing

the time the colon wall is exposed to potential carcino-
gens. Examples of foods containing a good amount of
fiber are listed below.

Food Content of Some Common Foods

Food	Grams of Fiber
Fruits	
Blackberries (½ cup)	4.0
Apple, with skin (1 medium)	3.5
Pear, with skin (1 medium)	3.1
Banana (1 medium)	3.0
Vegetables (⅔ cup)	
Corn	6.2
Brussels sprouts	3.5
Carrots	3.1
Potatoes, cooked	3.1
Cereals (1 cup)	
Bran Buds	36.0
All Bran w/ Extra Fiber	30.0
Fiber One +	26.0
100% Bran	24.0
Breads	
Bran muffin (1)	4.0
Whole-wheat bread (2 slices)	3.2
Pumpernickel bread (2 slices)	3.2
Grains (⅔ cup, cooked)	
Rice, brown	3.0
Barley	2.1
Rice, white	1.1
Legumes (½ cup, cooked)	
Kidney beans	9.7
Lentils	9.0
Pinto beans	8.9
Lima beans	7.4

Foods rich in soluble fiber help to reduce blood cholesterol. As it moves through the digestive system, soluble
fiber forms a gel that interferes with the absorption of

cholesterol and helps to reduce it in the bloodstream. Soluble fiber is particularly effective in people who have high cholesterol. Studies at the University of Kentucky show that eating one cup of oat bran daily (about three bowls, cooked) could reduce cholesterol by 13% to 19%. Foods rich in soluble fiber include oat bran, oatmeal, dried beans and peas (black-eyed and split peas, lentils, kidney, navy and pinto beans), vegetables (carrots, peas, corn, sweet potato, zucchini, cauliflower, broccoli) and fruit (apples, bananas, pears, prunes, oranges).

KIDS' DIETS FALL SHORT

Fruits, grains and vegetables are woefully lacking in the American diet. One of the great modern tragedies is that they have been replaced by fatty refined foods. The orange (about 60 calories, no fat and 3 grams of fiber), it seems, has been replaced by the Almond Joy bar (about 230 calories, 14 grams of fat and no fiber).

While kids' diets tend to be short in all three, lack of vegetables presents the greatest problem. Most children and teens do at least drink juice and eat pasta and bread. But they are not eating their vegetables. Consider the following statistics from the National Cancer Institute:

- Some 25% of school-age children do not even consume one serving a day of vegetables.
- For those kids that do eat vegetables, French fries constitute one-quarter of all vegetables eaten.
- Only one in five children eats five or more servings of fruits and vegetables a day.

Juice aside, the situation with fruits isn't much better. It is estimated that more than 50% of the 2-to-18 age group eat less than a single serving of fruit a day. A USDA one-day survey found that one-third of elementary school children and two-thirds of teenagers had eaten no fruit at all. This translates into a diet where American kids on average eat just 12 grams of fiber daily.

"To put this into perspective," says Dr. Ernst Wynder of the American Health Foundation, "on any given day some 24% of children in grades 2 through 6 do not brush their teeth. Parents think this figure is atrociously high. But on that same day, more of those kids—about 25%—will eat no vegetables! The lack of fruits, vegetables, grains and beans in the diet pattern of U.S. youth is an enormous tragedy that will show up in later years with increased levels of obesity, heart disease and cancer."

The good news, however, is that kids do not have an innate distaste for vegetables. They simply don't think about eating vegetables or don't choose them when candy and cookies are available. But vegetables are easy to add to kids' meals—in soups, stir fries, casseroles, snacks and side dishes.

CHAPTER 9

WHY KIDS EAT THE WAY THEY DO

There is no doubt that the eating habits of today's children and teens are different from those of their counterparts a few decades ago. This is reflected in popular television shows over the years. The prototype television families back then—the Nelsons and the Cleavers—each ate dinner together every night at six o'clock. Everybody was home, there were two vegetables on the table, and family members talked to one another.

But Harriet Nelson of *Ozzie and Harriet* and June Cleaver of *Leave It to Beaver* hung up their starched aprons long ago. Today's typical TV family (which may not be a family but rather a loose association of friends and acquaintances) comprises characters that eat on the run and at odd times, survive on fast food and caffeine, and communicate only as they pass one another. The American family has moved away from traditional meals, and kids no longer eat as in the past. Why has this change come about? Parents need to understand what influences the dietary choices of their children so that they can help them form better dietary habits.

A SHIFT IN PRIORITIES: CONVENIENCE OVER NUTRITION

The modern era of high-speed living and significant societal shifts has contributed to dramatic changes in the eating patterns of children and teenagers. Essentially, many people feel as if they're out of time, that they have less "free time" than they once had. According to *Time* magazine, time is the scarcest and most coveted commodity in modern society. Extended work hours, longer commuting times, both parents working, single-parent households, increased organized activities for children and teens—these are just some of the factors that have produced a serious shortage of time and, in many families, an increase in stress. In such an environment, we buy, prepare and consume food differently than in the past.

Modern life is shaped by a hurried and harried pace, dictated in part by economic uncertainties. Surveys find people feeling that they're "running harder just to stay in place." This was illustrated in a recent *Wall Street Journal* article, which featured a two-income couple with two young children. She a CPA, he an engineer, both with beepers and cell phones, and each with 6:00 A.M. to 12 midnight commitments, they jostle activities. ("It's your turn to get breakfast," he says. "I'll drop the kids at school, you pick them up," says she.) They try to balance career, couplehood and family, and battle constant fatigue. In this fast and fleet environment, where do you think healthy eating ranks on the priority list (if it makes the list at all)? The fact is, according to a recent survey by

Prevention magazine, parents today are so busy that they're less likely to help their kids avoid fatty and sugary foods than they were in 1991.

Time, or lack of it, has brought about a change in our priorities. Eating competes with many other activities for time in our fragmented schedules. "People are no longer inclined to shop, cook or make food choices based on good nutrition," says registered dietitian Evelyn Tribole. We skip breakfast to get "an early start," run errands at lunch and bolt a sandwich on the run. In our hurry-up society, revolving dinner schedules are replacing family meals as more and more women work outside the home. A Gallup poll shows that 64% of the people surveyed combined eating with another activity such as working, reading or watching television.

Source: Beef Industry Council.

Says Dr. Lilian Cheung of the Harvard School of Public Health, "I think the rat race has a lot to do with the disengagement from the emotionally satisfying aspects of food that existed in the past. For example, many people fall into the trap of recognizing that they're hungry, they didn't have a decent breakfast, and so they grab anything to eat and eat it at their desks. Then they go home and find out that, although they physically ate, psychologically they really didn't. So it's easy to snack or eat again."

All of these factors have moved us away from traditional meals, a trend reflected in experts' predictions for the next decade:

- The dominant foods will be snack foods, frozen meals, plastic-wrapped prepared foods and microwavable foods.
- The delicatessen and bakery sections of supermarkets will expand.
- More foods, particularly meats, will be sold fully prepared. Some fresh fish will be available in grocery stores, but most will be sold as "ready to heat and eat."
- Half of U.S. kitchens will have two or more microwave ovens to make it easier to "grab, zap and gulp" our food.
- Fast-food restaurants will accept credit cards.
- Fast-food restaurants won't be fast enough for some of us. There will be more microwavable fast foods for home consumption.

Since kids eat what parents eat (and, perhaps more important, learn about eating and food from parents), is it any wonder that the diet of children and teens is also dictated by this pace of life?

Fewer Family Dinners

If Mom and Dad are on the run, who's feeding the kids? And today's children also have busy schedules—soccer practice, piano lessons, the school play, baseball, after-school jobs—which means the whole family is often on the run. "One of the greatest tragedies of modern life is that the family dinner has been sacrificed to other seemingly more important activities," says television chef Graham Kerr. "Not only has it moved us away from better prepared, more nutritious home-cooked meals, but we've lost the celebration of food as a family tradition, where the family comes together to share the same food." He continues:

Today, people not only come in and leave the kitchen at different times, but many do not even eat the same food. Dad eats meat and potatoes, Mom heats up a Lean Cuisine dinner, and the kids chow down on take-out fast food. We're losing the opportunity to communicate as a family. The dinner table is what bound many families together in the past. It was a chance to share the day, to listen to your children, and to teach them your values. Research shows that families who eat dinner together have kids that get into less trouble and do better in school. You can't tell a child to rip the top off an aluminum container, microwave for three minutes, and remember, 'Mommy loves you.' It doesn't work. And it certainly doesn't produce the healthy, balanced diet that our children require.

Less Home Cooking

A second result of this shift in priorities is that fewer people are cooking meals. What do today's families make for dinner? Reservations! It's an old joke, but it still works with a minor revision in the punch line . . . A phone call! In cities and towns throughout the country, American families (particularly two-career couples, parents of young children, and single parents) turn not to Mom in an apron but to supermarket take-out, pizza deliveries or microwave dinners. *Voilà,* dinner is served. "If you're brought up the way kids are now, cooking is not necessarily the first thing you think of when it comes to getting something to eat," says Betsy Leichliter, who researches dining patterns.

"We've become a nation that has denigrated the role of preparing, serving and sharing food in society. We've moved from eating to grazing to refueling," observes Joel Weiner of Kraft General Foods. Consequently, nutrition has taken a back seat. This is particularly interesting in light of surveys of parents of young children. On one hand, they report that the health of their child is among their highest priorities, and they see healthy eating as being "extremely important." But on the other hand, many choose not to cook. It is a puzzling dichotomy.

The fact is that a great many Americans no longer cook. Instead, they heat and reheat. This change is reflected in grocery stores. Look, for instance, at the shelf space reserved for so-called inventory foods like flour or shortening used in "cooking from scratch." Their space has shrunk to almost nothing. Then take a look at frozen meals and shelf-stable meals. Their space goes on forever. Indeed, deli take-out is the fastest-growing segment of the food store industry. In some locations, deli take-out even has a drive-through window. "We treat it as our own fast-food franchise," says one store manager.

There is some concern that younger parents, with little history in the kitchen themselves as children and teens, may not know *how* to cook. "They can make some things fine. They can make pasta, they can operate a grill," says Monica Doyle, president of the Consumer Network, a firm that surveys people about their buying and eating habits. "But they don't know how to make a sauce, they don't know how to braise."

Is cooking a lost art? "It's smoke and mirrors when they get in the kitchen," says Katherine Alford of Peter Krump's New York Cooking School. Alford says she grew up with lots of convenience food and understands its importance to women seeking time for careers or pursuits other than housekeeping. That legacy has to some extent changed the definition of cooking. "People like to assemble foods now, more than prepare them," says Jo Natale, a supermarket chain spokesperson. "They might buy an entrée and make a salad. But," she adds, "it astonishes me that their culinary traditions are nonexistent."

More Prepared Food

With less cooking being done, modern society has developed a greater reliance on prepared foods. Almost 50% of the people in a Gallup survey stated that on a typical night they depended on frozen, packaged or take-out meals for dinner. The advent of microwave ovens has made it easy to use prepared foods. Speed is no longer the privilege of the wealthy. Over two-thirds of American households, including nearly half the households with incomes under $10,000, now have at least one microwave.

The last decade has seen a dramatic increase in the availability and variety of processed, ready-made foods. Boxed, bottled and frozen—a few years ago half the manufactured food items did not exist. But today, in response to our hurry-up lifestyle, these products have become dietary staples for kids and adults. Yearly sales for frozen meals alone amount to more than $1 billion.

These foods may be convenient, and may even taste fine, but many of them have high levels of fat, calories, sodium and sugar. And that's bad news for kids who eat a steady diet of processed foods. They can hardly avoid taking in too many calories and too much fat. A child who eats a Stouffer's Chicken Pot Pie takes in 530 calories and 34 grams of fat. Banquet's Beans & Franks frozen meal provides 510 calories and 25 grams of fat. And Oscar Mayer's Lunchable package of bologna and American cheese, so convenient to slip in a lunch box, has 450 calories and 34 grams of fat.

A relatively new wrinkle is that many processed foods now are directed at young children. Speedy Gonzales Enchiladas, Ghostbusters cereal, Daffy Duck Spaghetti, Looney Tunes Frozen Meals. The trend is for best-selling toys, cartoons or movies to become food. Too often this leads to a lot of advertising razzle without the important nutritional dazzle. The names and the characters may be cute, but these foods often contain adult levels of fat and sodium, and virtually all of them come with a cookie or brownie for dessert.

More Snack and Junk Foods

With family meals diminishing, snack and junk foods are on the rise. The typical American consumes over 22 pounds of snack foods annually, according to the Snack Food Association. Many children and teens more than double that number. To appreciate the impact of snack foods on eating habits, consider the following:

- Americans pay about $2 billion every year for sports tickets. We spend the same amount on just five candy products—M&M's, Snickers, Reese's Peanut Butter Cups, Milky Ways and Hershey's Kisses.
- We spend $3.9 billion annually on cookies.
- We buy more than $8 billion worth of potato chips, pretzels, corn chips and taco chips each year.

It isn't that kids have just discovered candy, potato chips and cookies. After all, snacks were around in the 1960s. But kids today have more disposable income, and they're willing to spend it on snack foods. Moreover, these foods are widely available. At convenience stores, movie houses and even schools, it's easier to get a cookie than an apple. And kids have more opportunity for unsupervised snacking. Many are home alone a lot of the time. A parent who feels guilty about not being there when her daughter comes in the door will compensate by leaving a bag of doughnuts (in front of the TV) for her. With no parent available to impose limits, the daughter is free to eat the whole bag.

Finally, the role of snacking has changed. In the past, it was something done between meals; today, for adults and kids on the run, it may be the meal.

More Restaurant Meals

Another result of our modern lifestyle is an increase in the consumption of restaurant meals, especially fast food. In fact, more people are eating in restaurants today than ever before. The American Restaurant Association reports that Americans eat out about 3.5 times a week and spend over 40% of their food budget on restaurant fare. "People have to eat somewhere," says one pediatrician. "If they're not cooking at home, restaurants become the logical choice." But many sit-down restaurant meals feature fatty meat, fried chicken and fish, oil-drenched salads, creamy sauces and rich desserts that often provide an excess of fat, calories, sodium and sugar.

Why Families Eat Out

- 36% say "to get the family together."
- 22% say "to have quality time with the family."
- 16% say "to treat the kids."

Source: MasterCard Dining Out Survey.

By far the greatest influence on contemporary eating habits, however, is fast food. Its impact on American food habits is seen in the fact that 10% of all restaurant meals are consumed in cars. Fast food is a clear favorite of children and teens. The availability of fast, filling, inexpensive food is seen as a positive thing by many people. Most of the current population has never lived without fast food, so its inclusion in the diet seems natural. Indeed, it is estimated that more than one-fifth of the population eats at a fast-food restaurant every day. Some schools even offer national-brand fast food for lunch (more about that later).

It may be tasty and inexpensive, but fast food is not necessarily nutritious. Most of it contains an inordinate amount of fat, as well as too much sodium, sugar and total calories. According to data published in the *New England Journal of Medicine*, a typical fast-food meal gets 45% to 55% of calories from fat. A Jack in the Box Ultimate Cheeseburger, as an example, has 1,030 calories and 79 grams of fat—more than 15 teaspoons! A typical meal of a quarter-pound cheeseburger, fries and a shake can have more than 1,000 calories and 50 grams of fat, which is more than most people should have in an entire day.

Fast-food portions also pose a caloric problem, particularly for teenage boys whose interest in volume supersedes the importance of taste. In recent times, portion sizes and fat content have spun out of control. Size, often equated with better value ("getting more for less"), has become a popular marketing device, which means that the serving size of many fast foods has expanded greatly. Burgers are getting bigger and bigger to go along with "Biggie" fries and giant soft drinks. In addition, the fat content of many fast foods has skyrocketed. Cheese and bacon are routinely added to a long line of items. The Triple Decker pizza at Pizza Hut, for instance, has more fat than you'd find in a stick and a half of butter!

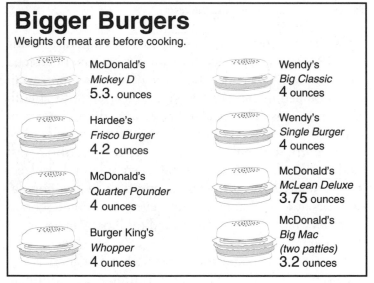

Bigger Burgers

Weights of meat are before cooking.

McDonald's
Mickey D
5.3. ounces

Hardee's
Frisco Burger
4.2 ounces

McDonald's
Quarter Pounder
4 ounces

Burger King's
Whopper
4 ounces

Wendy's
Big Classic
4 ounces

Wendy's
Single Burger
4 ounces

McDonald's
McLean Deluxe
3.75 ounces

McDonald's
Big Mac
(two patties)
3.2 ounces

Source: Individual companies.

Burger King is selling a Double Supreme Cheeseburger, along with large fries and a medium drink, for under $3. McDonald's can promote two Big Macs for less than $2. And burger chains are not alone. Everyone, it seems, is serving larger portions . . . pizza, soft drinks, chicken. A gargantuan Macho Meal at Del Taco weighs more than four pounds!

Will fast foods go away? I don't think so. They're part of the fabric of American life. But a steady diet of fast foods has destined many of our kids to an obese and unhealthy future.

Our contemporary way of life is a critical influence on our food habits. Dr. Kelly Brownell of Yale University blames America's paunch on what he calls "the toxic environment." "If you take a rat and toss food from the 7-Eleven into its cage," he says, "if you throw in candy bars, throw in Chee-tos, throw in marshmallows, things like that, you will get an enormously obese rat. Diet, exercise and personal responsibility are important, but we can give people information and work in the schools to prevent obesity until the cows come home. We won't begin to solve the problem with kids and teens until we deal with the environment. Until parents begin to think about high-fat, low-nutrition foods the way we think about alcohol and cigarettes, we can plan on continuing generations of overweight and unfit kids."

TELEVISION ADVERTISING

Television advertising exerts an enormous influence on the food selections of children and teens. Food advertisers know that if you can develop preferences in young children, you've gone a long way toward not only shaping their immediate dietary habits but also creating favorite foods for them as teens and adults. According to the USDA, eating habits are firmly established by age 12. This is why, particularly on Saturday morning, we see so much emphasis on TV advertising for children—by fast-food, soft drink, snack food and cereal companies. Their ads are upbeat, fun and high-quality, often costing more than $250,000 to develop. And once created, they're run over and over again (kids love repetition). Coca-Cola, for instance, spends about $200 million a year on TV commercials, while McDonald's and General Mills each spend about $400 million.

Younger kids can't always separate commercials from programs (particularly when their favorite cartoon character is also used to sell a product) and are unaware that they're being targeted. Advertisers know that this is the best way to bypass the parental filter and directly grab kids. Once the child is "hooked," the advertiser can rest. The child will ask the parents to buy whatever she saw advertised. Studies show that the more commercial television young children watch, the more foods they ask for when shopping with parents and the more they request to go to fast-food restaurants. And, eventually, even the strongest-willed parents will give in to fast food and sugar cereals, rather than do battle with their children over and over again.

"Television advertising is influencing the buying and eating habits of both children and their parents," observes Lisa Cohn, nutrition director of the Children's Cardiovascular Health Center at Columbia University. "Parents must be aware that their children are being exposed to a lot of advertising for high-sugar, high-fat foods—and that the children will continue to select these foods as teens and adults."

It is well established that American children not only watch a great deal of television but develop the TV habit early on. According to Nielsen surveys, by age 2 to 5 the average child watches nearly four hours of TV daily. By age 6 to 11, the figure drops slightly to some 3.5 hours (probably because the kids are now in school). And in the teen years, it stabilizes at about 3 hours a day. That's a lot of television viewing. And it's a lot of TV commercials. It is estimated that the average child can easily view between 30,000 and 40,000 commercials annually (or some 350,000 to 400,000 before graduating from high school).

The positive potential of television is that, like parents, schools and churches, it helps children to learn a tremendous amount about the world we live in. Research shows that a child's developing sense of what our culture deems fit to eat is influenced by the foods that he or she sees recommended in television commercials, which have become part of TV's socializing process. Unfortunately, it's safe to say that food commercials do not have the same standards as *Sesame Street*. A child watching television gets a truly perverted view of what society thinks are the best things to eat. But, quite simply, the young child doesn't know any better.

A new study of children's prime-time television found that of the 222 food commercials available to kids on any given Saturday morning, only eight ads promoted a "reasonably nutritious" product. The rest of Saturday's advertising pushes sugar-filled drinks and breakfast cereals, candy bars, snacks, chips, salty canned pastas and fast food—a junk food menu opposite the low-fat, low-sugar and low-salt diet recommended by the Surgeon General. "Over the past 20 years," says Dr. Thomas Starc, director of the study, "a growing body of research has linked diet to U.S. health problems such as obesity, heart disease and cancer. And U.S. dietary guidelines now say that children need the same low-fat, high-fiber diets to avoid those health risks. But you'd never know that from watching the food commercials on kids' TV shows."

What Dr. Starc found was that amid the barrage of ads for Chee-tos, Paws, Sprinkle, Chips Ahoy, Teenage Mutant Ninja Turtle Cereal, McDonald's Happy Meals and Twizzlers, there were virtually no spots that encouraged kids to eat fruits and vegetables, balance their diets or watch their fat intake. "A child can get up from the TV on a Saturday morning unscathed by nutritional information," says Congressman Ron Wyden. "This is particularly important given the impressionable age of the viewers and the typical lack of parental oversight on Saturday mornings."

While commercials set up children for poor food decisions, TV programs have an added effect on teens. This is because the food habits of characters on most top-ranked comedies and dramas are non-nutritious. It is estimated that 40% of food references in such shows are to coffee, alcohol and soft drinks; 18% to cookies, doughnuts, candy, ice cream and other sweets; and 7% to salty snacks like chips and pretzels. Less than 10% of the references are to fruits and vegetables.

This sends a mixed message, particularly to teens. According to TV, people can eat high-fat, high-sugar diets with no negative consequences. They can eat whatever they want and still stay thin. Says Dr. Nancy Signorelli of the University of Delaware, "Even though there are so many references to unhealthy and fattening foods, as well as numerous instances of eating sweets, obesity claims few victims on television." This is especially relevant to the kids seen on TV. Few of these children and teens are overweight.

SCHOOL FOOD

With so many kids eating lunch (and, for many low-income kids, breakfast as well) at school, cafeteria food can make up a significant portion of what kids eat. While some schools have improved, many school meals are a nutritional nightmare. Lamented Ellen Haas, assistant secretary of agriculture for food and consumer services, after visiting a Baltimore school recently: "The first thing you saw on the cafeteria line was French fries and pepperoni pizza. The second choice was French fries and a steak-and-cheese sandwich. The third choice was French fries and a fried-fish sandwich. The fourth choice was French fries and a submarine sandwich. If you were looking for something with low fat, low sodium and high fiber, there was *no* choice."

It's not that school lunches were better in the past; they were not. Despite parents' nostalgic recollections of life in the *Father Knows Best* era, school meals do not look better in retrospect. Most parents remember uniform lunches of mystery meat with pasty gravy, instant mashed potatoes, canned, tasteless vegetables and sickly-green gelatin desserts. Says former U.S. Senator Patrick Leahy, who worked to get low-fat federal guidelines in schools, "Like many people, I ate in school lunchrooms where the only choice was that you could have warm glop or cold glop. It's easy to see why children didn't want to eat it."

Indeed, school meals back in those days were an object of disgust and disbelief. But the aesthetic shortcomings of mystery meat and green gelatin are the least of the problems that plague cafeteria food in schools today. What our kids are getting on those plastic trays can be a shortcut to obesity, heart disease and other serious health problems.

There is no doubt that school lunches now are less fatty than in the past, when many meals got 35% to 45% of their calories from fat. But they have not gone far enough. A recent USDA study shows that public schools continue to serve lunches that contain more fat and sodium than is recommended for good health. The typical school lunch today

- Gets an average of 38% of calories from fat, well above the 30% guideline.
- Gets 15% of calories from saturated fat, also above the 10% guideline.
- Contains 1,480 milligrams of sodium, nearly two-thirds of the maximum daily intake of 2,400 milligrams.

"This study emphasizes the excesses," says Ms. Haas, "which are bad. But there are deficiencies, too. Kids aren't getting enough fruits and vegetables." Says Bonnie Liebman, a dietitian with the Center for Science in the Public Interest, "School lunches aren't promoting healthy eating but cultivating poor eating habits and loading our kids down with fat, saturated fat and sodium."

In an effort to change direction, the USDA has issued new nutrition guidelines that set limits on the fat and saturated fat content of meals for the school lunch program, which feeds 25 million children daily in 92,000 schools. Despite these guidelines, however, nutrition continues to be a low priority in many schools. And parents need to know why.

One reason is, quite frankly, that many school cooks have been reluctant to change their ways. The unfamiliarity of the new nutrition guidelines is partly responsible. One cafeteria manager told me that "these guidelines are too difficult to follow. We're cooks, not dietitians." This concern is echoed by Penny McConnell, food service director of the Fairfax (Virginia) County schools: "How on earth do you teach someone who might have an eighth-grade education to interpret all the nutritional data?" Another part of the reason, however, involves tradition. Many school cooks view their work as dealing more with nurturing than nutrition. Said one, "I've been cooking for these little kids for 30 years, and I've *always* made mashed potatoes with salt and butter. I'm not going to change now."

A second reason is pure economics. Cafeterias have to make money or they're a drain on school finances. Bob Honson, director of nutrition for the Portland (Oregon) Public Schools, states: "We have to operate cost-effectively. That's our number one goal. And to do that, we have to make sure that kids are eating in school. That's why we make sure we have foods that they like. Then, if we're operating in the black, we can think about our number two goal: meeting the U.S. dietary guidelines. Sometimes it's a struggle to reconcile both goals. But I guarantee you, if we don't make our first goal, we won't stay open, and nutrition will then go down the tubes."

It is in such an atmosphere that thousands of cafeterias offer pre-prepared chopped, pressed and formed foods such as hamburgers, hot dogs, corn dogs, Sloppy

Joes, pepperoni pizza, chicken nuggets, BBQ pork, French fries, tater tots, nachos, ice cream and other high-fat, high-sugar foods as part of the basic school lunch. That's because such foods reduce labor costs. Some do offer more nutritious selections, such as salads and bagels, in an à la carte line. But in many schools these same lines feature brand name fast-food items such as Taco Bell burritos, Subway sandwiches, McDonald's hamburgers and Pizza Hut pizza.

The issue is further complicated by school vending machines stocked with soft drinks, candy, gum, potato chips, cookies and other junk foods. These foods can also be found in many school stores.

When schools offer a nutritionally unbalanced menu, when the only thing you can get from a vending machine is a cola or a bag of chips, the message to students is that the good nutrition discussed in the classroom is not important enough to be practiced in the cafeteria. After all, if eating pizza, hamburgers and other fast food every day is so unhealthy, why are they offered each day in the school cafeteria?

But not all the news is bad. Parents should know that some schools are doing a wonderful job of improving meals. According to registered dietitian Pat Snyder, nutrition coordinator at the University of Minnesota School of Public Health,

> Many schools are making great progress in serving meals that are low in total fat and saturated fat and that are nutritious yet tasty enough to appeal to the students. School food service directors are using computers to analyze meals to make sure the new guidelines are met. They're offering more fruits and vegetables, and choices that include fat-free and light milk. Moreover, they're buying lower-fat cuts of ground meal and are using techniques such as draining and rinsing meat to further cut fat.

In addition, many school districts are using programs developed by organizations such as CATCH, Project LEAN and the Bogalusa Heart Study to train personnel, change menus and institute low-fat cooking techniques. But the parents of the students need to become more involved. Schools can dish up healthier foods, but they can't make kids eat them. Children come to school with dietary habits formed at home. If there is no emphasis on healthy eating at home, there will be no desire on the part of the child to eat healthfully in school.

This advice is echoed by George Bibbin, a food service director in Virginia: "I can work to meet the objective of 30% of calories from fat and make the appropriate foods available. But I cannot require the kids to eat those things in the cafeteria."

GOOD INTENTIONS, BAD RESULTS

Most parents are not surprised at many of the influences that move American kids to eat so much fat, including the societal changes that have resulted in fewer "home-cooked" meals, too much fast food and snacks as well as the effects of television advertising and school lunches. But two common sources of high fat for kids—meat and dairy products—come with healthful intentions. Parents know that growing children and teens need protein and calcium. They know that meat is a good source of protein and that dairy foods, such as milk and cheese, are good sources of calcium. But what many parents do not realize is how much fat comes with the protein and calcium.

The truth is that many meat and dairy foods are primarily sources of fat and serve only secondarily as sources of protein and calcium.

PROTEIN

There are a lot of fat sources on the American diet, and high-protein foods can be one of the worst. "How can that be?" parents ask. "Kids need protein for growth." That, of course, is true. It is well established that protein is a nutritional "building block," particularly for active children and teens. Although it can be used for fuel, its primary purpose is to build and repair muscle tissue; that's why it is recommended that 12% to 15% of total calories should come from protein.

But Americans overeat protein. The USRDAs for protein for children and adolescents are as follows:

Population	Age	Grams of Protein
Males	1–3	23
	4–6	30
	7–10	34
	11–14	45
	15–18	59
Females	1–3	23
	4–6	30
	7–10	34
	11–14	46
	15–18	44

To put this in perspective, a child between the ages of 7 and 10 could satisfy the entire day's protein requirement with a turkey sandwich (three ounces of turkey, two slices of whole-wheat bread) and an eight-ounce glass of milk.

Although too much protein is consumed in the United States, the problem is compounded by the fact that most of the protein we eat comes from animal foods rather than from vegetables—and most animal foods are high in fat. Nutritionists counsel that one-third of the protein that we consume should be from animals and two-thirds from plants, but our actual consumption is just the opposite. For many people, children and teens included, "high-protein" translates into "high-fat." As Dr. William Connor of the Oregon Health Sciences University has observed, "It's the company that protein keeps that is the health issue."

Three ounces of bacon, for example, get 17% of calories as protein but 81% of calories as fat. The same amount of ground round gets 28% of calories as protein but 70% as fat. Favorite kid foods such as bologna, hot dogs, pepperoni, sausage and luncheon meats are usually over 70% fat.

No two ways about it, protein is a critical element of a healthy diet, particularly for children. But those who get their protein mostly from fatty sources (hamburgers, luncheon meats, sausage, fried chicken) may be taking in far too much fat.

Fortunately, a number of low-fat sources of protein do exist. Small pieces of fish, skinless poultry or lean red meat (such as pork tenderloin or eye of round steak) added as a condiment to pasta, rice or vegetables can contribute valuable protein. So can nonfat milk and yogurt, beans, legumes (peas, lentils, soybeans) and tofu added to soups, rice and salads. The point is that it's possible for adults and children to get sufficient protein without over-consuming dietary fat.

CALCIUM

Like protein, calcium is an essential element for good nutritional health and is needed especially by children. This mineral helps to form strong bones and healthy teeth, and is important in warding off osteoporosis later in life. The optimal calcium intake for children and adolescents, according to figures from the National Institutes of Health, is as follows:

Optimal Calcium Intake
(Ages 1 to 24)

Ages	Milligrams of Calcium
1–5	800
6–10	800–1,200
11–24	1,200–1,500

Dairy products are one of the best sources of calcium. It is for that very reason that parents routinely incorporate milk and cheese into the diets of their children and teens. However, milk, cheese and other dairy foods can also be rich in fat.

A cup of whole milk, for example, provides about 288 milligrams of calcium but has 8 grams of fat—the same as two pats of butter! Fortunately, lower-fat milk choices do exist. Fat-free milk (also called skim and nonfat) has more calcium (300 milligrams) but contains less than one-half gram of fat.

Kids need a good supply of calcium, and dairy foods are a wonderful way to get it. But if their calcium source is fat-rich dairy products (whole milk, 2% milk, full-fat cheese, whole-milk yogurt, ice cream), their fat intake may be too high. Both the American Heart Association and the American Academy of Pediatrics advise that from the age of two on, children should get their calcium from low-fat and nonfat dairy sources—fat-free and light (1%) milk, nonfat yogurt and low-fat cheese. Additional sources of calcium include leafy green vegetables (such as spinach, broccoli and kale), tofu and bony fish (such as salmon).

The following are good examples of low-fat sources of calcium:

Food	Milligrams of Calcium
Calcium-fortified lactaid milk, fat-free (1 cup)	500
Yogurt, nonfat, plain (1 cup)	450
Milk, fat-free or light (1%), protein fortified (1 cup)	350
Yogurt, low-fat, fruit-flavored (1 cup)	250–350
Calcium-fortified orange juice (1 cup)	330
Milk, fat-free or light (1%) (1 cup)	300
Ricotta cheese, fat-free (¼ cup)	250
Total cereal (¾ cup)	250
Ice cream or frozen yogurt, fat-free or low-fat (1 cup)	200
Collards, frozen (½ cup cooked)	180
Sardines canned in water, drained (2 oz.)	175
Tofu (3 oz.)	100
Kale, frozen (½ cup cooked)	90
Soybeans (½ cup cooked)	90
Bok choy (½ cup cooked)	80
Cottage cheese, low-fat (½ cup)	75
Orange (1)	50
Bread, white or whole wheat (2 slices)	45
Broccoli (½ cup cooked)	35

To sum up, calcium is a critical part of a child's diet. But parents need to make sure the sources of calcium are low in fat.

CHAPTER 10

WHAT PARENTS CAN DO

U p to this point, the information on kids and food has been somewhat discouraging. The picture that has been painted shows our children gobbling their way into adult obesity, as well as heart disease and other diet-induced health problems. But it doesn't have to be that way. There are a number of simple, practical steps that parents can take to help their children (and themselves) to form better food habits.

First, however, it makes sense to plan for change. The desire to eat healthfully just isn't enough to make it happen in real life. Says Dr. Nancy Wellman, past president of the American Dietetic Association, "Many of us try to reduce fat in our diets, but our lifestyle overrides our good intentions. Demographic changes, the number of meals eaten away from home, the convenience pull, nutritional naiveté, and plain confusion confound our attempt."

There is no argument that the way kids eat has a great deal to do with their present and future health. The challenge to parents is to help their children form better food habits. And this is hard to do in a pro-fat environment where it's so easy to overeat or to eat too many fatty foods. You can replace a doughnut with an apple for a week. But making such a change stick as a permanent part of daily life is more difficult. The first step is for parents to adopt a perspective that focuses not on dieting but on healthy eating patterns.

KEEP A POSITIVE OUTLOOK

Before taking any action with respect to your child's eating habits, be certain the goal of "fit, not thin" is understood. This means getting rid of the word "diet" and replacing it with the concept of "balanced eating." Over the last 40 years, thousands of quick-weight-loss diet books have been published. (Remember the "grapefruit and cigarette diet"?) If any one of them had been effective, we'd be a nation of skinny folks. But we are not. Diets do not work. *And restrictive diets are particularly inappropriate for growing children and teens.* Says Bonnie Spear, a registered dietitian at the University of Alabama, "Kids need their calories to grow. Adolescents, for instance, may need 3,000 to 4,000 calories a day during growth spurts." So, dieting is definitely not recommended. We don't want kids to diet (a negative concept); we want them to eat better (a positive action). On the other hand, parents should avoid overfeeding their children. Experts recommend that the "clean plate club" be disbanded.

Remember, the purpose of making changes is to help your child create and maintain healthy dietary habits. That doesn't mean a rigid way of eating, eliminating certain foods and running a detailed nutritional analysis of every bite your child eats. The rule is "moderation in all things." Make sure you see the big picture. As long as the diet is basically balanced and healthy, an occasional Big Mac won't do any harm. Keep in mind that food is not only the main carrier of nutrition, but also the means by which family ritual and tradition are carried out.

Changing the way your child eats doesn't take place in a vacuum. Children learn by example. It's virtually impossible to teach children good eating habits if you eat poorly yourself. So when you institute changes, do it for the entire family, not just the child. "One clue to it all is positive exposure to healthy foods," says Mary Abbott Hess, a former president of the American Dietetic Association. "If parents have a lot of positive food choices easily available, and the kids see parents eating positively and it becomes a part of the family's habit, that's a powerful influence on what kids continue to do."

Start teaching your child as early as possible. It's easiest to teach good eating habits if you begin when your child is young. It gets progressively harder as kids get older. "If, at age two, kids are given a lot of fruits, vegetables and grains, and if they are not inundated with fried foods and cookies, they're a lot more likely to continue eating those healthful foods," Hess continues. "But if they see adults in their environment skipping breakfast, eating a doughnut at midmorning, eating nothing but cheeseburgers and French fries at lunch, and constantly talking about dieting, they're going to get those messages, too."

And finally, take your time. Remember, it's not a race. You're dealing with food habits, which are not easily changed over a week or two. Recognize that change doesn't progress in a straight line. It's more like "one step back, two steps forward." And it isn't the result of a single quantum leap. Small changes made over time cumulatively become a large change.

When we decided after my heart surgery that fat-free milk was a better choice for our family, the kids rebelled. "We don't want to drink 'blue milk,' " they told us. We listened to their complaints, but we knew they *were* going to drink fat-free milk. It was simply a question of how to get from here to there. We started by mixing 2% milk, which they usually drank, with fat-free milk. At the start it was lots of 2% milk and a little bit of fat-free milk. Gradually the amount of fat-free went up and the 2%

milk went down, until finally the kids were drinking 100% fat-free milk. It took about six weeks. But for those six weeks we served them the lower-fat mixtures in a 2% container. Once their taste buds had changed to accept fat-free milk, the need for the ruse evaporated. But the 2% container allowed us to change a significant dietary habit, trading high-fat milk for nonfat milk, with fewer hassles. Remember, permanent change is a process that is evolutionary, not revolutionary.

Building on this perspective, there are, I think, some basic actions and considerations that parents should take before attempting to change their children's food habits.

ESTABLISH A
FAT GUIDELINE

Fat typically makes up about 38% of a child's diet and about 34% of an adult's diet. Eating too much fat is clearly the biggest dietary concern in the United States. The most important action, therefore, is to reduce fat intake. This is a nice general concept, but it's one that doesn't carry much specific meaning. Parents should have a clear idea of what constitutes an appropriate fat intake for their child. Essentially, *you need to know how much fat your child can eat and still meet the guidelines for good health.* This puts you in a better position to help your child make smarter food selections.

The recommendation for all Americans over age two is for fat to make up no more than 30% of calories eaten. Many health professionals believe this is too liberal, particularly in light of the national obesity problem. They advise a diet closer to 25% fat. "Because of the unique nutritional needs of growing children and teens," says Dr. Theresa Nicklas, "a diet with 25% to 30% of calories from fat seems reasonable."

What does this recommendation mean for your child in practical terms? Unfortunately, not very much. It is simply not realistic to base a guideline on percentage figures. That's because translating such figures into everyday life is a difficult task. How, for example, do you estimate the percentage of fat in a dinner comprising three or four different foods? Most of us can't or won't do the necessary calculations, so we really never know whether or not we're within the guideline or if we've exceeded it. A better way is to express the guideline in grams of fat, not percentages.

By using the USDA figures for average calories consumed by youngsters, a fat guideline for kids of different ages can be estimated. The following gives the range of fat-grams in a diet where fat makes up 25% to 30% of calories.

Fat Guideline for Children and Adolescents

Age	Average Calories Consumed	Fat-Gram Range	
		From (25% Diet)	To (30% Diet)
2–3	1,300	36	43
4–6	1,800	50	60
7–10	2,000	56	67
11–18 (Females)	2,200	61	73
11–14 (Males)	2,500	69	83
15–18 (Males)	3,000	83	100

This guideline represents the maximum amount of fat recommended for your child. It is not a hard-and-fast rule, but rather a standard against which to measure your child's diet. It provides you with a simple, effective tool— a guideline to better manage dietary fat.

This is the way it works. Let's say your child, a 10-year-old girl, is eating about 2,000 calories per day, average for her age, but is consuming 80 grams of fat per day. She's exceeding the guideline by 13 grams. How hard would it be for you to help her trim those extra fat-grams? Not very. A hamburger with lettuce, tomato and ketchup instead of a Big Mac saves 14 to 16 grams of fat. A glass of light (1%) milk instead of whole milk saves another 6 grams. And a bowl of raisin bran instead of a Danish pastry for breakfast can save 10 to 12 grams. Small changes can add up to dramatic reductions in dietary fat.

Does it mean that her favorite foods—pizza, hamburgers, ice cream—will be forbidden? No. What it means is that small changes need to be made to better balance her diet. If pizza is on the menu for dinner, that's a day when cereal and fruit for breakfast is a better choice than a doughnut and chocolate milk. Just think in terms of little changes—nothing extreme. With some give-and-take, you'll find a balance that is sensible and satisfying.

Does this mean you have to teach your child to count calories and to budget for fat? Absolutely not. The point of the guideline is to give you some idea of the amount of fat that is appropriate for your child. This puts you in a better position to help your child make smarter choices and develop healthier eating habits.

LEARN HOW TO READ FOOD LABELS

It's important to raise a smart shopper. Use the grocery store to educate your child about healthy foods. Behavior expert Liz George advises starting when kids are young: "Let them compare foods at the store and choose unfamiliar fruits and vegetables to try. Teach them the basics—like what a portion size is, why foods with less fat are healthier or the fact that darker greens have more vitamins (and taste) than iceberg lettuce."

Teaching children about fresh fruits and vegetables is relatively simple. These foods offer few nutritional problems and usually carry no advertising to combat. But if you live in the real world, you buy more than fruits and vegetables at your grocery store—you buy processed foods. These foods make up much of what we eat, so it's necessary to know what's in them. *You cannot purchase foods in a grocery store with an eye to reducing fat if you have no idea how much fat they contain.* And that means learning how to read nutrition labels.

Unfortunately, much food advertising is more hype than information, often leading the consumer away from healthy choices. A good example is sandwich ham labeled "95% fat-free." What the claim actually means is that fat makes up just 5% of the ham's weight. It has nothing to do with the true measurement—the calories that come from fat. Sandwich ham actually derives about 40% to 60% of calories from fat, which is a long way from the low-fat claim. This is why a practical fat guideline should be expressed in grams of fat.

Visualize your child's fat guideline as a checkbook with fat-grams that can be "spent" for the day. Let's say your child has a maximum of 40 grams of fat as a guideline. If he stays below 40 grams, he'll have met the guideline for a low-fat day. So, a frozen chicken dinner with 8 grams of fat will not pose a problem for your child. But a chicken pot pie with 37 grams of fat will. Taking in that much fat at one meal would probably cause your child to exceed the guideline for the day. This technique will help you to better understand food labels and will help you teach your child to make lower-fat choices. More important, it will help you and your child to develop low-fat habits.

"Nutrition labels are simple enough even for younger kids to grasp," says Dr. Liz Applegate, a nutritionist at the University of California at Davis. "Show kids where to look for grams of fat and fiber. Older kids can understand the idea of a fat guideline. Then they can see from the label whether or not that food meets their guideline."

Most packaged foods have a label with a section called Nutrition Facts. This section summarizes food content.

Nutrition Facts

Serving Size ½ cup (114 g)
Servings Per Container 4

Amount Per Serving

Calories 90   Calories from Fat 30

	% Daily Value*
Total Fat 3 g	**5%**
Saturated Fat 0 g	**0%**
Cholesterol 0 mg	**0%**
Sodium 300 mg	**13%**
Total Carbohydrate 13 g	**4%**
Dietary Fiber 3 g	**12%**
Sugars 3 g	
Protein 3 g	

Vitamin A	80%	*	Vitamin C	60%
Calcium	4%	*	Iron	4%

* Percent Daily Values are based on a 2,000-calorie diet. Your daily values may be higher or lower depending on your calorie needs:

	Calories	2,000	2,500
Total Fat	Less than	65 g	80 g
Sat Fat	Less than	20 g	25 g
Cholesterol	Less than	300 mg	300 mg
Sodium	Less than	2,400 mg	2,400 mg
Total Carbohydrate		300 g	375 g
Fiber		25 g	30 g

Calories per gram:

Fat 9   Carbohydrate 4   Protein 4

More nutrients may be listed on some labels.

EXPLANATION

Calories tells how many total calories are contained in one serving (90 calories according to the sample label).

Total Carbohydrate. When you cut down on fat, you can eat more carbohydrates. Carbohydrates are found in foods such as bread, potatoes, fruits and vegetables. Information on simple sugars is important for people with blood sugar problems.

Dietary Fiber. Grandmother called it "roughage," but her advice to eat more is still up to date. That goes for both soluble and insoluble kinds of dietary fiber. Fruits, vegetables, whole-grain foods, beans and peas are all good sources and can help reduce the risk of heart disease and cancer.

Protein. Most Americans get more protein than they need. Where there is animal protein, there is also fat and cholesterol.

Vitamins & Minerals. Your goal here is 100% of each for the day. Don't count on one food to do it all. Let a combination of foods add up to a winning score.

Saturated Fat is listed separately because it's the key player in raising blood cholesterol. Since too much saturated fat is particularly likely to result in clogged arteries, it should supply no more than one-third of total fat intake. Note that one type of cholesterol-raising fat not covered is **trans fatty acids.** These are not broken out as a category but are included in the "Total Fat" figure.

Cholesterol. Too much cholesterol—a second cousin to fat—can lead to heart disease. Challenge yourself to eat less than 300 mg each day.

Sodium. You call it "salt"; the label calls it "sodium." Either way, it may add up to high blood pressure in some people. So, keep your sodium intake low—2,400 mg or less each day.

Daily Values are listed for people who eat 2,000 to 2,500 calories each day. If you eat more, your personal daily value may be higher than what's listed on this label. If you eat less, your personal daily value may be lower.

For fat, saturated fat, cholesterol and sodium, choose foods with a low **% Daily Value.** For total carbohydrate, dietary fiber, vitamins and minerals, your daily value goal is to reach 100% of each.

g = grams (about 28 g = 1 ounce)
mg = milligrams (1,000 mg = 1 g)

The Nutrition Facts provide a wealth of information that can be used to make healthier choices, and this information can be shared with your child.

- *Pay attention to calories*, particularly in "fat-free" foods. The label will tell you if the food is too calorically dense for a healthy diet.
- *Pay attention to serving size.* The Nutrition Facts will tell you how many calories per serving and how many servings in the container. If you buy a bag of chips that contains four servings, and your child eats half the bag, you'll have to double the calories and fat on the label since two servings have been eaten.
- *Pay attention to fat-grams.* Once you know your child's fat guideline, it's relatively easy to decide if any particular food "fits." If your child can "spend" a maximum of 50 grams of fat for the day, Kraft's frozen dinner of spaghetti and meatballs, with 15 grams of fat, should fit. But Stouffer's fettuccine Alfredo, with 40 grams of fat, most certainly would be a problem.
- *Watch out for fat described as a percentage.* This usually refers to the pecentage of fat in terms of the weight of the package. In other words, "15% ground round" means that fat constitutes 15% of the package weight. It has little to do with the calories that come from fat. Rely on fat-grams, not percentages.
- *Pay attention to fiber.* The recommendation is to eat 20 to 30 grams of fiber a day. There's a big difference between a serving of Post Raisin Bran with 8 grams of fiber and Kellogg's Frosted Flakes with none.
- *Pay attention to sugar.* Remember, 4 grams of sugar equals one teaspoon. Quaker Cap'n Crunch, for instance, lists 12 grams of sugar per serving. Think of it as three teaspoons.
- *Pay attention to sodium.* The recommendation is to consume 2,400 milligrams or less. That's about one teaspoon of salt. A cup of Newman's Own Pasta Sauce, for instance, can have 1,400 milligrams of sodium.

MAKE A MEAL PLAN

If you want your child to eat healthfully, be prepared to cook and eat most of your meals at home. There is no way around this. Homemade is best. To be sure, there's room for frozen meals and fast foods on occasion, but remember that these foods usually contain more fat, sodium and sugar than you would use in your own kitchen. Most do not contain enough complex carbohydrates and fiber to be eaten on a daily basis. And finally, they cost more than homemade meals. Convenience foods should not form the basis for your child's diet.

In addition, the traditional American home-cooked meal needs to be refocused. In the past, meals were centered around huge portions of meat. Typically, we'd enjoy a small salad, a moderate serving of potatoes, and a giant steak or slab of roast beef. Noticeably missing were fruits and vegetables. Today we know that this "meat and potatoes" style of eating is too high in fat and calories and needs to be lightened up. This simply means giving more room in the meal to vegetables, legumes, starches and fruit, with meat and other animal foods playing more of a supporting role. In place of the meal described above, a refocused meal would be a large salad, rice or potatoes, two other vegetables, half a chicken breast and fruit for dessert. (Obviously, younger children would have smaller portions.) This minimizes fat intake while allowing your child to eat to satisfaction and to consume valuable fiber and nutrients.

It's one thing, however, to talk about limiting convenience foods and refocusing meals, and quite another thing to make it happen. In our fast-paced modern society, simply preparing food is difficult enough, without figuring out how to make it healthy and flavorful. If it's 5 P.M. and you're shopping for dinner to be served at 6 P.M., you may be too pressed to make low-fat choices. It's very easy then to revert to old, familiar, high-fat favorites—hot dogs, pizza, frozen meals, the giant steak. Or, if you're making lunch for a child who's about to run out the door on the way to school, it's a little late then to think of low-fat alternatives.

You need to plan for change. As with most endeavors, planning is essential for success. Few people, for example, create economic security in retirement without a financial plan. It may call for them to put aside money, week after week, year after year, into a fund. Then, when they reach a certain age, their "nest egg" is as ready for retirement as they are. It's the same with establishing healthy dietary habits. By preselecting foods and meals that appeal to your family and meet your dietary guideline, you ensure the exclusion of high-fat foods and the inclusion of low-fat foods, and you minimize the selections left to chance.

Let's examine dinner, a main meal for most families, to see how it works. In many homes, Mom and Dad arrive home from work about 5:30 P.M., and need to prepare and eat dinner so they can be at a school event or another activity by 7 P.M. There's no time for pondering healthful food selections that also meet everyone's needs.

In our family, we addressed this problem by creating a general meal plan with categories of foods that we like— pasta, seafood, even meat. This is how it looked:

Day	Type of Food
Monday	Poultry
Tuesday	Pasta, soups, stews
Wednesday	Seafood
Thursday	Main-meal salads
Friday	Pizza, casseroles, chili
Saturday	Restaurants, take-out
Sunday	Meat

This plan was an overview. We then selected specific meals to fit into these categories for two weeks. So, on Monday—poultry night—we might have Chicken Fajitas, Southern Fried Chicken or Chicken Parmesan. Or, on

Tuesday we might plan for Penne with Meat Sauce, Cheesy Macaroni or Classic Lasagna, all kid-pleasers. Old-Fashioned Meat Loaf or Roasted Pork Tenderloin could be our Sunday dinner. (See the Cookbook section for all these recipes.)

The point is that for two weeks we knew what we were going to do. Dinner was no longer something that happened to us. We were now in control. We could shop for ingredients and be prepared. If we ate according to the plan, our dinners would be healthful, tasty and appealing to our kids. We treated the plan not as a hard-and-fast rule but as a general guide. If the day got away from us, or if evening activities changed, we might alter the menu, eat out or have a healthful frozen meal. Meal planning did not go on forever in our house. But its use in the beginning was critical in helping us to create new food habits—ones that became second nature over time.

We also made it a priority to eat our meals together. It made no sense to go to the effort of planning, shopping and preparing a healthful meal, only to have the family eat it in shifts. If people are running in opposite directions, eating at different times or not at all, grabbing a bite on the run and then back to the races—that's not eating. It's refueling, and there is no enjoyment or pleasure in that. What message does it send to a child about the importance of healthy food and of sharing as a family?

MODIFY FOODS YOUR CHILD ALREADY LIKES

One of the benefits of meal planning is that it allows you to modify foods that your child already likes. *This is a key to changing your child's food habits.*

In an effort to reduce dietary fat, some parents have abandoned their traditional favorite foods for new low-fat or no-fat recipes. But research shows that the kids haven't gone along. Knowing the nutritional differences between broccoli and French fries hasn't kept children and teens from continuing to choose favorite foods—even if those favorite foods rank lower in nutritional value. Very few kids are choosing a steady diet of poached fish over a cheeseburger. Parents have to be careful not to turn healthy eating into a boring form of punishment.

One way to handle this is to plan to change the make-up of the meals kids like rather than introduce too many new foods. This was the premise of a successful study conducted by Dr. Robert Whitaker, a pediatrician at the Seattle Children's Hospital and Medical Center. Dr. Whitaker became concerned that students ate too many high-fat lunches. "It seemed to me," he said, "that the reason they were eating high-fat foods was because that's mostly what the schools were serving—things like hamburgers, hot dogs and pizza." He wondered whether the kids would eat leaner foods if they were disguised as familiar meals.

Working with 16 elementary schools, Dr. Whitaker had school cooks offer kids a choice between high-fat staples, such as a burger and fries, and slimmed-down versions of such old favorites as chili or spaghetti and meatballs, made with ground turkey breast instead of ground beef. The result: most of the students chose the low-fat meals about one-third of the time, and over a period of eight months the fat content of the average lunch fell from 36% to 30%. The most surprising observation: no one complained!

In effect, Dr. Whitaker had slipped them lower-fat meals. "The goal," he says, "should not necessarily be to have children eating a low-fat lunch every day. A better aim is to lower dietary fat by offering choices that will bring the averages down. Maybe the message ought to be that we can change kids' diets by modifying foods they already like."

This concept is critical to success. Sometimes it involves a simple substitution of low-fat ingredients for high-fat ingredients. For example, instead of making a tuna salad sandwich with regular mayonnaise, at 11 grams of fat per tablespoon, you can use light mayonnaise at 5 grams per tablespoon or fat-free mayonnaise with virtually no fat. Or, instead of a jumbo hot dog with 33 grams of fat, you can choose a low-fat or fat-free variety. In a bun, with mustard and relish, your child won't know the difference.

Sometimes it involves a change in cooking methods. Traditional French fries are loaded with fat. But made in the oven or in a nonstick pan with an oil spray, "French fries" can be both low-fat and tasty.

You can learn to modify foods that your kids already like by using many of the menus and recipes in this book. You'll find over a month of menus, created for palatability and balance, with kid-friendly foods such as Spaghetti with Meatballs, Noodle Casserole with Tuna, Chicken Taco Salad, Combination Pizza and Homemade Apple Pie. These recipes are lighter versions of mainstream American favorites. By making these dishes, you will learn techniques and tips for changing your own family favorites.

DISBAND THE CLEAN PLATE CLUB

Parents often push their children, especially young children, to eat more, but this usually isn't necessary. "Parents should understand," says registered dietitian Sheah Rarback, a spokesperson for the American Dietetic Association, "that a young child's bite of this and nibble of that add up to more than you think. If your child says she's full, don't push her to have just a few more bites." Parents should realize that excess calories count. Most nutritional or weight problems arise when you eat too much, even of a good thing.

It can also promote bad eating habits in your child by disrupting internal cues. "Kids who eat when they're full can grow up to be overweight adults," says Jo Ann Hattner, a pediatric nutritionist at Stanford University Medical Center. Many overweight middle-aged people today look back with disdain on the "clean plate club" of their youth. One told me, "I don't eat until I'm full. I eat until my plate is clean. Heck, I'm *still* eating for the kids in China." This is especially appropriate advice in an era when food is entertainment. Many teens hang around fast-food restaurants gobbling up hundreds of calories, but not necessarily because they're hungry.

Instead, let your child feel what it's like to have an appetite and also what it's like to be stuffed. Teach your child to honor hunger and respect fullness. This is one way children will learn to trust their instincts about when to eat. Bev Utt, R.D., M.P.H., provides a great perspective: "Don't worry about serving smaller portions. Your child can always ask for more, and you won't feel guilty about wasting food."

This advice is validated by research. Dr. Susan Johnson at the University of Illinois at Champaign-Urbana found that the more control parents have over their children's eating, the less self-regulation the children displayed. "Parents are still the gatekeepers, responsible for making sure children have and eat healthy food," she says. "But the children are capable of figuring out how much to eat. The most successful approach to raising a child with good eating habits is to have parents control the quality and type of food the child eats, but let the child have control over the amount eaten."

"It's also important to give your child a choice," says dietitian Mary Abbott Hess. No matter the age, allowing children to make their own decisions between healthful alternatives lets them control what they put in their mouth and can set a pattern for life. "Early on," Hess states, "you must keep it simple. When your child is a toddler, two healthful choices are enough. Tell him, 'You can have an apple or an orange.' That way your child has some control. As the child ages, you expand the choices. By giving your child some control, you can avoid starting a series of power and control games between parent and child. Food and eating become too much a part of the game."

Parents should also guard against using food as a reward. If you bribe your child with ice cream and cookies as a reward for eating his or her vegetables, that only makes the reward-foods more alluring. "When food is used to comfort children, to reward good behavior or to punish bad behavior, it teaches them to eat for emotional reasons rather than because their bodies need food," says Florine Mark, president of Weight Watchers. "When children do eat well, reward them with praise, encouragement and attention."

MAKE PALATABILITY A PRIORITY

While it's critical to make dietary recommendations based on nutritional science, parents should not lose sight of the fact that eating is about real food for real people. Putting together a healthy diet for your child is more than nutritional advice based on percentages and grams. If experience regarding food behavior has taught us anything, it is this: people will eat healthful, low-fat food only when it tastes good. Children and teens in particular will not trade taste for an elusive concept of good health. Eating well is necessary to establish low-fat dietary habits.

Today's cooks look for menu ideas that are simple and easy to prepare. But "simple" should not mean "dull." A low-fat dietary pattern should involve foods that are tasty, attractive and appealing. The trick is to make low-fat foods so tempting and satisfying that high-fat foods are not missed.

Be creative:

- Make a breakfast sundae for your kids with whole-wheat waffles, low-fat yogurt and sliced strawberries.
- For younger children, use a cookie cutter to create different shaped sandwiches so the focus is on the fun shapes rather than the food.
- Throw fruits into the blender with ice to make slushies, or add fat-free milk or frozen yogurt to turn them into smoothies.
- Introduce low-fat ethnic fare, such as bean burritos or minestrone soup, to the weekly menu.

The strong belief that good food and good health go together is the motivating force behind the recipes in this book. You'll find favorite foods made lighter, creative and balanced menus, and meals that can be made quickly and easily.

Bring your child into the kitchen. "Kids are motivated to eat healthy food they have helped to prepare," says columnist Mary Carroll, "rather than eating what's on a plate plunked down in front of them." Let kids help organize meals. Involve them in fixing meals, whether this means stirring the soup, snapping string beans, choosing the ingredients for a fruit salad or topping a pizza with fresh vegetables. With a little encouragement, your child's natural curiosity will come into play.

It may seem like a lot of trouble to involve your kids in food preparation, but consider the following statistic from the American Dietary Association on the changing American family: among children 6 to 14, 65% prepare food for themselves at least once a week. Why not take advantage of kitchen time for a lesson about food and cooking? The basic skills needed for healthy eating are ones that your children will use all their adult lives.

PART IV

DIET: THE SEVEN-STEP SOLUTION

CHAPTER 11

ZERO IN ON THE BASICS

T he last section ended with suggestions for planning changes in your child's food habits. The seven steps outlined in this section are actions that you can take to make these changes happen. *The key to success is establishing priorities.*

There's a saying in the business world that 10% of your customers provide 80% of your business. That is why important clients are treated like VIPs. It's the same in other walks of life. In Hollywood, for instance, it is estimated that 10% of movie actors earn 80% of all salaries. It's no wonder these actors are called "stars." This axiom is known as the "10–80 rule," and it can help parents to focus on the most important things to do.

The fact is, there are literally hundreds of suggestions that can be made about changing habits to produce a healthier diet and a healthier child. But it doesn't make much sense to heap all of them onto parents. It is unrealistic to expect multiple changes to be implemented immediately and simultaneously. Chances are, you'll try some new things for a week or so, then begin to feel overwhelmed and out of time, and revert to your old ways. Nothing will have changed for you or your child. But because you now know better, your guilt will increase every time your kid opens a bag of potato chips.

It makes more sense to prioritize along the lines of the "10–80 rule." There are a few basic things that you can focus on which will improve *most* of your child's food habits. Zero in on these first. They are the most important determinants of your child's diet. Once the basics are in place, you may choose to make further refinements. But even if you never have time for anything other than the basics, you will have helped your child to make a sea-change in eating habits.

Here are the seven most important actions that parents can take:

1. Pick a good breakfast cereal.
2. Switch to fat-free and low-fat milk and cheese.
3. Cut out fatty hamburgers and hot dogs.
4. Lighten up lunches.
5. Make fast food your friend.
6. Go for the best snacks.
7. Change the focus of your meals.

CHAPTER 12

1: PICK A GOOD BREAKFAST CEREAL

Grandmother was right. Breakfast is the most important meal of the day. And it's so easy to make breakfast a healthy meal if you choose a low-sugar, high-fiber cereal to go along with fruit, juice and milk.

The primary cereal grains—wheat, corn, oats, barley, rye and rice—contain 70% to 80% complex carbohydrates, about 13% to 15% protein, and very little fat. In addition, cereals are great sources of fiber as well as vitamins and minerals.

The five criteria for healthy cereal choices are outlined below:

- *A maximum of 5 grams of sugar* (a little more than one teaspoon) per serving unless the product contains dried fruit such as raisins. Fruits contribute sugar but also nutrients such as fiber. Don't get snookered by advertising claims like "lightly sweetened." Instead, check the grams of sugar on the Nutrition Facts label. If sugar is the first item on the ingredients list, reject the cereal.
- *Whole wheat, whole grain, whole-oat flour or rolled oats* near the top of the ingredients list. This means the prod-

uct has not been subjected to refining, a process that does away with essential nutrients.

- *At least 2 grams of fiber per serving.* Whole-grain products always contain some fiber. Refined cereals often do not. (Remember, by adding fruit such as raisins or berries to your child's cereal, you also increase fiber.)
- *No more than 2 to 3 grams of fat per serving.* Most cereals are low in fat, but granola and muesli can contain about 9 grams in a half-cup serving.
- *No more than 350 milligrams of sodium.*

Here are some recommendations that meet the five criteria:

Cereal	Calories	Grams of Fiber	Grams of Sugar	Milligrams of Sodium
Arrowhead Mills				
Amaranth (1 cup)	115	33	33	30
Multigrain Flakes (1 cup)	140	3	3	130
Nature O's (1 cup)	130	3	1	5
Barbara's				
Breakfast O's (1¼ cup)	110	3	2	115
Shredded Wheat (2 biscuits)	140	5	0	0
High 5 (¾ cup)	100	5	5	180
Shredded Spoonfuls (¾ cup)	120	4	4	20
Erewhon				
Fruit'N Wheat (¾ cup)	170	5	12	105
Kamut Flakes (⅔ cup)	110	4	1	75
Raisin Bran (1 cup)	180	6	11	103
Wheat Flakes (1 cup)	180	6	1	135
General Mills				
Cheerios (1 cup)	110	3	1	280

Cereal	Calories	Grams of Fiber	Grams of Sugar	Milligrams of Sodium
Fiber One (½ cup)	60	14	0	140
Total (¾ cup)	110	3	5	210
Wheaties (1 cup)	110	3	5	210
Health Valley				
Fat-Free Granola				
(⅔ cup)	190	6	5	125
Fat-Free Honey				
Clusters & Flakes				
(¾ cup)	130	4	4	20
100% Natural Bran				
with Apples &				
Cinnamon (¼ cup)	170	7	6	10
Organic Amaranth				
(¾ cup)	98	4	4	10
Organic Blue Corn	98	4	4	10
Organic Fiber 7	98	4	4	10
Organic Healthy Fiber	98	4	4	10
Organic Oat Bran				
Flakes	98	4	4	10
Organic Oat Bran O's	98	4	4	10
Real Oat Bran				
(½ cup)	200	5	5	60
Kellogg's				
All-Bran with Extra				
Fiber (½ cup)	50	15	0	150
All-Bran (½ cup)	80	10	5	280
Complete Bran				
Flakes (¾ cup)	100	5	6	230
Raisin Bran (1 cup)	170	7	18*	310
Lifestream				
Berry Granola				
(½ cup)	125	4	4	13
Fruit & Nut Muesli				
(½ cup)	119	5	5	23

Cereal	Calories	Grams of Fiber	Grams of Sugar	Milligrams of Sodium
Nabisco				
Shredded Wheat 'N Bran (1¼ cups)	200	8	1	0
Shredded Wheat (2 biscuits)	160	5	0	0
Nature's Path				
Multigrain Flakes (⅔ cup)	110	3	3	40
Millet Rice (¾ cup)	118	3	3	110
O's (¾ cup)	118	3	3	110
New Morning				
Bran Flakes (1 cup)	110	5	1	0
Oatios Apple-N-Cinnamon (1 cup)	90	3	1	0
Raisin Bran (1 cup)	90	6	7*	0
Ultimate Oat Bran (1 cup)	110	4	1	0
Post				
Bran Flakes (⅔ cup)	90	6	5	210
Fruit & Fibre (1 cup)	210	6	17*	265
Grape-Nuts Flakes (¾ cup)	100	3	5	140
Raisin Bran (1 cup)	190	8	20*	300
Quaker				
Shredded Wheat (3 biscuits)	220	7	1	0

* More than 5 grams of sugar because of fruit.

Some other cereals that meet all the criteria except for being a bit high in sugar are Kellogg's Bran Buds (8 grams), Nabisco 100% Bran (7 grams), Healthy Choice Multi-Grain Squares (8 grams), Post Grape-Nuts (7 grams), Healthy Choice Multi-Grain Flakes (6 grams), General

Mills Multi-Grain Cheerios (6 grams), Quaker Life (6 grams) and Health Valley Fat-Free Granola (8 grams.) The makeup of brands changes often, so be sure to check the label frequently.

As nutritious as these low-sugar, high-fiber cereals are, your child may not want to eat them every day. Remember, children are not moved by health arguments, so don't force the issue. If your child has a favorite cereal (perhaps the frosted kind) that doesn't meet the criteria, don't put it on a list of forbidden foods. It will only make it more alluring. Instead, let your child pick a cereal he or she likes, and you pick another, healthier variety. Then mix the contents together, or alternate the days each cereal is eaten. Be sure to round out the meal with fat-free or light (1%) milk, fruit and juice.

You can reason to a certain extent with teens. Studies show that teenage boys in particular are interested in athletic performance and that teenage girls are interested in body shape. Good breakfast cereals can often be "sold" to teens as an aid to performance and weight control.

CHAPTER 13

2: SWITCH TO FAT-FREE AND LOW-FAT MILK AND CHEESE

D airy foods are rich in vitamins, minerals, protein and calcium, and should be part of a balanced diet for growing children and teens. But many dairy foods also contain too much fat (and cholesterol-raising saturated fat), so fat-free and low-fat versions are better. Milk and cheese are two of the dairy foods most frequently consumed by children and teens. It makes sense to work on these foods first.

MILK

V irtually all children and teens drink milk. (The exception is teenage girls who trade milk for diet soft drinks in an effort to reduce calories—an osteoporosis nightmare.) But milk comes with a wide range of fat. To help consumers, the Food and Drug Administration has recently ordered labels changed to give more accurate descriptions. For example, "2% low-fat" milk is now called "2% reduced-fat." "1% low-fat" milk is now "light milk (1%)." And "skim" or "nonfat" milk has become "fat-free" milk.

Type of Milk (8 fl. oz.)	Calories	Grams of Fat	% Calories from Fat
Whole milk	150	8.5	51%
Whole chocolate milk	208	8.5	37
2% reduced-fat milk	125	5.3	38
2% chocolate milk	79	5.0	25
Light (1%) milk*	104	2.5	22
Buttermilk, fat-free*	88	.4	2
Fat-free milk *	81	.4	2

*Smartest choices.

After age two, fat-free milk is the best choice for your child. Replacing a cup of whole milk with the same amount of fat-free milk saves 8 grams of fat without losing the nutritional benefits of calcium and protein. Just think of a cup of whole milk as the same as a cup of fat-free milk—except for two pats of butter added. At three cups of milk a day, that's enough fat and calories saved in a year to equal 22 pounds of body fat! Fat-free buttermilk and light (1%) milk are also smart choices.

It takes about a month for most people to get used to the taste of fat-free milk. If your child is currently drinking whole milk or 2% milk, switching to fat-free milk overnight usually won't work. The best advice is to move gradually to allow your child's taste buds to change. Take it in steps. Change from whole milk to 2% milk, then to light (1%) milk, and finally to fat-free milk. A slow transition will make it easier for your child (and you) to adjust.

CHEESE

The annual per capita consumption of cheese in the United States stands at 26 pounds. We eat it melted, sprinkled, in cubes, in sandwiches, in casseroles, on burgers and for dessert. It's a favorite at every age, so it's one of the hardest foods for us to trim from our diet.

Cheese is a good source of protein and calcium, but it can also be a concentrated source of fat. Most regular cheese is about 60% to 80% fat. One ounce of cheddar cheese, for example, has 9 grams of fat. Even "part-skim" mozzarella is rich in fat—one ounce has about 5 grams. Indeed, a typical 1.5-ounce serving of American cheese, about two slices, contains as much fat as 3.5 pats of butter. What many people don't realize is that most cheese is as fat as—or fatter than—meat. Three one-inch cheese cubes, for instance, have more fat than 3.5 ounces of London broil. So, if your child regularly eats cheese, it's important to make lower-fat choices.

Fat-Grams in Cheese

- One ounce of regular or full-fat cheese has 9 to 11 grams of fat.
- One ounce of reduced-fat or part-skim cheese has 5 to 7 grams of fat.
- One ounce of light cheese* has 2 to 4 grams of fat.
- One ounce of fat-free cheese* has less than one-half gram of fat.

*Smartest choices.

In general, hard cheese is usually fatter than soft cheese because it has less moisture and a higher concentration of fat solids. That's why one ounce of cheddar is richer in fat than one ounce of Brie. Most whole-milk cheese, such as American, Monterey Jack, cheddar and Swiss, contain about 9 grams of fat per ounce. It wouldn't take many ounces to exceed your child's fat guideline—or yours, for that matter. Regular cheese, then, should be used sparingly as a garnish or occasional treat rather than as a dietary staple.

Switch your child to lower-fat and fat-free cheese. Fortunately, a great many brands are available today. The following table lists smart choices for some of the most popular types of cheese.

Cheese (1 oz.)	Calories	Grams of Fat	% Calories from Fat
American, processed			
Regular	105	9	77%
Alpine Lace Fat Free	45	0	0
Borden Fat Free	40	0	0
Borden Light	60	3	45
Borden Low Fat	45	1	20
Healthy Choice			
Fat Free Singles	40	0	0
Healthy Farms	40	0	0
Kraft Deluxe 25% Less Fat	93	7	68
Kraft Free Singles	40	0	0
Kraft ⅓ Less Fat Singles	67	4	54
Lifetime Fat Free	40	0	0
Light 'n Lively 50% Less Fat	67	3	40
Lucerne Fat Free	40	0	0
Smart Beat Fat Free Slices	38	0	0
Weight Watchers Fat Free	40	0	0
Weight Watchers Fat Free			
Reduced Sodium	40	0	0
Cheddar			
Regular	115	9	70%
Alpine Lace Free 'N Lean	40	0	0
Alpine Lace, Shredded	35	0	0
Cabot Light 50%			
Reduced Fat	70	5	64
Cabot Light 75%			
Reduced Fat	60	3	42
Cracker Barrel ⅓ Less Fat	80	5	56
Dorman's Reduced Fat	80	5	56
Healthy Choice Fat Free	45	0	0
Kraft Healthy Favorites			
Fat Free	45	0	0
Kraft ⅓ Less Fat	85	5	54
Weight Watchers Natural	80	5	56
Weight Watchers Natural			
Low Sodium	80	5	56
Sargento Preferred Light,			
Shredded	70	5	64

Cheese (1 oz.)	Calories	Grams of Fat	% Calories from Fat
Monterey Jack			
Regular	105	9	70%
Alpine Lace Reduced Fat	70	5	64
Dorman's Reduced Fat	80	5	56
Formagg	70	5	64
Kraft ⅓ Less Fat	80	5	56
Lite-line	50	2	36
Weight Watchers			
Natural	80	5	56
Mozzarella			
Regular	90	7	70%
Part-skim	80	5	56
Alpine Lace Free 'N Lean	40	0	0
Frigo Reduced Fat			
Part Skim	60	3	42
Healthy Choice			
Fat Free	45	0	0
Kraft Healthy Favorites			
Fat Free	50	0	0
Polly-O Free	40	0	0
Polly-O Lite	60	3	42
Precious Fat Free	30	0	0
Precious Lite	60	3	42
Sargento Preferred Light	64	3	42
Sorrento Fat Free	30	0	0
Sorrento Lite	60	3	42
Stella Reduced Fat			
Part Skim	60	3	42
Swiss			
Regular	105	8	69%
Alpine Lace Reduced Fat	90	6	60
Dorman's Reduced Fat	100	5	45
Jarlsberg Lite	70	4	51
Lifetime Fat Free	40	0	0
Sargento Preferred Light	80	4	45
Weight Watchers			
Reduced Fat	50	2	36

There are two issues concerning low-fat and fat-free cheeses. The first is that many types are "lower in fat" than original versions but are not truly "low-fat." A reduced-fat cheddar, for instance, may have 5 grams of fat per ounce. That's less than regular cheddar, but it's not really low in fat. Just because the label states that the cheese is "part-skim," "low-fat" or "semi-soft" doesn't necessarily make it low in fat. Parents need to read the Nutrition Facts for accurate fat-gram information.

The second issue is taste. Some of the "fat-reduced" and most of the "fat-free" varieties are not as tasty as regular cheeses. This is important because if family members don't like the taste, they won't eat the cheese—no matter how low-fat it is. You have to find a balance between taste and fat that works. We found the best way was to try a variety of different brands. If one low-fat cheddar tasted awful (and some did), we didn't give up on low-fat cheddar. We just tried other brands until we discovered one we liked. We found, for example, that our children did not like the taste of most fat-free cheeses. However, they liked the fat-free American cheese slices made by Kraft and Healthy Choice. This allowed us to reduce fat in a sandwich without sacrificing taste.

Watch for serving size as well. Be aware that one ounce of cheese is a pitifully small amount for a real cheese lover. One way to stretch cheese is to grate it, then use teaspoons—not cups—for flavoring vegetables, salads, soups and pasta. A sprinkle of cheese may be just the thing to get your child to eat more vegetables.

While it can be difficult to find a good-tasting yet low-fat hard cheese, that's not the situation with soft cheeses like cottage and ricotta, and other dairy products like sour cream, cheese spreads and dips. There are many low- and fat-free types that will appeal to your kids. If your family likes lasagna, using nonfat ricotta cheese instead of full-fat will save 8 grams of fat per ¼ cup. Many brands today offer fat-free choices: Frigo, Stella, Precious, Sorrento, Polly-O and Maggio, to name a few.

Kids generally like cottage cheese. Luckily, the low- and fat-free versions taste about as good as the full-fat ones. Good fat-free choices include Knudsen Free, Friendship Nonfat and Light n' Lively Free. If your child likes cottage cheese with fruit, find a good-tasting plain brand and cut in a little fresh fruit of your own. That way you'll avoid the corn syrup that is usually added to most fruit-flavored cottage cheeses. One concern our family had with fat-free cottage cheese is that many brands are high in sodium—350 to 450 milligrams per quarter-cup. So we chose brands with a little more fat but much less sodium. Good examples are Lucerne No Salt Lowfat and Friendship 1% Lowfat No Salt Added. Each has one gram of fat per quarter-cup, but with only 40 milligrams of sodium.

Regular cream cheese is a lot closer to cream than it is to cheese. Two tablespoons of Philadelphia Free will save you 10 grams of fat over the same amount of full-fat Philadelphia Cream Cheese. Alpine Lace, Healthy Choice and Lucerne also offer fat-free types, and Weight Watchers has a "light" cream cheese.

OTHER DAIRY FOODS

There are many dairy foods that will fit kids' diets. Once you've taken care of milk and cheese, you can deal with other dairy foods to ensure the most healthful choices.

ICE CREAM

Ice cream is arguably America's favorite dessert, particularly for children. Most ice cream provides fat content per serving on the label. The standard serving size is one-half cup. This is not realistic. With the exception of small children, most people are more likely to eat a cup, so use that measurement as a guide.

- One cup of premium ice cream contains 30 to 40 grams of fat.
- One cup of regular ice cream contains 12 to 20 grams of fat.
- One cup of light ice cream (or ice milk) contains 6 to 8 grams of fat.
- One cup of fat-free ice cream* contains no fat.

*Smartest choice.

Changing from a cup of Breyers regular ice cream to Sealtest Fat-Free Frozen Dessert will you save you 17 grams of fat. A switch from Häagen-Dazs ice cream to Breyers Light saves 23 grams of fat per cup. And an Eskimo Pie Fat Freedom Sandwich has 7 grams less fat than an Embassy Ice Cream Sandwich.

But as with cheese, taste is a determining factor with low-fat and fat-free ice cream. If you find a brand to be bad-tasting, select another and keep trying. Some of the best fat-free national brands include Borden, Lucerne, Sealtest and Breyers. Be sure to check your local brands as well. Remember, balancing taste against fat is a prime consideration in changing family food habits. In our house, for instance, the taste of fat-free ice cream has not been well accepted. We do enjoy it in a terrific fat-free milk shake (recipe in this book), but for eating we prefer low-fat ice cream, which is really ice milk. For us, that is the best balance between taste and low-fat considerations. Many national brands offer low-fat choices with 3 to 6 grams per cup, including Healthy Choice, Borden, Lucerne, Weight Watchers and Mattus.

If your child can't stand either the low-fat or fat-free versions, you may have to opt for the higher-fat types— but do so in very small amounts and infrequently. And use your child's fat guideline to make decisions regarding other foods eaten that day.

FROZEN YOGURT

The fat content of frozen yogurt can vary from 0 to 20 grams per one-cup serving, so read the label. Be aware that serving sizes are not standardized. One brand might list the serving size as three ounces, which makes it look lower than other brands that use four ounces as a serving. As with ice cream, neither is realistic. Figure on a one-cup serving. Regular frozen yogurt can be extremely rich in calories and fat. A cup of Stars Butter Pecan, for instance, has 28 grams of fat.

Look for fat-free and low-fat frozen yogurt. There are many that your child will find to be as creamy and satisfying as ice cream. Häagen-Dazs has a line of low-fat frozen yogurt bars in 14 flavors, each only 100 calories with one gram of fat. Here are some good national brands to choose from:

> *Fat-free frozen yogurt:* Stoneyfield Farm, Stars, Lucerne, Yoplait, Breyers, Kemp's, Colombo, Ben & Jerry's.

> *Low-fat frozen yogurt (less than 3 grams of fat per cup):* Cascadian Farm, Yoplait Light, Häagen-Dazs, TCBY, Sealtest, Colombo, Ciao Bella.

If you buy yogurt from a stand, order fat-free as a general rule. But ask for the nutritional brochure. (You might be surprised at how many calories come in fat-free products.) Also, watch out for toppings. Putting two tablespoons of sprinkles on a yogurt cone adds 6 grams of fat!

YOGURT

An excellent source of calcium, yogurt can be eaten by itself or used as a substitute for regular sour cream, mayonnaise and commercial dressings in salads, dips and toppings. But yogurt comes with a wide range of fat, so be certain to read the labels and choose fat-free varieties.

Fat-Grams in Yogurt

- One cup of regular yogurt contains 8 to 11 grams of fat.
- One cup of low-fat yogurt contains 5 to 6 grams of fat.
- One cup of fat-free yogurt* contains no fat.

*Smartest choice.

Some of the best national brands include Dannon, Colombo, Yoplait, Carnation, Borden, Lucerne, Breyers and Weight Watchers.

SOUR CREAM

Many brands of low-fat and fat-free sour cream are very tasty. They are a good alternative on baked potatoes, for instance. But what is great news for parents is that there are a number of low-fat and fat-free sour cream-based dips. There is a wide range of flavors—some good, some not so good—so it pays to test multiple brands. Some dips to consider include Guiltless Gourmet Nacho, Louise's Fat Free Nacho Queso Salsa, Guilt Free Honey Mustard and Dean's Light French Onion. And don't just think taco or tortilla chips, either. Dips can be instrumental in increasing the vegetables eaten by your child.

BUTTER

A few dairy foods are so rich in fat that they should be considered outside the prescription for low-fat eating. Butter is the best example. It can be a main source of fat for kids. It's used on pancakes, waffles and toast; on bread and rolls; in sandwiches; on potatoes, rice and vegetables; in baked goods; on popcorn; and in frying. Not only is butter rich in fat—a single pat has 4 grams, a tablespoon 11 grams—but over half its fat content is saturated.

Ounce for ounce, butter has more fat than prime rib.

Butter is insidious because it's eaten in small amounts. A pat here, a spread there—but it quickly adds up. The best advice is to avoid it altogether. Sometimes this is easy. When our family changed from English muffins with butter and jam to jam alone, no one missed the butter. But sometimes it's harder to accept. Our kids liked butter on pancakes, for example. Syrup by itself just wouldn't do, so we switched from butter to a heart-healthy soft margarine. (Remember, stick margarine contains trans fat, which can cause cholesterol to go up, so use tub-type or liquid margarine. Corn and safflower oil are good choices.) Many brands are available in reduced-fat varieties. Some include:

Margarine (1 Tbsp.)	Calories	Grams of Fat	% Calories from Fat
Diet Mazola	70	8	100%
Fleischmann's Light	70	8	100
I Can't Believe It's Not Butter! Light	60	7	100
Land O Lakes Country Morning Blend Light	50	6	72
Parkay Light	70	7	90
Promise Extra Light	50	6	72
Promise Ultra	35	4	100
Promise Ultra Fat Free Nonfat	5	0	0
Shedd's Spread Country Crock	60	7	100
Super Light Smart Beat	20	2	90
Weight Watchers Extra Light Spread	45	4	80

For those times when nothing but butter will do, try Land O Lakes Light Whipped Butter. It has 34 calories and 3.5 grams of fat per tablespoon, but whipping makes a tablespoon go further.

We also found mustard to be a good substitute for butter as a sandwich spread. And instead of frying in butter, you can use a nonstick pan with cooking spray, lemon juice, flavored vinegar, defatted broth or even a small amount of olive oil.

A dilemma most American families share is how to get kids to eat more vegetables. Butter has traditionally been used to make veggies more palatable. But that didn't seem like a smart choice to us, so we used herbs, spices, flavored vinegars and imitation-butter sprinkles like Butter Buds. The sprinkles often provide flavor on vegetables and baked potatoes, without adding fat, and make them more appealing to children.

EGGS

This is a good place to call attention to eggs, even though they're not really a dairy item. Most children and teens like eggs, and that's good because eggs provide protein, calcium and other nutrients. Unfortunately, they also come with fat and cholesterol. The American Heart Association recommends no more than 300 milligrams of dietary cholesterol a day. Since one whole egg can provide 200 to 250 milligrams, your child could be over the limit with two eggs for breakfast.

Should children eat eggs? Of course they should. For most people, two or three eggs a week is not a problem. But if your child likes eggs on a regular basis, consider using more egg whites and fewer egg yolks. The yolk of an egg contains 90% of the cholesterol and 79% of the fat; the egg white has most of the protein. So, an eight-egg omelet for a family of four can be made with four whole eggs and four additional egg whites, or with commercial egg substitute.

A problem greater than the egg itself is how to cook it. It makes no sense to scramble egg whites in butter or margarine, or to eat an omelet laced with fatty cheese. You're better off using a nonstick pan for the scrambled eggs and emphasizing vegetables, not cheese, in the omelet.

CHAPTER 14

3: CUT OUT FATTY HAMBURGERS AND HOT DOGS

Red meat is the chief source of fat on the American diet. But unlike adults, whose red meat choices most often include steaks, chops and roasts, kids generally show a preference for ground beef—in the form of hamburgers, meat loaf, meatballs and chili—and hot dogs. (Luncheon meats, a third major source of fat for kids, are discussed in the next chapter, which deals with ways to cut down on fatty lunch foods.)

Hamburgers and hot dogs are eaten frequently by both children and teens. So when parents consider reducing fatty meats, it makes sense to start with these two favorite foods.

HAMBURGERS

You can't trim fat from ground beef the way you can from a steak or other fresh meat. So in reality there is no such thing as a truly lean hamburger (or, for that matter, meat loaf or meatballs). The average burger made at home (fast-food burgers are discussed in a later chapter) from standard ground beef gets two-thirds of its calories from fat, and much of that fat is saturated. Add a slice of cheese and a dab of mayo, and it's relatively easy to have your child's burger top out at over 40 grams of fat.

Asking kids—or, indeed, anyone else—to give up hamburgers is unrealistic. This all-American sandwich is part of the fabric of our society. What makes more sense, particularly in light of the information in the section on modifying foods your child already likes, is to figure out how to lighten up his hamburger.

One option is to buy the leanest ground beef available. The current labeling law now defines ground beef in lean-to-fat ratios by weight. For a package to be labeled "ground beef," it must contain beef that is at least 70% lean and no more than 30% fat. According to the Beef Council, "regular" ground beef is 73% lean/27% fat, more commonly known as "73% lean." Many stores also offer varieties of ground beef up to "95% lean."

If lean ground beef is unavailable, a second option is to create your own. Pick a very lean cut of beef, preferably top round, trim all the visible fat and grind it yourself (or have the butcher grind it).

A third option (the one favored by most nutritionists) is to use lower-fat alternatives to ground beef. Try making patties with ground chicken or turkey breast and garnishing them with your favorite trimmings. As long as it doesn't contain any skin and fat, ground poultry can be a tasty, low-fat alternative.

The following table shows how the options stack up.

Patty	Calories	Grams of Fat	% Calories from Fat
Ordinary burger (3.5 oz. ground beef, "73% lean," cooked)	291	21	65%
Leaner burger (3.5 oz. ground beef, "90 % lean," cooked)	199	11	49
Leanest burger (3.5 oz. ground round, cooked)	189	6.3	30
Turkey or chicken burger (3.5 oz. lean, skinless breast meat, cooked)	135	< 1	6

Vegetarian burgers are also available, but read the label. Some, such as Boca Burger, contain no fat. Others, such as LaLoma Meatless Sizzle Burger, have as much as 12 grams of fat. Although many people like them, I cannot recommend veggie burgers from personal experience.

Cooking methods count. Be certain to broil or grill (never fry) patties to medium or well done so that the maximum amount of grease drips off. Hold the mayo, bacon and cheese. They can add up to as much fat as is in the meat itself.

Here's the difference if you make the right choices:

Hamburger #1	Hamburger #2
4-oz. (raw weight) medium-lean ground beef patty	4-oz. (raw weight) extra-lean ground beef patty
Bun	Bun
1 oz. American cheese	No cheese*
1 tbsp. mayonnaise	No mayonnaise*
Ketchup, lettuce, tomato, onion	Ketchup, lettuce, tomato, onion
Calories 564	Calories 290
Grams of fat 39	Grams of fat 7

*Fat-free cheese and fat-free mayonnaise can also be used. They will add calories but not fat.

For pasta sauces, chili or casseroles, be sure to sauté the ground beef in a nonstick pan, then drain it on paper towels. Drain well before adding other ingredients to browned meat.

HOT DOGS

Kids may love them, but from a health standpoint hot dogs are in the nutrition doghouse. Ounce for ounce, most franks rack up more fat than ground beef. Consider that an Oscar Mayer Quarter Pound Beef Frank, *minus* the bun and any trimmings, contains a whopping 33 grams of fat—13 more than a McDonald's Quarter Pounder. If you can't see eliminating hot dogs from your child's diet, serve the healthiest hot dogs available (and balance out the rest of the day with lower-fat meals). Fortunately, some manufacturers are producing fat-free and low-fat hot dogs. To be sure, when fat is skimmed, some of their juicy texture and flavor is lost. But when these hot dogs are served inside a bun with all the trimmings, few children will complain.

How do you find the healthiest hot dogs? Read the label. Regular hot dogs average about 15 to 16 grams of fat, while reduced-fat hot dogs have about 10 to 12 grams. Don't assume that turkey or chicken hot dogs are automatically lower in fat. Some poultry franks have more fat than their beef and pork counterparts. It's rare, for example, to find a chicken hot dog with less than 7 grams of fat. Also, be aware that even fat-free and low-fat hot dogs have a fair amount of sodium.

Some of the smartest choices are listed in the table that follows. Many are fat-free or truly low in fat. Others are simply lower in fat than traditional franks. Keep in mind that many kids, particularly teenage boys, will easily consume two hot dogs. Also, many of the side dishes traditionally served with hot dogs, such as macaroni salad and potato salad, can be rich in fat.

Listed below are choices with less than 9 grams of fat.

Patty	Calories	Grams of Fat	% Calories from Fat
Smartest Choices			
Ballpark Fat Free (1.8 oz.)	45	0	0%
Ballpark "Lite," beef (2 oz.)	110	8	65
Butterball Fat Free!, turkey (1.6 oz.)	45	0	0
Dubuque Extra Lean Plumpers, pork (2 oz.)	60	2	30
Eckrich Fat Free, beef (1.8 oz.)	50	0	0
Eckrich Fat Free, turkey & pork (1.8 oz.)	50	0	0
Eckrich Reduced Fat Bun Size, pork and turkey (2 oz.)	120	8	60
Empire Kosher, chicken (2 oz.)	100	7	63
Empire Kosher, turkey (2 oz.)	90	6	60
Healthy Choice Low Fat, beef (1.8 oz.)	60	1.5	22
Hormel Light & Lean 97, beef (1.6 oz.)	45	1	20
Hormel Light & Lean 100, beef (1.8 oz.)	45	0	0
Jennie-O Extra Lean, turkey (1.6 oz.)	45	2	40
Jennie-O, turkey (1.2 oz.)	70	6	77
Louis Rich Bun-Length, turkey and chicken (2 oz.)	110	8	65
Oscar Mayer Light, beef (2 oz.)	110	9	74
Oscar Mayer Light, pork, turkey & beef (2 oz.)	110	9	74
Oscar Mayer Free, beef and turkey (1.8 oz.)	40	0	0
Perdue Turkey Franks (1.6 oz.)	100	8	72

The following choices fall between 10 and 15 grams of fat, so you might choose them on an occasional basis.

Patty	Calories	Grams of Fat	% Calories from Fat
Occasionally O.K.			
Armour Premium,			
chicken & pork (1.6 oz.)	140	12	77%
Butterball Bun Size,			
turkey (2 oz.)	130	10	69
Dubuque, beef (1.2 oz.)	110	10	82
Dubuque Supreme Plumpers,			
pork & chicken (1.6 oz.)	150	13	90
Eckrich, pork & turkey			
(1.6 oz.)	150	13	90
Hebrew National,			
beef (1.7 oz.)	150	14	84
Hebrew National Reduced-Fat,			
beef (1.7 oz.)	120	10	75
Hormel Wranglers, beef (2 oz.)	170	15	79
Hygrade Grillmasters,			
chicken (2 oz.)	180	11	55
Hygrade Grillmasters,			
turkey (2 oz.)	140	12	77
Oscar Mayer, beef (1.6 oz.)	180	16	80
Oscar Mayer,			
pork & turkey (1.6 oz.)	150	13	78
Perdue Chicken Frank (2 oz.)	140	11	71

Below are examples of hot dogs with over 16 grams of fat. It would be best to avoid them.

Patty	Calories	Grams of Fat	% Calories from Fat
Best to Avoid			
Armour Premium Jumbo,			
beef (2 oz.)	170	15	80%
Ball Park, beef (2 oz.)	180	16	80
Ball Park, beef,			
pork & turkey (2 oz.)	180	16	80

Patty	Calories	Grams of Fat	% Calories from Fat
Ball Park Stadium Classics, beef & pork (2 oz.)	170	16	85%
Dubuque Supreme Plumpers, beef (2 oz.)	180	17	85
Hygrade, beef (2 oz.)	180	17	85
John Morrell Bigger than the Bun (2 oz.)	180	16	80
Oscar Mayer Bun-Length, pork & turkey (2 oz.)	190	17	80
Oscar Mayer Deli Style, beef (2.7 oz.)	230	22	86
Oscar Mayer Original, beef (2.7 oz.)	240	22	83
Oscar Mayer Quarter Pound, beef (4 oz.)	350	33	85

The lower-fat choices for hamburgers and hot dogs provide parents with good options. If, however, your child eats a greasy burger or a giant full-fat hot dog on occasion, all is not lost. Just be sure to help your child make low-fat choices at other meals that day. The burger might be too fat, but the day doesn't have to be.

CHAPTER 15

4: LIGHTEN UP LUNCHES

L unches, both at home and at school, are often a
source of excessive fat and calories. For many
children and teens, lunch usually means a sandwich. And luncheon meats are a sandwich staple.
Unfortunately, many popular choices in regular (full-fat)
varieties are too rich in fat. (Fast-food sandwiches are
treated in a later chapter.)

Fat Content of Regular (Full-Fat) Luncheon Meats

Over 60% Fat	Over 70% Fat	Over 80% Fat
Corned beef	Bratwurst	Beef bologna
Picnic loaf	Chopped ham	Bockwurst
Turkey bologna	Italian sausage	Liverwurst
	Kielbasa sausage	Knockwurst
	Pastrami	Pepperoni
	Pork bologna	Polish sausage
	Salami	Sausage stick
	Smoked sausage	
	Summer sausage	

Some deli meats, like hard salami, can have 12 grams
of fat per ounce, while regular bologna can have 8 or
9 grams. With the average sandwich containing three
ounces of meat, fat-grams can quickly add up.

THREE ACTIONS
FOR PARENTS

The most basic thing you can do is to avoid regular high-fat cold cuts altogether and instead select low-fat versions or alternative fillings. An ounce of full-fat corned beef, for instance, has about 5 grams of fat. But Oscar Mayer Corned Beef has about one gram of fat. Hillshire Farm Deli Select Pastrami has just one gram of fat per ounce, which compares very well with an ounce of full-fat pastrami at 8 grams. "Chopped" ham has between two and eight times more fat than "boiled," "cooked," "smoked" or "baked" ham. Read food labels carefully. (You may also want to purchase a fat-gram guide, such as my fat-gram guides to supermarket and restaurant foods.)

In addition, there are many alternative low-fat fillings to choose from, including roasted turkey breast, roasted chicken breast, lean roast beef and lean boiled or baked ham. These are easy to make at home, or you can purchase them in the deli section of your supermarket in the amount that you desire. Water-packed tuna made with light or fat-free mayonnaise is another good alternative.

A number of national brands offer packaged, lower-fat versions of luncheon meats and alternative fillings.

Item (1 oz.)*	Calories	Grams of Fat	% Calories from Fat
Bologna			
Regular, full-fat	90	8	80%
Butterball Fat Free!	25	0	0
Butterball, turkey	60	5	75
Foster Farms, chicken	60	5	75
Foster Farms, turkey	60	5	75
Healthy Choice	30	1	30

Item (1 oz.)*	Calories	Grams of Fat	% Calories from Fat
Louis Rich, turkey	50	3.5	63%
Mr. Turkey Bologna, turkey	70	5	64
Oscar Mayer Free	20	0	0
Oscar Mayer Light	60	4	60
Chicken			
Skinless breast, roasted	*45*	*1*	*20%*
Foster Farms Oven Roasted	25	.5	18
Foster Farms Smoked	25	.5	18
Healthy Choice Deli- Thin Smoked	30	.5	15
Healthy Choice Smoked	35	1	26
Hebrew National Oven Roasted	25	.5	18
Louis Rich Carving Board	25	.5	18
Mr. Turkey Fat Free Deli Cuts Oven Roasted	25	0	0
Tyson Fat Free	25	0	0
Corned Beef			
Regular, full-fat	*70*	*5*	*64%*
Healthy Choice	30	1	30
Hebrew National	40	1.5	34
Hillshire Farm Deli Select	30	.5	15
Ham			
Regular, roasted	*50*	*2.5*	*45%*
Butterball, turkey	35	1.5	39
Carl Buddig Lean Oven Roasted Honey	35	1	25
Carl Buddig Lean Oven Roasted Smoked	30	1	30
Foster Farms, turkey	30	1	30
Healthy Choice Deli Thin Sliced Smoked	30	1	30
Healthy Choice Deli Thin Sliced Baked Cooked	30	1	30
Healthy Choice Honey	30	1	30

Item (1 oz.)*	Calories	Grams of Fat	% Calories from Fat
Hillshire Farm Deli Select	30	1	30%
Hillshire Farm Deli Select Baked	30	1	30
Hillshire Farm Deli Select Honey	30	1	30
Hormel Light & Lean 97	25	1	36
Jones Lean Choice	25	1	36
Louis Rich Carving Board, Baked	25	1	36
Louis Rich Carving Board, Smoked	25	1	36
Louis Rich Turkey Ham	30	1	30
Oscar Mayer Free	20	0	0
Oscar Mayer Baked Cooked	30	.5	15
Oscar Mayer Boiled Cooked	30	1.5	45
Oscar Mayer Honey Cooked	30	1.5	45
Pastrami			
Regular, full-fat	95	8	76%
Carl Buddig	40	2	45
Empire Kosher, turkey	30	1.5	45
Foster Farms, turkey	35	1	26
Hillshire Farm Deli Select	30	.5	15
Louis Rich, turkey	30	1	30
Salami			
Regular, full-fat, dried	110	10	82%
Regular, beef, cooked	70	5.5	70%
Gallo, 96% Fat Free	40	2.5	56
Louis Rich Cotto, turkey	40	2.5	56
Hebrew National Reduced Fat	55	4	65
Turkey			
Skinless breast, roasted	45	.8	18%
Butterball Fat Free! Oven Roasted	25	0	0
Butterball Fat Free! Smoked	20	0	0

Item (1 oz.)*	Calories	Grams of Fat	% Calories from Fat
Carl Buddig Lean Oven			
Roasted	30	.5	15%
Empire Kosher Oven Prepared	25	0	0
Empire Kosher Smoked	20	0	0
Foster Farms Smoked White	30	.5	15
Healthy Choice Deli Thin			
Honey Roasted & Smoked	30	1	30
Healthy Choice Deli Thin			
Smoked	30	1	30
Healthy Choice Oven Roasted	30	1	30
Hebrew National Oven Roasted	30	.5	15
Hebrew National Smoked	30	.5	15
Hillshire Farm Deli Select			
Smoked	30	0	0
Jones Lean Choice	25	.5	18
Louis Rich Deli-Thin Hickory	25	.5	18
Oscar Mayer Deli-Thin			
Smoked Honey Roasted	25	.5	18
Roast Beef			
Top loin	58	2.5	38%
Carl Buddig Smoked	40	2	45
Healthy Choice	30	1	30

*Remember, most sandwiches contain about 3 ounces of meat.

Avoid high-fat packaged "all-in-one" lunches, which typically contain meat, cheese, crackers and dessert. Oscar Mayer's Lunchables "Bologna & American Cheese" package is a good example. It has 450 calories and 34 grams of fat. Even the lunches that sound healthier may not be. Their "Lean Smoked White Turkey & Monterey Jack" with wheat crackers has more fat than a McDonald's Quarter Pounder . . . plus twice as much sodium. Be sure to read the label. Their "Ham & Cheddar" package has 390 calories and just 11 grams of fat.

A second step you can take is to eliminate added fat— full-fat cheese, butter, margarine and full-fat mayonnaise.

If you use cheese, choose a low-fat or fat-free variety for your child's sandwich. Avoid butter as a sandwich spread because of its saturated fat as well as calories. Hardened stick margarine is no better. Rich in trans fat, it can also raise cholesterol. If you do use margarine, choose one of the soft, tub or liquid squeeze types; they're better for cardiac health, but watch out for calories. Regular margarine has about the same fat content as butter (11 grams per tablespoon), so be judicious in its use. You may want to experiment with the many brands of "calorie-reduced," "fat-reduced" and "diet" margarine, most of which have about 6 grams of fat per tablespoon.

Few foods are fatter than regular mayonnaise, with 11 grams of fat per tablespoon. Ounce for ounce, it contains more fat than spareribs. Mayonnaise can make even healthful tuna into a high-fat, high-calorie sandwich. Fortunately, there are options. "Light" or "calorie-reduced" mayonnaise has 4 to 5 grams per tablespoon, and "fat-free" mayonnaise has less than one-half gram of fat per tablespoon.

A safety issue arises when mayonnaise is used on a school-lunch sandwich. If mayonnaise sits all morning in a backpack or locker, there is a possibility that it can go bad. A good tip is to freeze a juice drink the night before and include it with the sandwich. By lunchtime, the juice will be thawed and ready to drink, but it will have kept the rest of the food at a safe temperature.

As with cheese, taste is a key consideration. Some brands of "light" and "fat-free" mayonnaise have neither the rich taste nor the consistency of regular mayonnaise. Your family has to taste them and make decisions. In our house, "fat-free" mayonnaise is very acceptable on sandwiches, particularly when a spicy mustard is used. But for salads—tuna, potato, macaroni—only a "light" version will do. The point is that there now exists a range of choices from nonfat to full-fat mayonnaise. Choose the best one to balance taste and low fat in your sandwich.

Fat-Grams in Mayonnaise

Item (1 Tbsp.)	Grams of Fat
Regular mayonnaise	
Hain Canola	11
Hellmann's/Best Foods	11
Hollywood Safflower	12
Kraft	12
Hain	12
"Light" mayonnaise	
Hellmann's/Best Foods Lowfat	1
Hellmann's/Best Foods Reduced Fat	3
Nasoya Nayonnaise	3
Miracle Whip Light	3
Smart Beat Light	4
Hellmann's/Best Foods Sandwich Spread	5
Kraft Light	5
Weight Watchers Light	5
Miracle Whip	7
"Fat-Free" mayonnaise	
Kraft Free	0
Miracle Whip Free	0
Smart Beat Fat Free	0
Weight Watchers Fat Free	0

And finally, take action to regulate portion sizes. The type of pastrami sandwich made famous at the Carnegie and Stage delis in New York City could feed an entire family. Don't overfill your child's sandwich. If peanut butter and jelly sandwiches are a favorite, for instance, use a thin smear of peanut butter and more jelly. If it's a turkey sandwich, give it more substance by adding lettuce, onion and tomato—not more turkey.

A good tip is to use different types of breads—whole wheat, pita, onion roll. Our children said this made it taste like a different sandwich, even if it was roasted chicken breast for the second time that week.

SCHOOL LUNCHES

A previous chapter described many of the problems with the typical school lunch. Parents should never assume that the meals their children eat at school will be nutritious and balanced. Nor should they assume that the meals are just one step removed from fast food. Instead, parents need to investigate what is regularly being offered.

Nutritionist Pat Snyder, an expert on school lunches, advises parents to check the lunch menu in the local paper or, better yet, go eat lunch at the school. Are fresh fruit and vegetables served, particularly in elementary school? Or is it just a steady menu of pizza, corn dogs and fries? Are fat-free and light (1%) milk available? Is there an à la carte line with a self-serve salad bar? Are fast-food companies dominating the cafeteria? Communicate your concerns in a positive way to the principal and food service director. If there are problems, offer to help. Get the PTA involved. Remember, food habits are not changed overnight. But when parents and school administrators work together, change can be achieved.

You don't have to become an expert on school nutrition, but you must know enough about the food being served to your child to make a determination. Says Kay McManus, director of food services for the North Kitsap School District in Washington State, "Many schools are making an effort to provide healthier choices, to lighten entrées and include more vegetables and fruit. Parents should take advantage of a good lunch program." She suggests some things that parents can do:

- Make sure your child's school is allowing enough time for school meal service and eating.
- Introduce your child to a variety of foods at home so he or she will try them when they're offered at school.
- It's a good idea to prepay for school meals so you'll be assured that your child is eating the meals and not

using the money for cookies, ice cream and other high-fat treats.

▪ Most elementary schools send home monthly menus. Take the time to read and discuss them with your child.

▪ Encourage your child to try school meals. But remember, your child eats only about 180 meals at school (or 360, if breakfast is included) out of a 1,095 total meals a year. Set a standard of eating at home so your child will understand what constitutes a well-rounded meal when the family eats way from home.

▪ If you have suggestions for meal improvement, talk to the food service director. Many schools have a nutrition advisory council on which parents are welcome to serve.

Cafeteria lunches may be a good choice for your child. But if high-fat, low-fiber fare is the rule, you'll want to consider sending your child off to school with a brown-bag lunch. The key is finding a good combination of nutrition and taste. Says one mother, "I've switched from bologna and salami to sliced turkey breast on whole-wheat bread for my son's lunch. Stacked high with vegetables and mustard, it tastes great and is low in fat. I always put a piece of fruit in the lunch or include a fruit salad as a side dish. He uses low-fat yogurt as a dip. And I always include dessert such as a bag of pretzels, a bag of sweet, chewy dried fruit, fat-free pudding or Jell-O."

Another option is to have your child take a sandwich to school and then buy fruit and salad from the à la carte line in the cafeteria.

Whatever youngsters carry in their bags and boxes, here are a few tips for their parents:

▪ *Try for variety.* Kids often want the same item for lunch every day. This can be a problem if they're not eating a varied, balanced diet. Encourage additional choices by using different types of bread: whole wheat, pita, rolls, bagels and tortillas for a change.

- *Remember their habits.* If your child races through lunch to get out to recess (the most common problem concerning wasted food in elementary schools), take this into account. (You might also consider getting the school to reschedule recess so that it precedes lunch.) Pack a meal that can be eaten quickly.
- *Think about other meals.* Go for overall nutritional balance. If your son doesn't drink milk for breakfast, add low-fat cheese to his lunch for needed calcium. If your daughter had French fries at lunch, you may want to drop a fatty food at dinner. If lunchtime dessert was a cupcake, finish off your dinner with fresh fruit.
- *Give your kids some control.* Keep lunches interesting by letting kids choose from a variety of foods—apple sauce or low-fat yogurt, crackers or bread sticks, string cheese or turkey roll-ups, carrot sticks or a box of raisins. The more kids are involved in planning and preparing their lunch, the more likely they are to eat it. Kids who pack their own lunches are less apt to trade or toss out their own creations.

Parents should also be aware of organizations that offer programs to help schools serve tasty, nutritious food. Some include LUNCHPOWER, from the University of Minnesota; "Eat Smart," the CATCH school nutrition program; the Bogalusa Study's "Heart Smart" program; and Project LEAN from San Diego State University.

CHAPTER 16

5: MAKE FAST FOOD YOUR FRIEND

By its nature, fast food is practically irresistible. It's quick, cheap and tastes pretty good. Unfortunately, much of it is laden with fat and sodium. In a perfect world, knowing what we know about nutrition and health, we wouldn't eat in fast-food restaurants ourselves, and we wouldn't take our kids, either. But this isn't a perfect world. Sometimes parents are too busy to cook, or are running late with the soccer car pool. Sometimes it's the only food teens, out for the evening, can afford. Other times we may just crave the stuff.

According to the National Restaurant Association, fast-food restaurant sales account for nearly 50% of total dining-establishment revenues. A national Gallup poll found that 37% of all Americans say they eat fast food eight or more times a month.

Television advertising and peer pressure dictate a prominent place for fast food in the diet of American children. It doesn't make sense, then, to think that your children will never eat fast food. A smarter way to handle this reality is to make fast food your friend. You can do this by helping your child to make better fast-food choices.

Most fast foods are extremely rich in calories and fat . . . and getting fatter. Not too long ago, a McDonald's Quarter Pounder, with 21 grams of fat, was pretty much the king of hamburgers. Today, it looks positively lean next to the Double Western Bacon Cheeseburger at Carl's Jr., with 63 grams of fat and 1,030 calories, or Wendy's Big Classic Double with Cheese—820 calories and 51 grams of fat. And while McDonald's has phased out its low-fat McLean Deluxe because of slow sales, it has cooked up the Arch Deluxe, an extra-large burger with bacon and mayonnaise sauce on top.

Other fast foods have followed suit. A McDonald's McChicken sandwich has 29 grams of fat. Subway's six-inch tuna salad sub racks up 36 grams of fat. One of Del Taco's Macho Burritos will set you back 31 grams of fat. Even Taco Bell's Taco Salad (*a salad!*) has 87 grams of fat and 1,170 calories, providing more fat in a single meal than most people should consume in an entire day. Fast food is usually fat food, and no child or teen should eat a steady diet of this greasy stuff.

But not all fast-food choices are fatty. The industry has responded to public pressure by offering a number of lower-fat items:

- McDonald's has the McGrilled Chicken Classic Sandwich with just 4 grams of fat. That's less than their small shake, still a bargain at just 5 grams of fat.
- Roy Rogers' roast beef sandwich has 4 grams of fat, the same as Boston Market's ¼ white-meat chicken sandwich.
- A regular hamburger at Burger King has only 15 grams of fat.
- At El Polo Loco, the chicken is flame-broiled, so much of the fat is removed.
- At Subway, the Veggies & Cheese and the Ham & Cheese sub sandwiches contain less fat than comparable sandwiches elsewhere because they have lower-fat ham, less cheese and no mayonnaise.
- Low-fat salads can be found at Arby's, Burger King, Wendy's, Carl's Jr., McDonald's and Jack in the Box—all available with nonfat salad dressing.

▪ Jack in the Box has a Chicken Teriyaki Rice Bowl, very popular among teens, with only 2 grams of fat.

If you look, you can find low-fat salad dressing, nonfat frozen yogurt, and baked fish. So, there are plenty of ways to help your child make smarter choices. The trick is knowing how to work today's fast-food menus, because it's easy to make mistakes. Compare the fat and calories of these two meals at McDonald's:

Meal # 1

	Calories	Grams of Fat
Hamburger	255	9
Small fries	220	12
1% milk	110	2
Total	585	23

Meal #2

	Calories	Grams of Fat
Quarter Pounder		
w/ Cheese	510	28
Large fries	400	22
Strawberry shake	340	5
Apple pie	280	15
Total	1,530	70

Either way, your child ate at the Golden Arches. But while meal #1 did minimal fat damage, meal #2 was a fat disaster. And remember, if nothing but the Quarter Pounder with Cheese will do for your child, be sure to lighten up the rest of the day's meals.

Or, let's say your teenager is at Jack in the Box and wants to order chicken. After all, he's heard from you that it's healthier than a burger. And chicken is chicken, isn't it? Not so. If your teen has the Really Big Chicken Sandwich, he'll eat 56 grams of fat. The Chicken Fajita Pita, a better choice by far, has just 8 grams.

Most fast-food restaurants offer a brochure that contains nutritional information. Take it and use it to frame
better choices. Or, for more complete information on fast
food, refer to my fat-gram guides to supermarket and
restaurant foods.

The following examples will get you started. The list is
not all-encompassing. Moreover, foods are frequently
changed by fast-food chains, and new items are introduced, so it always makes sense to seek out the most current nutritional information.

HAMBURGERS AND
HOT DOGS

Most kids love hamburgers, cheeseburgers and hot
dogs, but not all choices are the same. My recommendations for "Smartest Choices" contain 15 grams of
fat or less. This gives your child some room for the ever-
present side dishes such as French fries.

Those designated "Occasionally O.K." range from 16
to 20 grams of fat, still not too bad for a main-meal burger. But those beyond 20 grams fall into the "Better to
Avoid" category.

Item	Calories	Grams of Fat	% Calories from Fat
Smartest Choices			
Carl's Jr.			
Hamburger	320	14	39%
Happy Star Hamburger	200	8	36
Burger King Hamburger	330	15	41
Dairy Queen			
Hamburger	310	13	38
Homestyle Hamburger	290	12	37
Jack in the Box			
Cheeseburger	320	15	42
Hamburger	280	11	35

Item	Calories	Grams of Fat	% Calories from Fat
McDonald's			
Cheeseburger	320	14	39%
Hamburger	270	10	33
Wendy's			
Plain Single	350	15	39
Jr. Cheeseburger	320	13	37
Jr. Hamburger	270	10	33
Occasionally O.K.			
Burger King Cheeseburger	380	19	45%
Carl's Jr.			
Big Burger	470	20	38
Old Time Star Hamburger	400	17	38
Original Hamburger	460	20	39
Dairy Queen			
Cheeseburger	365	18	44
Homestyle Cheeseburger	340	17	45
Regular Hot Dog	280	16	51
Regular Hot Dog w/ Chili	320	19	53
Hardee's			
Cheeseburger	390	20	46
Hamburger	340	16	42
Hot Dog	300	17	51
Large Hot Dog	450	20	40
McDonald's			
McLean Deluxe w/ Cheese	400	17	38
Quarter Pounder	420	20	43
Wendy's Deluxe			
Cheeseburger	360	16	40
Better to Avoid			
Burger King			
Cheeseburger Deluxe	390	23	53%
Double Cheeseburger	600	36	54
Double Cheeseburger			
w/ Bacon	640	39	55
Double Whopper	860	56	57
Double Whopper w/ Cheese	950	63	60
Whopper	630	39	56

Item	Calories	Grams of Fat	% Calories from Fat
Whopper w/ Cheese	720	46	58%
Whopper Jr.	410	24	53
Whopper Jr. w/ Cheese	460	28	55
Carl's Jr.			
All Star Hot Dog	540	35	58
Chili Dog	720	47	59
Double Western Bacon			
Cheeseburger	1,030	63	55
Famous Star Hamburger	610	38	56
Super Star Hamburger	820	53	58
Western Bacon			
Cheeseburger	730	39	48
Dairy Queen			
Bacon Double			
Cheeseburger	610	36	53
Double Cheeseburger	570	34	54
Double Hamburger	460	25	49
Homestyle "Ultimate"			
Hamburger	700	47	60
Hounder Hot Dog	480	36	68
Hounder Hot Dog			
w/ Cheese	535	40	68
Hounder Hot Dog w/ Chili	575	41	64
Quarter Pound Hot Dog	590	38	58
Regular Hot Dog w/ Cheese	330	21	57
Triple Cheeseburger	820	50	55
Triple Hamburger	710	45	57
Super Hot Dog w/ Cheese	580	34	53
Super Hot Dog w/ Chili	570	32	51
Hardee's			
Bacon Cheeseburger	530	34	57
Big Deluxe Burger	510	29	51
Big Double Cheeseburger	630	38	54
Big Hardee Cheeseburger	690	43	56
Big Hardee Hamburger	590	35	53
Big Twin Hamburger	450	25	50
Frisco Burger	740	49	60
Jr. Hardee Cheeseburger	450	25	50

Item	Calories	Grams of Fat	% Calories from Fat
Jr. Hardee Hamburger	400	21	47%
Mushroom 'N' Swiss Burger	610	36	53
Quarter-Pound			
Cheeseburger	420	22	47
Jack in the Box			
Bacon Bacon			
Cheeseburger	710	45	57
Colossus Burger	1,100	84	69
Double Cheeseburger	450	24	48
Grilled Sourdough			
Hamburger	670	43	58
Jumbo Jack Cheeseburger	650	40	55
Jumbo Jack Hamburger	560	32	51
Outlaw Hamburger	720	40	50
Quarter Pound Hamburger	510	27	48
Swiss Cheese &			
Bacon Burger	680	47	62
Ultimate Cheeseburger	1,030	79	69
McDonald's			
Arch Deluxe	570	31	49
Big Mac	530	28	47
Quarter Pounder	420	21	45
Quarter Pounder			
w/ Cheese	530	30	51
Wendy's			
Bacon Cheeseburger	410	21	46
Big Bacon Classic	640	36	51
Double Big Bacon Classic	680	39	52
Double Cheeseburger	620	36	52

- *Watch out for the size and number of patties.* As size and number increase, so does the fat. Single hamburgers have about two ounces of meat; quarter-pounders, about three ounces; triples, four or more ounces. Order items identified as "small," "single" or "junior." Avoid those labeled "jumbo," "super," "double," "triple," "extra-large," "ultimate" and "big."

■ *Watch out for fatty add-ons.* Opt for a plain hamburger with lettuce, tomato, onion and ketchup (10 to 15 grams of fat) instead of the supreme version loaded with cheese, bacon, mayonnaise or mayo-based "special sauces" (50 to 60 grams of fat). Each slice of cheese racks up about 100 calories. Mayonnaise adds 100 calories per tablespoon.

■ *Watch out for side orders.* A large order of McDonald's French fries contains 22 grams of fat and 450 calories—more than a Quarter Pounder. That's a lot of fat for a side order. A baked potato with broccoli and cheddar has about 20 grams of fat. You might get away with that if it's the meal, but as a side order? No way. Some chains offer baked potatoes with steamed vegetables, corn on the cob or salad with nonfat and low-fat dressings—all better choices.

■ *Watch out for milk shakes.* They're always high in fat, right? Not so. The great-tasting shakes at McDonald's, Burger King and Jack in the Box are made with low-fat and nonfat milk and have just 5 to 7 grams of fat.

FRENCH FRIES AND OTHER POTATOES

Potatoes are a favorite side dish for hamburgers, chicken and other fast-food entrées. Only the baked potatoes are really low-fat choices, and even then you'll have to watch the toppings. For the purpose of categorizing, French fries and hash browns that fall between 10 and 15 grams of fat per serving are listed as "Occasionally O.K." That's still a lot of fat for a side dish, so be sure to make smart choices in other food selections. Potatoes with more than 15 grams of fat are "Better to Avoid."

Item	Calories	Grams of Fat	% Calories from Fat
Smartest Choices			
Arby's Baked Potato, Plain	355		0%
Carl's Jr. Lite Baked Potato	290	1	3
Hardee's Mashed Potatoes, Small	70	1	12
Wendy's			
Baked Potato, Plain	310	0	0
Hot Stuffed Sour Cream			
& Chives Baked Potato	380	6	14
Occasionally O.K.			
Arby's			
Curly Fries	300	15	45%
French Fries	245	13	48
Potato Cakes	205	12	53
Burger King			
French Fries, Regular	230	13	52
Hash Browns	220	12	49
Carl's Jr.			
French Fries, Small	280	13	42
Dairy Queen			
French Fries, Regular	300	14	42
French Fries, Small	210	10	43
Hardee's			
French Fries, Small	240	10	38
French Fries, Medium	350	15	39
Hash Rounds	230	14	55
Jack in the Box Hash Browns	160	11	62
KFC			
French Fries, Crispy	210	11	47
French Fries, Regular	245	12	44
Kentucky Fries	270	13	44
McDonald's			
French Fries, Small	210	10	43
Hash Browns	130	8	55
Wendy's			
French Fries, Small	260	13	45
Hot Stuffed Broccoli &			
Cheese Baked Potato	470	14	27

Item	Calories	Grams of Fat	% Calories from Fat
Better to Avoid			
Arby's			
Baked Potato w/ Broccoli			
& Cheddar	570	20	32%
Baked Potato w/ Margarine			
& Sour Cream	580	24	37
Baked Potato Deluxe	735	36	44
Cheddar Fries	335	18	49
Hash Brown Nuggets	270	17	57
Burger King French Fries,			
Medium	400	20	45
Carl's Jr.			
Bacon & Cheese			
Baked Potato	730	43	53
Broccoli & Cheese			
Baked Potato	590	31	47
Cheese Baked Potato	690	36	47
Fiesta Baked Potato	720	38	48
French Fries, Criss-Cut	330	22	60
French Fries, Regular	420	20	43
Sour Cream & Chive			
Baked Potato	470	19	36
Dairy Queen French Fries,			
Large	390	18	42
Hardee's			
"Big Fry" Fries	500	23	41
Crispy Curls	300	16	48
French Fries, Large	430	18	38
Jack in the Box			
French Fries, Jumbo	395	19	43
French Fries, Regular	350	17	44
French Fries, Small	220	11	45
French Fries, Super Scoop	590	29	44
Seasoned Curly Fries	360	20	50
Wedges, Bacon & Cheddar	800	58	65
McDonald's			
French Fries, Large	450	22	44
French Fries, Super Size	540	26	43

Item	Calories	Grams of Fat	% Calories from Fat
Wendy's			
Biggie Fries	460	23	45%
French Fries Medium	380	19	45
Hash Browns	360	22	55
Hot Stuffed Bacon & Cheese Baked Potato	540	18	30
Hot Stuffed Cheese Baked Potato	570	23	36
Hot Stuffed Chili & Cheese Baked Potato	620	24	35

CHICKEN AND TURKEY

Poultry should be one of the healthiest items your child can order, but often it's not. Preparation methods make all the difference. I've treated chicken and turkey like hamburgers and hot dogs—only those with 15 grams of fat or less per serving get to be "Smartest Choices." The one exception is nugget-type chicken. It contains a lot of fat in a small amount of food, so it's deemed "Occasionally O.K."

Item	Calories	Grams of Fat	% Calories from Fat
Smartest Choices			
Arby's			
Grilled Barbecue Chicken Sandwich	390	13	30%
Light Roast Deluxe Chicken Sandwich	275	6	22
Roast Turkey Light Deluxe	260	7	21
Boston Market			
Chicken Breast	430	4	8
Skinless Rotisserie Turkey Breast Sandwich	400	4	8

Item	Calories	Grams of Fat	% Calories from Fat
¼ White Meat Chicken w/o Skin	160	4	23%
¼ Dark Meat Chicken, w/o skin	220	12	49
Burger King Broiled Chicken Salad	200	10	45
Carl's Jr.			
BBQ Chicken Sandwich	310	6	17
Charbroiled Chicken Salad	260	9	31
Lite Chicken Salad	200	8	36
Teriyaki Lite Chicken Sandwich	330	6	16
Dairy Queen			
Grilled Chicken Fillet Sandwich	300	8	24
Hardee's			
Chicken & Pasta Salad	230	3	12
Chicken Fillet Sandwich	420	15	32
Grilled Chicken Salad	150	3	18
Grilled Chicken Sandwich	290	9	28
Jack in the Box			
Chicken Teriyaki Bowl	580	2	3
Chicken Fajita Pita	290	8	25
Kenny Rogers Roasters			
BBQ Chicken Pita Sandwich	400	7	16
Chicken Caesar Salad (no skin)	285	9	27
Roasted Chicken Salad (no skin)	290	10	30
Turkey Sandwich	385	12	28
¼ Chicken, Dark Meat w/o Skin	170	7	39
¼ Chicken, White Meat w/o Skin & Wing	145	2	14
¼ Chicken, White Meat w/ Skin	245	11	39
½ Chicken w/o Skin	315	10	26

Item	Calories	Grams of Fat	% Calories from Fat
KFC			
BBQ Chicken Sandwich	256	8	28%
Extra Tasty Crispy Drumstick	190	11	52
Hot & Spicy Drumstick	190	11	52
Original Recipe Drumstick	130	7	48
Rotisserie Breast w/o Skin	199	6	27
Rotisserie Thigh w/o Skin	220	12	49
Long John Silver's			
Baked Chicken, Light Herb	120	4	30
Chicken Planks	120	4	30
Flavorbaked Chicken	110	3	27
McDonald's			
Grilled Chicken Deluxe	330	6	16
McGrilled Chicken Sandwich	260	4	14
Subway 6-inch Turkey Sandwich	273	4	13
Taco Bell			
Light Chicken Soft Taco	180	5	5
Chicken Soft Taco	223	10	40
Wendy's			
Grilled Chicken Sandwich	290	7	22
Grilled Chicken Salad	200	8	36
Occasionally O.K.			
Arby's Grilled Chicken Deluxe	430	20	42%
Burger King Chicken Tenders (6 pcs.)	250	12	43
Carl's Jr.			
Chicken Strips (6 pcs.)	260	19	66
Chicken Stars (6 pcs.)	230	14	55
Church's			
Fried Chicken Breast	280	17	55
Fried Chicken Breast & Wing	305	20	55
Nuggets (6 pcs.)	330	19	51
One Leg w/ Cajun Rice	270	16	53
One Chicken Breast w/ Corn	280	16	42

Item	Calories	Grams of Fat	% Calories from Fat
Dairy Queen			
Breaded Chicken Fillet			
Sandwich	430	20	42%
Chicken Nuggets	275	18	59
Del Taco Chicken Salad	254	19	67
Hardee's Turkey Club	390	16	37
Jack in the Box			
Chicken Sandwich	400	18	41
Chicken Strips (4 pcs.)	290	13	40
(6 pcs.)	450	20	40
Grilled Chicken Fillet	430	19	40
Kenny Rogers Roasters			
Chicken Caesar Pita			
Sandwich	605	35	53
Roasted Chicken Pita			
Sandwich	685	35	47
¼ Chicken, Dark Meat			
w/ Skin	270	17	56
½ Chicken w/ Skin	515	28	48
KFC			
Chicken Sandwich	497	22	40
Crispy Strips	323	20	56
Original Recipe Breast	360	20	50
Original Recipe Thigh	260	17	59
Rotisserie Breast w/ Skin			
& Wing	335	19	51
Rotisserie Thigh w/ Skin	335	24	65
McDonald's Chicken			
McNuggets (4 pcs.)	200	12	54
Wendy's			
Breaded Chicken Sandwich	440	18	37
Chicken Nuggets (6 pcs.)	280	20	64

Better to Avoid

Item	Calories	Grams of Fat	% Calories from Fat
Arby's			
Chicken Cordon Bleu			
Sandwich	623	33	48%
Breaded Chicken Fillet			
Sandwich	535	28	46

Item	Calories	Grams of Fat	% Calories from Fat
Roast Club Chicken Sandwich	545	31	50%
Roast Deluxe Chicken Sandwich	435	22	46
Roast Sante Fe Chicken Sandwich	435	22	43
Turkey Sub	550	27	44
Boston Market			
Chicken Caesar Salad w/ 4 tbsp. dressing	670	47	63
Chicken Pot Pie	750	34	41
Chicken Salad Sandwich	680	33	44
½ Chicken w/ Skin	630	37	53
¼ Dark Meat Chicken w/ Skin	330	22	60
Burger King			
BK Broiler Chicken Sandwich	540	29	48
Fried Chicken Sandwich	700	43	55
Carl's Jr.			
Bacon Swiss Chicken Sandwich	670	36	48
Charbroiler Club Chicken Sandwich	570	29	46
Sante Fe Chicken Sandwich	530	29	49
Turkey Club Sandwich	530	23	39
Church's			
Chicken Breast Fillet	610	34	50
Two Chicken Thighs w/ Biscuit	710	49	62
Two Chicken Wings w/ Biscuit	750	49	59
DQ Chicken			
Breaded Chicken Fillet Sandwich w/ Cheese	480	25	47
Strip Basket w/ Gravy	860	42	44
Hardee's Grilled Chicken 'Frisco	620	34	49

Item	Calories	Grams of Fat	% Calories from Fat
Jack in the Box			
Chicken Wings (6 pcs.)	845	44	47%
(9 pcs.)	1,270	66	47
Really Big Chicken			
Sandwich	900	56	56
Kenny Rogers Roasters			
½ Chicken w/ Skin	515	28	48
KFC			
Chicken Pot Pie	700	36	46
Extra Tasty Crispy Breast	470	28	54
Extra Tasty Crispy Thigh	370	25	61
Hot & Spicy Breast	530	35	59
Hot & Spicy Thigh	370	27	66
Hot Wings (6 pcs.)	471	33	63
McDonald's			
Crispy Chicken Deluxe	530	26	44
McChicken Sandwich	510	30	52
Wendy's Chicken Club			
Sandwich	500	23	41

- *Watch out for fried chicken*—it's extremely high in fat. If you eat fried chicken, choose the white-meat breast and remove the skin and breading. Exercise portion control.
- *Skip the skin and the wing*, the fattest piece.
- *Watch out for sandwiches that use fried chicken*. The best choice for a chicken sandwich is a skinless grilled breast. As with other sandwiches, cut out the extras such as mayonnaise, mayo-based sauces, cheese and cheese sauces.
- *Watch out for chicken nuggets*. They're usually battered and fried, so most of their calories come from fat. If you must have them, dip them in barbecue sauce instead of creamier condiments to save 10 or more grams of fat.
- *Watch out for fatty add-ons*. Mayo, bacon, cheese and "special sauce" can turn healthy chicken into an unhealthy sandwich.
- *Watch out for side dishes*. Mayonnaise- and oil-based salads, which often accompany chicken, will add much

fat to the meal. Skip the coleslaw, onion rings, potato and macaroni salads, and French fries. Order corn bread instead of biscuits, and you'll cut the fat in half. Better side dishes include green beans, baked beans, baked potato, corn on the cob, rice and green salads with light or fat-free dressing. KFC's red rice and beans, with only 3 grams of fat, is a great side dish.

- *Watch out for some roasted, rotisserie and flame-broiled marinated chicken.* Chicken prepared this way may sound a lot leaner than breaded fried chicken, but it can be rich in fat.

FISH AND SEAFOOD

With fish and seafood, as with chicken, it's a matter of preparation. Some restaurants offer low-fat choices on the menu. A serving of Flavorbaked Fish at Long John Silver's, for instance, has just 3 grams of fat. But most fish and seafood come deep-fried. Fried and deep-fried fish, oysters, scallops, shrimp and clams are popular fast-food choices.

Unfortunately, fried seafood usually comes with high-fat side dishes such as coleslaw or French fries. A good example is Long John Silver's Fish, Shrimp & Clams Dinner (with fries, hush puppies and coleslaw), with 70 grams of fat. Instead, choose low-fat items such as Long John Silver's Flavorbaked Fish & Chicken (1 piece each) over Rice (with baked potato and green beans). The cost to your budget is only 10 grams of fat.

A fried fish fillet sandwich is not a good choice. Breaded, fried in grease, and covered with mayonnaise and fatty sauces, this is an item to be avoided. Wendy's Fish Fillet Sandwich, for example, will set you back 27 fat-grams.

And finally, watch out for tartar sauce and mayonnaise. They add pure fat and calories to the meal.

Item	Calories	Grams of Fat	% Calories from Fat
Smartest Choices			
Arthur Treacher's Cod Fillet	245	14	52%
Long John Silver's			
Baked Fish w/ Sauce	150	2	12
Batter-Dipped Fish	180	11	55
Catfish Fillet	205	12	53
Crispy Fish	150	8	48
Flavorbaked Fish	90	3	28
Kitchen Breaded Fish	120	5	37
Lemon Crumb Fish (3 pcs.)	150	1	6
Light Paprika Fish (3 pcs.)	120	1	6
Skipper's			
Fish Fillet	175	10	51
Salmon, Baked	270	11	37
Shrimp w/ Seafood Sauce	170	3	16
Shrimp & Seafood Salad	170	3	16
Occasionally O.K.			
Arthur Treacher's Fried Fish	355	20	50%
Church's			
Fish Filet	430	18	38
Fried Catfish (3 pcs.)	200	12	54
Dairy Queen Fish Fillet			
Sandwich	370	16	39
Hardee's Fisherman's Fillet			
Sandwich	450	20	40
McDonald's			
Filet-O-Fish Sandwich	360	16	20
Fish Filet Deluxe	510	20	35
Better to Avoid			
Arby's Fish Fillet Sandwich	530	27	46%
Arthur Treacher's			
Fish Sandwich	440	24	49
Shrimp (7 pcs.)	380	24	58
Burger King			
BK Big Fish	720	43	54
Fish Fillet	495	25	45

Item	Calories	Grams of Fat	% Calories from Fat
Carl's Jr.			
Carl's Catch Sandwich	560	30	48%
Fish Fillet Sandwich	550	26	43
Church's Fish Filet			
w/ Cheese	485	22	41
Dairy Queen Fish Fillet			
Sandwich w/ Cheese	420	21	45
Jack in the Box Fish			
Supreme Sandwich	590	34	52
Long John Silver's			
Clams, Breaded	525	31	53
Fish & Chicken Kid's Meal			
w/ Fries, Hush Puppies			
& Coleslaw	620	34	49
Shrimp, Breaded	390	23	53
Skipper's			
Clam Strips w/ Fries	1,005	70	63
Cod, Thick cut (3 pcs.)			
w/ Fries	665	32	43
Create A Catch Sandwich	525	33	57
Create A Catch Sandwich,			
Double	700	73	94
Fish Fillet w/ Fries	560	28	45
Oyster Basket w/ Fries	1,040	51	44
Shrimp Basket w/ Fries	725	36	45
Wendy's Fish Filet Sandwich	460	25	49

OTHER SANDWICHES

Chicken and fish are not the only sandwiches available. Many fast-food restaurants and delis offer a variety of sandwiches. Some are healthy choices; others are nutritional disasters.

The criterion for the "Smartest Choices" category is a sandwich with 15 grams of fat or less. Many types are

available—turkey, ham, roast beef. Often it's the addition
of mayo and cheese that makes a healthy pick into a
"Better to Avoid" sandwich. And, as with other fast
foods, watch out for side orders with oil or mayonnaise
and those that have been fried.

Item	Calories	Grams of Fat	% Calories from Fat
Smartest Choices			
Arby's			
Ham 'n Cheese Melt	329	13	36%
Roast Beef Lite Deluxe	296	10	30
Boston Market Ham			
Sandwich (no sauce)	450	9	18
Hardee's			
Hot Ham 'N Cheese			
Sandwich	300	11	33
Regular Roast Beef			
Sandwich	270	11	37
McDonald's Egg McMuffin	290	13	40
Subway (6-inch)			
Club	297	5	15
Ham	270	4	13
Ham & Cheese	322	9	25
Light Tuna	368	15	37
Meatball	408	14	31
Roast Beef	295	5	15
Steak & Cheese	360	10	25
Turkey	273	4	13
Veggie	219	2	8
Veggies & Cheese	272	9	29
Typical Deli Sandwiches			
Turkey w/ Mustard	370	6	14
Roast Beef w/ Mustard	460	12	22
Occasionally O.K.			
Arby's			
Arby-Q	431	18	37%
Regular Roast Beef	388	19	44

Item	Calories	Grams of Fat	% Calories from Fat
Subway (6-inch) Cold Cut			
Combo	379	16	37%
Typical Deli Sandwiches			
Corned Beef w/ Mustard	500	20	36
Turkey w/ Mayo	475	19	35
Better to Avoid			
Arby's			
Bacon 'n Cheddar Deluxe	539	34	57%
Philly Beef 'n Swiss	755	47	55
Burger King Croissan'wich			
w/ Ham, Egg & Cheese	350	22	56
Jack in the Box Supreme			
Croissant	570	36	57
Subway (6-inch)			
BMT	491	28	51
Spicy Italian	458	24	47
Tuna	519	32	55
Ham & Cheese			
w/ Mayo or Oil	440	22	45
Roast Beef w/ Mayo or Oil	463	25	48
Turkey w/ Mayo or Oil	426	22	47
Veggies & Cheese			
w/ Mayo or Oil	389	22	51
Cold Cut Combo			
w/ Mayo or Oil	497	29	52
Typical Deli Sandwiches			
Bacon, Lettuce & Tomato	600	37	56
Chicken Salad	535	32	54
w/ Mayo	655	46	63
Corned Beef, Overstuffed,			
w/ Mustard	760	37	44
Egg Salad	545	31	51
w/ Mayo	665	44	60
Grilled Cheese	510	33	58
Ham w/ Mayo	665	40	54
w/ Mustard	565	27	43
Reuben	920	50	49

Item	Calories	Grams of Fat	% Calories from Fat
Roast Beef w/ Mayo	565	4	38%
Tuna Salad	715	43	54
w/ Mayo	835	56	61
Tuna Salad, Overstuffed	860	50	53
w/ Mayo	975	63	59
Turkey Club	740	34	42
Vegetarian	755	40	48

▪ *Roast beef sandwiches* can be a good alternative to hamburgers. Stick with the regular or junior sizes, and avoid high-fat extras such as mayonnaise, mayo-based sauces and cheese.

▪ *Avoid croissant sandwiches.* The croissant averages 200 to 500 calories, with as much fat as you'll find in four pats of butter. A whole-grain or white bun runs about 135 calories.

▪ *Extra-lean corned beef, pastrami and beef brisket* are available at many delis, but watch out for portion size. Sandwiches can be large enough to feed two people, so order a half-sandwich or split the sandwich with a friend. Also, be careful with side dishes such as creamy coleslaw and potato salad.

▪ *High-fat sub sandwiches* are those made with bologna, hard or Genoa salami, pepperoni, mortadella and cheese. Instead of these fatty fillers, opt instead for turkey, smoked turkey, ham and lean roast beef. Avoid oil and mayonnaise in favor of mustard, onions, lettuce, pickles and hot peppers.

▪ *Stick with low-fat sandwich fillers,* such as roasted turkey breast, roasted or grilled chicken breast, lean roast beef and lean ham. Avoid cold cuts, tuna or chicken with mayonnaise, egg salad, cheese sandwiches and cheese melts.

▪ *Watch out for fatty condiments.* A Subway six-inch Roast Beef Sandwich without oil has about 12 grams of fat; with oil, it has 19 grams. Use mustard, horseradish or ketchup to moisten the sandwich, but skip oil, butter, cheese, margarine and mayonnaise.

PIZZA

Pizza can be a good bet if you order wisely. Choose thin-crust instead of deep-dish. Pass up fatty meat toppings such as pepperoni, ground beef and sausage, which drive up the fat content to the level of a cheeseburger. Avoid extra-cheese and "four-cheese" pizzas, as well as double- and triple-deckers. (Two slices of Pizza Hut's Triple Decker Pizza with Ham have over 800 calories and 34 grams of fat.) And blot slices with a paper napkin to remove excess oil.

The table below shows what toppings can mean in terms of added fat. Estimated figures are based on two slices of a 14-inch pizza (about a quarter of a large pizza).

Topping	Calories	Grams of Fat
Pepperoni	80	7
Sausage	97	8
Bacon	135	12
Salami	57	5
Ham	41	2
Black olives	56	5
Onions	11	<1
Extra cheese	168	8
Green peppers	5	0
Fresh mushrooms	5	0

What do you order? Choose a cheese pizza with half the cheese and extra tomato sauce, and load up on vegetables—tomatoes, peppers and onions. Lean ham on occasion is a good choice. You'll have a fast food that you and your kids can live with.

SALADS

Try to avoid mayonnaise- or oil-based salads, including coleslaw, potato salad, and pasta and macaroni salads. Taco salads usually run in excess of 30 grams of fat.

Better choices include side salads, garden salads, green salads with strips or chunks of chicken (no mayonnaise) and chef's salads. The critical element is the dressing. Choose the wrong kind and you might as well be eating Ben & Jerry's Premium Ice Cream. Top off your salad with a two-ounce packet of ranch dressing at Burger King, and you'll add about 37 grams of fat. It's a far better idea to ask for diet or no-oil dressings. McDonald's Lite Vinaigrette, for instance, has just 2 grams of fat in each packet.

A comparison of dressings shows you why. Remember, the following nutritional information is for one packet of dressing.

Item	Amount	Calories	Grams of Fat	% Calories from Fat
Smartest Choices				
Carl's Jr.				
French, Reduced Calorie	1 oz.	40	2	45%
Hardee's				
French, Fat Free	1 pkt.	70	0	0
French, Reduced Calorie	1 pkt.	130	5	35
Jack in the Box				
French, Reduced Calorie	1 pkt.	175	8	41
Italian, Low Calorie	1 pkt.	25	2	72
McDonald's				
Lite Vinaigrette	1 pkt.	50	2	36

Item	Amount	Calories	Grams of Fat	% Calories from Fat
Occasionally O.K.				
Hardee's Italian,				
Reduced Calorie	1 pkt.	90	8	80%
McDonald's				
Red French,				
Reduced Calorie	1pkt.	160	8	45
Better to Avoid				
Burger King				
Bleu Cheese	1 pkt.	300	32	96%
French	1 pkt.	290	22	68
House	1 pkt.	260	26	35
Light Italian	1 pkt.	170	18	95
Olive Oil & Vinegar	1 pkt.	310	33	96
Ranch	1 pkt.	350	37	95
Thousand Island	1 pkt.	290	26	81
Carl's Jr.				
Bleu Cheese	1 oz.	150	15	90
House	1 oz.	110	11	90
Italian	1 oz.	120	13	98
Thousand Island	1 oz.	110	11	90
Hardee's				
Blue Cheese	1 pkt.	210	18	77
House	1 pkt.	290	29	90
Ranch	1 pkt.	290	29	90
Jack in the Box				
Bleu Cheese	1 pkt.	260	22	76
Buttermilk House	1 pkt.	360	36	90
Thousand Island	1 pkt.	310	30	87
McDonald's				
Bleu Cheese	1 pkt.	190	17	81
Peppercorn	1 pkt.	400	44	98
Ranch	1 pkt.	230	21	82
Thousand Island	1 pkt.	190	13	62

Many restaurants offer a salad bar, but don't assume that your salad-bar creation is automatically low in fat. It's a good idea to heap your plate with greens and beans. Avoid deli meats and cheeses. Skip anything mixed with oil, mayonnaise, cheese or whipped cream. Complement your salad with soup and bread. And don't get carried away with sampling.

Always approach dressings with a wary eye. Be aware that the average salad bar ladle holds four tablespoons of salad dressing (and many people spoon two ladlefuls of dressing on top of their salads.) Here's what you get with one ladle:

Topping	Calories	Grams of Fat
Blue cheese	308	32
Caesar	280	28
French	268	26
Golden goddess	272	28
Italian	276	28
Oil and vinegar	276	30
Ranch	216	23
Russian	304	31
Thousand Island	236	22

MEXICAN FOOD

Mexican fast food is one of the most popular choices. The basic components of Mexican food (tomatoes, lettuce, salsa, tortillas, beans and rice) start out low in fat, but preparation techniques as well as fatty extras can ruin the picture. However, a number of chains are offering a selection of low-fat choices.

The "Smartest Choices" are those with 15 grams of fat or less.

Item	Calories	Grams of Fat	% Calories from Fat
Smartest Choices			
Del Taco			
Breakfast Burrito	255	11	39%
Chicken Burrito	265	10	34
Chicken Fajita Taco, Deluxe	210	10	43
Deluxe Double Beef			
Soft Taco	211	11	47
Green Burrito	229	8	31
Green Burrito, Large	330	11	30
Soft Taco, Regular	210	10	43
Soft Taco, Small	145	6	37
Red Burrito	235	8	31
Red Burrito, Large	340	11	29
Refried Beans w/ Cheese	120	7	52
Tostado	140	8	51
El Polo Loco			
Chicken Burrito	310	11	32
Chicken Taco	180	7	35
Steak Taco	250	12	43
Vegetarian Burrito	340	7	19
Jack in the Box Taco	190	11	52
Macheezmo Mouse			
Cheese Quesadilla	380	13	32
Chicken Burrito	580	11	17
Chicken Quesadilla	450	15	31
Combo Burrito	630	12	17
Veggie Burrito	655	8	11
McDonald's Fajita			
Chicken Salad	160	6	33
Taco Bell			
Bean Burrito	390	12	28
Beef Tostadas	240	11	41
Chicken Soft Taco	223	10	40
Chicken Tostadas	265	15	51
Light Bean Burrito	330	6	16
Light Burrito Supreme	350	8	21
Light Chicken Burrito	290	6	19

Item	Calories	Grams of Fat	% Calories from Fat
Light Chicken Soft Taco	180	5	25%
Light Supreme Burrito	350	8	21
Light Supreme Soft Taco	200	5	23
Light Supreme Taco	160	5	28
Light Taco	140	5	32
Light Soft Taco	180	5	25
Light Taco Salad w/o Chips	330	9	25
Light Taco Supreme	160	5	28
Light 7 Layer Burrito	440	9	18
Soft Taco Supreme	270	15	50
Taco Time			
Bean Burrito, Soft, w/o Cheese	460	14	27
Chicken Taco, Soft	390	12	28
Chicken Taco, Soft, w/o Cheese	335	8	21
Combo Burrito, Soft, w/o Cheese	460	14	27
Refried Beans, w/o Cheese	295	11	34
Occasionally O.K.			
Del Taco			
Beef Burrito	440	20	41%
"Big Del" Burrito	455	20	40
Combination Burrito	413	17	37
El Polo Loco			
Classic Burrito	560	20	32
Spicy Hot Burrito	570	20	32
Macheezmo Mouse			
Chicken Enchilada	545	16	26
Chili Enchilada	560	16	25
Jack in the Box Super Taco	280	17	55
Taco Bell			
Beef Burrito	430	19	40
Burrito Supreme	440	19	39
Chili Cheese Burrito	390	18	42
Combo Burrito	410	16	35
Nachos	345	18	47

Item	Calories	Grams of Fat	% Calories from Fat
Taco Time			
Meat Tostada,			
w/o Sour Cream			
or Cheese	410	17	37%
Taco Salad, w/o Dressing	350	16	41
Better to Avoid			
Del Taco			
Chicken Fajita Burrito,			
Deluxe	435	22	46%
Macho Combo Burrito	774	31	36
Regular Quesadilla	483	27	50
El Polo Loco			
Loco Grande Burrito	680	30	40
Grilled Steak Burrito	740	29	35
Jack in the Box			
Cheese Nachos	570	35	55
Chimichanga (4 pcs.)	570	28	44
(6 pcs.)	855	42	44
Taco Salad	505	31	55
Taquito (7 pcs.)	510	22	39
Taco Bell			
Bellgrande Nachos	635	34	48
Big Beef Supreme Burrito	525	25	43
Light Taco Salad w/ Chips	680	25	33
Taco Salad	860	55	58
w/ Shell & Dressing	1,170	87	67
Steak Supreme Burrito	500	23	41
Supreme Nachos	365	27	66
Taco Time			
Bean Burrito, Soft	550	21	35
Combo Burrito, Soft	550	24	39

- *Watch out for* cheese, sour cream and guacamole; refried beans made with lard; deep-fried or crispy taco or salad shells, tortilla chips, nachos, chimichangas, flautas and quesadillas.

▪ *Better choices* are soft-shell tacos or corn tortillas, burritos, enchiladas, fajitas, and grilled chicken and/or fish. The plain bean burrito or tostada is a good choice for your child. It has far less fat than the loaded versions. Look for light versions.

BREAKFAST

M any fast-food restaurants offer cereal and juice. That's the best choice. But if your child wants more than cereal, opt for pancakes and syrup (no butter, margarine, or side orders of bacon or sausage). McDonald's Hot Cakes have only 7 grams of fat; Hardee's Pancakes have just 2 grams. These are better choices than a breakfast sandwich that combines cheese, egg and/or meat filling with a muffin, croissant or biscuit. Such a switch saves about 30 grams of fat. Also, watch out for French Toast Sticks. An order at Burger King contains 27 grams of fat.

In the following table, if an item is a meal, such as hotcakes, and it has 15 grams of fat or less, I've categorized it as a "Smartest Choice." But if it's not a full meal, such as Arby's Danish Pastry or Carl's Jr.'s Scrambled Eggs, I've not included it. My rationale is that more than 10 grams of fat in a side dish is hard to justify as a smart choice. It's the same with breakfast sandwiches. They simply provide too much fat in too little food to be "Smartest Choices."

Item	Calories	Grams of Fat	% Calories from Fat
Smartest Choices			
Arby's Blueberry Muffin	230	9	35%
Burger King Bagel, Plain	270	6	20
Carl's Jr.			
English Muffin w/ Margarine	180	6	30
Hot Cakes, w/ Margarine,			
w/o Syrup	360	12	30

Item	Calories	Grams of Fat	% Calories from Fat
Muffin, Blueberry	340	9	24%
Muffin, Bran	310	7	20
Hardee's			
Pancakes (3)	280	2	6
Pancakes (3)			
w/ 2 Bacon Strips	350	9	23
McDonald's			
Apple Bran Muffin, Fat Free	180	0	0
Blueberry Muffin, Fat Free	170	0	0
Cheerios, w/o Milk	70	1	13
English Muffin	140	2	13
English Muffin w/ Margarine	170	4	21
Hotcakes, Plain	310	7	20
Wheaties, w/o Milk	80	1	5

Occasionally O.K.

Item	Calories	Grams of Fat	% Calories from Fat
Arby's			
Bacon Biscuit	320	18	51%
Biscuit, Plain	280	15	48
Croissant, Plain	220	12	49
Danish, Cinnamon Nut	360	11	28
Ham Biscuit	325	17	47
Burger King			
Bagel w/ Cream Cheese	370	16	39
Bagel w/ Bacon,			
Egg & Cheese	455	20	40
Bagel w/ Egg & Cheese	410	16	35
Bagel w/ Ham,			
Egg & Cheese	440	17	35
Biscuit, Plain	330	17	46
Biscuit w/ Bacon	380	20	48
Croissant, Plain	180	10	50
Croissan'wich			
w/ Egg & Cheese	315	20	57
Danish, Apple Cinnamon	390	13	30
Danish, Cheese	405	16	35
Danish, Cinnamon Raisin	450	18	36
Mini Muffins Blueberry	290	14	43

Item	Calories	Grams of Fat	% Calories from Fat
Mini Muffins,			
Lemon Poppyseed	320	18	51%
Mini Muffins,			
Raisin Oat Bran	290	12	37
Carl's Jr.			
Cinnamon Roll	460	18	35
Danish, all types			
except cheese	520	16	28
Scrambled Eggs	120	9	68
Sunrise Sandwich	300	13	39
Sunrise Sandwich w/ Bacon	370	19	46
Hardee's			
Ham & Egg Biscuit	370	19	46
Pancakes (3)			
w/ 1 Sausage Patty	430	16	33
Jack in the Box Breakfast Jack	300	12	36
McDonald's			
Apple Danish	360	16	40
Egg McMuffin	290	13	40
Hotcakes w/ Margarine			
(2 pats) & Syrup	580	16	24
Scrambled Eggs (2)	170	12	64
Wendy's			
Apple Danish	360	14	35
Breakfast Sandwich	370	19	46
French Toast	400	19	43
Mushroom, Green Pepper			
& Onion Omelet	210	15	64
Scrambled Eggs	190	12	57

Better to Avoid
Arby's

Item	Calories	Grams of Fat	% Calories from Fat
Sausage Biscuit	460	32	62%
Bacon & Egg Croissant	430	30	63
Ham & Cheese Croissant	345	21	54
Mushroom/Cheese Croissant	495	38	69
Sausage & Egg Croissant	520	39	68
French Toastix	420	25	54

Item	Calories	Grams of Fat	% Calories from Fat
Bacon Platter	595	33	50%
Egg Platter	460	24	47
Ham Platter	520	26	46
Sausage Platter	640	41	58
Burger King			
Bagel w/ Sausage,			
Egg & Cheese	625	36	52
Biscuit w/ Bacon & Egg	470	27	52
Biscuit w/ Sausage	480	29	55
Biscuit w/ Sausage & Egg	570	36	52
Croissan'wich w/ Bacon,			
Egg & Cheese	350	24	62
Croissan'wich w/ Ham,			
Egg & Cheese	350	22	56
Croissan'wich w/ Sausage,			
Egg & Cheese	530	41	70
French Toast Sticks	500	27	49
Mini Muffins			
Scrambled Egg Platter,			
Regular	550	34	56
Scrambled Egg Platter			
w/ Bacon	610	39	58
Scrambled Egg Platter			
w/ Sausage	770	53	62
Carl's Jr.			
Danish Pastry Cheese	520	22	38
French Toast Dips,			
w/o Syrup	480	26	48
Sunrise Sandwich w/ Sausage	500	32	58
Hardee's			
Bacon & Egg Biscuit	530	30	50
Bacon, Egg & Cheese Biscuit	610	37	54
Big Country Breakfast			
w/ Bacon	820	49	53
Big Country Breakfast			
w/ Ham	500	25	45
Big Country Breakfast			
w/ Sausage	1,000	66	59

Item	Calories	Grams of Fat	% Calories from Fat
Biscuits 'N Gravy	510	28	49%
Canadian Rise 'N'			
Shine Biscuit	570	32	51
Country Ham & Egg Biscuit	400	22	50
Ham, Egg & Cheese Biscuit	540	30	50
Sausage & Egg Biscuit	600	37	55
Jack in the Box			
Canadian Bacon Crescent	450	31	62
Pancake Platter	610	22	32
Sausage Crescent	585	43	66
Sausage Croissant	670	48	64
Sausage Sandwich	585	43	66
Scrambled Egg Platter	560	32	52
Scrambled Egg			
Pocket Sandwich	431	21	44
Supreme Crescent	545	40	66
Supreme Croissant	570	36	57
Ultimate Sandwich	620	35	51
McDonald's			
Biscuit w/ Bacon,			
Egg & Cheese	450	27	54
Biscuit w/ Sausage	430	29	61
Biscuit w/ Sausage & Egg	520	35	61
Cheese Danish	410	22	48
Sausage McMuffin	360	23	58
Wendy's			
Breakfast Sandwich			
w/ Bacon	430	23	48
Breakfast Sandwich			
w/ Sausage	570	37	58
Cheese Danish	430	21	44
Ham & Cheese Omelet	290	21	65

CHAPTER 17

6: GO FOR THE BEST SNACKS

Americans of all ages are snacking more than ever. It's estimated that the average person snacks over 200 times a year. For children and teens, however, snacks are not incidental; in fact, snacking is vital in ensuring that they get enough calories to supply their growing needs. It's hard for children to get all their nutritional needs satisfied in three meals because of their small stomachs and appetites. Snacking may be even more important to teens, supplying about 30% of the calories they eat.

Says registered dietitian Stephanie Campbell, "If kids in junior high never snacked, I don't know how they would fill their nutritional needs. So it's important to make snacks count. Potato chips, cookies, cakes and ice cream are empty-calorie snacks. Go for nutrient-packed snacks that include fruits, vegetables and whole grains. Eating at least five servings a day of fruits and vegetables becomes a lot more realistic if your kids eat them for snacks."

How often your child snacks is less an issue than what your child snacks on. Unfortunately, despite an increase in nutritional awareness, for many children and teens the most popular snacks continue to be rich in fat (as well as calories, salt and sugar).

Potato chips, a particular favorite of children and teens, illustrate the problem. Over half their calories are from fat. Think of it this way: if your child eats eight ounces of chips, it's the same as eating a baked potato drenched in 12 to 20 teaspoons of oil.

A one-cup serving of the following snacks, just a handful or two during a television program, would surely strain any fat guideline.

Item	Calories	Fat-Grams
Cheese combos	510	21
Cheese puffs/twists	235	15
Chex mix	180	7
Corn chips	230	14
Corn nuts	375	12
Doo-Dads	260	11
Potato chips	150	10
Potato sticks	190	12
Pork rinds	115	7
Tortilla chips	180	9

It's even worse for peanuts. The small bags offered on airplanes have 9 to 10 grams of fat, and we usually eat two bags! A jelly-filled Dunkin' Donut has 22 grams of fat. A large Snickers bar has 24 grams of fat. Even Trail Mix has 24 grams of fat (and 570 calories) per cup! And the list goes on and on.

Experts advise that the first thing parents should do is clean out the cupboard and refrigerator. Get rid of the cookies, chips, ice cream and other tempting high-fat, empty-calorie munchies. It's much easier to avoid such snacks than to resist them. Be careful not to completely forbid any food, because forbidden foods become even more desirable.

Restock the cupboard and refrigerator with healthier, nutrient-packed snacks. Don't just think of traditional snacks. A cup of vegetable soup or a bowl of cereal makes for a nutritious after-school snack. Registered dietitian Bev Utt suggests using the following chart to pick snacks for your kids.

Carbo-Rich Snacks	Calcium-Rich Snacks	Protein-Rich Snacks	Once-in-a-While Snacks
Low-fat popcorn	Frozen yogurt	Turkey jerky	Sponge
Chex mix	Vanilla pudding	Bean dip on	cake
Whole-grain	Light ice cream	tortilla chips	Fruit
crackers	Tapioca	Lean meat	roll-ups
Cracker sandwiches	Yogurt and	roll-ups	Cookies
(low-fat cheese,	fresh fruit	Peanut butter	Cupcakes
fruit spread)	Hot chocolate	on: veggies,	
Fruit dipped in fat-	made w/ fat-free	crackers,	
free caramel	or light (1%)	apples,	
Frozen bananas,	milk	English	
grapes, berries,	Flavored low-fat	muffins,	
mango	milks (chocolate,	bagels,	
Veggies and dip	strawberry)	cracker	
(low-fat yogurt,	Veggies w/ fat-free	bread	
black bean, salsa)	cream cheese	Sliced turkey	
Fruit juice popsicles	English muffin	breast	
Cereal by the handful	w/ low-fat or		
Rice pudding	fat-free cheese		
Twice-baked potatoes			
Raisins			
Caramel-covered			
rice cakes			
Cracker Jacks			
Pretzels			
Dried fruits			

Kids are natural grazers, so they tend to eat what's handy. If the cupboards are bare, your child will be more likely to hit the local candy store. "Kids are inundated with television and other advertisements for unhealthy things," says Tammy Baker, R.D. "Making nutritious foods readily available, though, can combat some of that propaganda. Put out a bowl of fruit instead of a jar full of cookies. Popcorn, pretzels and fruit juice are nutritious options to high-fat foods such as potato chips, ice cream and cookies. Accessibility is a key. It's important not just to have the right snack, but to have it in the right location, which for younger children often means in an easy-to-reach cupboard or a low refrigerator shelf."

You need to plan ahead for snacks that fit into your family's nutritional scheme. Replace high-fat snacks with lower-fat alternatives, and save the high-fat stuff for special occasions.

MAKE FRUITS AND VEGETABLES THE PREMIUM SNACKS

F ruits and vegetables are great to snack on. They can be sweet, tart, chewy or crunchy, and can keep your jaws occupied. Fresh fruits are a real deal. Their sugar content provides a satisfying taste without excessive fat or calories. One hundred calories will get you any of the following:

> an apple * 5 apricots * a banana * half a cantaloupe * 20 cherries * one grapefruit * 29 grapes * 1 to 2 oranges * a nectarine * 2 peaches * a pear * 3 plums * a cup of raspberries * 2 cups of strawberries * 2 to 3 tangerines * 10 ounces of watermelon * ⅕ of a honeydew melon

Keep fresh fruits on hand and accessible to children and teens. Try frozen treats, such as frozen grapes and bananas, for a refreshing alternative to fatty snacks. Dried fruits are higher in calories but provide a valuable source of fiber and nutrients.

Vegetables are the same. Cucumbers, radishes, celery, zucchini, red and green peppers, cauliflower, mushrooms and broccoli—all are under 10 calories per ounce.

Children should be encouraged to snack before they get too ravenous and eat anything in sight. Planning is often the key. Asked if they're hungry when they come home from school, most kids will say yes. Don't make the mistake of then asking, "What would you like?" It may be a chocolate bar or a doughnut. Then your fruit and vegetable offerings may pale by comparison.

In our house, we learned to have cut-up fruit and vegetables ready when our children walked through the door after school. The kids would attack them immediately, while talking about their day. There were no requests for candy and cookies because they were occupied with food that was at hand.

MAKE SMARTER CHOICES

Make nutrient-packed snacks part of your child's eating plan. However, when you do choose to eat processed snacks, be sure to read labels for calorie, fat and sodium information. Then make the smartest choices. Many low-fat alternatives to favorite high-fat snacks now exist. Be careful of volume. Kids who eat too many fat-free cookies will consume a lot of calories. Below are some suggestions for favorite snacks of children and teens. (Ice cream and frozen yogurt were covered in an earlier chapter.)

CANDY

By its nature, most candy is rich in calories, fat and sugar. A regular-size Baby Ruth, for instance, gets its 300 calories from 3 teaspoons of fat and 10 teaspoons of sugar. A 3 Musketeers bar has 1.75 teaspoons of fat and 11.5 teaspoons of sugar in its 260 calories.

The best bet is to severely limit candy. But this is difficult to do because children are born with a preference for the taste of sugar, the proverbial "sweet tooth," and they will tend to choose sugary items over other foods if given the opportunity.

So, what do you do when your child lobbies for a

chocolate bar? Try sweet and smooth snacks like fruit sorbet, frozen bananas or grapes, fruit-flavored gelatin, nonfat yogurt, nonfat frozen yogurt, ice milk, angel food cake, sherbet, sorbets, tapioca, juice and low-fat applesauce. Many of these snacks will satisfy your child's "sweet tooth" without an overdose of fat and calories.

If nothing but a chocolate bar will do, look to reduce the size. You can do this by using mini-bars, called "fun-size." Some mini-bar brands include Almond Joy, Butterfingers, Hershey's Milk Chocolate, Milky Way, Mounds, Nestle Crunch, Reese's Peanut Butter Cup, Snickers and 3 Musketeers. They can satisfy your child's craving with far less fat and calories than found in a regular-size bar. The trick, of course, is not to eat 5 or 10 mini-bars.

One technique we used is our family was to cut a favorite candy bar (regular size) into bite-size pieces and keep them in the freezer. Then we'd dole them out one piece at a time. It takes several minutes to thaw a piece in your mouth. By that time, the kids had satisfied their "sweet tooth."

Don't be fooled by many of the so-called "energy bars." While energy bars do provide energy or, more precisely, calories, many have the same profiles as candy bars. A 2.5-ounce Hardbody bar, for example, racks up 300 calories and 10 grams of fat, making it more or less the nutritional equivalent of a Milky Way bar. A 1.75-ounce Hoffman's Energy Bar is as high in fat (14 grams) as a Snickers bar.

CHIPS

With 8 to 10 grams of fat per ounce, traditional potato, taco and tortilla chips are among the fattest of snacks. But there's no shortage of new and improved chips on supermarket shelves, many of which have been baked or microwaved, not fried. Guiltless Gourmet Nacho Chips, for instance, have just one gram of fat per ounce. Check out the labels. Make sure the serving size is realistic (one ounce is the standard). And remember to avoid chips made with hydrogenated oil, which can elevate your child's cholesterol.

Be aware that "lite" varieties do not always deliver a substantial cut in fat. One ounce of Ruffles Light Potato Chips has 6 grams of fat—3 grams less than the same amount of Ruffles Original Potato Chips. So, if you "can't eat just one" (ounce, that is), keep in mind that fat and calories add up quickly, even for "lite" chips.

The taste test is critical. As is the case with low-fat cheese, you and your child may have to sample a number of different brands before finding a chip that balances low fat with good flavor. Some low-fat brands to consider include:

Item	Calories	Grams of Fat	% Calories from Fat
Baked Lay's Low Fat Original Potato Chips	110	1.5	12%
Baked Lay's Low Fat Bar BQ Potato Chips	110	1.5	12
Baked Tostitos	110	1	8
Baked Tostitos Cool Ranch	120	3	23
Bearitos Baked Harvest Snackers	120	1.5	11
Boston's 40% Less Fat Potato Chips	130	6	42
Boston's No Oil Tortilla Chips	120	1	8
Grande Baked Low Fat Corn Chips	120	1.5	11
Guiltless Gourmet Chili & Lime Tortilla Chips	110	1.5	12
Guiltless Gourmet Nacho Chips	110	1	8
Louise's Fat-Free Potato Chips, Original	110	0	0
Louise's Fat-Free Potato Chips, Maui Onion	110	0	0

Item	Calories	Grams of Fat	% Calories from Fat
Padrino's Low-Fat Tortilla Chips	110	1	8%
Pacific Grain No Fries Ranch-O's Snacks	110	2	16
Pop Secret Pop Chips, Butter	120	3	23
Pop Secret Pop Chips, Cheddar	120	3	23
Pop Secret Pop Chips, Sour Cream & Onion	120	3.5	26
Snack Appeal Sour Cream & Onion Potato Crisps	110	1.5	12

COOKIES

If your child likes cookies and baked goods, you can choose from a wide range of "fat-free" and reduced-fat versions. New brands of cookies, cupcakes and other baked goods are being introduced every day, so be sure to look carefully when you're at the supermarket. And, of course, always read the food label.

The table below shows how low-fat and fat-free cookies stack up to their standard counterparts.

Type (1 oz. unless otherwise noted)	Calories	Grams of Fat	% Calories from Fat
Standard Cookies			
Chocolate chip (2)	130	6	41%
Fig bar (2)	106	2	17
Cream-filled sandwich	140	6	39
Ginger snap (4)	120	2	15
Oatmeal raisin (2)	120	4	30
Low-Fat Cookies			
Archway, Cinnamon Honey Gems (3)	100	.5	5%

Type (1 oz. unless otherwise noted)	Calories	Grams of Fat	% Calories from Fat
Bakery Wagon Iced Molasses (1)	90	1.5	15%
Bakery Wagon Soft Iced Oatmeal (1)	100	1.5	14
Keebler Honey Graham Selects (9)	120	1.5	11
Pepperidge Farm Wholesome Choice Oatmeal Raisin (1, or ½ oz.)	60	1	15
Raspberry Tart (1, or ½ oz.)	60	1	15
SnackWell's Chocolate Sandwich (1)	110	2.5	20
Weight Watchers Fruit-Filled Apple (1)	80	1	11
Fat-Free Cookies			
Entenmann's Chocolate Brownies (2, or ¾ oz.)	80	0	0%
Mother's Fat Free Fig Bars (1)	70	0	0
Nabisco Fat-Free Fig Newton's (1)	70	0	0
Health Valley Fat-Free Raisin Oatmeal (3)	80	0	0
Pepperidge Farm Chocolate Fudge Brownie (1)	120	0	0
SnackWell's Devil's Food (1)	50	0	0
SnackWell's Double Fudge Chocolate Cakes (1)	50	0	0

Be aware that fat-free products are not calorie-free. Overeating fat-free baked goods is a good way to gain weight, so keep one eye on calories. In some instances, it may be better to have a smaller amount of the original version and be satisfied than to have an enormous amount of the fat-free type and not be satisfied.

CRACKERS

Just because crackers are flat doesn't mean they're skinny. Some, like Ritz crackers, can contain several grams of fat in a handful. Fortunately, manufactures now make a wide variety of low-fat versions. The Nabisco SnackWell's line of crackers offers fat-free Cracked Pepper Crackers and Wheat Crackers, and Reduced Fat Cheese Crackers, Classic Golden Crackers, French Onion Crackers and Salsa Cheddar Crackers.

Other lower-fat choices include graham crackers, Nabisco Reduced Fat Triscuits, Armenian cracker bread, Ak-Mak, melba toast, Wasa, Kavli flatbreads, Pogens krisprolls, Finn Crisp, Ryvita Crisp Bread, Lavosh and RyKrisp.

DOUGHNUTS

There are no low-fat doughnuts. In fact, many doughnuts supply more calories and fat than many frozen dinners. A glazed chocolate ring at Dunkin' Donuts has 21 grams of fat, while their Almond Croissant contains 27 grams. Try to avoid doughnuts, period. Bagels are often a good alternative.

MUFFINS

It is often assumed that a muffin is a better choice than a doughnut or Danish pastry. But muffins can be deceptively high in fat. Many derive over half their calories from fat, and most are low in fiber.

If you buy national brands, be sure to read the label for serving size, calories and fat. The selection of truly low-fat and nonfat muffins from national companies has been growing. The following chart gives several examples.

Item	Calories	Grams of Fat	% Calories from Fat
Au Bon Pain Cinnamon			
Cranapple (4.5 oz.)	280	3	10%
Triple Berry (4 oz.)	270	3	10
Dunkin' Donuts			
Banana (3.4 oz.)	240	1.5	5
Blueberry (3.4 oz.)	220	1.5	6
Entenmann's Fat Free			
Blueberry (2 oz.)	120	0	0
McDonald's Apple Bran (2.8 oz.)	180	5	3

If you're buying a locally baked muffin without a nutrition label, look at the ingredients list. If oil, shortening, cream cheese, chocolate, nuts or other fatty items rank high on the ingredients list, you can assume it has a lot of fat and calories.

POPCORN

Popcorn is as American as apple pie—and can be a whole lot leaner. A four-cup serving (one ounce) of plain air-popped popcorn has only one gram of fat. For a richer taste, use one teaspoon of oil to pop one-half cup of kernels; this will add much more flavor for very little fat. If you buy microwave popcorn, choose one of the "lite" versions—such as Orville Redenbacher's Low Fat Smart Popcorn, Jolly Time Light or Pop Secret 94% Fat Free—and be sure to check the label.

Watch out for ready-to-eat popcorn, such as that found in movie theaters. It's generally high in fat, about 5 to 7 grams per cup. A study by the Center for Science in the Public Interest found that a medium-size bucket of movie popcorn could contain 43 grams of fat and almost 650 calories. Hit it with "butter" topping, and it climbs to 71 grams of fat and 910 calories. While total fat itself is enough to condemn movie popcorn, a greater problem is that most of the fat used is saturated. This is because many theaters pop their corn in coconut oil and use hydrogenated oils in their "butter" topping. Compare the following:

Item	Grams of Saturated Fat
Bacon, eggs, toast with butter	11
Big Mac and fries	14
Steak, baked potato with sour cream, salad with dressing, roll and butter	20
Movie popcorn, "buttered," medium size (11 cups)	41

PRETZELS

Pretzels are the fastest-growing snack food in the United States. They are much lower in fat than chips because they're baked, not fried. Few have more than a gram of fat in a one-ounce serving. Fat-free choices include:

Rokeach Dutch
Brachmann Hard
Eagle Sourdough Hard
   Bavarian
Michael Season's Organic
   Minis

Snyder's of Hanover Old
   Fashioned
Snyder's of Hanover Sour
   Mister Salty Twists

Brands that contain one gram of fat or less per ounce include:

Mr. Salty Butter Flavored
Mr. Salty Dutch
Reisman Mini
Reisman Thins
Snyder's of Hanover
   Fat Free Hard

Eagle Plain
Rold Gold Sticks
Rold Gold Twists
Quinlan Thins

Some brands are quite high in sodium, so be sure to check the label.

CHAPTER 18

7: REFOCUS YOUR MEALS

Many of the suggestions listed in the preceding chapters will help you to select more nutritious fast food, smarter snacks and such. But these are one-by-one actions. The most crucial aspect of creating long-term healthier food habits for your child and you is refocusing meals to create better nutritional balance. Specifically, this means decreasing the position of animal foods in the meal in favor of grains, beans, fruits and vegetables.

DECREASE ANIMAL FOODS

Since World War II, the U.S. diet has been based on animal foods, particularly red meat. Our philosophy of eating has been that animal foods should occupy center stage and everything else is a bit player. Meals have centered on large portions of meat (although in the past few years more health-conscious Americans have chosen poultry and seafood). Typically, we've enjoyed a small salad, a moderate serving of potatoes, and a giant steak or slab of roast beef. Noticeably missing have been fruits, vegetables, starchy carbohydrates, grains, beans, peas and other legumes. Today we know that this "meat-and-potatoes" style of eating is too rich in fat and calories and therefore should be modified.

Note that I've chosen the word "modified," not "eliminated." There is room for red meat and other animal foods on a healthy diet. But in light of our national weight and cholesterol problems, we need to lighten up our meals by shifting priorities. This simply means giving more room in a meal to vegetables, legumes, starches and fruit, with meat and other animal foods playing more of a supporting role. Instead of the meal described above, a refocused meal would look more like this: a large salad, rice or potatoes, two other vegetables, half a chicken breast, and fruit for dessert. (Obviously, smaller children would have smaller portions.) This perspective allows us to enjoy tasty food and family favorites—including red meat—to satisfaction yet consume valuable fiber and nutrients and minimize fat intake.

RED MEAT

Red meat can fit into a healthy diet for you and your children if you do four things. First, don't serve red meat as frequently. In many American homes, it's still bacon for breakfast, a bologna sandwich for lunch, and meat loaf for dinner. That's simply too much fat (and saturated fat) for most kids. On days that you eat red meat, have it at just one meal. This is where meal planning can help. And go for the best. Why use up your fat budget on a greasy burger when you and your family could enjoy roasted pork tenderloin?

Look for opportunities to go meatless with poultry, fish, beans, grains and vegetables. There are excellent recipes in this book to help you do this. Your family doesn't have to give up meat, but nor does meat have to be eaten on a daily basis.

Second, make the portions reasonable. It's easy to overeat red meat if it's the center of the meal. But when you increase other foods, a three- or four-ounce serving of lean red meat will satisfy. Since this amount of cooked lean meat often contains fewer than 200 calories, it will not upset most people's fat guidelines. The recommended serving size for red meat is 3.5 ounces—about the size of a deck of cards, an audio cassette or a woman's palm.

One way to moderate serving size is to "stretch" meat in chili, casseroles and stir-fries. You can also substitute grains and beans for part of the meat in many recipes. In our home, we borrowed a page from Asian cooks who use red meat as a condiment. In place of our traditional four steaks for four people, we now thinly slice one steak and cook it with crisp vegetables in a stir-fry to feed four people. This is also a great way to increase veggies on the menu.

Third, select lower-fat meats. Avoid fatty cuts like beef short ribs or pork spareribs, which can contain 20 to 30 grams of fat per 3.5-ounce serving. Instead, look for leaner cuts and trim them of all excess fat. Always check for marbling, the fat that cannot be trimmed. For beef, choose "Select" grade over "Choice" and "Prime." Cuts that are labeled "round" or "loin" are the leanest. Some of the best lower-fat choices include tenderloin, London broil, flank steak, club steak, and round, eye of round and sirloin tip roasts. According to the Beef Council, the "skinniest six" include:

Cut of Beef (3.5 oz.)	Calories	Grams of Fat	% Calories from Fat
Top round, broiled	179	4.9	25%
Eye of round, roasted	166	4.9	27
Round tip, roasted	183	6.9	34
Top sirloin, broiled	192	7.1	33
Top loin, broiled	205	9.3	41
Tenderloin, broiled	208	9.9	43

For pork, lamb and veal, the leanest cuts are labeled "loin" or "leg." Some smarter choices include extra-lean canned ham, pork tenderloin, Canadian bacon, pork center loin, fresh ham, lamb loin chop, lamb leg, veal leg and veal cutlet. Also, most cuts of game such as buffalo, elk and deer are lower in fat than either beef or chicken.

Always be careful to read labels on frozen meals. Meat entrées are typically among the fattest of the prepared meals, since many come smothered in fatty sauces or surrounded by other high-fat foods. Use your child's fat guide as a basis for comparison. Another good rule is "no more than 3 grams of fat per 100 calories." Some smart choices include Healthy Choice Beef Pepper Steak Dinner, Stouffer's Lean Cuisine Salisbury Steak, The Budget Gourmet Light and Healthy Oriental Beef, and Weight Watchers Swedish Meatballs. One brand's Salisbury Steak in Gravy with Macaroni and Cheese contains over 400 calories and 32 grams of fat.

And finally, use low-fat cooking methods—roasting, broiling, grilling, baking and stewing. These methods allow fat to drip off, whereas frying seals fat in. In general, the longer meat cooks, the more fat it loses, so medium and well-done are preferable to rare.

POULTRY

Poultry offers a great opportunity for nutritious, delicious low-fat meals. An added benefit is that virtually all kids like chicken. That's one of the reasons we've included so many quick-to-fix menus that feature chicken in the recipe section.

A simple rule will lead you to the leanest cuts of chicken and turkey: choose a skinless white breast. Unlike red meat, poultry is not marbled with fat. Instead, fat is concentrated just beneath the skin. So, if you remove the skin before cooking, you remove most of the fat. If you cook poultry with the skin on, be sure to remove it before serving your child. White (light) meat contains less fat than dark meat.

Poultry Meat (3.5 oz., roasted)	Calories	Grams of Fat	% Calories from Fat
Chicken			
Light meat, skinless	163	3.5	19%
Light meat, w/ skin	194	7.7	36
Dark meat, skinless	207	10.8	47
Dark meat, w/ skin	245	15.4	57
Turkey			
Light meat, skinless	155	3.1	18
Light meat, w/ skin	220	10.1	41
Dark meat, skinless	185	7.1	36
Dark meat, w/ skin	219	11.4	47

Cooking methods count. Frying a chicken breast in oil or smothering it in fatty gravy will offset any low-fat benefit. Use cooking methods that allow fat to drip off, such as roasting, broiling, barbecuing, baking, steaming and stewing. If you do fry, use a nonstick pan with cooking sprays or a small amount of oil.

Be sure to read labels on processed poultry products like hot dogs and bacon. Many contain dark meat, skin and fat as well as white meat and are high in fat. One of the worst offenders is ground turkey. Some brands contain 13 to 16 grams of fat in a four-ounce serving. Be sure the label reads "ground turkey breast." It has just 3 to 4 grams of fat per serving.

Look for frozen meals with no more than 3 grams of fat per 100 calories, such as Healthy Choice's Chicken Dijon and Teriyaki Chicken Dinners, Le Menu Herb Roasted Chicken, Stouffer's Lean Cuisine Honey Mustard Chicken Breast and Weight Watchers Smart Ones Chicken Mirabella.

And finally, pay attention to portion size. "People have gotten the message to eat less fat," says Dr. Walter Willett of the Harvard University School of Public Health. "But instead of replacing fatty animal foods with grains, beans, vegetables and fruit, as they should, they're eating more low-fat animal foods. A huge chunk of chicken has replaced the 12-ounce steak in our culinary repertoire. This may seem sensible, but only if the steak is replaced by a moderate amount of chicken—say, three or four ounces—surrounded by rice, pasta, vegetables and other foods rich in complex carbohydrates and fiber."

SEAFOOD

"Fish is very hard to beat as a food item," says heart expert Dr. William Castelli. "Fish oil tends to reduce the risk of heart attack, so eating seafood at least twice a week is recommended." While your child may not have a heart problem today, eating seafood more often can develop a food habit that will help to reduce cardiac risk in the future.

Since fish oil is so heart-healthy, making the leanest selection of seafood is less important than it is where red meat and poultry are concerned. Some types of fish, such as Dover sole, are low in fat. Some, such as Chinook salmon, are rich in fat. Fish with 3 grams or less of fat per 3.5-ounce serving include:

Abalone	Flounder	Ocean perch
Clams	Grouper	Oysters
Cod	Haddock	Pike
Crab (Alaskan	Halibut	Scallops
king and blue)	Lobster	Shrimp
Monkfish	Snapper	Sole (Dover)
Crayfish	Mussels	Squid

The fat content of fish is usually far less important than the cooking and preparation methods. Frying or deep-frying in oil or butter adds more than one gram of fat per ounce. Better cooking methods include grilling, baking, broiling, barbecuing, poaching and microwaving. Avoid basting with butter or margarine.

A low-fat seafood meal can be turned into a high-fat disaster with fatty condiments—butter, butter sauce, mayonnaise and tartar sauce. Better choices include fresh lemon and lime, tomato salsa, low-sodium soy sauce, flavored vinegars and oil-free dressings.

Tuna salad is a particular favorite of children. Buy water-packed tuna to save fat and calories. A four-ounce can of oil-packed tuna has 20 grams of fat; the same amount of water-packed has just one gram. Watch out for mayonnaise. Used too liberally, it can change a low-fat choice into a high-fat salad or sandwich. Better to use light or fat-free mayonnaise, a blend of fat-free yogurt and mayonnaise, and fat-free salad dressings.

Unfortunately, many parents report that it is hard to get their kids to eat seafood. This may be because of the quality of the seafood served. Always make sure the fish is extremely fresh. A "fishy," ammonia-like smell is a turnoff for kids, and it's a sure sign that the fish is past its prime. Fresh fish should have a mild, seaweedy or cucumber-like smell. You maight be surprised at how your child takes to meals with quality seafood.

Also, use firmer species such as fresh tuna and swordfish. Their texture is more like that of poultry, which your family is probably used to eating. And finally, be sure the fish is boneless. This is very important for kids of all ages, but particularly for small children.

INCREASE GRAINS, BEANS, FRUITS AND VEGETABLES

If animal foods become the bit players in a meal, what is to become the star? The answer is complex carbohydrates—beans, legumes, whole grains—and fruits and vegetables. Dietitian Joan Rupp suggests, "Instead of the traditional serving plate of ½ meat, ¼ starch and ¼ vegetable, change to ¼ meat, ¼ starch and ½ vegetable."

You can increase these foods in your child's diet in two practical ways. First, you can surround a smaller entrée of meat, poultry or fish with larger servings of pasta, rice, potatoes, fruits and vegetables. These foods are easy to eat, are bulky, and provide satisfaction. Here is a good example from a menu in this book.

Grilled Teriyaki Steak

Loaded Baked Potatoes

Stir-Fried Broccoli and Cauliflower with Red Peppers

Strawberries and Blueberries

This is a great way to balance a favorite food—steak—with fruits and vegetables that provide fiber, vitamins, minerals and other nutrients.

A second way to increase complex carbohydrates is to center some of your meals on plant foods. Recipes such as our Penne with Meat Sauce will show you how. These recipes are so tasty that your kids will be occupied with the food at hand and not miss what they're not eating.

PASTA

Pasta has developed a reputation as an important health food, and rightfully so. One cup cooked of enriched pasta (almost all varieties are enriched) provides starch, riboflavin, niacin, thiamin, about 10% of the USRDA for protein, and less than one gram of fat—all for just over 200 calories. And, perhaps of more importance to parents, kids of all ages love pasta.

Available in over 600 shapes and sizes, and almost every color of the rainbow, pasta lends itself to an assortment of meals:

- Linguine, rigatoni, penne, fettucine and, of course, spaghetti are great main dishes.

- Rotelle, fusilli, rotini and shells make terrific salads with fresh vegetables.
- Totellini and pastina make hearty soups.
- Orzo is a tasty side dish.

The type of pasta you choose is less important than what you put on it. Even the healthiest pasta will turn into a high-fat dish if drenched in Alfredo sauce (butter, cream and cheese) or served with a pound of sausage. We've found that simple sauces, such as marinara or red clam sauce, work well for kids of all ages. They're delicious yet low in fat and calories. One cup of pasta with a quarter-cup of marinara sauce and a tablespoon of grated Parmesan cheese has about 260 calories, or about the same as a cup of low-fat yogurt sweetened with fruit preserves.

We've also included kid-favorite recipes such as Spaghetti with Meatballs in the book. It is a great way to teach your child about balance. The pasta is the main dish; the meatballs are the condiment. The same is true of our recipe for Classic Lasagna, which uses a small amount of sausage for flavoring. These are good examples of how healthy food can be delicious.

A simple, low-fat sauce is easy to make, but if you're too busy to cook, consider one of the fat-free or low-fat brands of pasta sauce that are available. Be sure to check the label for sodium. Many brands are moderate, but some are sky-high. Some national brands to try include:

Pasta Sauce (½ cup)	Calories	Grams of Fat	% Calories from Fat
Classico Tomato & Basil	60	1.5	23%
Del Monte Traditional	80	1	2
Del Monte w/ Peppers & Mushrooms	70	1	13
Enrico's Fat Free Traditional	60	0	0
Enrico's Fat Free Bountiful Basil	50	0	0
Healthy Choice	50	.5	9
Hunt's Light Traditional	40	1	23

Pasta Sauce (½ cup)	Calories	Grams of Fat	% Calories from Fat
Millinina's Finest	45	0	0%
Pomodoro Fresca Fat Free			
Original	25	0	0
Pomodoro Fresca Original	40	1.5	34
Prego Extra Chunky Garden			
Combination	90	1	10
Quinn's Marinara Sauce	70	1	13
Ragu Light	50	.5	9
Tree of Life Fat Free	35	0	0

For tasty, low-fat pasta salad, use fat-free and low-fat salad dressings; for macaroni salad, be sure to choose a fat-free or light mayonnaise. And don't overlook introducing your child to Oriental noodles such as soba (buckwheat) and saifun (cellophane). These noodles are particularly good in chicken broth with vegetables and make a tasty main course.

RICE AND OTHER GRAINS

Rice is a low-fat, nutrient-rich food that makes for excellent side and main dishes. Polished white rice is the most popular in the United States. Unfortunately, the polishing process strips some protein, fiber, vitamins and minerals from the rice. Parboiled, or converted, white rice is a better choice because parboiling causes less nutrient loss. Instant and "minute" rice cook quickly but are lowest in nutritional content. The best choice is whole-grain brown rice. Not subject to processing, it retains all its nutrients.

As with pasta, rice is a food that is often adulterated by fatty add-ons like butter, butter sauce and gravy. Serve it instead as a side dish with a few drops of sodium-reduced soy sauce or as a main dish covered with beans or stir-fried chicken and vegetables.

Watch out for packaged rice dishes that contain added fat. Most rice can be prepared without the butter or oil suggested in the directions on the box. Don't be fooled into thinking that a packaged rice dish is fat-free because the Nutrition Facts list fat content as zero. Some manufacturers give nutritional information "as packaged," so that the fat called for in cooking directions is not reflected.

Look for chances to introduce your child to other grains such as barley (excellent in hearty soups and as a side dish), bulgur (a tasty alternative to rice) and couscous (the main ingredient in tabbouleh, a delicious salad). Don't overlook corn. Your child will love cornmeal, polenta (Italian cornmeal) and corn bread.

FRUITS AND VEGETABLES

The importance of fruits and vegetables in the diet of your child cannot be overstated. That is why health professionals recommend five servings of fruits and vegetables be eaten daily. These foods are important because they're low in calories and high in bulk, thus aiding weight control by creating a feeling of satisfaction before overeating occurs.

In addition, many fruits and vegetables provide protection from heart disease and cancer. Especially important are those that contain vitamin C (such as oranges, strawberries and broccoli) and beta-carotene (such as spinach, carrots, cantaloupe and broccoli).

Working more fruits and vegetables into your child's daily diet can be difficult. Most kids like fruit, so with some planning it's fairly easy to get two or more servings a day into the their diet—an apple with lunch, a banana on cereal in the morning, a cut-up peach as an after-school snack. One thing parents can do is to take advantage of the many fruits with natural sugars for desserts and snacks. They will satisfy your child's "sweet tooth" craving without loading up on calories. One medium apple, a banana, 30 fresh cherries and two cups of strawberries have the same calories as 15 jelly beans.

Vegetables are much harder to include in the food habits of most children. Raw vegetables as an after-school snack work very well—many children who don't like cooked vegetables will eat them raw. So does serving two vegetables at dinner. If you must "zip them up," do so without butter, margarine, bacon fat or melted cheese. Instead, try imitation butter sprinkles, flavored vinegars and a sprinkle of grated cheese. Look for ways to add veggies to foods your child already likes, such as adding pureed vegetables to soup, adding finely chopped vegetables to casseroles, spaghetti sauce and omelets, and using grated carrots in muffins.

An easy way to incorporate more vegetables and fruits is to use the menu suggestions and recipes in this book. Most of the menus are quick to fix, and all are nutritionally balanced. Here is an example:

Chicken and Bean Burritos

Long-Grain Basmati Rice

Corn on the Cob

Tropical Fruits

This is a menu your child will love, yet it's designed to make it simpler for parents to include fruits and vegetables at most meals.

POTATOES

Potatoes provide high nutritional value at a low-calorie cost. A medium-size potato with only 90 to 110 calories is bursting with vitamins, minerals and high-quality protein. Again, added fat can be a problem. How you cook potatoes, and what you put on them, determines whether they're a low-fat or high-fat food.

Most kids love potatoes. Figure out how to modify the potatoes that your child already likes, without altering taste.

■ If your child likes baked potatoes, skip the fatty add-ons like butter, margarine, sour cream, bacon bits and cheese. Instead, use toppings like fat-free sour cream, imitation-butter sprinkles, nonfat yogurt, salsa and herbs.

■ If your child likes mashed potatoes and gravy, use a defatted gravy. A number of brands are available commercially. Or you can make your own by refrigerating homemade gravy for a few hours so that fat can congeal and be skimmed off.

■ And if your child likes French fries (and what child doesn't?), a good alternative is to coat potatoes lightly with an oil-based cooking spray, then "fry" by cooking in the oven. (See the Cookbook section.)

BREADS

Breads can be high in fiber, low in calories and nutritious—or just the opposite. The best choice for your child is whole-grain bread made from stone-ground flour. The next-best choice is 100% whole-wheat or other whole-grain bread such as rye or pumpernickel. These breads provide much better fiber and nutrients than white bread. It's important to read the label or you won't know what's in the bread. Look for the terms "whole wheat," "whole grain" and "stone ground."

Here are some to try:

100% whole-wheat bread * Whole-grain bread * Multi-grain bread * Rye bread (dark) * Whole-wheat pita * Corn tortilla * Oat-bead with whole wheat * Cracked-wheat bread * Stone-ground grain bread * Whole-wheat bagels * Whole-grain English muffins * Fat-free or reduced-fat whole-wheat flour tortilla

BEANS, PEAS AND LEGUMES

Beans, peas and legumes are great sources of fiber, protein, complex carbohydrates, B vitamins, iron, potassium, zinc and magnesium, and yet they're low in fat and sodium. In addition, the soluble fiber contained in many of these foods have been found to reduce cholesterol. A drawback in the past was that it took so long to prepare dried beans. Now, however, canned beans are available in supermarkets.

Look to lighten up the foods that your child likes and eats. Switch from pork and beans to vegetarian baked beans. Serve low-fat versions of favorite dishes such as bean chili, bean soup and refried beans. This is an easy way to cut fat.

Another good way to include beans, peas and legumes in your child's diet is to mix them with other foods. Examples are black beans and rice, white bean and tuna salad, and pasta and beans. Or add lentils, split peas or black beans to heart soups and stews. Use pinto beans instead of ground beef in tacos and burritos. And add navy, kidney and garbanzo beans to salads.

CHAPTER 19

A LAST WORD

Business guru Tom Peters tells us that instead of researching and researching, we might be better off to focus on the goal, get off the mark and adapt as we get new information and experience. I think he's right.

Not all the information is in on children and teens, but it's becoming clearer all the time that the lifestyle of your child, particularly physical activity and eating habits, has a tremendous influence on present and future health. And, to the point made early in the book, it may dictate present and future weight as well.

There is still much to be learned about children, lifestyle habits and health. But sufficient information does exist to create two well-accepted goals for parents.

The first goal is, quite simply, *to help your child become physically active*. This is more easily done if parents are physically active themselves. You need not be a marathoner, but walking for exercise on a regular basis sends a clear message to your child that physical activity is important. Your role modeling will help to offset the unhealthy messages delivered by our society to vegetate in front of the television and pig out on high-fat junk food.

Parents need to encourage and support the physical activities of their child. With a young child, it may be as simple as spending time outdoors on a daily basis. That's all it takes to get young children to move. For older kids, it may be driving them to a team practice, helping them develop a skill, or washing cars to raise funds for the team. No one else cares about your child as much as you do. If you don't make physical activity a priority, who else will?

The second goal is *to help your child establish balanced, low-fat eating habits*. Again, it starts with you. If you skip breakfast, regularly eat cheeseburgers for lunch, overeat at dinner and constantly talk about dieting, what kind of example are you setting for your child? Use the tips, menus and recipes to lighten up eating habits for your whole family.

Because there are so many things that can be done to improve the way we eat, it is imperative to zero in on the basics. Don't tie yourself in a knot trying to change everything. Instead, work with the areas that will give you the biggest return. Help your child to eat a solid breakfast. Work to make low-fat dairy products the standard in your family. Make low-fat lunches a priority. And when fast food and snacks are a must, help your child make the smartest choices.

A key to success for parents is to understand that your child is more willing to accept familiar, favorite food that has been made lighter, rather than unfamiliar food. Pushing soyburgers won't go very far in most households. That's why this book includes over a month of menus based on kid-friendly foods—lasagna, macaroni and cheese, and fried chicken, to name but a few. But the recipes have been lightened up. And the menus have been balanced to include more fruits, vegetables, grains and beans.

Changing lifestyle habits is not always easy. But it is critical to the health and fitness of our children. You as a parent can be the greatest influence on your child's habits. It is my hope that this book will make it easier for you to make your influence a positive one.

COOKBOOK

COMMENTS FROM THE COOK

by Bernie Piscatella

O ne of our main goals in putting together this book was to create good-for-you recipes that also taste good. Our intent was to be practical and realistic. Real food without fuss was our catchphrase. We looked for balance between time and effort spent and quality mealtimes, between finding time to plan ahead and the context of leading very busy lives.

The guidelines from the USDA's Food Guide Pyramid shaped each recipe and menu. Our underlying theme was to maximize the use of carbohydrates (breads, pasta, rice, cereal, fruit and vegetables) while moderating protein-rich foods (meat, poultry, fish and dairy products). We minimized the use of fat.

We tried to show that no particular food or meal has to be ruled out as long as it's in balance. Higher-fat foods must be paired with low-fat foods. A serving of meat should be joined with greater amounts of vegetables and starches.

PLANNING AHEAD

Planning ahead is the key because eating healthfully requires a change in habits as well as menus. It is vitally important to spend a few minutes each week making a meal plan. Take into account the menu, the beverages, the company, preparation time and the schedule of family members. We like to use a weekly format as a guide: pasta on Monday, chicken on Tuesday, soup on Wednesday, main-meal salads on Thursday, and so on. If you plan to have French Market Soup on Wednesday, for example, cook a ham for a weekend meal and then use the leftover ham bone to make the stock. If the beans need to be soaked overnight, remember to do that on Tuesday. Being organized and planning ahead saves time in the end.

It also helps to have backup plans for meals that you know can be prepared quickly. If you remember at the office that you've forgotten to take the meat out of the freezer for dinner, your alternative could be Pasta Marinara; with preplanning, most of the ingredients (a good olive oil, a tasty brand of canned tomatoes, a package of pasta) are easy to have on hand. Served with a green salad and a loaf of French bread, it offers a simple alternative and is much more healthful than picking up fast food or cooking hot dogs.

Planning ahead could mean carrying at least two menus in your purse or briefcase so that you make good shopping choices once in the market. It will help you to stick to a plan rather than buy on a whim as often happens when you get hungry as you shop.

When planning meals, it's important to be realistic about the needs of each family member. If your daughter has soccer practice and won't be home until late, and your son has band practice, plan to serve a soup that can be made ahead and has holding power. This is a better choice than grilled steak, which tastes best just after it's been cooked. With flexible meal planning, each family member's needs can be met.

CHANGE YOUR FAVORITE RECIPE

Planning ahead may mean choosing your family's 10 to 12 favorite meals and then becoming an expert at modifying them to be more heart-healthy. Research shows that most American families prepare 12 recipes 80% of the time. You may find that these favorites satisfy and nurture your family's needs better than a meal prepared at the last minute with no plan at all.

Modifying foods that children already like is the key to changing their eating habits. Kids want familiar foods like pizza, fried chicken and spaghetti. Instead of throwing away your old recipes, analyze them for ways to reduce fat and increase carbohydrates without sacrificing taste. To modify a recipe, you first need to identify the sources of excessive fat and ask two key questions: "Why is this ingredient in the recipe?" and "How can I reduce the fat in this dish without sacrificing taste?" Many of us learned to cook from our mothers or grandmothers, or from a book. Ingredients or cooking methods were never questioned. Today, such inquiry is important.

We are advised today by nutritional experts to eat more fresh fruits and vegetables, more seafood and more complex carbohydrates in the form of rice, pasta and grains, and to consume only moderate amounts of meat, poultry and dairy products. Most of this advice is directed at getting us to eat less fat.

While no one argues with the goal, let's face it—fat tastes good. Simply omitting all high-fat foods can make your meals bland and boring. The chances of "sticking with it" are slim indeed. A better perspective is "How can I reduce the fat in this dish without sacrificing taste?" After all, taste is what eating is all about.

USE LOW-FAT SUBSTITUTES

Switching to low-fat versions of the foods in your own recipes is one of the easiest modification strategies. This involves simple "one-for-one" exchanges of lower-fat foods for those higher in fat. If, for instance, your favorite chili recipe calls for hamburger, substitute extra-lean ground round or shredded chicken breast. There will be very little change in taste from the original recipe, but the fat content will plummet. Choose the leanest cuts of meat, poultry and fish, and look for the lowest-fat dairy products that will still satisfy your taste buds.

A second method involves more use of low-fat ingredients. For example, if your child's favorite lunch is a tuna salad sandwich, make it with "light" mayonnaise instead of the regular full-fat version. You'll get half the fat and more than enough "real" mayonnaise flavor to keep your taste buds happy.

Check the labels for products that are low in fat, then try them. If one brand of fat-free sour cream or low-fat cheese doesn't meet your taste requirements, try others. Keep looking until you find the one that works for you and your family. There's a whole new world of products available in the grocery store to help in healthy low-fat cooking and eating.

Table of Low-Fat Ingredient Substitutions

INSTEAD OF:	USE:
Dairy Products	
Sour cream	Low-fat or nonfat sour cream or yogurt
Yogurt	Low-fat or nonfat yogurt
Whipping cream	Pressurized light whipped cream— used sparingly
Milk, whole or 2%	Fat-free or 1% milk
Buttermilk	1% buttermilk
Evaporated milk	Light (1%) evaporated milk
American, cheddar, Colby, Havarti, Edam, Swiss	Cheeses with 5 grams of fat or less per ounce
Mozzarella	Part-skim mozzarella; mozzarella with 5 grams of fat or less per ounce
Cottage cheese	Nonfat or 1% cottage cheese
Cream cheese	Nonfat or light processed cream cheese
Ricotta cheese	Nonfat, light or part-skim ricotta cheese

Ice cream	Low-fat, light or reduced-fat ice cream; nonfat or low-fat frozen yogurt or sherbet; sorbet; frozen fruit bars
Frozen yogurt	Reduced-fat or nonfat frozen yogurt

Fats and Oils

Butter and/or margarine	Reduced-calorie tub-style margarine made with water; whipped butter; reduced-calorie tub-style margarine made with safflower, soybean, corn, canola or peanut oil; reduced-calorie stick margarine (made with safflower oil) in baked products
Mayonnaise	Nonfat or reduced-calorie mayonnaise
Oil	Olive oil; safflower, soybean, corn, canola or peanut oil in reduced amounts

Meats and Poultry

Bacon	Canadian bacon, lean ham
Beef, veal, lamb, pork	Skinless chicken or turkey breast; lean cuts of meat trimmed of all visible fat
Ground beef	Leanest ground beef
Luncheon meats	Sliced skinless turkey or chicken breast; lean cooked Black Forest ham; lean roast beef
Poultry	Skinless breast
Turkey, self-basting	Turkey basted with fat-free broth
Tuna packed in oil	Tuna packed in water

Miscellaneous

Fudge sauce	Fat-free fudge sauce or chocolate syrup
Nuts	One-third to one-half less, toasted
Soups, canned	Reduced-fat or fat-free condensed cream soups
Soy sauce	Reduced-sodium light soy sauce

COOKING WITHOUT EXTRA FAT

How you cook is as important as *what* you cook. Look for ways to cook without added fat. A well-made heavy-gauge nonstick skillet is indispensable for stir-frying or sautéing in minimal fat. You can use one tablespoon of olive oil, for example, rather than an inch of oil to "fry" potatoes. Or cook your pancakes in a nonstick pan rather than the traditional skillet with added fat. There will be no change in taste, but the fat content will be cut substantially. Grilling fish is more flavorful (and healthful) than frying it in deep fat. If you're using ground beef, brown and drain it before adding it to your recipe. Learn to use fresh herbs and spices like fresh ginger, cilantro, curry powder, mustard and flavored vinegar to add flavor to food without the fat. Fresh herbs and the good tastes from using quality ingredients will help you to rely less on large amounts of fat to carry the taste. Change your focus to make grains, legumes, fruits and vegetables the center of your meals.

On the pages that follow, you'll find a number of recipes that have been modified. Each example provides the original recipe and a modified version. The intent is to show you how simple it is to make low-fat changes that pay off with big dividends. The goal is home-cooked meals that are delicious but won't fill your child with fat. Modifying your own recipes will help you reach that goal.

Deciding to eat more healthfully is a lifestyle change, and no lifestyle change is easily accomplished. Remember, this is a long-range plan. If you blow it on one day, don't be discouraged. Simply vow to start over again the next day. Small changes, made gradually over time, can add up to a tremendous difference. The important thing is to make steady progress. Remember that good food means good nutrition, which will help our children develop into healthy grown-ups.

CHICKEN DIVAN

Original Recipe (6 servings)

3 chicken breasts, halved
   and boned
½ cup butter
2 10-ounce packages frozen
   asparagus spears
1 10-ounce can cream of
   chicken soup
⅔ cup mayonnaise
⅓ cup evaporated milk
⅔ cup grated cheddar
   cheese
1 teaspoon lemon juice
½ teaspoon curry powder
½ cup bread crumbs
1 tablespoon butter

Modified Recipe (6 servings)

3 whole chicken breasts,
   skinned, boned and
   halved
¾ pound asparagus spears or
   2 cups broccoli florets
2 10¾-ounce cans fat-free
   (1%) cream of chicken
   soup
⅓ cup nonfat mayonnaise
⅓ cup light evaporated milk
¼ cup grated reduced-fat
   cheddar cheese
1 teaspoon lemon juice
½ teaspoon curry powder
2 tablespoons bread crumbs

Brown chicken breasts in butter. Cook asparagus according to package directions. Drain and arrange in casserole dish. Top with chicken. Combine cream of chicken soup, mayonnaise, milk, cheese, lemon juice and curry. Pour over chicken. Top with bread crumbs. Dot with 1 tablespoon butter. Bake at 350°F for 25 to 30 minutes.

Brown chicken lightly on both sides in nonstick skillet. Steam asparagus in vegetable steamer basket over boiling water for 1 minute. Arrange in 8-inch-square baking dish and top with chicken. Combine soup, mayonnaise, milk, cheese, lemon juice and curry. Pour over chicken. Sprinkle with bread crumbs. Cover lightly with aluminum foil. Bake at 350°F for 25 to 30 minutes.

Each serving approximately
630 calories, 53 g total fat, 75%
calories from fat, 126 mg cholesterol,
17 g carbohydrates, trace dietary
fiber, 27 g protein, 957 mg sodium.

Each serving approximately
264 calories, 6 g total fat, 21%
calories from fat, 86 mg cholesterol,
18 g carbohydrates, 1 g dietary fiber,
33 g protein, 755 mg sodium.

Modifications:
• Eliminate butter for sautéing by
  using nonstick skillet.
• Use skinless chicken.
• Use fat-free cream of chicken
  soup.
• Use nonfat mayonnaise.

• Use light evaporated milk.
• Use reduced-fat cheddar cheese.
• Reduce amount of bread crumbs.
• Eliminate dots of butter.

Calories saved per serving: 366
Fat saved per serving: 47 grams

CHICKEN ENCHILADAS

Original Recipe (8 servings)

2 tablespoons butter
2 whole chicken breasts,
   boned
1 small ripe tomato,
   chopped
1 onion, chopped
1 8-ounce can chopped
   green chilies
1½ cups grated cheddar
   cheese
1 cup tomato salsa
8 flour tortillas
1 8-ounce can tomato
   puree
3 cloves garlic
3 drops Tabasco sauce
½ cup sour cream

Melt butter in heavy skillet. Add chicken and sauté 10 to 15 minutes, or until chicken is cooked. Let cool, and tear into shreds.

Combine chicken, tomato, ¼ cup chopped onion, 1 tablespoon green chilies, 3 tablespoons cheese and 1 tablespoon salsa. Set aside.

Heat tortillas on nonstick baking sheet in 350°F oven for about 3 minutes on each side to soften.

Put 3 tablespoons chicken filling in center of each tortilla and roll. Arrange seam side down in shallow ovenproof baking dish. Set aside.

Place tomato puree, garlic and remaining onion in blender. Puree until smooth. Stir in remaining green chilies and Tabasco sauce. Pour over enchiladas. Bake at 375°F for 15 minutes. Sprinkle with remaining

Modified Recipe (8 servings)

4 cups reduced-fat chicken
   broth
2 whole chicken breasts,
   skinned and boned
1 small ripe tomato,
   chopped
1 onion, chopped
1 8-ounce can chopped
   green chilies
¾ cup grated reduced-fat
   cheddar cheese
1 cup tomato salsa
8 corn tortillas
1 8-ounce can tomato puree
3 cloves garlic
3 drops Tabasco sauce
½ cup nonfat sour cream

In saucepan, bring chicken broth to boil. Add chicken breasts and bring to second boil. Reduce heat to medium. Cook 20 minutes, or until chicken is done. Remove chicken, and tear into shreds. Reserve broth for later use.

Combine chicken, tomato, ¼ cup chopped onion, 1 tablespoon green chilies, 1 tablespoon cheese and 1 tablespoon salsa. Set aside.

Heat tortillas on nonstick baking sheet in 350°F oven for about 3 minutes on each side to soften.

Put 3 tablespoons chicken filling in center of each tortilla and roll. Arrange seam side down in shallow ovenproof baking dish. Set aside.

Place tomato puree, garlic and remaining onion in blender. Puree until smooth. Stir in remaining green chilies and cheese. Bake 10 minutes longer. Remove from oven. Top each enchilada with remaining salsa and dollops of sour cream.

Each serving approximately 349 calories, 17 g total fat, 45% calories from fat, 60 mg cholesterol, 30 g carbohydrates, 1 g dietary fiber, 19 g protein, 653 mg sodium.

Modifications:
• Eliminate butter for sautéing by using nonstick skillet.
• Remove skin from chicken.

Tabasco sauce. Pour over enchiladas. Bake at 375°F for 15 minutes. Sprinkle with remaining cheese. Bake 10 minutes longer. Remove from oven. Top each enchilada with remaining salsa and dollops of sour cream.

Each serving approximately 191 calories, 4 g total fat, 19% calories from fat, 31 mg cholesterol, 22 g carbohydrates, 1 g dietary fiber, 17 g protein, 568 mg sodium.

• Use reduced-fat cheddar cheese and reduce amount.
• Use nonfat sour cream.

Calories saved per serving: 158
Fat saved per serving: 13 grams

BEEF STROGANOFF

Original Recipe (8 servings)

3 tablespoons butter
¾ cup onion, finely chopped
1 clove garlic, minced
1½ pounds sirloin steak, cut into bite-size pieces
½ pound fresh mushrooms, sliced
½ teaspoon salt
⅛ teaspoon pepper
⅛ teaspoon rosemary
2 tablespoons all-purpose flour
2 cups cream of chicken soup
1 cup sour cream
1 pound bow tie pasta, cooked al dente
3 tablespoons poppy seeds
fresh parsley for garnish

Modified Recipe (8 servings)

¾ pound extra-lean ground round
¾ cup onion, finely chopped
1 clove garlic, minced
½ pound fresh mushrooms, sliced
¼ teaspoon salt
⅛ teaspoon pepper
⅛ teaspoon rosemary
1½ cups reduced-fat (1%) cream of chicken soup
1 cup nonfat sour cream
1 pound bow tie pasta, cooked al dente
2 tablespoons poppy seeds
fresh parsley for garnish

(continued on next page)

(continued from preceding page)

Melt butter in heavy skillet. Add onion and garlic, and sauté 3 to 4 minutes. Add beef and continue to cook 3 to 4 minutes. Add mushrooms. Cook 2 to 3 minutes. Sprinkle with salt, pepper, rosemary and flour. Stir in soup. Simmer, uncovered, for 5 minutes. Stir in sour cream. Heat, but do not boil.

Arrange pasta around edges of large platter. Spoon sauce into center. Sprinkle pasta with poppy seeds. Garnish with fresh parsley.

Each serving approximately 604 calories, 30 g total fat, 45% calories from fat, 89 mg cholesterol, 53 g carbohydrates, 2 g dietary fiber, 29 g protein, 734 mg sodium.

Sauté ground round, onion and garlic in nonstick skillet. Drain off any excess fat.

Add mushrooms. Cook 3 to 5 minutes. Stir in salt, pepper and rosemary. Simmer, uncovered, for 10 minutes. Add soup, and heat. Stir in sour cream. Heat, but do not boil.

Arrange pasta around edges of large platter. Spoon sauce into center. Sprinkle pasta with poppy seeds. Garnish with fresh parsley.

Each serving approximately 331 calories, 6 g total fat, 15% calories from fat, 30 mg cholesterol, 51 g carbohydrates, 2 g dietary fiber, 18 g protein, 288 mg sodium.

Modifications:

- Eliminate butter for sautéing by using nonstick skillet.
- Use low-fat cream of chicken soup.

- Use nonfat sour cream.
- Reduce fat in meat by changing cut.

Calories saved per serving: 273
Fat saved per serving: 24 grams

LUNCH-BOX SUGGESTIONS

Kindergarten through high school means lots of meals for the lunch box. Since you have to make lunches time and again, you might as well make them fun. Over the years, I've learned that if you ask kids what they want for lunch, they'll usually say they don't know. But there are ways to get them involved. I think it helps kids to see things. Try posting a list on the refrigerator once a week with lunch meat suggestions and types of bread, spreads and greens. Also include snacks, beverages and fruits. Have your kids circle their three favorites in each category—just like a room-service menu. Below are some guidelines and suggestions for specific items on the lunch-box list.

When selecting lunch meats, always carefully read the labels or ask the delicatessen server which brands are the lowest in fat. There is a wide range. Boar's Head and Healthy Choice, for instance, make relatively low-fat cuts of smoked turkey, chicken breast and Black Forest ham.

I try to use store-bought lunch meats only once or twice a week. For Saturday or Sunday dinner, I prepare a homemade entrée of Roasted Herbed Chicken Breast, Roasted Turkey with Bread Stuffing, Spicy Barbecued Chicken, Roasted Chicken with Garlic, Old-Fashioned Meat Loaf (see recipes), roast beef tenderloin or eye of round. Then I use the leftovers for lunch-box sandwiches the rest of the week.

When preparing sandwiches, it's a good idea to include a variety of breads—rye, French, sour dough, Italian, whole wheat and multi-grain. Alternate with baguettes, pretzel rolls, focaccia, pizza bread, lefse (Scandinavian flat bread), different types of rolls, a variety of bagels, and even crackers.

Try to keep butter, margarine and mayonnaise to a minimum. Some brands of light or fat-free mayonnaise are better than others. I like Best Foods or Hellmann's light mayonnaise. Try several brands until you find one you like. To cut fat in a sandwich, use nonfat cream cheese or put a light smear of margarine or mayonnaise on one slice of bread and mustard on the other. Better yet, put mustard on both slices. Try flavored mustards for extra zip. The following chart illustrates the point.

Spread (1 tbsp.)	Calories	Fat-Grams
Regular mayonnaise	100	11
Light or calorie-reduced mayonnaise	40–50	4–5
Fat-free mayonnaise	10–20	less than 5
Regular butter or margarine	100	11
Reduced-fat butter or margarine	50	5
Fat-free butter or margarine	10	0
Mustard	15	0
Nonfat cream cheese	13	0

For added nutrients, try substituting young baby spinach for lettuce or including it in addition to lettuce. We've come to like it even better than lettuce. And remember to pack the tomatoes separately to keep sandwiches from getting soggy.

Most days a simple sandwich, milk and fresh fruit make a great lunch, but once or twice a week try to include a homemade treat such as Black Bottom Cupcakes, Chewy Molasses Cookies, Peanut Butter Cookies or Angel Food Cake with Seven-Minute Icing (see recipes).

Examples of store-bought treats that work for the lunch box include baked (not fried) tortilla chips with salsa or Black Bean Dip, baked (not fried) potato chips with Sour Cream Dip, pretzels, popcorn, Chex mix, all varieties of rice cakes, licorice, peppermint candy, lemon drops, kids' fortune cookies. See our healthy-snack section for many more suggestions.

For special days like Valentine's Day, include little balls of chocolate, cinnamon candies, gummy bears or whatever is festive for the season. Prepare a fun fruit treat by filling a small container with fat-free caramel topping and packing some apple slices for dipping, or send along some Tropical Fruit Salad or Hawaiian Fruit Salad with our Raspberry Sauce (see recipes).

Having cookies/desserts at lunch rather than dinner or bedtime gives the kids a chance to burn the fat and calories off during the day.

Two or three times a week include cut-up celery and carrots and some vegetable dip. Don't include them every day or your children may tire of them. Having a chance to eat veggies at lunch helps to ensure they get the recommended servings for the day.

Instead of a sandwich or in addition to a sandwich, include a thermos of boiling water and a container of their favorite Cup of Noodle Soup or fill their thermos with leftover homemade soup.

Include fun drinks like lemonade, sparkling fruit juices, blackberry juices, and seltzers. Freeze cartons of juice to pack with their lunch. (If the juice is fresh, be sure it's pasteurized.) The frozen juice is slushy by lunch and helps to keep the lunch cold. Kids like bottled waters, and they're a benefit because they encourage kids to drink water.

Once in a while, tuck a special note in the lunch bag telling about a surprise after-school snack such as Pain au Chocolat (see recipe) and have the ingredients waiting when they get home.

AFTER-SCHOOL SNACKS

Potato chips, cookies, cakes and ice cream are "empty-calorie" snacks. Try to make a shift toward nutrient-packed snacks that include fruits, vegetables and whole grains. Eating five servings a day of fruits and vegetables becomes a lot more realistic if in addition to serving them at breakfast, lunch and dinner you figure out how to include them in snacks as well.

The secret is to have favorite fruits and vegetables cut up and ready when the kids get home from school. If my children ask "What is there to eat?" and I say "How about an apple or some celery," their reply is a big "YUK!" On the other hand, if they see a plate of sliced apples or pears, or heaping bowls of grapes, strawberries or raspberries, or a tray of vegetables with salsa or healthy dips, they unconsciously start munching while telling about their day. And if I'm not there when they get home and they open the refrigerator and see these things all cut up and ready to eat, they're apt to eat them because it's convenient. Before they realize it, they've eaten a lot of fruit and/or vegetables—and they're no longer hungry and looking for junk food.

The key is planning. If you expect your family to eat healthfully, you have to plan for healthy snacks. Some of our favorite heart-healthy snacks are listed below.

Nonfat pretzels
Cracker Jacks
Baked (not fried) tortilla chips with tomato salsa
    or our Black Bean Dip, baked (not fried) potato
    chips with our Sour Cream Dip

SOUPS—such as Progresso's chicken noodle,
    chicken with rice, chicken barley, rice and
    bean, black bean, split pea, lentil, tomato and
    rice, and vegetable. Many brands, such as
    Progresso and Campbell's, Health Valley
    and Healthy Choice, offer low-fat and low-
    sodium choices.

BREAKFAST CEREALS—such as Cheerios,
    Rice Krispies, Raisin Bran, Special K, Wheaties,
    low-fat granola. Many brands offer cereals that
    are low in fat and reasonably low in sugar.
    Other breakfast foods, such as pancakes, French
    toast and crêpes, will also work well as snacks.

SANDWICHES—see the Lunch-Box section (page 287).

BEVERAGES—Homemade lemonade, lemon-limeade or lemon spritzer, fresh orange juice, apple juice, apple cider, grape juice, pineapple juice, seltzers, mineral water.

VEGETABLES—Cut-up celery, carrots, radishes, cucumbers, zucchini dipped in our Black Bean Dip, White Bean and Garlic Dip, Sour Cream Dip (see recipes) or tomato salsa; celery stuffed with non-hydrogenated peanut butter or fat-free cream cheese.

FRUITS—Apples, apricots, cantaloupe, water-melon, honeydew, grapes, cherries, peaches, plums, tangerines, bananas, satsumas, pears, strawberries, blackberries, raspberries; frozen grapes, watermelon or berries; apples with low-fat or nonfat cheese or apples with non-hydro-genated peanut butter; raisins.

MUNCHIES—English muffin with melted low-fat or nonfat cheese or with peanut butter, toasted bagel with peanut butter, crumpets with jam, jelly or apple butter, cracker bread, Scandinavian flat breads, rye crisp, pocket bread, rice cakes (the caramel ones are great!), popped corn cakes, popcorn.

NOW AND THEN—Puddings, popsicles, frozen fruit and juice bars on sticks, frozen fruit ices, nonfat frozen yogurt bars, sherbets, sorbets, light or reduced-fat ice-cream with chocolate or fruit syrup. Be sure to read labels. Häagen-Dazs sorbet and yogurt bars, for instance, make a great low-fat treat.

Your children can get fat on "no-fat" foods. Many of the new "fat-free," "reduced-fat" and "low-fat" snack foods on the market have nearly as many total calories as their higher-fat counterparts—and sometimes even more! The American Dietetic Association advises us to ignore the flashy labels on the front of packaged food and to check the Nutrition Facts on the back of the package.

Sometimes a special treat just sounds good, and if you haven't already included one in the lunch box and are planning on fresh fruit for the main-meal dessert, try Black Bottom Cupcakes, Peanut Butter Cookies, Molasses Cookies, Angel Food Cake, Berry Cobbler or Berry Pie (see recipes).

NUTRITIONAL ANALYSIS

A nutritional analysis is provided for each recipe, usually on a per-serving basis and listing number of calories, grams of total fat, grams of saturated fat, milligrams of cholesterol, grams of carbohydrates, grams of dietary fiber, grams of protein, and milligrams of sodium.

In the interest of consistency and clarity, the analyses were based on the following factors:

- When a range is given for an ingredient, the midpoint amount is analyzed.
- When the ingredients listing gives one or more options, the first ingredient is the one analyzed.
- Figures are rounded off to whole numbers, so there might be slight discrepancies between an analysis for a whole meal and the sum of its parts.
- Fat-grams are rounded off to whole numbers. A total of less than 0.5 grams of fat is considered a trace amount.
- In many cases, salads and dressings have been analyzed separately. The amount of dressing, which is an individual choice, can greatly alter the calories and fat content of a salad.
- We have used the leanest ground beef that is 90% lean/10% fat, which according to the USDA has no more than 11 grams of fat per 3.5 ounces, cooked.
- Recipes that call for "light" soy sauce use a soy sauce yielding 600 milligrams of sodium per tablespoon (about half that of regular soy sauce).

- Recipes calling for a dash of salt are analyzed using ¼ teaspoon salt.
- Recipes that call for a "dollop" of something (e.g., sour cream) are analyzed using ¼ cup.
- Recipes using a "reduced-fat" cheese call for a cheese containing 5 grams of fat and 80 calories per ounce.
- Recipes that call for a "nonfat" cheese use a cheese containing 0 grams of fat and 40 calories per ounce.
- In recipes using oil-based marinades, only a quarter to a half of the marinade was used in the nutritional analysis if the marinade is drained off before cooking.
- Portions are based realistically on average-size servings and have not been shaved to make the numbers appear more favorable.
- For most recipes, the decision was made not to measure the amount cup by cup, since this is not the way most families eat. The analysis per serving is to be understood as an approximation since serving size most likely varies among family members.

The menus and recipes in this book are designed to ensure that meals fall well within the American Heart Association's guidelines for fat, cholesterol and sodium. Bear in mind that on occasion, in order to give a particular recipe the proper taste and texture, the fat guideline (no more than 30% of calories from fat) may be exceeded even in its fat-reduced version. The great majority of recipes keep well below this percentage, and all of them are significantly below the fat content of conventional recipes. However, while accommodating as healthy a diet as possible, this must be balanced with foods that give pleasure as well, rather than simply adhere to strict numerical rules.

Whatever health guideline you use, whether it's 30%, 25% or 20% calories from fat, keep in mind that the reference is to total daily caloric intake, which means that not every recipe or single food must be below that fat percentage. How the meal or the foods for the day go together is more to the point. Thus a low-fat meal might be capped off with a dessert that is relatively higher in fat. The more important perspective is how many grams of fat you're eating for the day, and whether or not that figure falls within your fat budget.

Every effort has been made to ensure the accuracy of nutritional data information; however, we cannot guarantee suitability for specific, medically imposed diets. People with special dietary needs should consult their physician and/or a registered dietitian.

Recipes have been analyzed for nutritional content by Beverly Utt, M.D., M.P.H., R.D., using Nutri-Calc Plus by Camde Corporation. Each analysis is based on the entry of nutritional data for all ingredients in each recipe. The primary sources of values used in the analyses include the *Agriculture Handbook 8 Series* and information from manufacturers. In the few cases where data are incomplete or unavailable, substitutions of similar ingredients have been made.

RECIPES

SOUPS AND CHILI

CURLY NOODLE SOUP

A sian noodles, also called buckwheat or soba noodles, are curly Japanese-style noodles made with wheat flour. They're available in Asian markets and in the Asian section of most supermarkets.

4 servings

> 3 *15-ounce cans chicken broth or*
>   *6 cups homemade (page 310)*
> 2 *cups water*
> 1 *8-ounce package soba noodles or rotini pasta*
> 1¼ *cups thinly sliced crimini mushrooms (optional)*
> 1¼ *cups snow peas, halved lengthwise (optional)*
> 1 *tablespoon reduced-sodium soy sauce*

In a medium saucepan, bring 1 can of the chicken broth and the 2 cups of water to a boil. Add soba noodles and cook 5 to 6 minutes, or until noodles are tender. Drain and rinse.

In a 4-quart stockpot, heat the remaining 2 cans of broth just to boiling. Add mushrooms and snow peas, if desired, and cook 1 to 2 minutes. Add cooked noodles and soy sauce. Serve at once.

Note: To save time, use canned broth instead of homemade; however, in this recipe you can tell the difference. And remember, using canned broth will substantially increase the sodium.

Each serving approximately 299 calories, 4 g total fat, 1 g saturated fat, 0 mg cholesterol, 52 g carbohydrates, 2 g dietary fiber, 12 g protein, 377 mg sodium using homemade chicken broth, 1,203 mg sodium using canned chicken broth.

A NOTE ON BASIC SOUP STOCKS AND BROTHS

Stock or broth—whether chicken, beef, ham hock or vegetable—will have the maximum flavor and quality when it's homemade and then reduced by one-third (see homemade broth recipes). Commercially canned stock or broth is convenient to have on hand and can be substituted for homemade broth in most recipes. Be sure to refrigerate it overnight or place it in the freezer for 30 minutes. The fat will congeal and rise to the top, and can then be skimmed. Remember, using commercially prepared broth instead of homemade will significantly increase the milligrams of sodium.

CHICKEN AND PASTINA SOUP

This is one of our family's favorite recipes. When our children were sick, I often made it without the mushrooms and peas. I think simply the good smells alone helped them to feel better.

Makes 2½ quarts (6 servings)

> **1 6-ounce package egg pastina**
> **2 quarts chicken broth, preferably homemade**
> **   (page 310)**
> **1 cup finely chopped carrots**
> **½ cup finely chopped fresh parsley**
> **1 7-ounce can mushroom stems and pieces,**
> **   drained (optional)**
> **1 pound peas in the pod, shelled (optional)**

Cook pastina in boiling water according to package directions. Rinse and drain.

In a 3-quart saucepan, heat chicken broth. Add pastina and carrots; simmer 5 minutes. Add parsley, mushrooms and peas; simmer 3 to 5 minutes longer.

Note: To save time, use canned broth instead of homemade; however, in this recipe you can tell the difference. And remember, using canned broth will substantially increase the sodium.

Each serving approximately 173 calories, 3 g total fat,
1 g saturated fat, 40 mg cholesterol, 25 g carbohydrates,
3 g dietary fiber, 12 g protein, 549 mg sodium using homemade
broth, 1,858 mg sodium using canned chicken broth.

TORTELLINI VEGETABLE SOUP

An abundant meal in a single dish. This soup is an example of pyramid eating. It offers starchy potatoes and pasta and a moderate amount of protein as well as leafy green vegetables.

Makes 3 quarts (6 servings)

> 4 cups chicken broth, preferably homemade
>   (page 310)
> 2 cups spicy vegetable juice (we like Snappy Tom)
> 4 large garlic cloves, minced
> 1½ cups peeled and diced russet potatoes
>   (1 very large potato)
> ½ skinned and boned chicken breast, diced
> ½ cup diced carrots (about 3 carrots)
> ½ pound cheese tortellini, cooked al dente
> 2 cups chopped fresh young spinach leaves

In a 4-quart stockpot, combine chicken broth, vegetable juice and garlic; heat to boiling. Add potato and chicken. Reduce heat and simmer over medium heat 15 minutes. Add carrots; simmer 10 minutes. Add tortellini and spinach; simmer 1 minute, or just until spinach wilts.

Each serving approximately 243 calories, 5 g total fat,
2 g saturated fat, 30 mg cholesterol, 36 g carbohydrates,
3 g dietary fiber, 14 g protein, 586 mg sodium using homemade
broth, 1,069 mg sodium using canned chicken broth.

THREE-BEAN CHILI

Full of B vitamins as well as minerals, beans are one of the best sources of dietary fiber. Beans are especially good for you because they are a vegetable source of protein without the hidden fat. If you want a vegetarian meal, simply omit the ground beef.

8 *servings*

    1 *pound leanest ground beef*
    1 *medium onion, chopped*
    2 *garlic cloves, minced*
 1½ *teaspoons Lawry's Chili Seasoning (optional)**
    1 *28-ounce can plum tomatoes, with liquid*
   ⅛ *teaspoon ground cumin (¼ teaspoon for spicy)*
   ½ *teaspoon cayenne for a spicier flavor*
    1 *tablespoon chili powder*
   ¾ *teaspoon Lawry's Seasoned Salt*
    2 *15-ounce cans red kidney beans, drained and
        rinsed*
    1 *15-ounce can black beans, drained and rinsed*
    1 *15-ounce can cannellini beans, drained and
        rinsed*

In a nonstick skillet, brown ground beef with onion and garlic; drain excess fat and pat with paper toweling to remove any additional fat. Sprinkle meat with Lawry's Chili Seasoning, if desired.

Meanwhile, in a food processor puree tomatoes until smooth, 2 to 3 minutes. Pour tomatoes into a 3-quart saucepan and add seasonings. Heat just to boiling; reduce heat to simmer. Add ground beef and beans; simmer 10 minutes.

*If Lawry's Chili Seasoning (found in the spice section of the supermarket) is unavailable where you shop, just leave it out. The recipe is delicious either way.

Each serving approximately 255 calories, 7 g total fat,
2 g saturated fat, 35 mg cholesterol, 30 g carbohydrates,
11 g dietary fiber, 22 g protein, 651 mg sodium.

BEEF AND BEAN SOUP

The beef, beans and corn will be very filling in this hearty soup. Filling equals satisfaction.

6 main-dish servings

½ *pound leanest ground beef*
1 *onion, chopped*
1 *28-ounce can plum tomatoes, with liquid, diced*
1½ *cups chicken broth, preferably homemade (page 310)*
1 *packet (1¼ ounce) Lawry's Taco Seasoning*
1 *15-ounce can black beans, drained and rinsed*
1 *15-ounce can red kidney beans, drained and rinsed*
1 *4-ounce can diced green chilies (optional)*
2 *cups fresh or frozen corn*
1 *cup black olives, pitted and sliced (optional)*

In a nonstick skillet, sauté ground beef and onion. Drain on paper towels; pat with additional paper toweling to remove excess fat. Set aside.

In a 2-quart saucepan, combine remaining ingredients and heat through. Add ground beef and heat soup to serving temperature.

Each serving approximately 313 calories, 7 g total fat,
2 g saturated fat, 23 mg cholesterol, 45 g carbohydrates,
10 g dietary fiber, 19 g protein, 1,168 mg sodium.

TOMATO AND BEAN SOUP

The beans in this soup are packed with the kind of fiber that protects against clogged arteries. By combining them with a tomato soup, you will help your body absorb more of the nutrients. Simply omit the ham for an equally delicious, meatless soup.

Makes 2½ quarts (5 main-dish servings)

3 15-ounce cans cannellini beans
1 28-ounce can plum tomatoes, including liquid, diced
2 cups chicken broth, preferably homemade (page 310)
1 fresh rosemary sprig
1 fresh thyme sprig
2 teaspoons olive oil
1 large carrot, diced
1 clove garlic, minced
1 medium onion, chopped
¼ pound extra-lean ham, diced
½ teaspoon salt
¼ teaspoon pepper
¼ teaspoon Tabasco sauce
¼ cup freshly grated Parmesan cheese

Place cannellini beans in a colander; rinse with cold water and drain thoroughly.

In a 6½-quart stockpot, combine tomatoes, chicken broth, rosemary and thyme; heat just to boiling. Reduce heat and let simmer.

In a nonstick skillet, heat olive oil; add diced carrots and sauté 3 to 4 minutes. Add garlic and onions, and continue sautéing until the carrot is tender and the onion is soft. Add ham and sauté 2 to 3 minutes longer. Add to tomato mixture.

Add rinsed beans to tomato mixture and heat to serving temperature. Season with salt, pepper and Tabasco sauce. Serve
in individual soup bowls. Sprinkle with Parmesan cheese.

Each serving approximately 325 calories, 5 g total fat,
2 g saturated fat, 18 mg cholesterol, 48 g carbohydrates,
13 g dietary fiber, 20 g protein, 1,306 mg sodium.

A NOTE ON BEANS

*In most cases, we use canned beans in our recipes.
Home-cooked dried beans are preferable, but canned
beans shorten cooking time. The Progresso brand offers
heart-healthy canned black beans, as well as cannellini
beans, red kidney beans and fava beans. Canned beans
tend to be higher in sodium than home-cooked beans, so
watch the sodium intake in the other foods consumed
throughout the day. Rinsing canned beans will reduce their
sodium content by one-half.*

THE BEST TURKEY SOUP

S tretch your food dollars. Cook a turkey not just on
Thanksgiving but now and then on a weekend. The leftovers make great lunch-box sandwiches, and the carcass makes
the best turkey soup.

Makes 4 quarts

Basic Stock
>1 *turkey carcass with meaty bones*
>5 *quarts water or enough to cover turkey parts*
>   *by about 2 inches*
>3 *garlic cloves, peeled*
>1 *large yellow onion, quartered*
>3 *carrots, peeled*
>3 *celery stalks with leaves*
>3 *tablespoons fresh basil leaves or 1 teaspoon*
>   *dried*
>1 *tablespoon salt*

Place turkey carcass in a stockpot (pull carcass apart so it will
fit); add enough water to cover. Bring slowly to a boil,
removing scum and fat that floats to the top. Add remaining
ingredients and simmer 3½ hours. Do not boil or fat will be
reabsorbed into the stock, making it cloudy. Cover only partially with lid so that steam can escape. Strain stock; discard
bones and vegetables, as they will be very greasy. Refrigerate
overnight. Skim and discard fat that floats to the top.

Return stock to stockpot. Simmer, uncovered, 1 hour or until
stock is reduced by one-third. Test seasoning. Sparingly add
more salt, if needed. Use stock at once, or store in refrigerator or freezer for later use. Freeze some stock in ice-cube trays
for stir-frying or sautéing vegetables.

Hearty Soup

1 recipe Basic Turkey Stock (facing page)
3 carrots, peeled and diced
2 celery stalks, diced
1 large onion, finely chopped
2 garlic cloves, minced
4 cups cooked elbow macaroni
½ pound fresh mushrooms, sliced (optional)
½ cup chopped fresh parsley

Bring reduced basic stock just to boiling; add carrots, celery, onion and garlic. Cover; reduce heat and simmer until vegetables are tender, about 30 minutes. Add macaroni and mushrooms; heat to serving temperature, about 2 to 3 minutes. Sprinkle with parsley.

Each 1-cup serving approximately 95 calories, 2 g total fat, 1 g saturated fat, 0 mg cholesterol, 13 g carbohydrates, 1 g dietary fiber, 4 g protein, 287 mg sodium.

Soup is a great comfort food. By its nature, soup has to be eaten slowly, giving the family time to talk. Remember, too, that leftover soups make perfect after-school snacks.

FRENCH MARKET SOUP

This recipe makes good use of commercial multi-bean soup packages. Because the homemade Basic Bean Soup Stock is made with a ham hock, our kids used to call this "ham hock" soup. It's one of our family's favorite soups.

Makes 8 quarts

> 1   *12-ounce package multi-bean soup mix*
> 3   *quarts Basic Bean Soup Stock (facing page) or*
>   *canned chicken, beef or vegetable broth*
> ¼   *cup dry pearl barley*
> 1   *28-ounce can plum tomatoes, with liquid, diced*
> 2   *medium yellow onions, finely chopped*
> 6   *stalks celery, finely chopped*
> 2   *garlic cloves, minced*
> 1½ *skinned and boned chicken breasts, diced*
> ¼   *pound extra-lean Italian sausage*
>   *(as lean as you can find)*

Thoroughly sort and wash bean soup mix and place in a large bowl. Cover with water. Soak overnight. Drain.

In a stockpot, heat Basic Bean Soup Stock just to boiling (do not boil). Add bean soup mix, barley, tomatoes, onions, celery, and garlic. Reduce heat; cover and simmer 3 hours, or until beans are tender. Uncover, add chicken and cook 30 minutes, or until chicken is cooked.

Meanwhile, slit open, remove and discard casing on Italian sausage. Preheat a nonstick skillet over medium-high heat; add sausage and brown 6 to 8 minutes, or until cooked, breaking the sausage apart as it browns. Drain on paper towels; pat with additional paper toweling to remove all excess fat. Add to stockpot, when chicken is nearly cooked.

Each 1-cup serving approximately 85 calories, 1 g total fat,
0 g saturated fat, 11 mg cholesterol, 10 g carbohydrates,
1 g dietary fiber, 7 g protein, 294 mg sodium.

BASIC BEAN SOUP STOCK

U se this Basic Bean Soup Stock with the many prepackaged multi-bean soup mixes on the market. Your family
will love how much better they taste using this as a base rather
than water or the canned broths recommended on the boxes.
To stretch your food dollars, cook a lean ham for a Sunday dinner. Make lunch-box sandwiches with the leftover ham. Use
the bone for this delicious stock.

Makes 3 quarts

> 2 *tablespoons dried parsley*
> 1 *tablespoon thyme*
> 1 *tablespoon marjoram*
> 2 *dried bay leaves*
> 2 *tablespoons celery seed*
> 1 *very meaty ham hock, about 2½ to 3 pounds*
> 3 *quarts water*
> 1 *tablespoon salt*

Measure parsley, thyme, marjoram, bay leaves and celery seed
into a square of cheesecloth; tie cloth securely at the top
with a string.

In a stockpot, combine seasoning pouch with ham hock,
water and salt. Bring slowly to a boil, removing scum and fat
that floats to the top. Cover and simmer 2½ to 3 hours. Do
not boil or fat will be reabsorbed into the broth, making it
cloudy. Refrigerate overnight. Skim and discard fat that floats
to the top. Cut ham off bone, reserving only very lean meat.
Dice meat and return to stockpot with seasoning pouch.
Discard ham bones and ham fat. Use stock at once, or store
in refrigerator or freezer for later use.

Each 1-cup serving approximately 33 calories, 0 g total fat,
0 g saturated fat, 5 mg cholesterol, trace g carbohydrates,
trace g dietary fiber, 3 g protein, 240 mg sodium.

HOMEMADE CHICKEN BROTH

Homemade chicken broth is worth the effort. Not only is the taste delicious, but the whole house smells wonderful while the broth is simmering on the stove. It freezes well and is nice to have on hand. Plus the amount of sodium you cut by not using canned broth is truly amazing. For a quick-to-fix vegetable-based meal, just add beans, rice or leftover pasta along with any vegetables in your refrigerator. Serve with oyster crackers or crusty French bread and seasonal fruit.

Makes 4 quarts

> 1 *3- to 4-pound chicken, cut up, plus 2 additional*
>   *whole chicken breasts*
> 1 *large onion, peeled and quartered*
> 2 *carrots, peeled*
> 2 *garlic cloves, peeled*
> 1 *tablespoon chopped fresh basil leaves or*
>   *½ teaspoon dried*
> 1 *tablespoon salt*
> ½ *teaspoon pepper*
> 5 *quarts cold water*

Wash chicken parts and put all except the breast meat into an 8-quart stockpot. Add onion, carrots, garlic, basil, salt, pepper and enough water to cover (add additional water if necessary so that the chicken parts are totally covered by 1 to 2 inches of water).

Heat gradually to boiling point; add whole chicken breasts. Reduce heat to simmer and cook 20 to 30 minutes, or until breast meat is tender. Remove chicken breasts. Cool slightly. Reserve breast meat in refrigerator for later use in sandwiches, salads or other dishes.

Simmer remaining chicken, partially covered with a lid, so that steam can escape, for 2 to 2½ hours, or until chicken is tender and pulls away from the bone. Strain. Remove meat from bones (save meat for later use unless it's way too greasy). Refrigerate broth overnight; fat will float to the top. Skim and discard the fat.

Return broth to stockpot. Simmer, uncovered, 1 hour, or until broth is reduced by about one-fourth. Test seasonings. Sparingly add salt, if needed. Use broth at once, or store in refrigerator or freezer for later use.

Each 1-cup serving approximately 27 calories, 1 g total fat, 0 g saturated fat, 2 mg cholesterol, 0 g carbohydrates, 0 g dietary fiber, 4 g protein, 275 mg sodium.

PASTA

SALLY'S NOODLE CASSEROLE

The combination of light and nonfat dairy products reduces calories and fat dramatically while still keeping the great taste and integrity of the recipe.

8 servings

> 1 *pound leanest ground beef*
> 3 *large garlic cloves, pressed*
> 1 *tablespoon sugar*
>   *salt and pepper to taste*
> 2 *15-ounce cans tomato sauce*
> 1 *8-ounce package light cream cheese*
> 1 *8-ounce package light sour cream with chives*
> 1 *12-ounce package spinach noodles or rotini*
>   *cooking spray*
> 2 *tablespoons nonfat cheddar cheese, shredded*
> 2 *tablespoons nonfat jack cheese, shredded*

In a preheated nonstick skillet, sauté beef and garlic 4 to 5 minutes, or until beef is browned. Add sugar, salt and pepper. Stir in tomato sauce; simmer 20 minutes.

Using a wire whisk or an electric mixer, combine the cream cheese and the sour cream with chives.

Meanwhile, cook noodles according to package directions. Drain and set aside.

Spray an 8-inch round x 3½-inch deep ovenproof baking dish with cooking spray. Add a layer of noodles. Spread a layer of the cream cheese mixture, then a layer of the tomato sauce mixture. Repeat 2 more times. Bake, covered, at 350°F for 30 to 40 minutes until sauce is bubbly. Top with cheddar and jack cheese. Bake, uncovered, until cheese melts, about 5 minutes.

Each serving approximately 379 calories, 15 g total fat, 6 g saturated fat, 101 mg cholesterol, 39 g carbohydrates, 3 g dietary fiber, 25 g protein, 610 mg sodium.

A NOTE ON PASTA

Pasta brands can differ greatly in quality. It's important to use the best pasta available, since the quality of the meal is only as good as the quality of the pasta. Many supermarkets and Italian markets offer high-quality imported and domestic brands. Pasta should be cooked al dente, which in Italian means "firm to the tooth," or just barely tender.

PASTA MARINARA

A ny pasta with marinara sauce makes great leftovers for after-school snacks.

8 servings

> 1 *pound mostaccioli or other tube-shaped pasta*
> 1 *28-ounce can crushed, peeled tomatoes in heavy puree*
> 2 *tablespoons extra-virgin olive oil*
> 10 *fresh basil leaves or 1 teaspoon dried*
> 1 *teaspoon finely chopped fresh oregano or ½ teaspoon dried*
> 1 *teaspoon salt*
> ½ *teaspoon pepper*

Cook pasta according to package directions. Drain and set aside.

Meanwhile, in a saucepan over medium-high heat, warm the tomatoes. Add the olive oil, 4 leaves fresh basil, or all the dried basil, oregano, salt and pepper. Simmer 10 minutes. Serve over pasta while pasta is still warm. Garnish with remaining whole basil leaves.

Each serving approximately 263 calories, 4 g total fat,
0 g saturated fat, 0 mg cholesterol, 43 g carbohydrates,
3 g dietary fiber, 9 g protein, 459 mg sodium.

OLIVE AND MUSHROOM MARINARA:

While the sauce is simmering, add 1 cup pitted Calamata olives and one 7-ounce can mushroom stems and pieces, drained.

Each serving approximately 284 calories, 6 g total fat,
0 g saturated fat, 0 mg cholesterol, 45 g carbohydrates,
4 g dietary fiber, 9 g protein, 609 mg sodium.

LITTLE EAR PASTA
WITH SAUSAGE

This recipe provides a good way to enjoy the taste of sausage without all the calories and fat you would get from an entrée-size portion.

8 servings

> 1 *pound orecchiette (little ear) pasta or medium shell-shaped pasta*
> ¾ *pound extra-lean sweet Italian sausage (as lean as you can find)*
> 4 *medium garlic cloves, minced*
> 1 *28-ounce can plum tomatoes, with liquid, diced*
> 2 *tablespoons tomato paste*
> 1½ *teaspoons minced fresh oregano or ½ teaspoon dried*
> 2 *tablespoons chopped fresh basil leaves or ½ teaspoon dried*
> ½ *teaspoon salt*
> ¼ *teaspoon pepper*
> ⅛–¼ *teaspoon crushed red pepper (optional) fresh basil leaves for garnish*

Cook pasta according to package directions. Drain and set aside.

Slit open, remove and discard the casing on the Italian sausage. In a preheated nonstick skillet over medium heat, brown the sausage 6 to 8 minutes, or until cooked, breaking it apart as it browns. Drain on paper towels; pat dry with additional toweling to remove all excess fat. Set aside.

Meanwhile, in a medium saucepan, combine garlic, tomatoes, tomato paste, oregano, basil, salt, pepper and crushed red pepper. Simmer 10 to 15 minutes; stir sausage into sauce. Serve over pasta. Garnish with fresh basil leaves.

Each serving approximately 346 calories, 9 g total fat,
1 g saturated fat, 33 mg cholesterol, 45 g carbohydrates,
3 g dietary fiber, 17 g protein, 629 mg sodium.

CLASSIC LASAGNA*

Save your fat calories for another day by making your own lasagna. Compare this homemade version with a store-bought type and you'll see that not only does it taste better but you save 5 to 10 grams of fat per serving. Omit the sausage to prepare an equally delicious meatless lasagna that saves 100 calories and 8 grams of fat.

12 servings

1   *12-ounce package lasagna noodles*
1   *pound extra-lean Italian sausage*
    (as lean as you can find)
2   *garlic cloves, minced*
1   *small onion, chopped*
3   *16-ounce cans plum tomatoes, with liquid*
2   *tablespoons extra-virgin olive oil*
3   *8-ounce cans tomato sauce*
½   *teaspoon dried oregano*
1   *teaspoon dried basil*
1   *teaspoon salt*
¼   *teaspoon pepper*
2   *bunches fresh spinach*
2   *cups nonfat ricotta cheese*
½   *pound reduced-fat mozzarella cheese, grated*
½   *pound fat-free mozzarella cheese, grated*

Cook the lasagna noodles according to package directions. Drain and set aside.

Meanwhile, slit open, remove and discard the casing on the Italian sausage. In a preheated nonstick skillet over medium heat, brown sausage with garlic and onion until sausage is done and onion is tender. Drain on paper towels; pat dry with additional paper toweling to remove all excess fat. Set aside.

In a food processor, puree tomatoes; add olive oil, tomato sauce, oregano, basil, salt and pepper. Process 2 to 3 minutes, or until smooth. Set aside.

Wash spinach; shake dry and remove any tough stems. Steam in a covered skillet 2 to 3 minutes, or until wilted. Squeeze dry; chop. Combine spinach, sausage and ricotta.

Combine reduced-fat mozzarella with fat-free mozzarella.

Cover bottom of a 13 x 9 x 2-inch pan with some tomato sauce. Add a layer of lasagna noodles. Spread with meat mixture. Add a layer of mozzarella. Cover with a little more sauce. Repeat layers two or three more times. Pour remaining sauce over final layer. Top with additional cheese. Bake, covered, at 350°F for 60 minutes. (For a smaller group, use two 8-inch square pans and freeze one.)

*Sodium alert: Choose low-sodium foods at other meals throughout the day to offset the higher sodium in this recipe.

Each serving approximately 346 calories, 14 g total fat, 3 g saturated fat, 43 mg cholesterol, 31 g carbohydrates, 6 g dietary fiber, 23 g protein, 1,185 mg sodium.

A NOTE ON STORE-BOUGHT CANNED TOMATO PRODUCTS

Italian plum tomatoes are the best substitute for fresh tomatoes. It is important to buy the best quality available. Progresso Plum Tomatoes and S&W Pear Tomatoes are especially good, as are many of the imported brands such as Di Napoli. The better the grade, the more flavorful the sauce. For recipes in this book that call for diced plum tomatoes, buy the whole plum tomatoes and simply dice them yourself.

Store-bought tomato sauce, tomato puree and tomato paste should also be of the highest grade available. Progresso and Contadina brands are among the best. Freeze any leftover paste by the tablespoonful on a sheet of waxed paper; once frozen, remove to a plastic freezer bag and store in the freezer for later use.

LINGUINE WITH CLAM SAUCE

Tired of the same old spaghetti sauce? Here's a quick, tasty variation on a red sauce. This recipe is delicious even without fresh clams.

8 servings

> 1   *pound linguine*
> 1   *28-ounce can plum tomatoes, with liquid, diced*
> 1½ *tablespoons extra-virgin olive oil*
> 4   *large garlic cloves, finely minced*
> 1   *cup dry white wine*
> ¾   *teaspoon salt*
> ¼   *teaspoon pepper*
> 2   *6½-ounce cans chopped clams with liquid*
> 2   *pounds shell clams (steamers)*
> ¼   *cup chopped fresh parsley*
>   *crushed red pepper (optional)*

Cook linguine according to package directions. Drain and set aside.

Meanwhile, in a 1½-quart saucepan, combine tomatoes, olive oil, garlic, wine, salt, pepper and chopped clams. Simmer, uncovered, for 15 to 20 minutes.

Wash steamers thoroughly, discarding any clams with broken or open shells. Place in steamer with ½ cup hot water; cover tightly and steam 5 to 10 minutes, or until clams open. Discard any shells that do not open.

Divide linguine into individual pasta bowls; ladle sauce over pasta. Top with steamed clams in their shells. Sprinkle with fresh parsley. Accompany with crushed red pepper.

Each serving approximately 304 calories, 4 g total fat,
0 g saturated fat, 12 mg cholesterol, 45 g carbohydrates,
3 g dietary fiber, 14 g protein, 551 mg sodium.

PENNE WITH MEAT SAUCE

8 servings

> 1 *pound penne*
> 1 *28-ounce can plum tomatoes, with liquid, diced*
> 1 *15-ounce can tomato sauce*
> ¼ *cup dry white wine (Orvieto is good)*
> 1½ *teaspoons extra-virgin olive oil*
> 2 *garlic cloves, minced*
> ½ *pound ground veal (as lean as you can find)*
> ½ *cup fresh basil leaves, chopped*
>   *salt and pepper to taste*

Cook penne according to package directions. Drain and set aside.

Meanwhile, in a 4-quart saucepan, heat tomatoes, tomato sauce and wine; allow to simmer.

In a nonstick skillet, heat olive oil; add garlic and ground veal, and sauté until veal is cooked. Drain excess fat; pat veal with paper toweling to further remove any fat. Add veal to tomato sauce. Season with fresh basil, salt and pepper.

Divide penne into individual bowls; top with sauce.

Each serving approximately 288 calories, 4 g total fat,
1 g saturated fat, 22 mg cholesterol, 49 g carbohydrates,
4 g dietary fiber, 4 g protein, 460 mg sodium.

CHEESY MACARONI

Substitute leaner cheese and add the Parmesan at the end to lower the fat and maximize the flavor.

12 servings

    1 *pound large elbow macaroni*
    ¼ *cup all-purpose flour*
    2½ *cups nonfat milk*
    1 *tablespoon margarine*
    ¼ *teaspoon paprika*
    1 *teaspoon dry mustard*
    ½ *teaspoon hot sauce*
    2 *teaspoons Worcestershire sauce*
    1 *teaspoon salt*
    ¼ *teaspoon pepper*
    1 *pound reduced-fat cheddar cheese, shredded*
    1 *large ripe tomato, sliced*
    3 *tablespoons freshly grated Parmesan cheese*

Cook macaroni according to package directions. Drain and set aside.

In a screw-top jar, combine flour with ½ cup of the nonfat milk to form a smooth paste. Set aside.

In a saucepan over medium heat, melt margarine; add the remaining nonfat milk, paprika, mustard, hot sauce, Worcestershire sauce, salt and pepper, stirring constantly. When milk is hot, gradually stir in reserved flour mixture.

Cook, stirring constantly, until slightly thickened and bubbly. Add cheddar cheese; stir until melted. Stir macaroni into cheese sauce. Transfer to a 2-quart casserole. Arrange tomato slices over top, pushing edges of each slice into the macaroni. Bake, uncovered, at 350°F for 45 minutes. Sprinkle with Parmesan the last 5 minutes of cooking.

Each serving approximately 294 calories, 9 g total fat,
4 g saturated fat, 29 mg cholesterol, 33 g carbohydrates,
2 g dietary fiber, 20 g protein, 541 mg sodium.

NOODLE CASSEROLE
WITH TUNA

Serve this dish with broccoli so your kids can dip the vegetables into the sauce. It will help teach them to like all vegetables, even broccoli.

8 servings

> 1 *pound elbow macaroni*
> 2 *10¾-ounce cans reduced-fat Campbell's*
>   *Cream of Chicken Soup**
> 1 *cup nonfat milk*
> 1 *6-ounce can water-packed tuna*
> 1 *8-ounce can sliced water chestnuts, drained*
> 2 *tablespoons freshly grated Parmesan cheese*

Cook macaroni according to package directions. Drain and
set aside.

Meanwhile, in a saucepan, heat Cream of Chicken Soup;
gradually stir in nonfat milk and cook, stirring, until mixture
is smooth and bubbly. Gently stir in tuna, water chestnuts
and the cooked macaroni. Transfer to a 2-quart casserole.
Bake at 375°F for 15 minutes; sprinkle with Parmesan. Bake
5 minutes longer. Serve at once.

**Simply using reduced-fat cream of chicken soup yields fat and calorie savings that make this old
favorite fit into today's eating plan. Substitute Campbell's Healthy Request Cream of Chicken Soup
for the reduced-fat soup to save an additional 2 grams of fat and 470 mg of sodium per serving.*

Each serving approximately 288 calories, 3 g total fat,
0 g saturated fat, 15 mg cholesterol, 46 g carbohydrates,
0 g dietary fiber, 16 g protein, 296 mg sodium.

SPAGHETTI WITH MEATBALLS

If you asked any member of our family to name his or her favorite recipe, the answer would be this one—with the sausage variation. Because it has more fat and calories than we recommend, we save it for special occasions such as family birthdays. We wanted to include it here because it's a favorite and also to illustrate that with moderation and portion control even Grandma's Spaghetti with Meatballs and Sausage is acceptable now and then. When you eat high-fat foods, just be sure to budget for them by eating low-fat or nonfat foods at other meals that day and serve fruit or other low-fat accompaniments with the high-fat meal so you won't break your fat budget for the day.

16 servings

> 1   *28-ounce can plum tomatoes*
> 1   *28-ounce can tomato puree*
> 1   *12-ounce can tomato paste*
> 1   *8-ounce can tomato sauce*
> 3   *cups water*
> 1½ *teaspoons salt*
> 2   *tablespoons chopped fresh basil leaves or*
>   *1½ teaspoons dried*
> 1½ *tablespoons minced fresh oregano leaves or*
>   *¾ teaspoon dried*
> ½   *pound boneless pork loin chops*

Meatballs
> 1   *pound ground beef (as lean as you can find)*
> 1   *cup dry bread crumbs*
> 5   *cloves garlic, finely minced*
> 1   *egg*
> ¼   *cup nonfat milk*
> ½   *cup chopped fresh parsley*
>   *salt and pepper to taste*

> 2   *pounds spaghetti or corkscrew-shaped pasta*
>   *fresh basil sprigs for garnish*
>   *crushed red pepper (optional)*

In a food processor, puree tomatoes until smooth; transfer to a stockpot. Add canned tomato puree, tomato paste, tomato sauce, water, salt, basil and oregano. Stir thoroughly to combine ingredients. Heat sauce just to boiling (do not allow to boil). Reduce to a simmer.

Trim all visible fat from pork chops. In a nonstick skillet, brown chops 3 to 4 minutes on each side. Remove from skillet and drain on paper towels; pat dry with additional paper toweling to remove all excess fat. Add chops to sauce.

Meanwhile, put ground beef in a medium bowl. Add bread crumbs, garlic, egg, nonfat milk, parsley, salt and pepper. Knead until mixture is smooth and ingredients are combined, adding additional nonfat milk if needed for moisture. Form 20 firm golf ball-size meatballs and add to the sauce. Continue to simmer sauce for 2 to 2½ hours.

One half-hour before serving, cook pasta according to package directions. Drain and transfer to a pasta bowl. Pour one cup of sauce over the top—just enough for color. Garnish with sprigs of fresh basil. Serve with meatballs and additional sauce. Accompany with crushed red pepper, if desired.

VEGETARIAN SAUCE: Omitting the pork chops and the meatballs saves 106 calories and 5 grams of fat.

ITALIAN SAUSAGE SAUCE: In a nonstick skillet over medium-high heat, sauté 6 extra-lean (as lean as you can find) Italian sausages 8 to 10 minutes or microwave the sausages on full power in a covered dish 8 to 10 minutes, turning once. Drain and pat with paper towels to remove excess fat. Cut each sausage lengthwise into thirds. Add to spaghetti sauce along with the meatballs. Simmer as directed above. Add 97 calories and 7 grams of fat per ⅓ sausage.

Each serving (1 cup pasta, ¾ cup sauce, and 1 meatball)
approximately 365 calories, 8 g total fat, 2 g saturated fat,
40 mg cholesterol, 55 g carbohydrates, 5 g dietary fiber,
20 g protein, 462 mg sodium. (Add 62 calories and 3 grams of
fat for each additional meatball).

BOW TIE PASTA WITH CHICKEN

This dish is a quick variation on Penne with Meat Sauce (page 319).

8 *servings*

> 1 *pound farfalle (bow tie pasta)*
> 1½ *pound skinned and boned chicken breasts,*
> *cut into 1-inch cubes*
> 1½ *tablespoons extra-virgin olive oil*
> 2 *large garlic cloves, minced*
> ¼ *cup finely chopped onion*
> 1 *28-ounce can crushed, peeled tomatoes in*
> *heavy puree*
> ½ *cup water*
> ¼ *cup chopped fresh Italian flat-leaf parsley plus*
> *additional whole leaves of Italian parsley*
> *for garnish*
> ¾ *teaspoon salt*
> ¼ *teaspoon pepper*

Cook farfalle according to package directions. Drain and set aside.

In a nonstick skillet over medium-high heat, brown chicken breasts. Remove from pan; set aside.

In the same skillet, heat the olive oil. Add garlic and onion, and sauté 4 to 5 minutes. Transfer to a large saucepan. Add tomatoes, water and chopped Italian parsley; cook over medium heat 5 to 10 minutes. Add the chicken. Partially cover and allow the sauce to simmer gently for 20 minutes, stirring occasionally. Season with salt and pepper. Serve over pasta. Garnish with remaining whole Italian parsley leaves.

Each serving approximately 365 calories, 6 g total fat,
1 g saturated fat, 55 mg cholesterol, 48 g carbohydrates,
4 g dietary fiber, 29 g protein, 403 mg sodium.

PASTA PRIMAVERA

This recipe is a great way to get your children to eat and to actually love cruciferous vegetables, such as cauliflower and broccoli.

6 side-dish servings

Sauce
> 1¼ *cups fresh basil leaves*
> 2 *large garlic cloves, peeled*
> ¼ *teaspoon salt*
> 2 *tablespoons pine nuts*
> ¼ *cup extra-virgin olive oil*

Combine basil, garlic, salt and pine nuts in a food processor and process until fairly smooth, 2 to 3 minutes. With machine running, add olive oil one tablespoon at a time. Process until the oil is incorporated and mixture is smooth, 2 to 3 minutes longer.

> ½ *pound rotini*
> 1 *6½-ounce jar marinated artichoke hearts,*
> *drained*
> 2 *cups broccoli florets*
> 2 *cups cauliflower florets*
> ¾ *cups thinly sliced baby carrots*
> 1½ *cups diced plum tomatoes*

In a large pot of boiling water, cook pasta according to package directions. Drain. While pasta is still hot, toss it with artichokes, including their marinade. Add broccoli, cauliflower and carrots. Add basil sauce and toss. Add tomatoes and toss again.

Each serving approximately 284 calories, 10 g total fat,
1 g saturated fat, 0 mg cholesterol, 39 g carbohydrates,
6 g dietary fiber, 10 g protein, 372 mg sodium.

SALADS

CHICKEN TACO SALAD

This taco salad is juicier and tastier than the fast-food version. Your kids will want to eat it with a spoon.

8 servings

1   28-ounce can plum tomatoes, with liquid
2   garlic cloves, peeled
¾   teaspoon salt
¾   teaspoon dry mustard
1¼ teaspoons chili powder
½   teaspoon Lawry's Chili Seasoning (optional)
⅛   teaspoon ground cumin (¼ teaspoon for spicy)
⅛   teaspoon cayenne pepper (¼ teaspoon for spicy)
2   skinned and boned chicken breasts
       (1 pound chicken)
1   tablespoon sake*
2   tablespoons potato starch (available in the
       Asian section of the supermarket)**
1   teaspoon olive oil
3   15-ounce cans red kidney beans, drained and
       rinsed
8–12 cups shredded lettuce
2   large ripe tomatoes, coarsely chopped
1   medium white onion, coarsely chopped
½   cup grated nonfat cheddar cheese
½   cup grated reduced-fat cheddar cheese
½   cup nonfat sour cream
1   cup commercially prepared tomato salsa
8   6-inch warm flour tortillas (page 388)

Put canned tomatoes and garlic into the work bowl of a food processor and process until smooth. Transfer to a 3-quart saucepan and add seasonings. Heat just to boiling (do not allow to boil). Reduce heat and let simmer 8 to 10 minutes.

Cut chicken into ½-inch strips. Toss with sake. Sprinkle with potato starch. Heat olive oil in a nonstick skillet over medium-high heat. Add chicken strips and stir-fry 8 to 10 minutes, or until done.

Add chicken and kidney beans to tomato mixture. Heat to serving temperature.

Meanwhile, line shallow soup bowls with shredded lettuce (this shredded lettuce replaces the fried tortilla shell used in fast-food taco salads). Spoon chicken-and-bean mixture over lettuce. Top with chopped tomatoes, onion and each type of cheese. Accompany with sour cream and salsa. Serve with warm tortillas.

SHRIMP TACO SALAD: Omit chicken, sake, potato starch and olive oil. Just before serving, add ½ pound cooked baby shrimp to bean-and-tomato mixture. Garnish salad with sliced avocado, if desired.

*White wine may be substituted.
**Corn starch or flour may be substituted.

Each serving approximately 359 calories, 6 g total fat,
1 g saturated fat, 43 mg cholesterol, 47 g carbohydrates,
11 g dietary fiber, 29 g protein, 973 mg sodium.

A NOTE ON SALAD DRESSINGS

*S*alads provide an attractive, easy and tasty way to add
nutrients and fiber to your children's diet. They are filling, satisfying, and low in fat and calories. Salad dressings, however, are a different thing altogether. With few
exceptions, salad dressings are rich in fat and calories. Too
much dressing can turn a low-fat salad into a high-fat
food. There are many fat-free and low-fat dressings on the
market. Some brands taste much better than others but
many are not tasty enough to provide satisfaction. We
have found that spraying the salad greens lightly with an
olive-oil spray moistens the greens with a minimum of oil
and less dressing is needed. (Tossing the greens with a
small amount of fat-free dressing and then adding the full-
fat dressing accomplishes the same thing.) The point is,
whatever dressing you choose, be moderate in its use.
Don't spoil a healthful salad with added fat. Remember,
the more dressing you use, the more fat and calories you
take in.

When high-fat dressings are used, be sure that low-fat
foods are on the menu. This will help keep the fat in the
meal in balance.

Many of our dressings are made with olive oil, considered by many the most healthful of all oils. It may be better
for your heart, but it's still rich in fat and calories and
must be used sparingly. Virgin and extra-virgin olive oils
are richer and have a more powerful taste than multipur-
pose or light olive oil; however, they provide no additional
health benefit. Be aware also that "light" olive oil has no
less fat and no fewer calories than regular olive oil.

BUILD-YOUR-OWN SALAD

W hen kids make their own salads, they often eat more vegetables than they do when someone serves them. They'll love this home salad bar.

6 servings

Buttermilk Dressing
½ cup nonfat sour cream
½ cup nonfat cottage cheese
1 cup low-fat (1%) buttermilk
1 0.4-ounce package Hidden Valley Ranch
*   Original Ranch Salad Dressing Mix*
*   (Buttermilk Recipe)*

Combine sour cream, cottage cheese, buttermilk and salad dressing mix. Chill. Makes 2 cups.

6 cups mixed greens (make at least 2 cups of
*   them spinach)*
1 cup broccoli florets
1 cup cauliflower florets
4 large carrots, cut into julienne strips
1 bunch chopped green onions
1 large cucumber, peeled and diced
1 large ripe tomato, coarsely chopped

Arrange mixed greens in a medium salad bowl. In separate bowls, arrange the broccoli, cauliflower, carrots, green onions, cucumber, tomatoes, and ¾ cup of the Buttermilk Dressing. Each person can then build his or her own salad. Reserve remaining dressing for later use.

Each serving approximately 128 calories, 1 g total fat, 0 g saturated fat, 2 mg cholesterol, 26 g carbohydrates, 7 g dietary fiber, 8 g protein, 182 mg sodium, 135 mg calcium. Each additional one tablespoon dressing about 8 calories, 0 g fat, 29 mg sodium.

CLASSIC PASTA SALAD

This classic pasta salad is an example of a recipe that offers red, yellow, green and dark green leafy vegetables all in one dish.

Makes 5 quarts

Dressing
    9 *tablespoons extra-virgin olive oil*
    3 *tablespoons red wine vinegar*
    ¾ *teaspoon salt*
    ¼ *teaspoon pepper*

Measure ingredients into a small bowl; mix with wire whisk or fork until well blended.

    1 *pound pennette (little penne), small shells or*
       rotini
    1 *6½ ounce jar marinated artichoke hearts**
       (with marinade)
    1 *15-ounce can water-packed artichoke hearts,*
       drained and quartered
    1 *cup finely chopped red pepper*
       (1 medium pepper)
    1 *cup finely chopped green pepper*
       (1 medium pepper)
    1 *15-ounce can whole spears baby corn on the*
       cob, drained
    1 *7-ounce can mushroom stems and pieces,*
       drained
    4 *cups tiny broccoli florets*
    4 *cups cherry tomatoes, halved*
    ½ *cup black olives, halved, for garnish*
    1 *cup fresh basil leaves for garnish*

Cook pasta according to package directions; rinse, drain and transfer to large salad bowl. While pasta is still warm, add marinated artichoke hearts with their marinade. Toss until pasta is well coated. Let cool to room temperature. Layer remaining vegetables over pasta. Chill. Just before serving, toss with dressing. Garnish with olives and fresh basil leaves.

*The most heart-healthy brands of marinated artichoke hearts available are those in which the oil is a non-hydrogenated soybean oil.

CHICKEN PASTA SALAD: Add 2 cups diced poached chicken or ¾ pound diced, smoked turkey breast. An excellent main-meal salad.

Each 1-cup serving approximately 164 calories, 7 g total fat,
1 g saturated fat, 0 mg cholesterol, 21 g carbohydrates,
2 g dietary fiber, 5 g protein, 220 mg sodium.

A NOTE ON PARMESAN CHEESE

*P*armesan cheese should be used only sparingly. Avoid preground, packaged varieties, which are very expensive and almost flavorless. Buy a small wedge of fresh Parmesan and grate as needed, or buy freshly grated in the amount you need.

PASTA AND SMOKED TURKEY SALAD

8 servings

Dressing
6 *tablespoons extra-virgin olive oil*
2 *tablespoons white wine vinegar*
2 *garlic cloves, finely minced*
½ *teaspoon salt*
¼ *teaspoon pepper*

Measure ingredients into a small bowl; mix with wire whisk or fork until well blended.

1 *pound rotini, small shells, or fusillette*
    (little fusilli) pasta
2 *cups fresh broccoli florets*
2 *cups fresh cauliflower florets*
1 *6-ounce jar roasted red peppers, drained and*
    diced
½ *cup sliced black olives*
1 *pound smoked turkey breast, diced*
⅓ *cup freshly grated Parmesan cheese*
½ *cup fresh basil leaves for garnish*

Cook pasta according to package directions; rinse, drain, and transfer to a large bowl. Top with broccoli, cauliflower, peppers and olives. Do not toss. Chill for at least 1 hour. Just before serving, toss with dressing. Add turkey and toss again. Sprinkle with Parmesan. Garnish with fresh basil.

Each serving approximately 423 calories, 14 g total fat,
2 g saturated fat, 52 mg cholesterol, 45 g carbohydrates,
3 g dietary fiber, 29 g protein, 317 mg sodium.

CORN AND BLACK BEAN SALAD

This salad is high in carbohydrates, from the more complex bean to the simple tomato. Carbohydrates provide fuel for our everyday energy needs.

8 servings

> 2 *15-ounce cans black beans, drained and rinsed*
> 2 *cups cooked corn kernels (from 5 cobs)**
> 2 *tablespoons finely chopped jalapeño pepper*
> *(optional)*
> 1 *cup finely chopped red bell pepper*
> *(1 medium pepper)*
> ½ *cup finely chopped red onion*
> 1 *cup coarsely chopped ripe tomato*
> *(1 large tomato)*
> ¼ *cup extra virgin olive oil*
> 3 *tablespoons fresh lime juice*
> ½ *teaspoon ground cumin*
> ⅛ *teaspoon cayenne pepper*
> ¾ *teaspoon salt*
> ¼ *cup finely chopped fresh cilantro for garnish*
> *(optional)*

Combine all ingredients except cilantro in a medium salad bowl. Toss. Serve at once, or cover and chill in refrigerator. Just before serving, garnish with the cilantro, if desired.

*This salad is a good way to use leftover corn.

Each serving approximately 194 calories, 8 g total fat,
1 g saturated fat, 0 mg cholesterol, 26 g carbohydrates,
7 g dietary fiber, 8 g protein, 555 mg sodium.

TUSCAN BEAN SALAD

This salad is a good way to get kids to eat more beans.

8 *servings*

Dressing
> 2 *garlic cloves, minced*
> 3 *tablespoons fresh lemon juice*
> ¼ *cup extra-virgin olive oil*
> ½ *teaspoon salt*
> ¼ *teaspoon pepper*

Combine garlic, lemon juice, olive oil, salt and pepper in a covered jar and shake until well blended.

> 3 *15-ounce cans cannellini beans, rinsed*
> 1½ *cups coarsely chopped red onion*
> 2 *large ripe tomatoes, coarsely chopped*
> ½ *cup chopped celery*
> ¾ *cup coarsely chopped fresh flat-leaf parsley*

Arrange cannellini beans in a shallow salad bowl and toss with 2 tablespoons of the dressing. Chill beans and remaining dressing. Just before serving, toss beans with onion, tomatoes, celery, parsley and remainder of dressing.

Each serving approximately 245 calories, 8 g total fat,
1 g saturated fat, 0 mg cholesterol, 34 g carbohydrates,
9 g dietary fiber, 12 g protein, 167 mg sodium.

VARIATION: Sort and wash one 16-ounce package of small white beans and put them into a stockpot with 2 quarts of water; cover and bring to a boil. Remove from heat and let soak for 1 hour. Drain.

Bring beans and 6 cups water to a boil in a stockpot. Add 1 teaspoon salt, 1 quartered onion, 2 bay leaves and 1 teaspoon powdered coriander. Boil gently, uncovered, until beans are tender, 35 to 40 minutes (add water to keep beans covered). Drain. Remove onion and bay leaves. Rinse beans with cold water; drain again. Proceed with recipe as above.

ANTIPASTO*

I t's good to have the ingredients on hand for this easy salad or quick-to-fix hors d'oeuvre.

12 servings

> 1 *15-ounce jar pickled beans*
> 1 *15-ounce jar pickled asparagus*
> 1 *15-ounce jar pickled snap peas*
> 1 *15-ounce can whole spears baby corn on the cob*
> 1 *15-ounce can water-packed artichoke hearts, drained*
> 1 *15-ounce jar pepperoncini peppers (optional)*
> 1 *15-ounce can garbanzo beans, drained*
> 1 *15-ounce can black olives*
> 2 *bunches carrots*
> 2 *bunches radishes*
> 2 *cups ripe cherry tomatoes*
> 1 *bunch red leaf lettuce*

Chill beans, asparagus, snap peas, baby corn, artichoke hearts, peppers, garbanzo beans and olives in their individual jars or cans. Wash carrots; trim, peel and slice on the diagonal. Trim and wash radishes. Put carrots and radishes into a bowl of ice water and place in refrigerator to crisp. Wash tomatoes and lettuce.

Just before serving, thoroughly drain vegetables. Pat dry with paper towels. Arrange beans, asparagus, snap peas, corn, artichoke hearts, peppers, garbanzo beans, carrots, radishes and tomatoes in mounds in a lettuce-lined basket. Tuck olives among the mounds.

*Sodium alert: Choose low-sodium foods at other meals throughout the day to offset the high sodium in this recipe.

Each serving approximately 154 calories, 2 g total fat, 0 g saturated fat, 0 mg cholesterol, 26 g carbohydrates, 5 g dietary fiber, 6 g protein, 837 mg sodium.

TOMATOES WITH FRESH MOZZARELLA AND BASIL

This quick salad is especially good in the summer when tomatoes and basil are at their peak.

6 *servings*

> 1   *large bunch fresh basil leaves*
> 4   *large ripe tomatoes, sliced into ¼-inch slices*
> ½   *pound fresh mozzarella cheese, cut into ¼-inch slices*
> 1   *tablespoon extra-virgin olive oil*
>   *Salt and pepper to taste*

Wash and trim basil. Spread basil leaves on an oval platter. Arrange alternating slices of tomatoes and mozzarella over the basil. Drizzle with olive oil. Season with salt and pepper.

Each serving approximately 139 calories, 9 g total fat, 4 g saturated fat, 13 mg cholesterol, 6 g carbohydrates, 2 g dietary fiber, 27 g protein, 212 mg sodium.

FRESH BASIL AND TOMATO SALAD: Spread 2 cups fresh basil leaves over 4 chilled salad plates. Arrange 1 sliced ripe tomato over each plate of basil. Drizzle each with 1 teaspoon extra-virgin olive oil. Season to taste with salt and pepper.

Each serving approximately 70 calories, 5 g total fat, 1 g saturated fat, 0 mg cholesterol, 7 g carbohydrates, 1 g dietary fiber, 2 g protein, 11 mg sodium.

SANTA FE SALAD

This dressing keeps a long time so you may want to double or even triple the recipe. Use a good grade of olive oil. The flavor is so intense, you'll find you need only a small amount of dressing to add flavor to your salads. A sliced, ripe avocado is a nice addition to this salad—with the fat coming from the healthy unsaturated type.

4 servings

Dressing
- 3 tablespoons *extra-virgin olive oil*
- 1 tablespoon *cider vinegar*
- 1 *garlic clove, minced*
- ¼ teaspoon *salt*
- ⅛ teaspoon *pepper*
- dash *bottled hot sauce*

In a screw-top jar, combine all the ingredients. Cover and shake well.

- 2 cups *torn mixed greens*
- 3 cups *fresh baby spinach leaves*
- 1 *chopped ripe tomato*

In a medium salad bowl, combine mixed greens, spinach leaves and tomato. Pour dressing over. Toss lightly to coat.

Each serving approximately 104 calories, 10 g total fat,
1 g saturated fat, 0 mg cholesterol, 3 g carbohydrates,
2 g dietary fiber, 2 g protein, 169 mg sodium.

ANTIPASTO SALAD

Pair the canned ingredients with some fresh vegetables to create a nutritious, balanced salad in no time.

6 servings

Garlic Vinaigrette
>   3 *tablespoons extra-virgin olive oil*
>   1 *tablespoon cider vinegar*
>   2 *garlic cloves, finely minced*
>   ¼ *teaspoon salt*
>   ⅛ *teaspoon pepper*

In a screw-top jar, combine all the ingredients. Cover and shake until well blended.

>   1 *cup torn red leaf lettuce*
>   1 *cup torn green leaf lettuce*
>   1   *cup torn fresh spinach*
>   2 *ripe tomatoes, cut into wedges*
>   1 *small zucchini or cucumber, diced*
>   1   *8-ounce can water-packed artichoke hearts,*
>   *drained and quartered*
>   1 *5-ounce can whole spears baby corn on the cob,*
>   *drained*
>   1 *8-ounce can garbanzo beans, drained*

In a large salad bowl, combine lettuces, spinach, tomatoes, zucchini, artichoke hearts, baby corn and garbanzo beans. Top with dressing; toss to mix.

Each serving approximately 127 calories, 8 g total fat, 1 g saturated fat, 0 mg cholesterol, 12 g carbohydrates, 3 g dietary fiber, 4 g protein, 276 mg sodium. Each additional 1 tablespoon dressing approximately 74 calories, 8 g fat, 107 mg sodium.

SPINACH SALAD

Making your own dressing in a jar is quick and tastes so much better than commercial dressing. You'll find you'll use this dressing because the flavor is so intense.

4 servings

Dressing
> 3 *tablespoons extra-virgin olive oil*
> 1 *tablespoon fresh lemon juice*
> ¼ *teaspoon salt or to taste*
> ⅛ *teaspoon pepper*

In a screw-top jar, combine all the ingredients. Cover and shake until well blended.

> 8 *cups fresh baby spinach leaves*
> 3 *tablespoons pine nuts*

Put spinach in a medium salad bowl. Toss with dressing. Sprinkle with pine nuts.

SPINACH TOSSED SALAD: Prepare as above, omitting the pine nuts and adding ½ cup crisp croutons, 6 fresh white mushrooms, thinly sliced, and ½ of a purple onion, cut crosswise into ½-inch slices and separated into rings.

Each serving approximately 153 calories, 14 g total fat,
1 g saturated fat, 0 mg cholesterol, 5 g carbohydrates,
3 g dietary fiber, 5 g protein, 221 mg sodium.

ASIAN STIR-FRY

This dish comes together in minutes once the vegetables are cut up. Buckwheat or soba noodles are a great way to get your kids to eat whole grains.

4 servings

Sauce

1 cup chicken broth (preferably homemade, page 310)
1 tablespoon plus 1 teaspoon cornstarch
2 tablespoons reduced-sodium soy sauce
1 teaspoon spicy Thai chili sauce*
  (2 teaspoons for extra spicy flavor)

1 15-ounce can chicken broth or
  2 cups homemade (page 310)
2 cups water
1 8-ounce package soba noodles
1 tablespoon Asian sesame oil
1 10-ounce package firm Chinese tofu
1 tablespoon extra-virgin olive oil
2 tablespoons peeled and minced fresh ginger
2 cups cauliflower florets
¼ pound mushrooms, sliced
½ cup chopped green onions
½ cup baby carrots
2 cups snow peas, ends and strings removed
4 cups baby bok choy leaves, chopped

To make the sauce, combine the 1 cup chicken broth with cornstarch in a small bowl; stir until smooth and no lumps remain. Stir in soy sauce and Thai chili sauce. Set aside.

In a medium saucepan, bring chicken broth and water to a boil. Add soba noodles and cook until just tender, 3 to 4 minutes. Drain. Transfer to shallow serving bowl. Toss with sesame oil. Set aside.

Available in the Thai section of the supermarket.

Drain tofu in a colander for 30 minutes. Cut into ½-inch squares.

Heat a nonstick wok over medium-high heat. When wok is hot, add olive oil. When oil is hot, add ginger and stir-fry for 30 seconds. Add cauliflower and stir-fry, uncovered, for 2 minutes. Add mushrooms, green onions, carrots, snow peas, and bok choy and stir-fry 1 to 2 minutes. Cover and cook 1 minute. Uncover, add tofu and sauce. Stir gently and cook 2 to 3 minutes or until sauce thickens. Pour vegetables over noodles and toss.

Each serving approximately 336 calories, 12 g total fat, 2 g saturated fat, 0 mg cholesterol, 41 g carbohydrates, 6 g dietary fiber, 18 g protein, 898 mg sodium.

A NOTE ON OILS

Of the monounsaturated oils, olive and canola oils are the most highly recommended. Canola oil is the lowest in saturated fat, has a light taste and is particularly good in recipes calling for butter, margarine or lard. Olive oil ranges from mild-flavored to rich-flavored. Use a lighter variety for cooking and a stronger one for salads. The finest quality, labeled "extra-virgin" or "virgin," has a more intense flavor, so the amount of oil can be reduced. Remember, light olive oil has no less fat or fewer calories than regular olive oil.

Of the polyunsaturated oils, safflower oil is the least saturated of all, followed in order by soybean, sunflower, corn, cottonseed and sesame.

POULTRY

SPICY BARBECUED CHICKEN

Your family and guests will rave about this Barbecue Sauce. Double the chicken quantity and use the leftovers for BBQ chicken sandwiches in pita pockets.

6 servings (makes 2 cups sauce)

Barbecue Sauce
- 1 *cup tomato ketchup*
- ¼ *cup brown sugar*
- 2½ *tablespoons pure maple syrup*
- 2 *tablespoons tomato paste*
- 2 *tablespoons Dijon mustard*
  (we like Grey Poupon)
- ½ *teaspoon Tabasco sauce*
- 2 *tablespoons chopped fresh sage*
- 1½ *teaspoons ground cinnamon*
- ¼ *teaspoon Hickory Smoke*
- 1 *tablespoon red wine vinegar*

Combine all ingredients and stir until well blended. Use at once or store in the refrigerator for up to 2 weeks.

Each 1 tablespoon sauce approximately 111 calories, 1 g fat.

6 *whole chicken breasts (about 1½ pounds),*
  skinned, boned, halved and pounded to
  a ½-inch thickness
  extra-virgin olive-oil cooking spray
1 *bunch fresh cilantro for garnish*

Spray chicken breasts lightly on both sides with cooking spray, about 5 seconds. Grill chicken over hot coals 4 to 5 minutes, or until opaque around the edges. Turn and cook 3 to 4 minutes longer, or until opaque throughout. Brush with sauce while grilling. Reserve remaining sauce for later use. Transfer the chicken to a cilantro-lined platter and serve.

Each serving approximately 253 calories, 4 g total fat,
1 g saturated fat, 73 mg cholesterol, 27 g carbohydrates,
0 g dietary fiber, 28 g protein, 611 mg sodium.

A NOTE ON POULTRY

*T*he most healthful poultry is skinless white breast *(white meat is leaner than dark). The skin should always be removed from poultry, since that's where the fat is. Three ounces of skinless chicken breast contains just 3 grams of fat; with skin, it contains twice that amount. Similarly, 3 ounces of skinless turkey breast has just 2.7 grams of fat; with skin, it has 8.7 grams of fat. Watch out for ground turkey and ground chicken—both can be higher in fat than ground round.*

CHICKEN PARMESAN

Try this homemade version of Shake-and-Bake Chicken. You'll love the taste.

4 servings

> 1 *cup oyster crackers or saltines*
> ¼ *cup freshly grated Parmesan cheese*
> 2 *tablespoons finely chopped fresh parsley*
> ½ *teaspoon ground thyme*
> ½ *teaspoon dried oregano*
> ½ *teaspoon dried basil*
> ½ *teaspoon paprika*
> ½ *teaspoon salt*
> ½ *teaspoon pepper*
> 2 *whole skinned and boned chicken breasts,*
>   *halved*
> 1 *teaspoon olive oil*
> ½ *cup low-fat (1%) buttermilk*

Put the oyster crackers in a gallon or jumbo-size zip-lock plastic bag and crush them with your hands or a rolling pin. Add Parmesan cheese and seasonings. Shake the bag to combine the ingredients.

Brush chicken with olive oil, dip in buttermilk and place in the plastic bag; shake bag until chicken pieces are evenly coated with seasonings. Put chicken in a nonstick pan and bake at 400°F for 30 minutes. Reduce heat to 350°F and bake 10 minutes longer, or until chicken is tender.

Each serving approximately 240 calories, 7 g total fat,
2 g saturated fat, 78 mg cholesterol, 11 g carbohydrates,
0 g dietary fiber, 31 g protein, 645 mg sodium.

CHICKEN AND BEAN BURRITOS

This recipe decreases the chicken (animal protein) and increases the black beans (vegetable protein).

6 *servings*

Marinade
- ¼ *cup freshly squeezed orange juice*
- 1 *tablespoon freshly squeezed lime juice*
- 2 *tablespoons cider vinegar*
- 1 *tablespoon extra-virgin olive oil*
- 1 *teaspoon fresh oregano or ½ teaspoon dried*
- ½ *teaspoon salt*
- ¼ *teaspoon pepper*

Combine marinade ingredients in a screw-top jar and shake to blend.

- 2 *whole skinned and boned chicken breasts, cut into ½-inch strips*
- 1 *cup Black Bean Dip (page 400)*
- 6 *cups shredded lettuce*
- 6 *6-inch warm flour tortillas (page 388)*
- ⅓ *cup commercial tomato salsa (optional)*
- ½ *cup nonfat sour cream (optional)*

Pour marinade over the chicken strips; marinate 10 minutes. Drain and set aside.

Heat a nonstick skillet over medium-high heat. Add chicken strips and stir-fry 8 to 10 minutes, or until done. Transfer chicken to a serving platter. Accompany with Black Bean Dip, shredded lettuce, warm tortillas and, if desired, tomato salsa and sour cream.

To prepare burritos have each person spoon Black Bean Dip along the center of a tortilla. Top with shredded lettuce and chicken. Add salsa and sour cream, if using. Fold opposite sides of the tortilla over filling, then fold ends over folded sides.

Each serving approximately 284 calories, 5 g total fat, 1 g saturated fat, 49 mg cholesterol, 32 g carbohydrates, 7 g dietary fiber, 26 g protein, 657 mg sodium.

CHICKEN FAJITAS

Fajitas are the perfect food to get everything you need in proper balance. The tortilla and the variety of vegetables offer an abundance of carbohydrates, while the chicken provides moderate amounts of protein. For a spicier chicken dish, mince a canned chipotle chili and add it to the marinade.

6 servings (makes 1½ cups sauce)

Pico De Gallo Sauce
½ pound ripe plum tomatoes
¼ cup white onion
2 garlic cloves
1 tablespoon extra-virgin olive oil
2 tablespoons freshly squeezed lime juice
¼ teaspoon salt

In a food processor, combine tomatoes, onion, garlic, olive oil and lime juice. Pulse 1 to 2 minutes until tomatoes and onion are finely chopped. Season with salt.

2 garlic cloves, minced
3 tablespoons freshly squeezed lime juice
¼ cup loosely packed cilantro
    plus additional cilantro for garnish
1 tablespoon plus 1 teaspoon extra-virgin olive oil
2 whole skinned and boned chicken breasts, cut
    into ¼-inch strips
2 white onions, halved and sliced lengthwise into
    ⅓-inch-thick slices
1 yellow bell pepper, cut into ⅓-inch strips
1 red bell pepper, cut into ⅓-inch strips
1 green bell pepper, cut into ⅓-inch strips
½ cup nonfat sour cream
6 warm flour tortillas (page 388)

In a medium bowl, combine garlic, lime juice and ¼ cup-cilantro with 1 tablespoon of the olive oil. Add chicken and toss to coat. Let sit 20 to 30 minutes.

Heat a nonstick skillet over medium-high heat. Add chicken strips and stir-fry 8 to 10 minutes, or until done. Remove from pan and set aside.

In the same skillet, heat remaining teaspoon olive oil over medium-high heat. Add onions and stir-fry 2 minutes. Add peppers and stir-fry until crisp-tender, 3 to 4 minutes.

Arrange chicken with onions and peppers on a platter or in a shallow serving bowl. Accompany with Pico de Gallo sauce, sour cream and warm tortillas. Serve with steamed long-grain rice.

Each serving approximately 289 calories, 9 g total fat,
1 g saturated fat, 49 mg cholesterol, 29 g carbohydrates,
4 g dietary fiber, 23 g protein, 254 mg sodium.

A NOTE ON NONSTICK PANS

Investing in high-quality nonstick frying pans allows you to fry and stir-fry with ease and yet use only a minimum amount of fat and in many cases no fat at all. The heavier pans work best. Often frying pans come in sets of three: an 8-inch, a 10-inch and a 12-inch. Although you can stir-fry in the frying pans, a good nonstick wok is a wonderful addition, as are nonstick cake pans and cookie sheets.

CHICKEN STIR-FRY

Stir-fry dinners are your answer to the question "What's for dinner?" You can use any vegetables you happen to have on hand. This wonderful assortment of food then tops a generous amount of good-for-you rice.

4 servings

>   1 *whole skinned and boned chicken breast,*
>   *cut into 1-inch pieces*
>   1 *tablespoon sake*
>   1 *tablespoon potato starch*
>   1½ *teaspoons extra-virgin olive oil*
>   1 *cup very cold water*
>   1 *tablespoon cornstarch*
>   2 *tablespoons reduced-sodium soy sauce*
>   ½ *cup chicken broth, preferably homemade*
>   *(page 310)*
>   1 *garlic clove, minced*
>   2 *cups small broccoli florets*
>   1½ *cups snow peas, halved lengthwise*
>   1 *8-ounce can sliced water chestnuts,*
>   *drained*
>   3 *cups cooked Sticky Rice (page 387)*

Put chicken in a medium bowl and toss with sake. Sprinkle with potato starch and toss again to coat.

In a nonstick wok or skillet, heat ½ teaspoon of the olive oil over medium-high heat. Add chicken and stir-fry 8 to 10 minutes, or until done. Remove pan from the heat and set aside.

Meanwhile, in a small saucepan, combine the cold water with cornstarch and stir until there are no lumps. Add soy sauce and chicken broth. Cook and stir over high heat until sauce thickens; reduce heat and allow to simmer.

In a nonstick wok or skillet, heat another ½ teaspoon of the olive oil over high heat. Add garlic and stir-fry 30 seconds. Add broccoli and stir-fry 2 to 3 minutes, just until broccoli is crisp-tender. Remove from pan and set aside. Drain any liquid from the broccoli that remains in the pan. Add and heat the remaining ½ teaspoon of the olive oil. Add snow peas and water chestnuts, and stir-fry 1 to 2 minutes, or just until snow peas are crisp-tender. Remove from heat. Add the cooked broccoli and chicken. Pour sauce over. Toss gently. Serve with rice.

Each serving approximately 308 calories, 4 g total fat,
1 g saturated fat, 37 mg cholesterol, 46 g carbohydrates,
4 g dietary fiber, 21 g protein, 480 mg sodium.

GRILLED HERBED CHICKEN BREASTS

Cooking with fresh herbs makes such a difference! Try this recipe on your family and enjoy the compliments.

4 servings

> 2   *tablespoons extra-virgin olive oil*
> 1   *tablespoon fresh lemon juice*
> 1   *tablespoon minced fresh thyme*
> ½   *tablespoon minced fresh rosemary*
> ¾   *teaspoon salt*
> ½   *teaspoon pepper*
> 2   *whole skinned and boned chicken breasts*

In an 8 x 8 x 2-inch Pyrex casserole, combine olive oil, lemon juice, thyme, rosemary, salt and pepper. Add chicken breasts and turn chicken over in the marinade so both sides are coated. Marinate 10 minutes.

Heat the grill. When coals are ready, grill chicken breasts about 5 minutes on each side, or until chicken is cooked. When chicken is done, it will feel firm to the touch but not hard.

Each serving approximately 184 calories, 8 g total fat, 1 g saturated fat, 73 mg cholesterol, 1 g carbohydrates, 0 g dietary fiber, 27 g protein, 327 mg sodium.

A NOTE ON HERBS AND SPICES

Fresh herbs and spices are much more flavorful than the dried varieties and should be used whenever possible. More and more supermarkets today stock commonly used fresh herbs such as basil, rosemary, sage, and oregano all year long. Look for them in the fresh vegetable section of the store. In the past we were told that 1 part dried equaled 3 parts fresh, but today most cooks agree that you can be pretty generous with the amount of a fresh herb but very judicious with the amount of the dried.

GRILLED CHICKEN BURGERS

E njoy the taste of a lean burger made with chicken.

4 servings

1 recipe Grilled Herbed Chicken Breasts
   (facing page)
4 sesame hamburger buns, split
4 teaspoons Best Foods or Hellmann's light
   mayonnaise (optional)
1 large tomato, sliced
4 large Boston or Bibb lettuce leaves
4 slices of red or white onion (optional)
2 tablespoons sweet pickle relish (optional)

Prepare chicken breasts according to recipe. Toast buns, cut
side down, on the grill during last 1 minute of cooking.
Spread the mayonnaise on top of each bun half. Arrange a
chicken breast on bottom half of each bun; add tomato, lettuce, onion, if using, and top with other bun half. Transfer
burgers to dinner plates. Garnish with pickle relish.

Each burger approximately 335 calories, 12 g total fat,
2 g saturated fat, 75 mg cholesterol, 25 g carbohydrates,
1 g dietary fiber, 31 g protein, 671 mg sodium.

SOUTHERN FRIED CHICKEN

I magine not having to give up fried chicken! Follow the braising technique in this recipe to enjoy an old favorite.

4 servings

> 1   *cup low-fat (1%) buttermilk*
> 2   *whole chicken breasts, skinned, boned and*
>   *halved*
> 1   *cup all-purpose flour*
> 1½ *teaspoons salt*
> ½   *teaspoon pepper*
> 2   *teaspoons paprika*
> 2   *teaspoons extra-virgin olive oil*

Pour buttermilk into an 8 x 8 x 2-inch pan. Dip chicken in buttermilk, turning once to coat.

Combine flour, salt, pepper and paprika in a paper bag. Add chicken and shake to coat.

In a nonstick skillet over medium-high heat, heat olive oil. Add chicken and cook 10 to 15 minutes, turning chicken frequently to brown evenly. Add 3 tablespoons water and cover. Reduce heat and cook 25 minutes longer. Uncover and cook 5 to 10 minutes more, or until chicken is tender. Remove to serving platter. Set the skillet aside so that the drippings and brown bits can be used for Old-Fashioned Gravy (see recipe at right).

Each serving approximately 304 calories, 6 g total fat,
2 g saturated fat, 75 mg cholesterol, 28 g carbohydrates,
1 g dietary fiber, 32 g protein, 392 mg sodium.

OLD-FASHIONED GRAVY

The combination of the chicken broth and the beef broth gives this gravy a richer flavor than it would have using only chicken broth or only beef broth. It's a quick gravy that can be made in a saucepan. It tastes good even without the drippings and brown bits from the Southern Fried Chicken recipe.

Makes 2 cups (6 servings)

> 1 *cup chicken broth, preferably homemade*
>   *(page 310)*
> 1 *cup beef broth*
> ½ *cup all-purpose flour*
> ¼ *cup very cold water*
> ¼ *teaspoon salt*
> ⅛ *teaspoon pepper*

Pour broths into the skillet used for Southern Fried Chicken recipe, or into a nonstick skillet and bring to a boil. In a screw-top jar, combine flour and water and shake to form a smooth paste; gradually add to boiling broth. Reduce heat to medium and cook, stirring constantly, 3 to 5 minutes, or until gravy has thickened and the remaining brown bits in the skillet are loosened. Season with salt and pepper.

Each serving approximately 46 calories, 1 g total fat,
0 g saturated fat, 1 mg cholesterol, 8 g carbohydrates,
0 g dietary fiber, 2 g protein, 393 mg sodium.

ROASTED CHICKEN
WITH GARLIC

Double this recipe and use the leftovers for sandwiches. Encourage your family to enjoy every bit of flavor in this dish by dipping Tuscan bread in the sauce.

6 servings

> 1½ *teaspoons olive oil*
> 3 *whole skinned chicken breasts, halved (bone in)*
> 30 *garlic cloves (about 3 heads), unpeeled*
> 1¼ *cups dry white wine (Orvieto is good)*
> 1½ *teaspoons fresh rosemary sprigs*
> 1½ *teaspoons fresh thyme sprigs*
> ¼ *cup fresh Italian flat-leaf parsley, chopped*
> *salt and pepper to taste*
> 6 *¼-inch-thick slices Tuscan-style bread*

In a nonstick skillet, heat the oil. Add chicken and cook over medium-high heat 4 to 5 minutes. Turn chicken, add garlic and cook 4 to 5 minutes longer, or until garlic cloves begin to brown. Transfer chicken and garlic to an ovenproof baking dish and set aside.

Pour the wine into the skillet to deglaze the pan; add rosemary and thyme and pour mixture over chicken. Cover tightly with foil. Bake at 350°F for 30 to 45 minutes, or until chicken is done. Sprinkle with parsley. Season with salt and pepper; set aside.

Under a preheated broiler, toast the Tuscan bread slices until bread is golden-brown on each side. Pass bread for dipping with chicken.

Each serving approximately 315 calories, 5 g total fat,
1 g saturated fat, 73 mg cholesterol, 27 g carbohydrates,
0 g dietary fiber, 31 g protein, 338 mg sodium.

EASY CHICKEN

This chicken is excellent for sandwiches and salads, as well as for an entrée dish. Double the recipe and serve part as a dinner entrée one night and the rest for lunch-box sandwiches the following day.

4 servings

> 1 15-ounce can chicken broth or 2 cups
>   homemade (page 310)
> 2 cups water
> 1 pound chicken breasts, skinned and boned,
>   or chicken tenderloins

In a 1½-quart saucepan, bring chicken broth and water to a boil. Add chicken and bring to a second boil. Reduce heat to medium and cook 20 minutes, or until chicken is done. ' Remove chicken and reserve stock for later use.

If chicken is to be used for sandwiches, cool 10 minutes and tear into strings or slice diagonally across top.

Each serving approximately 157 calories, 4 g total fat,
1 g saturated fat, 73 mg cholesterol, 0 g carbohydrates,
0 g dietary fiber, 28 g protein, 178 mg sodium.

ASIAN GARLIC CHICKEN: Combine 3 table-spoons rice wine vinegar, 1 tablespoon extra-virgin olive oil, 1 tablespoon reduced-sodium soy sauce and 2 finely minced garlic cloves in a small bowl. Pass with prepared Easy Chicken. Serve with Sticky Rice (page 387) and Stir-Fried Vegetables (page 393).

Each serving approximately 192 calories, 8 g total fat,
2 g saturated fat, 73 mg cholesterol, 0 g carbohydrates,
0 g dietary fiber, 28 g protein, 328 mg sodium.

ROASTED TURKEY

You can save fat and calories by choosing to eat white meat without skin instead of dark meat with skin. Save the dark meat and the skin for the soup pot.

Approximately 15 3-ounce servings

> **8- to 10-pound fresh turkey**
> **fresh or ground sage to taste**
> **salt and pepper to taste**
> **3 celery stalks, cut into 2-inch pieces**
> **2 onions, quartered**

Rinse inside and outside of turkey with cold water. Rub inside cavity with seasonings. Place celery and onions inside cavity. Skewer neck skin to back; tuck wing tips behind shoulder joints.

In a roasting pan, place turkey breast side up on a rack; roast at 325°F. Turkey is done when drumsticks move easily or twist out of joint. A meat thermometer should register 185°F. If turkey browns too quickly, cover it with a cap of aluminum foil. Remove skin before slicing.

ROASTING CHART
6–8 pounds: 2¾ to 3½ hours
8–12 pounds: 3¼ to 4 hours
12–16 pounds: 3¾ to 5 hours
16–20 pounds: 4¾ to 6½ hours
20–24 pounds: 6¼ to 8 hours

Note: To be heart-healthy, the turkey should not be stuffed, as the fat from the turkey will drip into the dressing. On the facing page is an excellent stuffing recipe that is cooked alongside the turkey.

TO ROAST A HALF- OR QUARTER-TURKEY:

Season as for roast turkey. Place skin side up in a shallow roasting pan. Insert a meat thermometer so tip is in the thickest part of the thigh muscle or breast meat and does not touch bone.

ROASTING CHART FOR HALVES AND QUARTERS

5–8 pounds: 2½ to 3 hours
8–10 pounds: 3 to 3½ hours
10–12 pounds: 3½ to 4 hours

Each 3-ounce serving approximately 143 calories, 4 g total fat,
1 g saturated fat, 64 mg cholesterol, 0 g carbohydrates,
0 g dietary fiber, 25 g protein, 59 mg sodium.

BREAD STUFFING

Made with vegetables, not meats, and moistened with chicken broth, not butter, this stuffing saves many calories and fat-grams.

26 ½-cup servings (enough to accompany a 10- to 14-pound turkey)

> 1 **tablespoon extra-virgin olive oil**
> 1 **large onion, chopped**
> 3 **celery stalks, chopped**
> ½ **pound fresh mushrooms, sliced (optional)**
> 10 **cups dried, unseasoned bread cubes**
> 1 **15-ounce can chicken broth or 2 cups homemade (page 310)**
> 1¼ **teaspoons ground sage or to taste**
> ½ **teaspoon salt or to taste**
> ¼ **teaspoon pepper or to taste**

In a nonstick skillet, heat olive oil. Add onion and celery, and sauté over medium heat until tender. Add mushrooms and sauté 2 to 3 minutes. Remove from heat. Add bread cubes. In a small saucepan, heat broth. Moisten bread gradually with broth, adding a little more or a little less as necessary. Bread cubes should be moist but not saturated. Add seasonings. Transfer to baking dish. Bake, uncovered, at 350°F for 30 to 40 minutes, or until piping hot.

Each serving approximately 43 calories, 1 g total fat, 0 g saturated fat, 0 mg cholesterol, 6 g carbohydrates, 0 g dietary fiber, 2 g protein, 176 mg sodium.

GRILLED TURKEY SANDWICHES

The taste of this sandwich wins hands-down when compared to the taste of a typical turkey sandwich—and you'll love the fat saved compared to that of a burger.

6 sandwiches

Lemon Mayonnaise
   ¼ *cup Best Foods or Hellmann's light mayonnaise*
1½ *teaspoons fresh lemon juice*
   1 *teaspoon grated lemon peel*

Combine ingredients in a small bowl and stir to blend. Set aside.

   1 *tablespoon extra-virgin olive oil*
   2 *tablespoons fresh lemon juice*
   1 *pound very thin turkey breast fillets*
   6 *sesame hamburger buns or sandwich buns, split*
12 *large butter lettuce leaves, washed and crisped*
   1 *large firm ripe tomato, sliced*
   6 *thin slices white onion*
     salt and pepper to taste

Prepare the grill.

In a shallow bowl, combine olive oil and lemon juice. Add turkey fillets and turn to coat on all sides with marinade.

Place turkey on a grill 4 to 6 inches above coals. Cook, turning only once, until turkey is white in center, 10 to 15 minutes total. Just before removing turkey from grill, arrange buns over top of turkey fillets to warm.

To assemble sandwiches, place turkey, lettuce, tomato and onion on bottom half of bun and season. Spread bun top with lemon mayonnaise.

Each serving approximately 252 calories, 7 g total fat,
1 g saturated fat, 50 mg cholesterol, 25 g carbohydrates,
1 g dietary fiber, 21 g protein, 350 mg sodium.

ROASTED HERBED
TURKEY BREAST

B uy the biggest turkey breast available and serve this dish as an entrée. Use any leftover turkey for lunch-box sandwiches the rest of the week.

8 servings

> *3 pounds fresh turkey breast*
> *extra-virgin olive-oil cooking spray*
> *2 heaping tablespoons fresh rosemary*
> *2 heaping tablespoons chopped fresh sage*
> *salt*
> *pepper*
> *paprika*

Spray turkey breast on both sides with olive-oil spray, about 5 seconds or until coated. Rub turkey with rosemary and sage. Sprinkle lightly with salt, pepper and a pinch of paprika for color. Position turkey breast on a rack in a roasting pan. Roast at 325°F for 1½ hours, or until juices have no trace of pink; a meat thermometer should register 170°F.

Each serving approximately 181 calories, 1 g total fat,
0 g saturated fat, 110 mg cholesterol, 0 g carbohydrates,
0 g dietary fiber, 39 g protein, 68 mg sodium.

BEEF, VEAL AND PORK

OLD-FASHIONED MEAT LOAF

This recipe is an example of how buying the leanest ingredients possible make a big difference. Finding 90% lean ground beef is worth the search! For an even leaner meat loaf, use a draining meat loaf pan available at most specialty kitchen stores. Serve leftover meat loaf slices on Kaiser rolls with Best Foods or Hellmann's light mayonnaise and lettuce.

8 servings

> 1   *teaspoon extra-virgin olive oil*
> 1   *large yellow onion, finely chopped*
> 2   *pounds leanest (90% lean) ground beef*
> 1½   *cups bread crumbs*
> 2   *eggs, lightly beaten*
> 1   *teaspoon salt*
> ½   *teaspoon pepper*
> 1   *teaspoon dry mustard*
> ¼   *teaspoon ground thyme*
> ¼   *cup finely chopped fresh parsley*
> ½   *cup evaporated skim milk (Carnation)*

In a nonstick skillet, heat olive oil over medium-high heat. Add onion and sauté until slightly soft, 4 to 5 minutes.

(continued on next page)

(continued from preceding page)

In a large bowl, combine ground beef, bread crumbs and sautéed onion. In a medium bowl, whisk together the eggs, salt, pepper, dry mustard, thyme, parsley and milk. Pour the egg mixture over the beef mixture. Using your hands, mix the ingredients together. Do not overmix or loaf will be too dry. Pat meat mixture into a 5½ x 9½ x 2½-inch loaf pan. Bake at 350°F for 1½ hours, or until meat loaf begins to shrink from sides of the pan. Cover pan with foil for the first ½ hour of baking. Then remove cover for the last hour. Remove from oven and let cool 5 to 10 minutes so the slices won't fall apart. Cut meat loaf into thick slices.

Each serving approximately 317 calories, 14 g total fat, 5 g saturated fat, 123 mg cholesterol, 19 g carbohydrates, 1 g dietary fiber, 28 g protein, 556 mg sodium.

A NOTE ON RED MEAT

According to the Beef Council, the "skinniest six" cuts of beef are top round, eye of the round, round tip, sirloin, top loin and tenderloin. The leanest cuts of beef are labeled "loin" or "round." The lowest-fat grade is "Select," followed by "Choice" and "Prime."

The leanest cuts of pork are labeled "loin" or "leg." With less than 5 grams of fat in a 3.5-ounce serving, pork tenderloin is the equivalent of skinless chicken breast.

The two leanest cuts of lamb are labeled "loin chop" and "leg."

Always trim all visible fat from meat before cooking—the difference between a 3-ounce trimmed T-bone steak and an untrimmed one of the same size is about 20 grams of fat. Cook meat to medium or well-done to allow fat to drip off. If you grill regular hamburger meat until it's well-done, you'll end up with as little fat as you'd have if you used lean ground beef.

STIR-FRIED BEEF

F or a spicier stir-fry, add 1 to 2 hot red-pepper pods along
with the garlic and ginger.

6 *servings*

Sauce

> 2 *tablespoons unseasoned rice vinegar*
> 2 *tablespoons oyster-flavored sauce**
> ¼ *cup reduced-sodium soy sauce*
> 1 *teaspoon extra-virgin olive oil*
> ¼ *teaspoon Asian hot chili oil (optional)*

In a small bowl, combine the rice vinegar, oyster-flavored
sauce, soy sauce, olive oil and, if using, chili oil. Set aside.

> 2 *cups beef broth*
> 2 *cups water*
> 1 *8-ounce package soba noodles*
> 1½ *teaspoons extra-virgin olive oil*
> 1 *teaspoon finely minced garlic*
> 1 *teaspoon minced fresh gingerroot*
> ¾ *pound boneless beefsteak such as top round,*
>   *flank or sirloin, cut into 1-inch stir-fry strips*
> ¾ *pound snow peas, ends and strings removed*
> 1 *red pepper, seeded and cut into ½-inch-wide*
>   *strips*
> ⅛ *teaspoon crushed red pepper*
>   *(optional, if you like spicy)*

In a medium saucepan, bring beef broth and water to a boil.
Add noodles and cook 5 to 6 minutes, or until noodles are
tender. Drain and set aside.

**Oyster-flavored sauce is a thick brown sauce that is available in the Asian section of most super-
markets.*

(continued on next page)

(continued from preceding page)

Place a nonstick wok or skillet over medium-high heat and add ½ teaspoon of the oil. When oil is hot, add garlic and ginger and cook 2 to 3 minutes; add beef and stir-fry until browned, 2 to 3 minutes. Remove from wok and set aside. Heat the remaining 1 teaspoon of oil. Add snow peas, red pepper and crushed red pepper; stir-fry 2 to 3 minutes, or just until crisp-tender. Arrange beef, noodles and vegetables on individual plates. Accompany with sauce.

Each serving approximately 199 calories, 5 g total fat,
1 g saturated fat, 37 mg cholesterol, 20 g carbohydrates,
2 g dietary fiber, 18 g protein, 740 mg sodium.

SUNDAY NIGHT STEW

This recipe is for another comfort food made easy—and lean!

4 servings

1   15-ounce can chicken broth or 2 cups
    homemade (page 310)
2   cups water
8   small white boiling onions, peeled
4   medium white new potatoes, diced
10 baby carrots, peeled
1½ cups sugar snap peas, ends and strings removed
¾   pound veal stew meat
1   cup Old-Fashioned Gravy (page 353) or
    1 8-ounce jar Heinz Homestyle or
    Pepperidge Farm 98% Fat-Free Beef Gravy

In a 4-quart stockpot, combine chicken broth and water and bring to a boil. Add onions and cook 3 to 4 minutes. Add potatoes and cook 8 to 10 minutes. Add carrots and cook 4 to 5 minutes. Add sugar snap peas and cook 1 to 2 minutes longer. (The above cooking times may vary depending on the freshness of the vegetables.) Check vegetables frequently during cooking and as they become tender remove them from the broth using a slotted spoon. Reserve remaining broth for soup at a later time.

While the vegetables are cooking, heat a nonstick skillet over medium-high heat. Add veal and brown 8 to 10 minutes, or until meat is cooked.

Meanwhile, prepare the gravy according to directions.

Arrange meat and vegetables on a serving platter. Serve with gravy.

Each serving approximately 326 calories, 7 g total fat,
2 g saturated fat, 68 mg cholesterol, 40 g carbohydrates,
7 g dietary fiber, 25 g protein, 395 mg sodium using homemade
gravy, 430 mg sodium with commercially prepared gravy.

COMBINATION PIZZA

The combination of the grated fat-free mozzarella cheese topped with slices of the part-skim mozzarella seem to be what makes this low-fat pizza work. As long as the cheeses are layered in the order given, any other toppings may be substituted. You can get all these pizzas on the table in less time than it takes to order a pie and have it delivered.

6 *servings*

> ¼ *pound extra-lean Italian sausage*
>   *(as lean as you can find)*
> 1 *12-inch commercially prepared pizza crust**
> 1 *teaspoon extra-virgin olive oil*
> 10 *fresh basil leaves, chopped*
> 1 *16-ounce can crushed, peeled tomatoes in*
>   *heavy puree (we like Progresso or Di Napoli)*
> 1 *7-ounce can mushroom stems and pieces,*
>   *drained*
> 1 *4-ounce can sliced black olives, drained*
> ½ *cup shredded fat-free mozzarella cheese*
> 3 *ounces part-skim mozzarella cheese, very thinly*
>   *sliced or ⅔ cup shredded*

Preheat the oven to 450° or 500°F (the highest setting, but not broil). Move oven rack to highest position. (If using a baking stone, place stone on rack and heat for at least 30 minutes.)

Slit open, remove and discard the casing on the Italian sausage. Preheat a nonstick skillet over medium-high heat. Add sausage and brown 6 to 8 minutes or until cooked, breaking the sausage apart as it browns. Drain on paper towels and pat dry with additional paper toweling to remove all excess fat. Set aside.

Slide the crust onto a nonstick pizza pan. Rub crust with olive oil, but do not dampen the edges with the oil. Combine basil and tomatoes. Spread crust with ⅓ to ½ cup of the sauce, again taking care not to dampen the edges. (Reserve remaining sauce for pizza at a later date, or serve it over pasta.)

Sprinkle pizza evenly with sausage, mushrooms and olives. Top with shredded fat-free mozzarella cheese and then the slices of part-skim mozzarella cheese. Bake 12 to 15 minutes, or until crust is golden brown.

Each serving approximately 274 calories, 10 g total fat, 2 g saturated fat, 23 mg cholesterol, 31 g carbohydrates, 1 g dietary fiber, 16 g protein, 771 mg sodium

VEGETARIAN MEXICAN PIZZA: Drain and rinse one 15-ounce can black beans. Toss beans with 1 teaspoon extra-virgin olive oil, 1 tablespoon chili powder, and salt to taste; set aside. Combine one 8-ounce can tomato sauce, ½ teaspoon ground cumin (use 1 teaspoon for a more spicy flavor), ¼ teaspoon chili powder, ¼ teaspoon salt and ¼ teaspoon pepper; spread over pizza dough. Sprinkle black beans over top. Add the shredded and sliced mozzarella cheese and bake as directed above. Top baked pizza with cherry tomato halves and avocado slices, if desired.

Each serving approximately 297 calories, 8 g fat, 650 mg sodium. Other amounts remain the same.

PIZZA GARLIC BREAD: Rub pizza crust with 1 tablespoon extra-virgin olive oil. Sprinkle with 1 teaspoon minced garlic and 2 teaspoons fresh rosemary. Sprinkle lightly with salt. Bake on pizza stone for 7 to 8 minutes.

Each serving approximately 154 calories, 4 g fat, 225 mg sodium. Other amounts remain the same.

When selecting a pizza crust, be sure to read labels. Some crusts have little or no fat, while others may be very high in fat. Once the crust is loaded with cheese and toppings, the low-fat crusts will taste just as good as the high-fat crusts.

GRILLED TERIYAKI STEAK

You can make leaner cuts of meat more tender by marinating them first in a lean marinade. Any leftover steak makes great lunch-box sandwiches.

6 servings

> ½ *cup reduced-sodium soy sauce*
> ½ *cup dry vermouth*
> 1 *tablespoon brown sugar*
> 1 *tablespoon Worcestershire sauce*
> 2 *garlic cloves, minced*
> 1 *1-inch piece of fresh gingerroot,*
>   *peeled and minced*
> 1½ *pounds flank steak, all visible fat removed*

In a small bowl, combine the soy sauce, vermouth, brown sugar, Worcestershire sauce, garlic, and gingerroot.

Arrange flank steak in a shallow glass casserole dish suitable for marinating; pour sauce over top. Cover with plastic wrap. Marinate in refrigerator 1 to 24 hours. Drain marinade.

Grill flank steak over hot coals for 6 to 8 minutes on each side, or to desired doneness. Remove to a cutting board. Cut beef across grain at a diagonal angle into thin slices.

Each serving approximately 194 calories, 9 g total fat,
4 g saturated fat, 57 mg cholesterol, 1 g carbohydrates,
0 g dietary fiber, 23 g protein, 244 mg sodium.

A NOTE ON REDUCED-SODIUM SOY SAUCE

Reduced-sodium soy sauce contains 46% less sodium than regular soy sauce, with little or no difference in flavor. Reduced-sodium soy sauce has 80 milligrams of sodium per ½ teaspoon. By comparison, ½ teaspoon of salt has 1,150 milligrams of sodium.

CLASSIC GRILLED BURGERS

Ground chuck is considered the best-tasting ground beef for burgers. Leaner cuts, such as round and sirloin, though more healthy (about 9% fat), dry out. Ask your butcher to select the leanest parts of a chuck roast and grind it especially for you. That way, the meat will be about 14% fat versus 25 to 30% fat in regular ground beef. Unfortunately, most commercial meat grinders are large so you need to buy a minimum of 2 pounds.

8 servings

> 2 *pounds ground chuck**
> 1 *teaspoon salt*
> ¼ *teaspoon pepper*
> 8 *large sesame hamburger buns*
> 2 *large firm ripe tomatoes, sliced*
> 8 *thin slices white onion*
> 1 *head Bibb lettuce, washed and crisped*

Prepare grill.

Season meat with salt and pepper and shape into 8 patties. Grill over hot coals, 3 inches from heat, 6 to 7 minutes per side for medium-rare and 10 to 11 minutes for well-done, turning meat when juices begin to form on top. Serve immediately on warm buns, French bread or French rolls with tomato slices, onion slices and lettuce.

*Remember, since ground chuck is not the leanest cut available, be sure to make low-fat choices for breakfast and lunch and always try to serve the burgers with low-fat accompaniments to keep the total fat content for the day in line.

Each serving approximately 318 calories, 17 g total fat, 1 g saturated fat, 61 mg cholesterol, 17 g carbohydrates, 1 g dietary fiber, 18 g protein, 365 mg sodium.

GRILLED STEAK SANDWICH

Your kids will be pleasantly surprised to find a steak sandwich on the dinner menu.

Makes 1 sandwich

> 3 ounces cubed steak
> 2 slices French bread
> 1½ teaspoons Best Foods or Hellmann's light mayonnaise
> 2 white onion slices
> 2 tomato slices
> 2 lettuce leaves
> young baby spinach leaves

Prepare grill.

Grill steaks over hot coals, 3 inches from heat, 2 to 3 minutes on each side. Serve on French bread with mayonnaise, onion, tomato, lettuce and spinach leaves.

Each serving approximately 261 calories, 7 g total fat,
2 g saturated fat, 52 mg cholesterol, 26 g carbohydrates,
1 g dietary fiber, 23 g protein, 368 mg sodium.

VEAL ITALIAN-STYLE

4 servings

2 *large tomatoes, diced*
1 *teaspoon extra-virgin olive oil*
2 *garlic cloves, finely minced*
1 *teaspoon fresh oregano leaves or*
   ⅛ teaspoon dried
2 *tablespoons fresh basil leaves or*
   ¼ teaspoon dried
   salt and pepper to taste
1 *pound veal, sliced very thin and*
   pounded extra-thin
2 *ounces very thinly sliced part-skim*
   mozzarella cheese

Prepare the grill.

In a saucepan, combine tomatoes, olive oil, garlic, oregano and basil. Heat just to boiling (do not allow to boil). Remove from heat, add salt and pepper and adjust seasonings. Cover to keep warm.

Grill veal over hot coals, 3 inches from heat, for 2 to 3 minutes. Turn when juices begin to form on top of meat. Cover with cheese; grill until cheese melts and veal is done. Top with sauce.

Each serving approximately 215 calories, 9 g total fat,
4 g saturated fat, 97 mg cholesterol, 5 g carbohydrates,
1 g dietary fiber, 26 g protein, 155 mg sodium.

ROASTED PORK TENDERLOIN

R oasts are an easy dinner solution and a cinch to prepare. The only requirements are to season the meat, put it in the oven and occasionally baste it. Small roasts cook in under 1½ hours and are an elegant main course.

4 servings

> 1 *pork tenderloin (about 1 pound)*
> 3 *cloves garlic, pressed*
> 1 *teaspoon extra-virgin olive oil*
> 1 *tablespoon minced fresh rosemary or*
>   1 *teaspoon powdered*
> 1 *tablespoon minced fresh sage or 1½ teaspoons*
>   *dried*
> ¼ *teaspoon salt*
> ½ *teaspoon pepper*
> ½ *pint sauerkraut*

Place tenderloin fat side up on a wire rack in a shallow roasting pan. Mix garlic with olive oil; rub all over roast. Combine remaining seasonings; rub all over roast. Insert meat thermometer horizontally so tip is in center of thickest part of pork. Roast, uncovered, at 325°F for about 1 hour, or until thermometer registers 160°F for medium or 170°F for well-done. Serve with sauerkraut.

Each serving approximately 164 calories, 5 g total fat,
2 g saturated fat, 79 mg cholesterol, 3 g carbohydrates,
0 g dietary fiber, 25 g protein, 751 mg sodium.

SEAFOOD

SAUTÉED SHRIMP

L ightly sautéing the shrimp in a small amount of oil gives them flavor, not heaviness.

4 servings

> 2 *teaspoons extra-virgin olive oil*
> 3 *large cloves finely minced garlic*
> 1 *pound large shrimp, peeled and deveined, tails left on*
> 2 *tablespoons finely chopped Italian flat-leaf parsley*

In a nonstick skillet, heat olive oil. Add garlic and cook over medium-high heat for 1 minute. Add shrimp and cook 3 to 4 minutes. Turn; sprinkle with parsley and cook 3 minutes more, or until opaque. Serve with rice.

Each serving approximately 143 calories, 4 g total fat,
1 g saturated fat, 172 mg cholesterol, 2 g carbohydrates,
0 g dietary fiber, 23 g protein, 169 mg sodium.

GRILLED SHRIMP KABOBS

The unique presentation of a grilled kabob varies the look and adds interest to your family mealtime.

4 servings

>   1 *large red pepper*
>   1 *large yellow pepper*
>   1 *large green pepper*
>   1 *medium white onion*
>   1 *medium red onion*
>   1 *pound large shrimp*
>   ¼ *cup extra-virgin olive oil*
> 1½ *teaspoons balsamic vinegar*
>   2 *tablespoons fresh lemon juice*
>   4 *garlic cloves, chopped*
>   2 *tablespoons chopped fresh basil leaves*
>   12 *cherry tomatoes*
>   1 *cup fresh or canned pineapple chunks, drained*

Prepare grill.

Wash peppers and remove seeds; cut into 2-inch chunks. Peel onions; cut into 2-inch cubes. Shell and devein shrimp; pat dry.

In a shallow bowl, combine olive oil, vinegar, lemon juice, garlic and basil. Add peppers, onions and shrimp; marinate 20 to 30 minutes, turning each two or three times to coat with sauce. Thread shrimp, vegetables, tomatoes and pineapple onto metal skewers. Grill over hot coals 8 to 10 minutes, turning frequently, until shrimp turn pink and are cooked.

Each serving approximately 231 calories, 8 g total fat,
1 g saturated fat, 172 mg cholesterol, 16 g carbohydrates,
3 g dietary fiber, 25 g protein, 180 mg sodium.

STIR-FRIED SCALLOPS WITH SHRIMP

I f you peel and devein the shrimp early in the day or buy pre-cooked shrimp that are already peeled and deveined, this dish can be prepared and on the table in under 10 minutes.

4 servings

½ *pound medium shrimp*
1½ *teaspoons extra-virgin olive oil*
2 *garlic cloves, minced*
½ *pound sea scallops*
1 *bunch fresh Italian flat-leaf parsley*
2 *fresh lemons, cut into wedges*

Peel and devein shrimp, leaving tails on. In a nonstick skillet, heat olive oil over medium-high heat. Add garlic and scallops, and sauté 2 to 3 minutes on each side; add shrimp and cook 2 to 3 minutes longer, or until scallops and shrimp are cooked. Serve on a parsley-lined platter. Garnish with lemon wedges.

Each serving approximately 134 calories, 3 g total fat,
0 g saturated fat, 106 mg cholesterol, 4 g carbohydrates,
0 g dietary fiber, 22 g protein, 182 mg sodium.

TERIYAKI SALMON

This marinade is very adaptable and works equally well on fresh swordfish and tuna.

4 servings

Marinade
¼ *cup reduced-sodium soy sauce*
1 *tablespoon Asian sesame oil*
1 *tablespoon Mirin sweet cooking sake*
     or 1 tablespoon sake and ½ teaspoon sugar
1 *tablespoon minced gingerroot*

1 *pound salmon steaks or fillets*
1 *bunch fresh spinach leaves*
½ *lemon, cut into wedges*
½ *lime, cut into wedges*

In a small bowl, combine the marinade ingredients.

Arrange the salmon in a 9 x 13 x 2-inch casserole. Pour marinade over top and marinate 10 minutes. Turn and marinate 10 minutes more.

While fish is marinating, prepare the grill. When grill is hot, brush grill with oil. Remove salmon from marinade and place on grill. Cook salmon 10 minutes per inch of thickness of fish. If grill has a lid, keep it down during cooking and you will not need to turn the salmon. If not, turn the salmon only once.

Line serving platter with spinach leaves. Arrange cooked salmon on top. Garnish with lemon and lime wedges.

Each serving approximately 232 calories, 13 g total fat,
2 g saturated fat, 75 mg cholesterol, 3 g carbohydrates,
1 g dietary fiber, 24 g protein, 234 mg sodium.

GRILLED SWORDFISH STEAKS

E ach year, seafood ranks higher on the popularity poll of Americans. Introduce fresh fish to kids to start them on their way to acquiring another healthy habit.

4 servings

Marinade
 2 *teaspoons extra-virgin olive oil*
 ¼ *cup fresh lemon juice*
 2 *garlic cloves, minced*
 1 *tablespoon minced parsley*
 1½ *tablespoons fresh rosemary sprigs*

 1 *pound swordfish steaks (about 1 inch thick)*
 fresh rosemary and thyme sprigs for garnish (optional)
 1 *lime, cut into wedges*
 ¼ *cup pitted and chopped Calamata olives (optional)*
 2 *teaspoons capers (optional)*

Prepare grill.

In a small bowl, combine the marinade ingredients.

Arrange swordfish in an 8 x 8 x 2-inch casserole. Pour marinade over swordfish and marinate at room temperature for 15 to 20 minutes.

When grill is hot, brush it with oil. Remove swordfish from marinade and place on grill. Grill, turning once, until just cooked, about 9 to 10 minutes. Place swordfish on a bed of fresh herb sprigs, if desired. Garnish with lime. Sprinkle with olives and capers.

Each serving approximately 163 calories, 7 g total fat,
0 g saturated fat, 57 mg cholesterol, 2 g carbohydrates,
0 g dietary fiber, 22 g protein, 168 mg sodium.

A NOTE ON FISH AND SHELLFISH

Fish and shellfish are high in protein, and many kinds are also low in fat. Unfortunately, varieties such as salmon and swordfish are rich in oil. Recipes that use oily fish can derive more than 30% of calories from fat. But a component of fish oil is Omega-3, which is beneficial to cardiac health, so eating a dish with over 30% fat from fish oil is not the same as eating one with over 30% fat from red meat. Though more healthful than saturated meat fat, fish oil is still rich in calories. Be sure to accompany oily fish with low-fat foods to control the fat content of the entire meal.

Some cuts of salmon are lower in fat than others. Three and one-half ounces of chinook (or king) salmon (the most popular type) has 10 grams of fat; sockeye, 9 grams; coho, 6 grams; chum, 4 grams; and pink, 3 grams. Three ounces of farm-raised Atlantic salmon has 9 grams of fat; chinook, 9 grams; coho, 6 grams; and wild, 5 grams.

The Canadian Department of Fisheries suggests measuring fish at the thickest point and allowing 10 minutes' cooking time per inch. For example, if a salmon measures 3 inches at its thickest point, the total cooking time would be 30 minutes, 15 minutes per side. A halibut fillet that is 1 inch thick would require 10 minutes' total cooking time, 5 minutes per side. Always test fish a few minutes early to avoid overcooking.

Fish is done the second it loses translucency and flakes easily when probed with a fork at its thickest point. When testing a whole fish, probe an inch or two below the base of the head, and again at the thickest point behind the abdominal cavity. When fish is opaque and milky and detaches easily from the bone, it is done.

SIDE DISHES

STUFFED POTATOES

There's more to potato toppings than sour cream and chives! If the potato shells fall apart when you scoop out the insides, just piece them together as best you can before placing the mashed potatoes on top. Once the cheese melts, they'll look perfect.

4 servings

>   2 *large baking potatoes*
>   1½ *teaspoons extra-virgin olive oil*
>   8 *sprigs fresh rosemary*
>   1 *small white onion, finely chopped*
>   2 *tablespoons finely chopped pickled jalapeño*
>   *nacho rings*
>   ¼ *cup low-fat (1%) buttermilk*
>   ½ *cup nonfat sour cream*
>   2 *tablespoons chopped green onions*
>   ¼ *cup shredded nonfat cheddar cheese*
>   ¼ *cup shredded nonfat mozzarella cheese*

Scrub potatoes; cut in half lengthwise. Lay each potato half, cut side down, on a piece of aluminum foil. Drizzle ½ teaspoon of the olive oil among the potato halves and rub each half on all sides with the oil. Tuck 2 sprigs of rosemary under each potato half. Wrap potato in aluminum foil. Bake at 425°F for 30 to 40 minutes, or until tender.

(continued on next page)

(continued from preceding page)

In a nonstick skillet, heat remaining 1 teaspoon olive oil. Add onion and sauté until golden, 3 to 5 minutes. Toss with jalapeños.

Carefully scoop the insides of each potato half into a large bowl, leaving a thin shell. Using a potato masher or electric mixer, mash hot potatoes thoroughly until no lumps remain. Gradually beat in buttermilk until potatoes are smooth and fluffy. Gently stir in the sour cream, green onions, sautéed onions and jalapeños. Divide the potato mixture among the 4 potato shells. Top with cheddar and mozzarella cheeses. Rebake the potatoes at 350°F until the cheese melts, about 10 minutes.

Each serving approximately 140 calories, 2 g total fat,
0 g saturated fat, 3 mg cholesterol, 23 g carbohydrates,
2 g dietary fiber, 7 g protein, 162 mg sodium.

COUNTRY FRIED POTATOES

Frying, as a cooking method, does not need to be a thing of the past. By using a nonstick skillet in combination with an olive-oil cooking spray, you can produce a lean variation on fried potatoes that tastes great!

4 servings

> 1½ *tablespoons extra-virgin olive oil*
> 1½ *tablespoons minced garlic*
> 4 *medium red potatoes with skins,*
>   *(about 1 pound), very thinly sliced*
>   *extra-virgin olive-oil cooking spray*

In a nonstick skillet, heat olive oil over medium-high heat. Add garlic and sauté 2 to 3 minutes. Spray potatoes lightly with cooking spray, about 5 seconds. Add potatoes to skillet and sauté 4 to 5 minutes, turning frequently. Reduce heat to medium, partially cover with lid so steam can escape, and cook 8 to 10 minutes longer, turning frequently. When potatoes are tender, remove lid and reduce heat to low. Sauté 2 to 3 minutes longer, or until nicely browned.

Each serving approximately 124 calories, 6 g total fat,
1 g saturated fat, 0 mg cholesterol, 16 g carbohydrates,
1 g dietary fiber, 2 g protein, 6 mg sodium.

JUMBO OVEN FRIES

R oasting the potatoes actually brings out their flavor. You won't miss the deep fat.

4 servings

> *extra-virgin olive-oil cooking spray*
> 3 *large russet potatoes (2 pounds)*
> *salt to taste*

Preheat oven to 450° or 500°F (the highest setting, but not broil). Move oven rack to highest position. Place a nonstick baking sheet on rack and heat at least 5 minutes.

Meanwhile, scrub potatoes. Cut each potato lengthwise into fourths. Cut each fourth lengthwise into ¼-inch strips. Spray preheated baking sheet with cooking spray until coated, about 5 seconds. Arrange potatoes cut sides down on cookie sheet and spray with cooking spray about 8 seconds, or until coated. Reduce heat and bake at 425°F for 15 to 20 minutes. Turn with a fork or tongs and bake 15 to 20 minutes longer, turning potatoes 2 to 3 times during cooking, until they are tender and evenly browned on all sides. Season with salt.

To speed up the cooking time, parboil the potatoes in boiling salted water to cover 5 to 6 minutes before baking.

ROSEMARY OVEN-FRIES: Prepare as directed above and after spraying the potatoes with olive oil, sprinkle them with 2 to 3 tablespoons chopped fresh rosemary sprigs and salt and pepper to taste.

Each serving approximately 157 calories, 3 g total fat,
0 g saturated fat, 0 mg cholesterol, 31 g carbohydrates,
3 g dietary fiber, 4 g protein, 11 mg sodium.

LOADED BAKED POTATOES

You won't miss the butter when you discover how much flavor is added by the fresh rosemary! And we think you'll find this sour-cream-cottage-cheese mixture just as pleasing as full-fat sour cream.

4 servings

> 2 *large russet potatoes*
> 1 *teaspoon extra-virgin olive oil or olive-oil*
>   *cooking spray*
> 8 *sprigs of fresh rosemary*
>   *salt and pepper*
> ¼ *cup nonfat sour cream*
> ¼ *cup nonfat cottage cheese*

Preheat oven to 425°F.

Meanwhile, scrub potatoes. Cut in half lengthwise. Lay each potato half, cut side down, on a piece of aluminum foil; rub on all sides with olive oil or spray with olive-oil spray. Tuck 2 sprigs of rosemary under each potato half. Wrap each half in aluminum foil. Bake at 425°F for 30 to 40 minutes, or until tender. Season with salt and pepper. Combine sour cream and cottage cheese; pass with potatoes.

Each serving approximately 102 calories, 1 g total fat,
0 g saturated fat, 1 mg cholesterol, 17 g carbohydrates,
1 g dietary fiber, 7 g protein, 118 mg sodium.

GARLIC ROASTED
RED POTATOES

The fresh rosemary and garlic add a whole new level of taste to these roasted potatoes.

4 servings

> 1 *pound small red potatoes*
> *extra-virgin olive-oil cooking spray*
> ½ *cup peeled and minced garlic*
> *(about 8 large cloves)*
> 2 *tablespoons chopped fresh rosemary sprigs or*
> 1 *teaspoon powdered rosemary*
> *salt and pepper to taste*

Preheat oven to 450° or 500°F (the highest setting, but not broil). Move oven rack to highest position. Place an 8 x 8 x 2-inch ovenproof nonstick baking pan on rack and heat at least 5 minutes.

Meanwhile, scrub potatoes and cut into quarters. Spray preheated baking pan with cooking spray until coated, about 5 seconds. Arrange potatoes cut sides down in pan. Sprinkle with garlic and rosemary. Spray with cooking spray until potatoes and garlic are well coated, about 8 seconds. Bake 15 minutes, or until potato tops begin to brown. Turn potatoes; spray lightly with cooking spray and continue baking 20 to 30 minutes more, turning frequently, until potatoes are tender and golden brown. Season with salt and pepper.

Each serving approximately 99 calories, 3 g total fat,
0 g saturated fat, 0 mg cholesterol, 17 g carbohydrates,
1 g dietary fiber, 2 g protein, 8 mg sodium.

MASHED POTATOES

Since these mashed potatoes don't call for butter and cream, you save calories and fat-grams. And the best part is that they taste just as delicious as their high-fat counterparts.

4 servings

> 1½ *pounds potatoes (about 4 medium-large)**
> *salt*
> ¼–⅓ *cup hot nonfat milk*

Wash potatoes, then pare and quarter. In a 2½-quart saucepan, cover potatoes with water, adding ½ teaspoon salt per 1 cup water, and heat to boiling. Cover and boil until tender, 20 to 25 minutes; drain cooking water.

Using a potato masher or electric mixer, mash hot potatoes thoroughly until no lumps remain. Gradually beat in hot milk (amount depends on kind and age of potatoes used) until potatoes are smooth and fluffy.

*Yukon Gold or Finn potatoes lend themselves nicely to this recipe. Their yellow flesh looks and tastes buttery without any added fat.

Each serving approximately 106 calories, 0 g total fat,
0 g saturated fat, 0 mg cholesterol, 24 g carbohydrates,
2 g dietary fiber, 3 g protein, 16 mg sodium.

GARLIC MASHED POTATOES

The key to this lean version of mashed potatoes is the substitution of chicken broth for butter, and nonfat milk for the typical addition of cream.

4 servings

> 1½ *pounds potatoes (about 4 medium-large)*
> *salt*
> 10 *large garlic cloves (about 1 head), peeled*
> ⅓–½ *cup hot chicken broth, preferably homemade (page 310)*
> ⅓ *cup hot nonfat milk*

Wash potatoes, then pare and quarter. In a 2½-quart saucepan, cover potatoes with water, adding ½ teaspoon salt per 1 cup water, and heat to boiling. Cover and boil 15 minutes. Add garlic. Continue boiling until potatoes are tender, 10 to 20 minutes; drain cooking water.

Using a potato masher or electric mixer, mash hot potatoes thoroughly until no lumps remain. Gradually beat in hot chicken broth (amount depends on kind and age of potatoes used). Gradually beat in hot milk. Beat until potatoes are smooth and fluffy.

Each serving approximately 120 calories, 0 g total fat,
0 g saturated fat, 0 mg cholesterol, 26 g carbohydrates,
2 g dietary fiber, 4 g protein, 103 mg sodium.

STICKY RICE

Short-grain rice is also called pearl or Japanese new-variety rice.

4 servings

1 cup short-grain rice

Pour rice into a 2-quart saucepan. Cover with cold water, stir and drain; repeat 2 to 3 times until water runs clear. Return drained rice to saucepan and add 1¼ cups cold water. Bring to a boil over high heat. Reduce heat to low, cover and simmer 20 minutes, or until rice is tender and liquid is nearly absorbed. Remove from heat and let stand, covered, for 5 to 10 minutes. Uncover; fluff with a fork.

CRUSHED RED PEPPER RICE: Sprinkle cooked rice with dried crushed red peppers.

Each 1-cup serving approximately 170 calories, 1 g total fat, 0 g saturated fat, 0 mg cholesterol, 39 g carbohydrates, 0 g dietary fiber, 3 g protein, 5 mg sodium.

WARM TORTILLAS

Both flour and corn tortillas are available. Always buy flour tortillas that are made with soybean oil, not with lard. Corn tortillas, generally made without oil or shortening, are more healthful and lower in fat and calories.

4 servings

4 7-inch flour or corn tortillas

OVEN METHOD: Wrap tortillas in aluminum foil and heat in a 325°F oven until warm, about 15 minutes.

MICROWAVE METHOD: Place tortillas between 2 slightly dampened paper towels. Microwave on high for 1 to 2 minutes, or until warm. Keep wrapped until ready to serve.

EASIEST METHOD: Invest in an inexpensive terra-cotta tortilla warmer available at your local kitchen store or by mail order.

Each serving approximately 114 calories, 2.5 g total fat,
0 g saturated fat, 0 mg cholesterol, 20 g carbohydrates,
1 g dietary fiber, 3 g protein, 167 mg sodium.

KID-FRIENDLY VEGETABLES

LITTLE GREEN TREES

When our niece and nephew Betsy and Guy Hedreen were young they referred to broccoli as green trees. That is how we came up with the name for this recipe.

4 servings

> 2 *tablespoons chicken broth, preferably*
>   *homemade (page 310), or water*
> 3 *cups broccoli florets*
>   *juice of ½ lemon (optional)*

STOVE TOP: In a nonstick skillet, heat broth or water over medium-high heat. Add broccoli florets; cover tightly and steam 3 to 5 minutes, or until broccoli is crisp-tender. Shake pan occasionally during cooking. Drain. Squeeze lemon juice over broccoli.

MICROWAVE: In a microwave-proof baking dish, arrange broccoli in a single layer, florets toward center. Cover with plastic wrap, and prick the plastic wrap to allow steam to escape. Cook at full power 3 to 4 minutes, or just until barely tender.

Each serving approximately 20 calories, 0 g total fat,
0 g saturated fat, 0 mg cholesterol, 4 g carbohydrates,
2 g dietary fiber, 2 g protein, 50 mg sodium.

SAUTÉED BABY CARROTS

Carrots are a great vegetable choice because they are high in vitamin A.

4 servings

> 2 teaspoons *extra-virgin olive oil*
> 1 *large garlic clove, thinly sliced*
> 20 *baby carrots, peeled*
> ¼ *cup chicken broth, preferably homemade*
> *(page 310)*
> 1 *tablespoon chopped fresh parsley*
> 1 *tablespoon chopped fresh mint*
> ⅛ *teaspoon ground nutmeg*
> ⅛ *teaspoon salt*

Heat a nonstick wok or skillet over high heat. When wok is hot, add olive oil. When oil is hot, add garlic and carrots; stir-fry, uncovered, for 1 minute. Add chicken broth; cover and cook 3 to 5 minutes, or until carrots are crisp-tender. Sprinkle with chopped fresh parsley and mint the last minute of cooking. Season with nutmeg and salt.

Each serving approximately 54 calories, 3 g total fat,
0 g saturated fat, 0 mg cholesterol, 8 g carbohydrates,
2 g dietary fiber, 1 g protein, 155 mg sodium.

POPEYE SPINACH

Check your produce market for baby spinach leaves. They are often tastier and more tender than regular spinach leaves.

4 servings

½ teaspoon extra-virgin olive oil
2 garlic cloves, peeled and minced
1 pound fresh spinach, trimmed
   and washed
2 tablespoons water
   salt and pepper to taste
1 teaspoon balsamic vinegar

Place a nonstick skillet over medium-low heat. When skillet is hot, add olive oil. When olive oil is hot, add garlic; sauté until golden, about 1 minute. Add spinach and water. Cover and cook over medium heat until spinach is wilted, 2 to 3 minutes. Remove spinach, shaking off excess water, and place on a serving platter. Season with salt and pepper. Sprinkle with balsamic vinegar and toss gently to mix.

Each serving approximately 31 calories, 1 g total fat,
0 g saturated fat, 0 mg cholesterol, 4 g carbohydrates,
3 g dietary fiber, 3 g protein, 89 mg sodium.

PARMESAN SPINACH: Omit the balsamic vinegar and sprinkle the cooked spinach with 2 tablespoons freshly grated Parmesan cheese.

Each serving approximately 42 calories, 2 g fat, 135 mg sodium.
The other amounts remain the same.

LEMONY SPINACH

The lemon in the spinach recipe will help the body absorb the iron in the spinach.

4 servings

> **2 pounds fresh spinach**
> **juice of ½ lemon**
> **salt and pepper to taste**

Remove spinach stems and wash. Place a metal steamer in a medium saucepan filled with 1 inch of water. Bring water to a boil. Add spinach, cover, and steam for 3 to 4 minutes, or until just wilted. Remove from steamer; season with lemon juice, salt and pepper.

Each serving approximately 43 calories, 0 g total fat, 0 g saturated fat, 0 mg cholesterol, 7 g carbohydrates, 4 g dietary fiber, 5 g protein, 126 mg sodium.

STIR-FRIED VEGETABLES

I nvesting in a nonstick skillet or wok will allow you to sauté in *minimal* fat with *ease.*

4 servings

1 teaspoon extra-virgin olive oil
½ teaspoon Asian sesame oil
3 medium carrots, cut diagonally into slices
⅛ inch thick
3 large garlic cloves, thinly sliced
¼ cup chicken broth, preferably homemade
(page 310)
1 teaspoon peeled, minced fresh gingerroot
½ pound snow peas, ends and strings removed
1 red pepper, seeded and cut into ½-inch-wide
strips
1 tablespoon reduced-sodium soy sauce

Place a nonstick wok or skillet over high heat. When wok is hot, add olive oil and sesame oil. When oils are hot, add carrots and garlic; stir-fry, uncovered, for 1 minute. Add chicken broth. Cover and cook 3 minutes. Add ginger, snow peas and red pepper. Cover and cook 1 minute longer, or until vegetables are crisp-tender. Drizzle with soy sauce.

Each serving approximately 76 calories, 2 g total fat,
0 g saturated fat, 0 mg cholesterol, 13 g carbohydrates,
4 g dietary fiber, 3 g protein, 235 mg sodium.

CHINESE SNOW PEAS

Cook the fresh snow peas just until they are crisp-tender. You will be preserving nutrients, and your kids will like their crunchy (not mushy) quality.

4 servings

>   2   teaspoons *extra-virgin olive oil*
>   1   teaspoon *finely minced garlic*
>   ¼   teaspoon *crushed red pepper*
>   ¾   pound *snow peas, ends and strings removed*

Place a nonstick wok or skillet over high heat. When wok is hot, add olive oil, garlic and crushed red pepper. When oil is hot, add snow peas; stir-fry, uncovered, just until crisp-tender, 2 to 3 minutes.

Each serving approximately 56 calories, 2 g total fat, 0 g saturated fat, 0 mg cholesterol, 7 g carbohydrates, 2 g dietary fiber, 2 g protein, 4 mg sodium.

STIR-FRIED BROCCOLI AND CAULIFLOWER WITH RED PEPPERS

This recipe offers a variety of color (green, white and red) as well as a variety of vegetables (green leafy, cruciferous, and vitamin C-rich).

4 servings

> 1 teaspoon extra-virgin olive oil
> 1 teaspoon Asian sesame oil
> 2 cups broccoli florets
> 2 cups cauliflower florets
> ¼ cup chicken broth, preferably homemade
>   (page 310)
> 1 cup red pepper, seeded and cut into
>   ¼-inch strips

Place nonstick wok or skillet over high heat. When wok is hot, add olive oil and sesame oil. When oils are hot, add broccoli and cauliflower; stir-fry, uncovered for 1 minute. Add chicken broth. Cover and cook 2 minutes. Add red peppers. Cover and cook one minute longer, or until vegetables are crisp-tender.

Each serving approximately 52 calories, 3 g total fat,
0 g saturated fat, 0 mg cholesterol, 6 g carbohydrates,
3 g dietary fiber, 3 g protein, 82 mg sodium.

GREAT GREEN BEANS

Steaming is an easy, low-calorie way to prepare all sorts of vegetables. Steamed vegetables keep their color and nutrients—and they taste fantastic.

6 *servings*

> 1 *pound fresh green beans*
> 1 *15-ounce can water-packed artichoke hearts,*
> *drained and quartered*
> ¼ *cup fresh lemon juice*
> 2 *teaspoons extra-virgin olive oil*
> ½ *teaspoon salt*
> ¼ *teaspoon pepper*

Wash beans; remove ends and strings. Place a metal vegetable steamer in a medium saucepan filled with 1 inch of water. Bring water to a boil. Add beans; cover and steam 15 to 20 minutes, or until beans are just tender (do not overcook). Remove beans from steamer. Add artichokes. Toss with lemon juice, olive oil, salt and pepper. Serve hot or cold.

Each serving approximately 57 calories, 2 g total fat,
0 g saturated fat, 0 mg cholesterol, 9 g carbohydrates,
3 g dietary fiber, 2 g protein, 437 mg sodium.

ROASTED MIXED VEGETABLES

Cooking spray coats vegetables with oil using far less fat than pouring it on as a dressing.

6 servings

> *extra-virgin olive-oil cooking spray*
> 2 *pounds selected vegetables, such as asparagus,*
>   *broccoli, carrots, cauliflower or green beans*
> 1 *tablespoon balsamic vinegar (optional)*
>   *salt and pepper to taste*

Preheat oven to 450° or 500°F (the highest setting, but not broil). Move oven rack to highest position. Place a nonstick baking sheet on rack and heat at least 5 minutes.

Meanwhile, trim and wash vegetables. Pat with paper towels to remove all excess moisture. Spray preheated baking sheet with olive oil cooking spray until coated, about 5 seconds. Arrange vegetables in a single layer on hot baking sheet and spray until lightly coated, about 8 seconds. Roast vegetables until tender, about 5 to 7 minutes depending on size and freshness. Turn vegetables with tongs 2 to 3 times during cooking. Transfer cooked vegetables to serving dish. Drizzle with balsamic vinegar, if desired. Season with salt and pepper.

ROASTED BABY VEGETABLES: Select a combination of baby eggplants, baby zucchini, patty pan squash, red, green or yellow pepper cut into squares, small white cremini or portobello mushrooms. Cook as directed above.

Each serving approximately 61 calories, 2 g total fat,
0 g saturated fat, 0 mg cholesterol, 10 g carbohydrates,
4 g dietary fiber, 2 g protein, 35 mg sodium.

HOLIDAY YAMS

These yams are lean due to no cream and butter. And your kids will love the apples and the marshmallow topping.

8 servings

> **2 large Red Delicious apples, sliced**
> **⅓ cup chopped pecans**
> **⅓ cup brown sugar**
> **½ teaspoon cinnamon**
> **1 28-ounce can yams, drained**
> **1 cup miniature marshmallows**

Preheat oven to 350°F.

Put apples and pecans in a medium mixing bowl. Combine brown sugar with cinnamon in a small bowl. Pour over apples and gently toss until apples are coated. Arrange yams in a 1½-quart ovenproof casserole. Poke apples in between yams. Cover with aluminum foil. Bake 35 to 40 minutes. Sprinkle with marshmallows. Broil 6 to 8 minutes, or until marshmallows are lightly browned.

Each serving approximately 206 calories, 4 g total fat,
0 g saturated fat, 0 mg cholesterol, 45 g carbohydrates,
3 g dietary fiber, 0 g protein, 32 mg sodium.

RAW VEGGIES IN A BASKET

K eep your kids' interest by experimenting with different dips for your vegetables. It will make eating them more fun. These fresh vegetables are particularly good with saucy entrées such as Classic Lasagna (page 316), Cheesy Macaroni (page 320) and Sally's Noodle Casserole (page 312). Encourage your family to dip the vegetables into the sauce.

6 *servings*

> 16 *baby carrots or 4 larger carrots, peeled and*
> *cut into thirds*
> 4 *stalks celery, trimmed and cut into thirds*
> 1 *bunch green onions, trimmed*
> 1 *small bunch radishes, rinsed and trimmed*
> 1 *small summer squash, cut crosswise into rings*
> 1 *English cucumber, cut crosswise into rings*
> 8 *cherry tomatoes, halved*
> 2 *cups sugar snap peas*
> 1 *small bunch fresh spinach, rinsed and trimmed*

Chill vegetables. Arrange in a spinach-lined basket.

VARIATIONS: Other options include blanched green beans or asparagus, red or green pepper strips, daikon radish, jicama strips, or steamed baby red potatoes.

Each serving approximately 55 calories, 0 g total fat,
0 g saturated fat, 0 mg cholesterol, 10 g carbohydrates,
3 g dietary fiber, 2 g protein, 52 mg sodium.

> A *s an after-school snack, you may want to experiment with various dips, including Black Bean Dip, White Bean and Garlic Dip, Artichoke Dip, Avocado Dip and Sour Cream Dip. These recipes can be found on the following pages.*

BLACK BEAN DIP

B lack bean dip is an interesting and tasty change to the typical ranch dip for vegetables. The fat and calories saved can be used at another meal.

Makes 1 cup

> **1 15-ounce can black beans,**
> **drained but not rinsed**
> **1 tablespoon chili powder**
> **½ teaspoon cumin**
> **¼ teaspoon salt**

Combine all ingredients in a food processor and process until smooth, 2 to 3 minutes. Taste. Add additional salt if needed.

Serve with cut-up celery, carrots, cucumber and jicama sticks, nonfat tortilla chips or warm flour tortillas (page 388).

RED BEAN DIP: Substitute red kidney beans for black beans.

Each 1-tablespoon serving approximately 24 calories, 0 g total fat, 0 g saturated fat, 0 mg cholesterol, 4 g carbohydrates, 2 g dietary fiber, 2 g protein, 126 mg sodium.

WHITE BEAN AND GARLIC DIP

Here's another dip for your vegetables, and because it's made with beans, you get some fiber.

Makes 1½ cups

> 1 **15-ounce can cannellini beans,**
>   **drained and rinsed**
> 2–3 **large cloves garlic, peeled**
> 1 **tablespoon fresh lemon juice**
> 1 **tablespoon extra-virgin olive oil**
> ½ **teaspoon salt**
> ¼ **teaspoon pepper**

Combine all ingredients in a food processor and process 2 to 3 minutes until smooth.

Serve with cut-up celery and carrot sticks, radishes, broccoli and cauliflower florets, warm breadsticks or pita bread, or sliced and toasted bagels.

Each 1-tablespoon serving approximately 17 calories, 1 g total fat, 0 g saturated fat, 0 mg cholesterol, 3 g carbohydrates, 1 g dietary fiber, 1 g protein, 45 mg sodium.

ARTICHOKE DIP

Great with raw vegetables or as a spread on grilled or toasted French or Tuscan bread.

Makes 1 cup

> 1 **15-ounce can artichoke bottoms,**
>   **drained**
> 3 **tablespoons extra-virgin olive oil**
> 3 **large cloves garlic, peeled**
> 2 **tablespoons freshly grated**
>   **Parmesan cheese**
> ½ **teaspoon salt**
> ¼ **teaspoon pepper**

Combine artichoke bottoms, olive oil and garlic in a food processor and process until smooth. Add cheese, salt and pepper and process until combined, about 30 seconds.

Each 1-tablespoon serving approximately 33 calories, 3 g total fat,
0 g saturated fat, 1 mg cholesterol, 1 g carbohydrates,
1 g dietary fiber, 1 g protein, 174 mg sodium.

AVOCADO DIP

Use this dip in moderation with fresh vegetables such as fresh carrots and radishes, or as a complement to Mexican food.

Makes 1 cup

> 1 *ripe avocado*
> 1 *tablespoon fresh lime juice*
> ⅛ *teaspoon salt*
> 1 *tablespoon grated onion (optional)*

In a small bowl, mash avocado with a fork. Add lime juice and salt. Stir with fork until avocado is smooth. Add onion, if desired.

Each 1-tablespoon serving approximately 22 calories, 2 g total fat, 0 g saturated fat, 0 mg cholesterol, 2 g carbohydrates, 0 g dietary fiber, 0 g protein, 18 mg sodium.

AVOCADO SHRIMP DIP: Add ½ cup cooked shrimp to mixture above.

Each 1-tablespoon serving approximately 26 calories, 3 g total fat, 0 g saturated fat, 8 mg cholesterol, 2 g carbohydrates, 0 g dietary fiber, 1 g protein, 28 mg sodium.

SOUR CREAM DIP

You may want to serve this dip as a condiment for baked potatoes, chili or Jumbo Oven Fries (page 382). It works equally well as a fresh vegetable dip.

Makes 2 cups

> 1 *cup nonfat sour cream*
> 1 *cup nonfat cottage cheese*
> 2 *tablespoons Best Foods or Hellmann's*
> *light mayonnaise*
> 1 *0.4-ounce package Hidden Valley Ranch*
> *Original Ranch Salad Dressing Mix*
> *(Buttermilk Recipe)*

Combine sour cream, cottage cheese, mayonnaise and salad dressing mix. Chill.

Each 1-tablespoon serving approximately 13 calories, 0 g total fat,
0 g saturated fat, 1 mg cholesterol, 0 g carbohydrates,
0 g dietary fiber, 1 g protein, 44 mg sodium.

OLD FAVORITES MADE LEAN

BLACK BOTTOM CUPCAKES

With no frosting, these cupcakes are convenient to pack in a lunch box or send along to the Brownie meeting or class picnic.

Makes 24 cupcakes

Filling

   1 *8-ounce package fat-free cream cheese, softened*
   1 *egg*
1⅓ *cups granulated sugar*
 ⅝ *teaspoon salt*
   1 *6-ounce package semisweet chocolate chips*

  ½ *cup sifted all-purpose flour*
   1 *teaspoon baking soda*
  ⅓ *cup Hershey's unsweetened cocoa powder*
   1 *cup water*
   1 *2½-ounce jar baby food prunes*
   2 *tablespoons canola oil*
   1 *tablespoon cider vinegar*
   1 *teaspoon vanilla extract*

(continued on next page)

(*continued from preceding page*)

Preheat oven to 350°F.

With an electric mixer on medium speed, combine cream cheese, egg, ⅓ cup of the sugar and ⅛ teaspoon of the salt in a mixing bowl. Stir in chocolate chips. Set cream cheese mixture aside.

In a small bowl, combine flour, remaining 1 cup sugar, baking soda, cocoa and remaining ½ teaspoon salt with a wire whisk. Add water, prunes, canola oil, vinegar and vanilla; whisk together until blended and smooth.

Fill 24 paper-lined muffin cups one-third full with batter. Top each with a heaping teaspoon of the cream cheese mixture. Bake for 25 minutes.

Each cupcake approximately 120 calories, 3 g total fat,
0 g saturated fat, 11 mg cholesterol, 19 g carbohydrates,
0 g dietary fiber, 3 g protein, 169 mg sodium.

GINGERSNAPS

This recipe is great for a crowd because it yields so many cookies.

Makes 8 dozen cookies

>   2 *cups granulated sugar plus sugar for rolling*
> 1½ *cups shortening*
>   2 *eggs*
>   ¾ *cup molasses*
>   4 *teaspoons baking soda*
>   4 *cups sifted all-purpose flour*
>   1 *heaping teaspoon ginger*
>   1 *heaping tablespoon cinnamon*
>   ½ *teaspoon salt*

Preheat oven to 375°F.

With an electric mixer on medium to high speed, cream sugar and shortening in a mixing bowl. Add eggs and molasses, and beat 2 to 3 minutes. Add baking soda, flour, ginger, cinnamon and salt, and beat until thoroughly combined. Form into small balls. Roll balls in granulated sugar (do not flatten); place on nonstick cookie sheet, 2 inches apart. Bake for 8 to 10 minutes. Cool slightly; remove from cookie sheet.

Each cookie approximately 71 calories, 3 g total fat,
0 g saturated fat, 4 mg cholesterol, 10 g carbohydrates,
0 g dietary fiber, 1 g protein, 66 mg sodium.

PEANUT BUTTER COOKIES

The applesauce reduces the need for more butter or margarine in this recipe for an old favorite.

Makes 5 dozen cookies

> ¾ cup creamy peanut butter
> 2 tablespoons margarine
> ⅓ cup plus 2 teaspoons applesauce
> 1¼ cups all-purpose flour
> ½ cup granulated sugar
> ½ cup brown sugar
> 1 egg
> 1 teaspoon baking soda
> ¼ teaspoon baking powder
>   dash of salt

Preheat oven to 350°F.

With an electric mixer on medium speed, combine peanut butter, margarine and applesauce in a mixing bowl. Add remaining ingredients and mix well.

Roll dough into 1-inch balls and arrange 3 inches apart on nonstick cookie sheets. Using a fork, press crisscross pattern on cookies. Bake until golden, about 10 to 12 minutes. Transfer to a wire rack to cool.

Each cookie approximately 47 calories, 2 g total fat,
0 g saturated fat, 4 mg cholesterol, 6 g carbohydrates,
0 g dietary fiber, 1 g protein, 43 mg sodium.

CHEWY MOLASSES COOKIES

B y using baby food prunes, less shortening is needed and fat is reduced without sacrificing taste.

Makes 8 dozen cookies

> 2 cups firmly packed dark brown sugar
> ¾ cup shortening
> 2 eggs
> ½ cup molasses
> 2 2½-ounce jars baby food prunes
> 4 teaspoons baking soda
> 4 cups sifted all-purpose flour
> 1 heaping teaspoon ginger
> 1 heaping tablespoon cinnamon
> ½ teaspoon salt
> granulated sugar for rolling

Preheat oven to 375°F.

With an electric mixer on medium to high speed, cream sugar and shortening in a mixing bowl. Add eggs and molasses, and beat 2 to 3 minutes. Add prunes and mix well. Add baking soda, flour, ginger, cinnamon and salt, and beat until thoroughly combined. Chill dough in refrigerator for 2 hours. Form into small balls. Roll balls in granulated sugar (do not flatten). Place on nonstick cookie sheets, 2 inches apart. Bake for 8 to 10 minutes. Cool slightly; remove from cookie sheets.

Each serving approximately 77 calories, 2 g total fat,
0 g saturated fat, 6 mg cholesterol, 13 g carbohydrates,
0 g dietary fiber, 1 g protein.

STRAWBERRY SHORTCAKE

To make a fun Valentine's Day dessert, cut the biscuits with a 3-inch heart-shaped cookie cutter.

8 *servings*

> **8 biscuits made from reduced-fat biscuit mix**
> **(such as Bisquick)**
> **4 cups hulled strawberries**
> **2 cups light vanilla ice cream**

Prepare biscuit batter according to package directions; let sit 20 minutes. Bake according to package directions.

Reserve a few whole berries for garnish. Place remaining berries in a bowl and slightly crush them.

Split the still-hot biscuits and put them on individual dessert plates. Add crushed berries and a dollop of ice cream to the bottom half. Cover with the other half. Add more ice cream and crushed berries. Garnish with reserved whole berries.

Each serving approximately 180 calories, 4 g total fat,
2 g saturated fat, 3 mg cholesterol, 31 g carbohydrates,
1 g dietary fiber, 5 g protein, 336 mg sodium.

PAIN AU CHOCOLAT

Pain au chocolat was the simple forerunner of the fancy chocolate croissant.

Makes 4 sandwiches

> **8 ¼-inch-thick slices of a 2 x 3-inch French baguette**
> **16 small squares (¼" x 1") Lindt Swiss Milk Chocolate Bar (½ of a 3-ounce bar)**

Place 4 chocolate squares on a baguette slice. Top with a second baguette slice. Wrap sandwich in a paper napkin. Cook in microwave for 1 minute, just until chocolate melts. Cut sandwich in half. Serve with milk.

Each sandwich approximately 137 calories, 4 g total fat,
2 g saturated fat, 0 mg cholesterol, 21 g carbohydrates,
0 g dietary fiber, 3 g protein, 201 mg sodium.

VARIATION: Use eight 2 x 2-inch graham crackers in place of baguette slices.

Each 2 x 2-inch sandwich approximately 114 calories,
5 g total fat, 2 g saturated fat, 0 mg cholesterol, 16 g carbohydrates,
0 g dietary fiber, 2 g protein, 86 mg sodium.

BEST-EVER CHOCOLATE SHAKES

Fat-free ice cream in combination with chocolate syrup makes a smooth and creamy shake. The integrity of the shake is not compromised by substituting leaner ingredients.

4 servings

> ¼ **cup nonfat milk**
> ¼ **cup Hershey's Chocolate Syrup**
> 1 **quart fat-free vanilla ice cream, softened**
> ¾ **teaspoon pure vanilla extract**

Combine milk, chocolate syrup and ice cream in a blender and blend until nearly smooth. Add vanilla and blend until smooth, about 30 seconds longer. Stir and pour into glasses.

Each serving approximately 253 calories, 0 g total fat, 0 g saturated fat, 0 mg cholesterol, 57 g carbohydrates, 0 g dietary fiber, 7 g protein, 197 mg sodium.

AWESOME STRAWBERRY SHAKES

You might be surprised at how much ice cream it takes to make a shake. However, when you taste this creamy milk shake, I think you'll find it very satisfying.

4 servings

1 10-ounce package sliced, fresh-frozen strawberries with sugar, thawed
¼ cup nonfat milk
1 quart fat-free vanilla ice cream, softened

Put ½ cup of the thawed berries in a blender; add milk and blend 30 seconds. Add ice cream and blend until nearly smooth. Stir and pour into glasses. (Reserve remaining ½ cup berries to serve over ice cream at a later meal.)

Each serving approximately 305 calories, 1 g total fat,
0 g saturated fat, 0 mg cholesterol, 68 g carbohydrates,
4 g dietary fiber, 7 g protein, 168 mg sodium

ANGEL FOOD CAKE WITH SEVEN-MINUTE ICING

Angel food cake is the cake of choice at our house because it's so low in fat.

12 servings

1 box angel food cake mix

Frosting
2 egg whites
1¼ cups granulated sugar
dash of salt
½ cup water
¼ teaspoon cream of tartar
1 teaspoon vanilla extract

Prepare angel food cake according to package instructions. When cake has thoroughly cooled, prepare frosting.

In bottom of a double boiler, bring 2 cups water to a boil. In the top of the double boiler, combine egg whites, sugar, salt, ½ cup water, and cream of tartar; beat 1 minute. Place over boiling water. Using highest speed of electric mixer, beat constantly for 5 to 7 minutes, or until frosting stands in stiff peaks. Remove from heat. Stir in vanilla. Spread frosting over top and sides of cake.

Each serving approximately 214 calories, 0 g total fat, 0 g saturated fat, 0 mg cholesterol, 51 g carbohydrates, 0 g dietary fiber, 4 g protein, 224 mg sodium.

CHOCOLATE GLAZE: In a small bowl, combine 1 cup confectioners' sugar, sifted, and 2 tablespoons cold non-fat milk; stir until smooth. Add 1 teaspoon unsweetened cocoa powder (Ghirardelli and Dröste are good); stir until smooth. Spread the glaze over the top of the cake and allow it to drizzle down the sides.

Each serving approximately 170 calories, 172 mg sodium.
The other amounts remain the same.

ORANGE GLAZE: In a small bowl, combine 1 cup confectioners' sugar, 2 tablespoons chilled, freshly squeezed orange juice and 1 tablespoon orange zest. Stir until smooth. Spread the glaze over the top of the cake and allow it to drizzle down the sides.

Each serving approximately 170 calories, 170 mg sodium.
The other amounts remain the same.

WITH FRESH STRAWBERRIES: Crush or slice 2 pints of strawberries. Top each slice of cake with berries, a dollop of light vanilla ice cream and one whole berry for garnish. If desired, substitute raspberries or peaches for strawberries. With this variation I like to use mini angel food cake pans, which are available at kitchen stores. They are on the order of muffins tins; each tin makes six mini angel food cakes.

Each mini cake approximately 340 calories, 2 g fat,
359 mg sodium. The other amounts remain the same.

VERY BERRY COBBLER

K eep some berries in the freezer and this delicious cobbler can come together in minutes—all year round.

8 *servings*

Cobbler Dough

>   1   *cup all-purpose flour*
>   ½   *teaspoon salt*
>   1½ *teaspoons baking powder*
>   ⅓   *cup nonfat milk*
>   3   *tablespoons canola oil*

Berry Filling

>   ½   *cup cold water*
>   2   *tablespoons cornstarch*
>   ½   *cup granulated sugar*
>   6   *cups strawberries, raspberries, blueberries or blackberries*

Preheat oven to 425°F.

To prepare the dough, sift flour, salt and baking powder into a small bowl. In a separate bowl, mix milk with canola oil. Add the milk-and-oil combination all at once to flour mixture. Using a fork or pastry blender, work dough into a ball. Knead the ball of dough with your hands once or twice until ball is smooth and all the flour mixture is worked in. If the dough seems dry add a few more drops of milk for moisture. Do not overwork the dough. With your fingers, pinch off 10 to 12 silver-dollar-size rounds of dough. Flatten each round very slightly between fingers and set aside.

In a medium saucepan, combine all the ingredients for the filling except for the berries; bring to a boil over high heat. Cook 1 minute, stirring constantly. Remove from heat and gently stir in berries. Pour into a 9-inch pie plate. Arrange the dough rounds over top. Bake for 20 to 25 minutes, or until topping is lightly browned.

Each serving approximately 186 calories, 6 g total fat,
0 g saturated fat, 0 mg cholesterol, 32 g carbohydrates,
2 g dietary fiber, 2 g protein, 232 mg sodium.

RED RASPBERRY PIE

This delicious pie works well with whatever berries are in season.

8 servings

1 9-inch double pastry crust, prepared from a mix such as Krusteaz
1 tablespoon all-purpose flour
½ cup granulated sugar
⅛ teaspoon salt
4 cups fresh raspberries, strawberries or blackberries
1 teaspoon freshly squeezed lemon juice

Prepare double pastry crust according to package directions. Line a 9-inch pie plate with bottom crust.

Preheat oven to 450°F.

Mix together flour, sugar and salt; sprinkle a quarter of the mixture on uncooked bottom crust. Coat berries with lemon juice and toss with remaining sugar mixture. Spoon into pie plate. Add top crust; seal and flute edges. Cover edges of crust with a 3-inch strip of aluminum foil to prevent excessive browning. Cut slits in top crust so that steam can escape. Bake at 450°F for 15 minutes. Reduce heat to 350°F and continue baking until crust is brown and juices begin to bubble through slits in crust, 20 to 25 minutes. Remove foil during the last 15 minutes of baking.

Each serving approximately 266 calories, 10 g total fat,
1 g saturated fat, 0 mg cholesterol, 41 g carbohydrates,
trace dietary fiber, 3 g protein, 234 mg sodium.

HOMEMADE APPLE PIE

T ry to make the day's other meals lean to save room for a
slice of this pie.

8 servings

> 1 *9-inch double pastry crust, prepared from*
> *a mix such as Krusteaz*
> 6 *cups pared and sliced tart apples, such as*
> *Granny Smith*
> 2 *tablespoons freshly squeezed lemon juice*
> ¼ *cup granulated sugar*
> ½ *teaspoon cinnamon*
> 1 *tablespoon all-purpose flour*

Preheat oven to 450°F.

Prepare double pie crust according to package instructions.
Line a 9-inch pie plate with bottom crust.

Toss apples with lemon juice. In a bowl, combine sugar, cinnamon and flour; mix with apples. Spoon into pie plate. Add
top crust; seal and flute edges. Cover edges of crust with a 3-
inch strip of aluminum foil to prevent excessive browning.
Cut slits in top crust so that steam can escape. Bake at 450°F
for 10 minutes. Reduce heat to 375°F and continue baking
until crust is brown and juices begin to bubble through slits
in crust, 30 to 40 minutes. Remove foil during the last 15
minutes of baking.

Each serving approximately 296 calories, 12 g total fat,
2 g saturated fat, 0 mg cholesterol, 46 g carbohydrates,
2 g dietary fiber, 2 g protein, 200 mg sodium.

PUMPKIN PIE

This pie saves calories and fat-grams because it's made with nonfat milk instead of whole milk. Best of all, you never taste the difference.

8 slices

> 1 9-inch pie shell, prepared from a mix such
>   as Krusteaz
> 1 1-pound can pumpkin
> ¾ cup firmly packed brown sugar
> 3 lightly beaten eggs
> ¼ teaspoon salt
> 1 teaspoon cinnamon
> ½ teaspoon ground ginger
> ½ teaspoon nutmeg
> ¼ teaspoon ground cloves
> 1 12-ounce can evaporated skim milk

Preheat oven to 400°F.

Prepare pie shell according to package instructions. Line a 9-inch pie plate with crust.

Measure remaining ingredients into a medium mixing bowl. Mix with wire whisk or spoon until well blended. Pour into pie shell. Cover edges of crust with a 3-inch strip of aluminum foil to prevent excessive browning. Bake for 50 minutes, or until knife inserted in center of pie comes out clean.

Each serving approximately 274 calories, 8 g total fat,
2 g saturated fat, 81 mg cholesterol, 44 g carbohydrates,
0 g dietary fiber, 8 g protein, 257 mg sodium.

FRESH STRAWBERRY PIE

This is a quick and easy dessert for the summer when strawberries are fresh.

8 servings

> 1 *9-inch pie shell, prepared from a mix such as Krusteaz*
> 2 *quarts big fresh strawberries (the bigger the berries, the more outstanding the pie), stemmed*
> ¾ *cup granulated sugar*
> 3 *tablespoons cornstarch*
> ½ *cup water*
> 2 *cups light vanilla ice cream*

Prepare and bake pie shell according to package instructions. Let stand until cool.

Arrange 1½ quarts of the strawberries, pointed tips up, in pie shell. Crush remaining berries. Mix sugar and cornstarch in a 2-quart saucepan. Gradually stir in water and crushed berries. Place pan over medium heat and cook, stirring constantly, until mixture thickens and boils. Boil and stir 1 minute. Pour over berries in pie shell. Chill at least 2 hours. Serve with vanilla ice cream.

Each serving approximately 289 calories, 7 g total fat,
1 g saturated fat, 2 mg cholesterol, 53 g carbohydrates,
2 g dietary fiber, 7 g protein, 233 mg sodium.

FRESH FRUIT ENDINGS

BAKED CARAMEL PEARS

This dessert is sure to satisfy the cravings of even the most serious sweet tooth.

4 servings

½ *cup water*
½ *cup brown sugar*
1 *vanilla bean, split open*
4 *ripe firm Bosc or Anjou pears*
¼ *cup caramel dessert topping*

In a small saucepan, combine water, brown sugar and vanilla bean. Simmer 5 minutes to dissolve sugar.

Meanwhile, carefully peel pears. With apple corer, remove cores. Slice a small piece off the bottom so each pear will stand alone. Arrange pears in a shallow ovenproof casserole. Pour brown sugar mixture over top. Cover casserole with aluminum foil and bake at 425°F, for 30 to 40 minutes, or until pears are tender, occasionally basting pears with syrup in casserole. Serve pears on deep-lip dessert plates. Warm caramel topping and drizzle 1 tablespoon over each pear.

Each serving approximately 243 calories, 1 g total fat,
0 g saturated fat, 0 mg cholesterol, 60 g carbohydrates,
4 g dietary fiber, 1 g protein, 111 mg sodium.

HOMEMADE APPLESAUCE

Your family will never be able to face another jar of commercial applesauce once they have tasted your homemade variety. Sprinkling red-hot cinnamon candies on top adds a kid-friendly touch to this nutritious dessert.

8 servings

> **8 to 10 large tart cooking apples, such as Granny Smith**
> **½ cup water**
> **½ cup granulated sugar**
> **1 teaspoon ground cinnamon**
> **1 tablespoon red-hot cinnamon candies (optional)**

Wash and peel apples. Core and cut into quarters. Put in a medium saucepan, add water and bring to a boil. Reduce heat, cover and simmer, stirring frequently, until apples are barely tender, 8 to 10 minutes. Add sugar and continue cooking until apples are tender and sugar is dissolved, about 10 minutes. Remove from heat. Stir in cinnamon. Serve in bowls. Sprinkle with red-hot cinnamon candies, if desired.

Each ½-cup serving approximately 130 calories, 0 g total fat,
0 g saturated fat, 0 mg cholesterol, 34 g carbohydrates,
3 g dietary fiber, 0 g protein, 1 mg sodium.

FRESH PINEAPPLE
WITH BERRIES

The papaya puree adds a nice touch to the presentation.

8 servings

> 1 *ripe pineapple*
> 2 *ripe papayas*
> 1½ *cups strawberries, raspberries or blueberries*

Cut off the top and bottom of the pineapple. Peel off the brown skin, cutting fairly deep. Remove any brown "eyes" that may remain. Cut into rings. Cut rings into quarters.

Pare papayas; cut in half and remove seeds. Place papaya halves in food processor and puree. Divide puree among individual dessert plates. Arrange pineapple quarters over the top. Garnish with berries.

Each serving approximately 86 calories, 1 g total fat,
0 g saturated fat, 0 mg cholesterol, 21 g carbohydrates,
4 g dietary fiber, 1 g protein, 3 mg sodium.

STRAWBERRIES WITH SOUR-CREAM TOPPING

4 servings

> 1½ *pints fresh strawberries, hulled*
> 4 *sprigs fresh mint (optional)*
> 4 *tablespoons brown sugar*
> ½ *cup nonfat sour cream*

Arrange strawberries in a pretty serving bowl. Garnish with mint, if desired. Accompany with small, custard-size bowls of brown sugar and sour cream.

Each serving approximately 99 calories, 0 g total fat,
0 g saturated fat, 0 mg cholesterol, 24 g carbohydrates,
2 g dietary fiber, 3 g protein, 27 mg sodium.

TROPICAL FRUIT SALAD

A great Sunday salad. Double the recipe and your fruit will be cut up and ready for the whole week. This fruit salad is especially high in vitamins A and C and in folic acid, a B vitamin.

8 servings

> ½ *grapefruit*
> ½ *cantaloupe*
> ¼ *watermelon*
> ½ *honeydew*
> ½ *pineapple*
> 1 *papaya*
> 2 *cups peach or raspberry sorbet*
> *fresh mint for garnish*

Peel and section grapefruit and remove membrane. Remove rind and seeds from melons and cut into 2-inch pieces. Peel pineapple; remove core and cut into 2-inch pieces. Peel and seed papaya and cut into 2-inch pieces. Arrange fruits in uniform rows on individual salad plates. Serve with sorbet garnished with mint.

Each serving approximately 157 calories, 1 g total fat,
0 g saturated fat, 0 mg cholesterol, 39 g carbohydrates,
3 g dietary fiber, 1 g protein, 13 mg sodium.

HAWAIIAN FRUIT SALAD

P resentation is so important to the whole eating experience.
Add to your family's pleasure by serving this fruit salad in a
pineapple boat.

10 servings

> 1 *fresh pineapple*
> 1 *cup strawberries, stemmed and halved*
> 1 *cup blueberries*
> ½ *small cantaloupe, peeled and cut into*
> *1-inch cubes*
> 1 *papaya, peeled, seeded and cut up*
> 1 *cup seedless green grapes*
> *fresh mint for garnish*

Cut pineapple in half horizontally, leaving the stem end
intact. Using a curved grapefruit knife, carefully remove
pineapple flesh from shell and cut into cubes. Place ½ of the
pineapple cubes in a salad bowl (reserve remaining half for
later use). Add remaining fruit and toss. Transfer fruit to
pineapple shells. Garnish with mint.

Each serving approximately 60 calories, 0 g total fat,
0 g saturated fat, 0 mg cholesterol, 15 g carbohydrates,
2 g dietary fiber, 1 g protein, 5 mg sodium.

FRESH PEACHES IN RASPBERRY SAUCE

For a "hands-on" after-school snack, in place of the peaches substitute 4 cups Tropical Fruit Salad (page 425) or Hawaiian Fruit Salad (facing page). Arrange the fruits in symmetrical piles on a serving plate with a cup-size bowl of the raspberry sauce in the center. Your kids will love the presentation, and dipping the fruit in the sauce adds to the fun.

4 servings

> 1 *10-ounce package frozen raspberries with*
>   *sugar, thawed*
> 2 *tablespoons freshly squeezed orange juice*
> 1 *teaspoon cornstarch*
> ½ *cup cold water*
> 4 *fresh peaches, seeded and thinly sliced*

In a 2-quart saucepan, combine raspberries and orange juice; heat to boiling. In a small bowl, combine cornstarch with cold water and stir until smooth; gradually add to boiling raspberries. Heat and stir until sauce thickens slightly. Pour mixture into a blender. Blend until smooth and frothy, about 2 minutes. If desired, pour mixture through a strainer to remove raspberry seeds. Chill. Serve in 4 chilled deep-lip dessert plates. Ladle ¼ cup sauce onto each plate. Arrange peaches symmetrically over sauce.

Each serving approximately 143 calories, 1 g total fat,
0 g saturated fat, 0 mg cholesterol, 35 g carbohydrates,
5 g dietary fiber, 1 g protein, 1 mg sodium.

BERRIES AND HÄAGEN-DAZS

The good news: you can definitely have dessert, even a Häagen-Dazs dessert, with calories this few.

4 servings

> 1½ *cups sliced fresh strawberries*
> 2 *cups Häagen-Dazs vanilla sorbet*
>   *and 2 cups yogurt*
> 1½ *cups fresh blueberries*
>   *fresh mint for garnish*

Divide strawberries among 4 stemmed dessert or champagne glasses. Add a scoop of vanilla sorbet and yogurt. Top with fresh blueberries. Garnish with fresh mint.

Each serving approximately 185 calories, 0 g total fat,
0 g saturated fat, 0 mg cholesterol, 40 g carbohydrates,
2 g dietary fiber, 7 g protein, 46 mg sodium.

STRAWBERRY SUNDAES

You won't miss "real" ice cream when you flavor light ice cream with delicious seasonal fruits.

6 servings

> 1½ *pints light vanilla ice cream, softened*
> 1 *10-ounce package fresh-frozen sliced*
>   *strawberries with sugar, thawed*

Scoop ice cream into 6 parfait glasses. Top with strawberries.

Each serving approximately 167 calories, 4 g total fat,
3 g saturated fat, 25 mg cholesterol, 29 g carbohydrates,
2 g dietary fiber, 3 g protein, 35 mg sodium, 100 mg calcium.

BAKED APPLES

Dried cranberries are plumper and sweeter than raisins. Your kids will love them.

4 servings

> **4 tart cooking apples, such as Granny Smith
>   or McIntosh**
> **⅓ cup brown sugar
>   zest of 1 orange**
> **1 tablespoon tub-style margarine**
> **½ cup dried cranberries or raisins**
> **¾ cup water**
> **2 tablespoons granulated sugar**
> **4 scoops light vanilla ice cream**

Preheat oven to 375°F.

Wash apples and remove core to ½-inch of the bottom. Arrange apples in an 8 x 8 x 2-inch ovenproof baking dish. Using a fork, combine brown sugar, orange zest and margarine; stir in the cranberries. Fill each apple center with the mixture.

In a small container, combine water and granulated sugar; pour around apples. Bake about 30 minutes, or until apples are tender but not mushy. Remove from oven and baste the apples several times with the pan juices. If the juices are thin, remove the apples to individual serving bowls and reduce the pan juices before glazing the apples. Serve warm with ice cream.

Each serving approximately 346 calories, 6 g total fat,
2 g saturated fat, 9 mg cholesterol, 75 g carbohydrates,
4 g dietary fiber, 3 g protein, 99 mg sodium.

MENUS

Many of our menus suggest seasonal fruits for desserts. Others specify a specific fruit such as fresh strawberries. There are lots of delicious fruits to choose from, so if strawberries or other specified fruits are not your favorite or are not available, substitute another dessert fruit that is in season and that sounds good to you.

In the menus that follow, asterisks indicate the names of recipes included in this book.

NEW AND LEAN OLD FAMILY FAVORITES

---

*Bonus meal: leftover meat loaf makes
great lunch-box sandwiches.*

LIKE DINNER AT GRANDMA'S HOUSE

One of the messages of the USDA's Food Guide Pyramid is to moderate the amount of animal protein we eat. We practice that advice by using 2 pounds of lean ground beef for 8 servings of meat loaf. The remainder of the menu is balanced with vegetables and fruit, allowing you to enjoy more old favorites without loading up on fat.

*OLD-FASHIONED MEAT LOAF

CORN ON THE COB • SUGAR SNAP PEAS

*STUFFED POTATOES

SLICED FRESH PEACHES WITH BLUEBERRIES

Easy meal: 40 minutes

YOUR KIDS WILL LOVE IT!

Grilled Chicken Burgers as a main-meal sandwich served with fries and a shake have less fat than a typical quarter-pound fast-food hamburger.

*GRILLED CHICKEN BURGERS

*JUMBO OVEN FRIES

RAW CURLY CARROTS AND SUGAR SNAP PEAS

*BEST-EVER CHOCOLATE SHAKES

---

30 minutes

MOM'S NIGHT OUT

Enjoy this casserole by using the reduced-fat version of cream-of-chicken soup instead of its fattier counterpart. Accompany the casserole with broccoli and sautéed baby carrots so your kids can dip the vegetables in the sauce.

*NOODLE CASSEROLE WITH TUNA

*LITTLE GREEN TREES

* SAUTÉED BABY CARROTS

APPLES • PEARS • GRAPES

*Easy meal: 45 minutes' baking time,
but only 15 minutes' preparation time.*

WHEN THE BABY-SITTER COMES

Remember, it's usually a too-fast fork, not a too-slow metabolism, that makes us fat. Help your kids slow down their eating habits by serving the all-time favorite, macaroni and cheese, with an assortment of raw vegetables to dip. Accompany it with their favorite fruit salad.

*CHEESY MACARONI

*RAW VEGGIES IN A BASKET

FRUIT SALAD

---

40 minutes

ALL-AMERICAN FAVORITE

Your family will want to eat at "mom's place" versus the local fast-food place after tasting this great combo of burgers, fries and shakes. You'll be happy to know that you've just given them less than a third of the fat.

*CLASSIC GRILLED BURGERS

*ROSEMARY OVEN FRIES

*RAW VEGGIES IN A BASKET

*WHITE BEAN AND GARLIC DIP

*AWESOME STRAWBERRY SHAKES

OLD-FASHIONED
SUNDAY DINNER

Creative ingredient substitutions and low-fat cooking methods are the keys to making this normally high-fat meal very lean yet still just as tasty. It's a super example of how you can still enjoy old favorites without all the fat.

*SOUTHERN FRIED CHICKEN WITH GRAVY

*GARLIC MASHED POTATOES

FRESH PEAS AND CARROTS

*STRAWBERRY SHORTCAKE

———

Easy meal: 40 minutes' baking time, but only 30 minutes' preparation time!

DINNER FOR A HOUSEFUL

This is an easy solution for feeding your kids and their friends. Crunchy raw vegetables add contrast to the soft texture of the casserole. It's a sure pleaser, even for picky eaters.

*SALLY'S NOODLE CASSEROLE

*RAW VEGGIES IN A BASKET

SEASONAL FRUIT PLATE

THANKSGIVING DAY MENU

This menu gives all the satisfaction of having family favorites without the heavy fat. Each of the recipes uses leaner, creative ways to cook and flavor traditional foods—without sacrificing taste.

*ANTIPASTO

*ROASTED TURKEY

*BREAD STUFFING

*MASHED POTATOES

*OLD-FASHIONED GRAVY

*HOLIDAY YAMS

FRESH CRANBERRY RELISH

BAKE-AND-SERVE BREAD

*PUMPKIN PIE

*Easy meal: 1 hour's roasting time,
but only 15 minutes' preparation time.*

GAME DAY DINNER

The tenderloin cut of pork is a lean choice. The apples for dessert can be cooking while the family is eating the main meal—the aroma from the cinnamon and apples will make everyone's mouth water!

*ROASTED PORK TENDERLOIN

*COUNTRY FRIED POTATOES

SNOW PEAS

*HOMEMADE APPLESAUCE

MAKE-AHEAD DINNERS

---

20 minutes, except for baking the apples

"SOUPER" QUICK

It's nice to serve soup for a family meal. Soup is a comfort food, and it also slows down the meal, giving time to enjoy each other's company.

*TOMATO AND BEAN SOUP

FRENCH BREAD

*SPINACH SALAD

*BAKED APPLES

30 minutes

QUICK AND HEARTY WINTER SUPPER

The soup in this menu offers a variety of vegetables (white, yellow and dark green) as well as significant protein all in one dish. The complex carbohydrates in the bread complete the meal. Not only does pudding provide a satisfying end to the dinner, but it also comes with an added bonus—calcium.

*TORTELLINI VEGETABLE SOUP

TUSCAN BREAD

TAPIOCA PUDDING

---

30 minutes

"MEETING NIGHT" MENU

Thanks to the convenience of canned beans, this chili can be prepared in just half an hour. The Santa Fe Salad is a great way to sneak spinach into your family's meal, and the tortillas provide another option for adding much-needed grains.

*THREE-BEAN CHILI

*SANTA FE SALAD

*WARM TORTILLAS

*STRAWBERRIES WITH SOUR-CREAM TOPPING

A MAKE-AHEAD CLASSIC

Compare this homemade lasagna with a store-bought type and you'll see that not only does it taste better but you save 5 to 10 grams of fat per serving. Because even our homemade lasagna is not low-fat, we serve it with a low-fat antipasto.

*ANTIPASTO

*CLASSIC LASAGNA

ITALIAN BREAD

APPLES • GRAPES • PEARS

BISCOTTI

30 minutes

AFTER-SOCCER DINNER

Get your kids to eat spinach by offering this spinach salad with dressing. The lean chicken soup allows us to pair it with the full-fat dressing on the salad. There's even room for dessert!

*CHICKEN AND PASTINA SOUP

ITALIAN BREAD STICKS

*SPINACH SALAD

*VERY BERRY COBBLER

A HEARTY SOUP MEAL

Prepare this soup and dessert ahead of time and treat yourself to dinner on the table in minutes.

*THE BEST TURKEY SOUP

*HOMEMADE APPLE PIE

A WARMING
"AFTER THE GAME" DINNER

Make this menu on a weekend and treat your family to inviting smells from the kitchen. Because the soup needs to be prepared ahead of time, supper can be put on the table with ease after the game.

*FRENCH MARKET SOUP

*PIZZA GARLIC BREAD

*BAKED CARAMEL PEARS

*Bonus meal: leftover meatballs make good
lunch-box sandwiches.*

ANYTIME FAVORITE

Here's an opportunity to practice moderation in all things!
Remember, meatballs are the condiment. The spaghetti is the <u>main</u>
dish. Eat accordingly. If you want second helpings, eat more
pasta—not meatballs.

We have offset the fat in the meatballs and salad by including
bread, which can be dipped in the sauce rather than buttered, and
suggest a lean dessert in order not to add additional fat to the meal.

*SPAGHETTI WITH MEATBALLS

*ANTIPASTO SALAD

CRUSTY ITALIAN BREAD

BASKET OF FROZEN FRUIT ICES ON STICKS

WATERMELON CHUNKS

WEEKLY TIME-SAVER

Good eating involves planning ahead. This menu is a quick-and-
easy way to make a delicious dinner and still have lots of leftovers
for lunch-box sandwiches. There's even room for dessert!

*ROASTED HERBED CHICKEN BREAST

LONG-GRAIN RICE

*CORN AND BLACK BEAN SALAD

LIGHT ICE-CREAM SANDWICHES

45 minutes

VEGETARIAN DINNER

This simple stir-fry, packed with taste, color, texture and sizzle, is a great alternative to high-fat casseroles. Satisfy your kids' sweet tooth with berries and Häagen-Dazs.

*Asian Stir-Fry

*Berries and Häagen-Dazs

A meal that hits the spot on certain warm summer days

THREE-SALAD SUPPER

Show your kids there's more to salads than just lettuce. These healthy salads incorporate all sorts of vegetables in combination with pasta, beans and turkey.

*Pasta and Smoked Turkey Salad

*Tuscan Bean Salad

Mixed Summer Fruit Salad

LAST-MINUTE SUPPERS

Main-meal sandwich: 30 minutes

FOR HOT SUMMER NIGHTS

Your family will love the taste of fresh grilled turkey instead of the usual processed, deli type. For a creative turn from the typical vegetable dips, try our Black Bean Dip. It's healthier and leaner than the usual mayonnaise-based dips and a perfect complement to this sandwich.

You can tell your kids it's O.K. to eat this meal with their hands!

*GRILLED TURKEY SANDWICHES

LETTUCE, TOMATO AND ONION

DILL PICKLES

*BLACK BEAN DIP

BITE-SIZE VEGGIES

SEASONAL FRUIT

---

30 minutes

SPUR-OF-THE-MOMENT SUPPER

Another kids' favorite is this variation of spaghetti with red sauce. Why open a jar of commercial spaghetti sauce, when you can make your own tastier version in minutes? Making this marinara sauce gives you the benefit of cutting the fat in half while getting twice as much sauce per serving as you do with the store-bought variety. The dark greens and seasonal fruit make it possible to reach our goal of more fruit and vegetables.

*PASTA MARINARA

MIXED GREEN SALAD

SEASONAL FRUIT PLATE

---

30 minutes

FOR BUSY MOMS WITH NO TIME TO COOK

This menu fits the bill when you're pressed for time but want something warm—and simple—to prepare.

*PENNE WITH MEAT SAUCE

MIXED GREEN GARDEN SALAD

ASSORTED FRESH FRUIT

---

30 minutes, except for chilling the pie

UPTOWN SANDWICH SUPPER

Celebrate this lean, main-meal sandwich with a slice of fresh pie!

*GRILLED STEAK SANDWICHES

*ANTIPASTO

*FRESH STRAWBERRY PIE

---

30 minutes

NEW FAMILY FAVORITE

Have fun with all the different shapes of pasta now available on the market. Surprise your kids! Dinner can be on the table in minutes with this quick-to-fix menu.

*LITTLE EAR PASTA WITH SAUSAGE

SOURDOUGH FRENCH BREAD

PEACHES • APRICOTS • BLUEBERRIES

30 minutes

SPEEDY DINNER FOR A SOFTBALL NIGHT

There's no need to call out for pizza when something this tasty and good for you can be prepared quickly at home. The key is a combination of nonfat and low-fat cheeses. Balance the dinner by encouraging family members to be creative in putting together their own hearty salad using as many of the vegetables choices as possible.

*COMBINATION PIZZA

*BUILD-YOUR-OWN SALAD

CHILLED WATERMELON

I'VE GOT
THE CHICKEN ... NOW
WHAT CAN I MAKE?

---

30 minutes

TWO-SALAD SUPPER

Kids love these salads. Moms and dads love how quick they are to prepare.

*CHICKEN TACO SALAD

*TROPICAL FRUIT SALAD

---

40 minutes

A SUMMERTIME FAVORITE

Chicken Parmesan tastes so good your family will think they are eating fried chicken. The protein it supplies is moderated by the carbohydrate-rich Pasta Primavera and fresh fruit.

*CHICKEN PARMESAN

*PASTA PRIMAVERA

RASPBERRY AND LEMON ICES

TROPICAL FRUITS

40 minutes
Bonus meal: leftover BBQ chicken makes great
sandwiches.

A MOTHER'S DAY DINNER THAT DAD CAN PREPARE

Wonderful backyard BBQ anytime! Grilling and using olive-oil cooking spray makes this BBQ chicken a food to enjoy anytime. Portioning the amount of dressing on the pasta salad adds another measure of leanness. If you still have room for dessert, enjoy a sundae, made light.

*SPICY BARBECUED CHICKEN

*CLASSIC PASTA SALAD

HERBED GRILLED CORN

*STRAWBERRY SUNDAES

---

30 minutes

A FAVORITE WITH THE KIDS

This menu is another example of "the way" to eat. The beans, rice and chicken combination offers a nutritious balance of 3 carbohydrates to 1 protein, verifying the principles of the pyramid: maximize carbohydrates; minimize proteins.

*CHICKEN AND BEAN BURRITOS

LONG-GRAIN TEXMATI RICE

CORN ON THE COB

TROPICAL FRUITS

30 minutes, except for marinating the chicken

A SIZZLING TREAT FOR THE WHOLE FAMILY

Fajita meals are a fun way to eat healthfully. This type of meal lends itself to nutritious eating habits because the main focus is on the vegetables, complemented by the lean chicken. Each person filling his or her individual tortilla adds to the fun and the togetherness of a family eating together.

*CHICKEN FAJITAS

LONG-GRAIN RICE

BOWL OF MANDARIN ORANGES

30 minutes

DINNER IN A HURRY

Kids love the interesting shape of this pasta and the addition of chicken in place of the more typical ground beef. Popeye spinach is a great complement to this dish. When you taste the way our spinach has been seasoned, you'll probably agree that Popeye never had it so good!

*BOW TIE PASTA WITH CHICKEN

*POPEYE SPINACH

BERRIES IN A MELON

30 minutes

FAST, EASY AND TASTY

This stir-fry menu is a good way to accomplish the pyramid approach to eating. You get three or more kinds of vegetables, along with starchy rice and lean protein. The messages with fortune cookies make a fun topic of conversation—all part of the experience of "breaking bread" together.

*CHICKEN STIR-FRY

*STICKY RICE

*FRESH PINEAPPLE WITH BERRIES

FORTUNE COOKIES

---

30 minutes

CHICKEN WITH STYLE

This meal is a good example of pyramid building: lots of carbohydrates to moderate protein intake, and lots of fruits and vegetables.

*GRILLED HERBED CHICKEN BREASTS

*STICKY RICE

*LEMONY SPINACH

*SAUTÉED BABY CARROTS

BOWL OF CHERRIES

A BIT ON THE FANCY SIDE

30 minutes

AN ELEGANT SUMMER DINNER

Light and refreshing describes this meal. You won't believe that it can taste and look this good and still be put together so quickly. Your kids will love winding down the meal with soft, satisfying pudding—one of those wonderful comfort foods.

*SAUTÉED SHRIMP

LONG-GRAIN AND WILD RICE

*TOMATOES WITH FRESH MOZZARELLA AND BASIL

ASPARAGUS

VANILLA PUDDING

30 minutes

QUICK COMPANY DINNER

This *"fish-friendly"* menu encourages children to give fish a try. Salmon has a firm texture like that of chicken—something your family is probably used to eating. The heart-healthy fat of the salmon is balanced with lean vegetables, rice and fruit.

*TERIYAKI SALMON

*STIR-FRIED VEGETABLES

*STICKY RICE

PINEAPPLE SORBET • SEASONAL FRUIT

45 minutes, except for marinating the steak

GRILLED STEAK DINNER

Steak and potatoes can be a healthy option for family meals. Step one is to choose a lean cut of meat, marinate it for tenderness and enjoy a smaller portion. Step two is to pair it with equally delicious and satisfying lean side dishes.

*GRILLED TERIYAKI STEAK

*LOADED BAKED POTATOES

*STIR-FRIED BROCCOLI AND CAULIFLOWER WITH RED PEPPERS

STRAWBERRIES AND BLUEBERRIES

30 minutes

LIFE AFTER MEATBALLS

Try this typical Italian meal for a delightful change of pace. Give your kids an opportunity to discover that they like clams.

*LINGUINE WITH CLAM SAUCE

ITALIAN BREAD

*TOMATOES WITH FRESH MOZZARELLA AND BASIL

*VERY BERRY COBBLER

40 minutes

KIDS MEET FISH

Introduce your kids to a fish dinner they'll love and a meal that follows the pyramid principles: lots of carbohydrates in the potatoes, corn, beans and peaches; and a moderate amount of protein due to portion control with the serving size of the swordfish.

*GRILLED SWORDFISH STEAKS

*GARLIC ROASTED RED POTATOES

GRILLED CORN ON THE COB

*GREAT GREEN BEANS

*FRESH PEACHES IN RASPBERRY SAUCE

FESTIVE SUMMER SUPPER

This chicken not only tastes delicious but also smells delicious. The accompanying salad and fresh berries pack the meal with nutrients, including approximately half a day's requirements for fiber.

Double the recipes and take the leftovers on a picnic. Bring along your favorite sandwich rolls, plenty of fresh lemonade, and homemade peanut butter or molasses cookies.

*ROASTED CHICKEN WITH GARLIC

*TUSCAN BEAN SALAD

WATERMELON • GRAPES • CHERRIES

BIBLIOGRAPHY

Alpert, B.S., and J.H. Wilmore. "Physical Activity and Blood Pressure in Adolescents." *Pediatric Exercise Science* 6, 1994.

American Academy of Pediatrics Committees on Sports Medicine and School Health. "Physical fitness and the schools." *Pediatrics* 80, 1987.

American Alliance for Health, Physical Education, Recreation and Dance. "Summary of Findings from National Children and Youth Fitness Study." *Journal of Physical Education, Recreation and Dance* 56: 45, 1985.

――――. "Summary of Findings from National Children and Youth Fitness Study. II." *Journal of Physical Education, Recreation and Dance* 58: 49, 1987.

American College of Sports Medicine: Position Stands and Opinion Statements. "Physical Fitness in Children and Youth." Indianapolis, 1988.

American College of Sports Medicine. *Guidelines for Exercise Testing and Prescription*. Philadelphia: Lea & Febiger, 1991.

American School Health Association. *The National Adolescent Student Health Survey: A Report on the Health of America's Youth*. Oakland, Cal.: Third Party Publishing, 1989.

――――. "School Health Policies and Programs Study (SHPPS): A Summary Report." *Journal of School Health*, October 1995.

Armstrong, N., and B. Simonds-Morton. "Physical Activity and Blood Lipids in Adolescents." *Pediatric Exercise Science* 6, 1994.

Association for the Advancement of Health Education. "Cardiopulmonary Behavioral Research: Focus on Youth, Gender, Ethnicity." *Journal of Health Education*, March/April 1995 Supplement.

Baranowski, T., et al. "Assessment, Prevalence, and Cardiovascular Benefits of Physical Activity and Fitness in Youth." *Medicine and Science in Sports and Exercise*, Vol. 24, No. 6 Supplement, 1992.

Baranowski, T., and P.R. Nader. "Family Involvement in Health-Related Behavior Change Programs." In *Health, Illness and Families*. New York: Wiley, 1985.

Bar-Or, O., and T. Baranowski. "Physical Activity, Adiposity, and Obesity Among Adolescents." *Pediatric Exercise Science* 6, 1994.

Beardall, S. "Today's Children: Fatter, Sicker and More Disturbed." *The Times*, London, November 9, 1985.

Bell, R.D., et al. "Health Indicators and Risk Factors of Cardiovascular Diseases During Childhood and Adolescence." *Children and Exercise. XII*, eds. J. Rutenfranz et al. Champaign, Ill.: Human Kinetics, 1986.

Berenson, G.S., et al. "Cardiovascular Disease Risk Factor Variables at the Preschool Age: The Bogalusa Heart Study." *Circulation* 57 (3): 603–12, March 1978.

———. *Cardiovascular Risk Factors in Children*. New York: Oxford University Press, 1980.

Blair, S.N., et al. "Exercise and Fitness in Childhood: Implications for a Lifetime of Health." *Perspectives in Exercise Science and Sports Medicine. Vol. 2: Youth, Exercise, and Sport*, eds. C.V. Gisolfi and D.R. Lamb. Indianapolis: Benchmark Press, 1989.

————. "How Much Physical Activity Is Good for Health?" *Annual Revenue of Public Health* 13, 1992.

Burghardt, John, and Barbara Devaney. "The School Nutrition Dietary Assessment Study: Summary of Findings," U.S. Department of Agriculture, October 1993.

Castelli, W.P. "Epidemiology of Coronary Heart Disease: The Framingham Study." *American Journal of Medicine* 76, 1984.

Children and Exercise. III, eds. S.C. Oseid and K.H. Carlson. Champaign, Ill.: Human Kinetics, 1989.

Cooper, Kenneth. *Kid Fitness.* New York: Bantam Books, 1991.

Despres, J.P., et al. "Physical Activity and Coronary Heart Disease Risk Factors During Childhood and Adolescence." *Exercise and Sport Science* 18, 1990.

Dietz, W.H. "Childhood Obesity: Susceptibility, Cause and Management." *Journal of Pediatrics* 61, 1983.

Dietz, W.H., and S.L. Gortmaker. "Do We Fatten Our Children at the Television Set? Obesity and Television Viewing in Children and Adolescents." *Pediatrics* 75, 1985.

Edmundson, E.W., et al. "CATCH: Classroom Process Evaluation in a Multicenter Trial." *Health Education Quarterly*, Supp. 2, 1994.

Elder, J.P., et al. "CATCH: Process Evaluation of Environmental Factors and Programs." *Health Education Quarterly*, Supp. 2, 1994.

Frank, G.C., et al. "Dietary Studies and the Relationship of Diet to Cardiovascular Disease Risk Factor Variables in 10-Year-Old Children—The Bogalusa Heart Study," *The American Journal of Clinical Nutrition*, February 1978.

Gruber, J.J. "Physical Activity and Self-Esteem Development in Children." In *Effects of Physical Activity on Children*, eds. G.A. Stull and H.M. Eckert. Champaign, Ill.: Human Kinetics, 1986.

Jacobson, Michael, and Bruce Maxwell. *What Are We Feeding Our Kids?* New York: Workman Publishing, 1994.

Johnson, C.C., et al. "CATCH: Family Process Evaluation in a Multicenter Trial." *Health Education Quarterly*, Supp. 2, 1994.

Kalish, Susan. *Your Child's Fitness*. Champaign, Ill.: Human Kinetics, 1996.

Kuntzleman, Charles T. "Childhood Fitness: What Is Happening? What Needs to Be Done?" *Preventive Medicine* 22, 1993.

———. *The Well Family Book*. San Bernardino, Cal.: Here's Life, 1985.

LeBow, Michael. *Overweight Children: Helping Your Child Achieve Lifetime Weight Control*. New York: Plenum Publishing, 1991.

McGraw, S.A., et al. "Design of Process Evaluation Within the Child and Adolescent Trial for Cardiovascular Health (CATCH)." *Health Education Quarterly*, Supp. 2, 1994.

McKenzie, T.L., et al. "CATCH: Physical Activity Process Evaluation in a Multicenter Trial." *Health Education Quarterly*, Supp. 2, 1994.

Meredith, C.N., and J.T. Dwyer. "Nutrition and Exercise: Effects on Adolescent Health." *Annual Revue of Public Health* 12, 1991.

Moore, L.L., et al. "Influence of Parents' Physical Activity Levels on Activity Levels of Young Children." *Journal of Pediatrics* 118, 1991.

Morgan, K.J. "The Role of Snacking in the American Diet." *Contemporary Nutrition* 17, 1982.

National Institutes of Health. "Report of the Second Task Force on Blood Pressure Control in Children—1987." *Pediatrics* 79, 1987.

National Research Council. *The Diet and Health Report.* Washington, D.C.: National Academy of Sciences, 1989.

———. *Recommended Dietary Allowances.* Washington, D.C.: National Academy of Sciences, 1989.

Newman, W.P., et al. "Relationship of Serum Lipoprotein Levels and Systolic Blood Pressure to Early Atherosclerosis: The Bogalusa Heart Study." *New England Journal of Medicine* 314, 1986.

Nicklas, T.A., et al. "Heart Smart School Lunch Program: A Vehicle for Cardiovascular Health Promotion." *American Journal of Health Promotion* 4, 1989.

Norris, R., D. Carroll, and R. Cochrane. "The Effects of Physical Activity and Exercise Training on Psychological Stress and Well-Being in Adolescent Population." *Journal of Clinical Psychology* 36, 1991.

North American Society of Pediatric Exercise Medicine. *Physical Activity Guidelines for Adolescents.* Pediatric Exercise Science, November 1994.

Pate, R.R., et al. "Association Between Physical Activity and Physical Fitness in American Children." *AJDC* 144, 1990.

Raizman, D.J., et al. "CATCH: Food Service Program Process Evaluation in a Multicenter Trial." *Health Education Quarterly,* Supp. 2, 1994.

Robinson, T.N., et al. "Does Television Viewing Increase Obesity and Reduce Physical Activity? Cross-Sectional and Longitudinal Analyses Among Adolescent Girls." *Pediatrics* 91, 1993.

Ross, J.G., and G.G. Gilbert. "The National Children and Youth Fitness Study: A Summary of Findings." *Journal of Physical Education, Recreation and Dance* 1, 1985.

Ross, J.G., and R.R. Pate. "The National Children and Youth Fitness Study II: A Summary of Findings." *Journal of Physical Education, Recreation and Dance* 58, 1987.

Sallis, J.F., et al. Determinants of Physical Activity and Interventions in Youth. *Medicine and Science of Sports and Exercise* 24, 1992

Sallis, J.F., and K. Patrick. "Physical Activity Guidelines for Adolescents: Consensus Statement." *Pediatric Exercise Science* 6, 1994.

Sallis, J.F., and P.R. Nader. "Family Determinants of Health Behaviors." In *Health Behavior*, ed. D.S. Gochman. New York: Plenum Publishing, 1988.

Simons-Morton, B.G., et al. "Promoting Physical Activity and a Healthful Diet Among Children: Results of a School-Based Intervention Study." *American Journal of Public Health* 81, 1990.

Snyder, M. P., M. Story, et al. "Reducing Fat and Sodium in School Lunch Programs: The LUNCHPOWER! Intervention Study." *Journal of the American Dietetic Association*, 1992.

Society for Public Health Education. "Process Evaluation in the Multicenter Child and Adolescent Trial for Cardiovascular Health (CATCH). *Health Education Quarterly*, Supplement 2, 1994.

Strong, W.B. "Physical Activity and Children." *Circulation* 81, 1990.

Suskind, R.M., et al. "Recent Advances in the Treatment of Childhood Obesity." *Annals of the New York Academy of Science* 699, 1993.

Suter, E., and M.R. Hawes. "Relationship of Physical Activity, Body Fat, Diet and Blood Lipid Profile in Youths 10–15 Years." *Medicine and Science of Sports and Exercise* 25, 1993.

Tappe, M.K., J.L. Duda and P.M. Ehrnwald. "Perceived Barriers to Exercise Among Adolescents." *Journal of School Health* 59, 1989.

Taylor, C.B., J.F. Sallis, and R. Needle. "The Relationship of Physical Activity and Exercise to Mental Health." *Public Health Report* 100, 1985.

The Surgeon General's Report on Nutrition and Health, Public Health Service, U.S. Department of Health and Human Services, 1988.

The Surgeon General's Report on Physical Activity and Health, Public Health Service, U.S. Department of Health and Human Services, 1996.

Tucker, L.A. "The Relationship of Television Viewing to Physical Fitness and Obesity." *Adolescence* 21, 1986.

U.S. Department of Health and Human Services. *Healthy Children 2000:* Washington, D.C., 1991.

———. *Healthy People 2000: National Health Promotion and Disease Prevention Objectives.* Washington, D.C., 1991.

———. *National Cholesterol Education Program Report of the Expert Panel on Population Strategies for Blood Cholesterol Reduction.* Washington, D.C., 1991.

Van Horn, L., and G. Frank. "Children and High Cholesterol: Prevention and Intervention. *Journal of the American Dietetic Association* 89, 1989.

Willis, Judith. "Good Nutrition for the Highchair Set," *FDA Consumer*, September 1985.

Wilmore, Jack. *Sensible Fitness*. Champaign, Ill.: Human Kinetics, 1986.

GENERAL
INDEX

establishing fat guideline for, 160–62, 163
going for best snacks in, 247–58
importance of, 100
increasing grains, beans, fruits and vegetables in, 265–72
incremental changes in, 159–60
and influences on children's food choices, 99, 135–56
learning to read food labels and, 162–66
lightening up lunches in, 203–12
making fast food your friend in, 213–46
meal plans and, 167–69, 277–78
modifying foods your child already likes and, 169–71, 278– 81
palatability and, 173–74
picking good breakfast cereal in, 179–83
positive outlook in changing of, 158–60
prioritizing along "10-80 rule," 177–78
protein and calcium sources in, 152–56
recent deleterious changes in, 101–2
refocusing meals and, 259–72
school food and, 101–2, 148–52, 170, 210–12
seven-step solution for, 175–272
switching to fat-free and low-fat milk and cheese in, 184–95
television advertising and, 76–77, 145–48, 213
too much fat in, 102–13
too much sodium in, 102, 113–20
too much sugar in, 102, 120–28
ways for parents to make improvements in, 157–74

Dietary Guidelines for Americans, 100–101, 120, 150
Dieting, 34, 35
banishing idea of, 158
body fat and, 46
crash, 29, 46, 49
metabolic rate reduced by, 49
subjecting children to, 37, 158
Dietz, William, 74, 75, 89–90
Dinner, 101, 102
family, demise of, 137, 138–39
frozen, packaged or take-out meals for, 140, 141. *See also* Fast food; Frozen meals
meal plans and, 167–69, 277–78
Doughnuts, 104, 256
Doyle, Monica, 140
DQ Chicken, 227
Dybahl, Thomas, 4

E

Eggs, 195
Elk, 262
El Polo Loco, 238, 239, 240, 241
Emotional eating, 173
Emotional health, 13–15
enhanced by exercise, 51–52
Endometrial cancer, 21–22
Endorphins, 51
Energy level, 44, 51
Epstein, Leonard, 10
Ernst, Nancy, 111
Estrich, Susan, 33
Ethnic fare, 174
Exercise, 4, 24, 32, 34, 39–96
activity pyramid and, 62–63
aerobic, 43, 79, 85
age and, 59–60, 66
for ages under 2, 58

National Research Council, 10, 23,
115, 129

National Restaurant Association,
213

New England Journal of Medicine,
10, 109, 143

Nicklas, Theresa, 113, 160

Nielsen Media Research, 74,
76–77, 146

Nonas, Cathy, 110

Nonstick pans, 282, 347

Nutritional analysis, for recipes,
293–95

Nutrition Facts, on food labels,
164–66

Nuts, 248, 281

O

Oat bran, 133

Obesity:
age at onset of, 10
in childhood, risk of obesity in
adulthood and, 7–8, 10–11
coronary heart disease and, 21
ethnic groups at greater risk
for, 9
"extremely obese" category and,
8, 9, 10
genetic predisposition to,
25–32
increase in, 4, 5, 8, 31
medical definition of, 8
physical inactivity and, 43, 45,
80
sugar and, 125–26
television viewing and, 74–77
see also Overweight

Oils, 103, 104, 107, 281, 341
hydrogenated, 108–9

Olestra, 111

Omega-3, 109, 378

Oparil, Suzanne, 5, 18

Osteoporosis, 113, 114, 154

Outdoors, maximizing time spent,
55–56, 72

Overweight:
cancer and, 12, 13, 21–23
among children, 3–4, 5, 7–9
coronary heart disease and, 12,
13, 20–21
criticizing children for, 36, 37
dietary fat and, 105–7
genetics and, 25–29, 30
geographic regions and, 9
health risks of, 4, 12–24
and inclination for physical
activity, 66–67
increase in, 4–9, 31
lifestyle vs. genes as cause of, 25,
29–32
physical inactivity and, 45
self-image/self-esteem and,
13–15
societal attitudes about, 13–15,
34–36
among teenagers, 6
see also Obesity

P

Paffenbarger, Ralph, Jr., 50–51

Page, Lot, 115–16

Palatability, 173–74

Pans, nonstick, 282, 347

Parents:
and blame for children's
unhealthy habits, 32–34, 37
exercise habits of, 65–66, 81–82,
83–85, 273
as role models, 33–34, 36, 37,
53, 65–66, 81–82, 83–85, 159,
273, 274
steps for, to help children form
better food habits, 157–74
strategies for, to increase
children's physical activity,
83–96
time pressures on, 42, 71–74,
136–37

Parents Magazine, 14

RECIPE INDEX

481

ACKNOWLEDGMENTS

This book could not have been written without the contributions and strong support of many people. The link between lifestyle habits and the health of children is a relatively new area of study. For that reason, we relied heavily on scientists and health professionals working in the field. Some of those in particular include Evelyn Stone, Ph.D., of the National Institutes of Health; William Roberts, M.D., of the Baylor University Medical School; Joan Rupp, R.D., and Paul Rosengard of the University of San Diego; and Carolyn Johnson, Ph.D., of the Bogalusa Heart Study.

Our thanks to Bev Utt, R.D., for her work on the nutritional analysis and her willingness to consult with us on nutritional content throughout the book. Many friends gave us good advice on food and on children: Malika Blair, former pastry chef at the Four Seasons Hotel in Seattle, provided creative suggestions for low-fat adaptations; Sally Barline offered great ideas for numerous old-favorites-made-lean recipes and shared her cooking expertise.

Many others contributed to the shape of the book, including Andrea and Peggy Paradise, Aija Ozolin, Gertrude Smothers, Kaye Bickford, Linda Clark, Del Berg, Bette and Mac Kirk, David Thayer, and Lou, Mike and Michelle Imhof. We owe many thanks to Joan Imhof for her help with recipe testing and proofreading. And we are particularly grateful to Chuck Eichten for all his contributions to the book as well as his willingness to come to our assistance over and over again.

Our children have been a part of every one of our books. Our daughter, Anne, and our son, Joe, helped in naming the recipes and the menus, and proved to be ace recipe testers.

And finally, our thanks to the Workman Publishing team—especially Peter Workman, Sally Kovalchick and Lynn Strong—for their support of our work.

ABOUT THE
AUTHORS

Joseph C. Piscatella is the author of four widely acclaimed books—*Don't Eat Your Heart Out Cookbook, Choices for a Healthy Heart, Controlling Your Fat Tooth* and *The Fat Tooth Fat-Gram Counter & Restaurant Guide*—all of which have been enthusiastically endorsed by health professionals. His books are used by more than 5,500 hospitals in cardiac rehabilitation, weight loss and prevention programs. Mr. Piscatella's recovery from open-heart surgery at age 32 and his successful approach to healthy lifestyle changes, which resulted in coronary regression at age 47, are welcome news to those interested in improving cardiac health.

President of the Institute for Fitness and Health, Inc., in Tacoma, Washington, Mr. Piscatella lectures on lifestyle management skills to a variety of clients, including Fortune 500 companies, professional associations, hospitals and health professionals. His seminar has been cited in *Time* magazine for its effectiveness.

As a spokesperson on behalf of a healthy lifestyle, Mr. Piscatella is a frequent guest on television and radio programs, contributes to national publications and has hosted a television series on making healthy lifestyle changes. He is the only nonmedical member of a National Institutes of Health Cardiac Rehabilitation Expert Panel charged with developing clinical practice guidelines for physicians. He is a also a member of the American Association for Cardiovascular and Pulmonary Rehabilitation.

Bernie Piscatella is vice president of the Institute for Fitness and Health and is responsible for all the recipes and nutritional analyses in this book as well as in those named above.